The
Green Line
THE CINCINNATI, NEWPORT & COVINGTON RAILWAY

By Terry W. Lehmann and Earl W. Clark, Jr.

Bulletin 134
of the
Central Electric Railfans' Association

The *Green Line*

THE CINCINNATI, NEWPORT & COVINGTON RAILWAY

By Terry W. Lehmann and Earl W. Clark, Jr.

Book Copyright 2000 by CERA
Manuscript Copyright 1997 by Terry W. Lehmann

Bulletin 134 of the Central Electric Railfans' Association

An Illinois Not-for-profit Corporation. Post Office Box 503, Chicago, Illinois 60690, U. S. A.

CERA Bulletins are technical, educational references prepared as historic projects by members of the Central Electric Railfans' Association, working without salary due to their interest in the subject. This Bulletin is consistent with this stated purpose of the corporation. To foster the study of history, equipment, and operation of electric railways.

Editor and Book Designer: G. Mac Sebree

Halftones, color separations and pre-press assembly by Jim Walter Color Separations, Inc., of Beloit, Wisconsin. Printed by Walsworth Press, of Marceline, Missouri. Manufactured in the United States of America.
Cartography by G. Mac Sebree

Library of Congress Card Catalog Number: 00-130324
ISBN: 0-915348-34-9

Cover Illustrations

FRONT: It was the Green Line because the cars and buses were green. Only the Ft. Mitchell line was left when the photographer encountered double-trucker 507 making the turn onto Pike from Hermes; it will soon be on private right-of-way heading southbound. 'Tis 1950, and the end of streetcars is near to hand. *Pat Cormody, Cliff Scholes Collection.*

REAR: Those with long memories treasure the *Kentucky*, built in 1892 by Brownell and converted into a parlor car in 1911. Shown here at Park Place, it was the last streetcar to run in Kentucky and is the third oldest preserved car in the U. S. The *Kentucky* was powered by two Westinghouse No. 3 single-reduction motors, the model which gave horsecar technology the coup-de-grace. After the *Kentucky*, buses took over. 41-S Twin Coach No. 482 typified the 1950's, and we have it here at Covington carbarn in its elaborate 1948-54 livery. Finally, the third century of public transit in Northern Kentucky is represented by TANK's first low-floor buses, delivered by Gillig in April, 2000. *Top: Dave Rummel, Phil Lind Collection. Middle: Pat Carmody, Cliff Scholes Collection. Bottom: Transit Authority of Northern Kentucky.*

Endsheet Illustrations

These two photos spotlight the important Cincinnati anchorage of the Green line before and after the advent of the Dixie Terminal.

FRONT: In late June of 1917, an almost new Cincinnati, Newport & Covington car 502 pauses at 5th & Walnut in downtown Cincinnati, about to start for Dayton. This is Fountain Square, with both the Tyler Davidson fountain and a World War I Red Cross fund drive sign prominent in the background. A Cincinnati Traction Co. car is on the left and the Emery Arcade Building is in the distance. *TANK Archives.*

REAR: It's April 6, 1937, in the rush hour. Remodeled 507 is bracketed by a single-truckers 265 and 267 as it inches along the ramp from the Suspension Bridge toward the upper level Dixie Terminal loading area. Below, on Third St., line 11 single-trucker 102 has just emerged from the lower level heading for Newport and Ft. Thomas. *James Gibson*

Table of Contents

Foreword

THE CINCINNATI, Newport & Covington Railway Co. was not a major player in the realm of public transit. The Green Line, so named to distinguish it from the orange cars of the much larger Cincinnati Street Railway, was comprised of only 58 or so route miles and it rostered only 200 streetcars during the heyday of its rail operation.

Yet the CN&C was remarkable, if not downright unique, in its field. Consider the contrasts between old and new. It clung to the last two-man, single-truck, hand-braked cars in the United States. Inaugurated the nation's first interstate trolley-coach service. Ran transit buses over Greyhound's intercity routes during World War II. Barged into the air age by holding the franchise to exclusively serve the Greater Cincinnati Airport for more than 25 years. And formed the nucleus for what would become one of the nation's largest transit conglomerates: American Transportation Enterprises. This is a company that somehow managed to reach into the past and into the future simultaneously. It was a wondrous thing to behold.

Successor Transit Authority of Northern Kentucky is today ranked as one of the finest small transit systems in the U. S. It is the old Green Line brought up to date.

Both of us drew extensively on our own collections of Green Line records and photographs and conducted original research. We looked at miles of local newspaper microfilm and microfiche and all sorts of regulatory documents. But our effort would have surely missed the mark without the efforts of many other folks.

To properly tell the Green Line's remarkable story would not have been possible without the foresight of retired Green Line President David Lear Ringo, who saw to it that many company records and photographs were safely entrusted to the Special Collections and Archives of the University of Kentucky Libraries. The tireless help of William J. Marshall, the Libraries' Director, made the task of sorting through the collection a rewarding and enjoyable experience. We also thank U. K.'s Phyllis Gillespie, Sallie Powell, and Lisa Carter.

We recognize Mark Donaghy, the general manager of TANK, who not only answered numerous questions about current operations, but graciously made available Green Line records discovered during the move to TANK's Ft. Wright facility. A kudo also to TANK's Carole Beach for all her help.

G. Mac Sebree provided valuable editorial insight borne of his many years as a book and magazine publisher. He put us in contact with other people, and drew a number of maps. Albert E. Meier, Eli Bail, P. Allen Copeland, and the late John Hoschek of the Motor Bus Society provided much information about the Green Line's motor bus fleet. Tom McNamara and Richard Segerer furnished both records and photographs which filled voids in our understanding of the 1960-1972 era. C. William "Bill" Myers came up with some remarkable photographs and the 1893 souvenir program. And, along with Tom McNamara, he thoroughly vetted the manuscript for both historical accuracy and language usage. John Niehaus gave us an important Covington traffic study, and James Jones drew the Dayton property map.

Assisting us at the Kenton County Library were Director Wayne Onst, Charles King, Steve Alpert, and Mike Averdick. Paul Vath of the Cincinnati-Hamilton Co. Public Library and Cynthia Keller and the librarians at the Cincinnati Museum Center were also most helpful. Van Wilkins gave some important encouragement.

Both Cliff Scholes and David McNeil opened up to us their photographic collections. As an aside, Cliff runs a small business dealing in historical transit and railroad photographs and slides. For further information write him at 1423 Kelvin Court, Cincinnati, Ohio 45240. The folks at the Provident Camera Shop in Cincinnati did some fine work copying numerous photographs. Also contributing photos, postcard views and/or data were Tom Tallentire, Dave Etienne, Dave Warning, Phil Lind, Bob Mason, Carl Rekow, Charles Tharp, Bill Sanders, John H. White, James Gibson, Dan Finfrock, Dave Arganbright, M. D. McCarter, Tom Taylor, George Krambles, Larry Fobiano, Don Hess, Jim Rodecker, Ron Hill, Charles Tharp, Mark Albert, Arnold Joseph, Mark Steffen, Kenneth Stewart, Mike Sweeney, Tad Winborne, Harvey Hylton, and Fred Bauer. We also thank Marie L. Potter for proofreading parts of the text, Elaine Shaw for typing the index, and Lisa Tingley for computer formatting.

Terry W. Lehmann thanks his wife, Hannah, for occasionally assuming "widow" status during this endeavor, and Mary Ann Arrasmith (whose aunt Grace Kruetzkamp was a longtime Green Line employee) for preparing numerous drafts. Mr. Lehmann would like to dedicate his part of his work to his daughters Corinne and Susan, his mother Catherine, to John Blakely, to William Cook, to Mary Ryan, and to Jessica and Pusser . . . loving cats and feline editorial assistants.

Earl W. Clark, Jr., has been taking, trading, and collecting photographs since 1935 and apologizes to anyone who has not received due credit because of the passage of time. Mr. Clark would like to remember his brother Jack and Fred Veith for their encouragement, interest and contributions over the years.

A special salute goes to Dr. George W. Hilton, professor emeritus of economics at the University of California, Los Angeles, for his grant to CERA which made the color sections possible. Lastly, the photographs attributed to George Krambles were provided by him just days prior to his passing, the last, generous gesture of a lifetime of devotion to the rich history of electric railroading.

All errors of commission and omission are those of the authors although we pray they are few and far between.

Terry W. Lehmann
Earl W. Clark, Jr.
Cincinnati, Ohio, 2000.

A Green Line Motorman at Work

As we crouch behind the motorman of this Green Line single-truck car we see that Clinton Smith's right hand is on the "stemwinder" hand brake. The car's controller was operated by his left hand. Since the last of the Green Line single-truck, two-man hand braked cars were not retired until 1947, the Cincinnati, Newport & Covington was the last transit property in the United States to operate such cars in daily revenue service. Could a transit company be staunchly progressive and backward at the same time? This photo dates from the late 1930s, prior to the Green Line's side trip into the airline business at the postwar Greater Cincinnati airport. Doesn't it boggle the mind to think that Green Line officials eventually found themselves occupied simultaneously with Convairs and DC-4 airliners, and single-truck streetcars with hand brakes? *Special Collections and Archives, University of Kentucky Libraries.*

JOHN A. ROEBLING ARCHITECT & BUILDER.
WORK COMMENCED SEPT 1ST 1856.
OPENED TO TRAVEL, DEC. 1ST 1866.
COST OF BRIDGE PROPER $ 1,500,000.
DISTANCE BETWEEN CENTRE TOWERS 1,057 FEET.
TOTAL LENGTH 2,252 FEET.
HEIGHT OF TOWERS 240 FEET.

DIAMETER OF CABLES 12.4 INCHES.
WIRE IN THE TWO CABLES 1,000,000 POUNDS.
STRENGTH OF STRUCTURE 15,264 TONS.
DEFLECTION OF CABLES 85 FEET.
NUMBER OF WIRES IN EACH CABLE 5,200.
HEIGHT OF BRIDGE IN CENTRE ABOVE LOW WATER 103 FEET.
WEIGHT SUPPORTED BY CABLES 1,900 TONS.

CINCINNATI & COVINGTON SUSPENSION BRIDGE.

'It Was Indeed a Work to Excite Amazement and Wonderment'

So said Thomas Kinsella, a journalist for the *Brooklyn Eagle.* This contemporary lithograph of the Cincinnati & Covington Suspension Bridge, designed, engineered and built by John A. Roebling, depicts a structure that became a dress rehearsal for Roebling's famed Brooklyn Bridge. Kinsella and other East Coast movers and shakers had been junketed to Cincinnati and Northern Kentucky to behold the great marvel, and buy into Roebling's grand plan for New York's East River. And a great marvel it was, too, for the citizens of Northern Kentucky. Soon after it opened to travel on December 1, 1866, public transportation between the Queen City and its neighbors across the Ohio River became a reality. And in the wake of that, the Cincinnati, Newport & Covington Railway Co., better known as the Green Line, began its remarkable existence. *T. W. Lehmann Collection.*

1.

Origins of the Green Line: 1867-1889

THE HISTORY of public transportation in the Northern Kentucky metropolitan area across the Ohio River from Cincinnati must necessarily start with that larger city. In the 30 years between 1830 and 1860 the Queen City had exploded in population from 24,831 to 161,044. It was now the largest city west of the Alleghenies and the fourth largest in the United States.

Across the deep and swiftly flowing Ohio, there were in 1860 two modest Kentucky cities: Covington with 16,471 and Newport with 10,046 souls. The first steamboat, on its way to New Orleans from Pittsburgh, passed by in 1811. With its natural harbor, Cincinnati by 1825 was a major port and had attracted a number of steamboat builders. By 1840, it was also the top meatpacking center in the nation. Chicago, which would eventually eclipse the Queen City, was but an upstart crossroads.

Everyone seemed to be heading for Cincinnati. The completion of the Miami and Erie Canal from Toledo in 1842 added another jewel to the Queen City's crown. And by 1860 it had become a railroad hub.

However, it was the Ohio River that kept Northern Kentuckians from easily holding jobs in Cincinnati or providing goods and services to that city. In 1860 the only way across the Ohio River from either Covington or Newport was by ferryboat,

a service often interrupted by high water, low water or solid water. Before the days of dams across the Ohio, the river frequently left its banks in the spring, became too shallow for passage during summer and in the winter could easily freeze

Even getting to the ferry was no easy matter. The streets were miserable, unpaved affairs with severe ruts and potholes that resembled the Sahara Desert in the summer and the Great Dismal Swamp during periods of inclement weather.

At the start of the Civil War the only public transportation in Northern Kentucky was the horse-drawn omnibus. However, the unpaved streets ensured a tortuous ride in these contraptions due to their primitive springs and narrow iron-rimmed wheels. And omnibuses tended to be operated on irregular schedules by generally unreliable operators.

But by 1860 hopes for bridges linking Covington (Kenton County) and Newport (Campbell County) with Cincinnati were improving markedly. The rumor in Newport was that the Pennsylvania Railroad was exploring possible sites for a combination road and railway bridge linking the two cities. In Covington a group of investors had approved the plans of famed civil engineer and wire rope specialist John Roebling for a suspension-type wagon bridge linking Cincinnati and Covington. Roebling was off the mark first; his company was well financed and construction commenced during the summer of that year.

Although the Civil War delayed the completion of both bridges, it was apparent that Cincinnati and Northern Kentucky interests would soon be tangibly united. This spotlighted another need: an improved public transportation system linking Northern Kentucky counties with the Queen City. Thoughts turned to new technology, a major advance over the omnibus,

After 1867 Campbell County residents could detour via Covington and the Suspension Bridge to reach Cincinnati and, after 1876, could use the Pennsylvania Railroad Bridge to reach Cincinnati. However, ferry service between the foot of York Street in Newport and the foot of Broadway in Cincinnati continued until the start of streetcar service in 1892 over the Central Bridge, opened only the year before. *Earl Clark Collection.*

consisting of two iron rails over which passenger cars having flanged wheels would be drawn at regular intervals by horses and mules.

Horsecars seem so quaint today. Not then; they were in the 1860s quite state of the art. Flanged wheels meant a much lower co-efficient of friction, allowing more people to be carried more smoothly and more rapidly for the same expenditure of horse-power (in the truest sense) compared to animal-drawn vehicles on ordinary roadways.

The Covington Street Railway Co.

On February 9, 1864, a group of Covington citizens incorporated the Covington Street Railway Co. with the purpose of building a horsecar line from Cincinnati over the soon to be completed Suspension Bridge and along Madison in Covington to 12th or 13th Streets. Then on August 15, 1865, the Covington City Council accepted the Covington Street Railway's bid to construct the Madison Street line in accordance with an ordinance enacted earlier that year which set out Covington routes to be bid for by private companies:

No. 1 - Greenup St.
No. 2 - Madison St.

Rough riding stagecoaches, or omnibuses, such as the one in the right foreground near Ninth & Washington in Newport, were the only means of public transit in Northern Kentucky prior to the coming of the horsecars. *Earl Clark Collection via Fred Bauer.*

No. 3 - Pike and Banklick Sts.
No. 4 - Main St.
No. 5 - Third St.

Meanwhile, an epochal event in the life of Northern Kentucky took place. The Suspension Bridge opened to pedestrian traffic in December of 1866 and to wagon traffic the next month. The Covington and Cincinnati Bridge Co. had installed streetcar tracks in the floor of the bridge during construction and then offered them, for a toll of 2 cents a passenger, to any street railway company wishing to utilize the bridge.

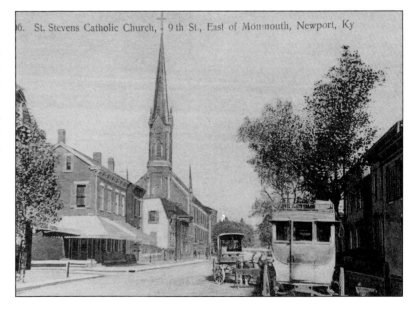

6. St. Stevens Catholic Church, 9th St., East of Monmouth, Newport, Ky

Construction of the Madison St. (later upgraded to "Avenue") line got underway in the spring of 1867 and revenue service started on August 5, 1867. From 12th & Madison in Covington this pioneer horsecar line operated north on Madison to Third, east on Third to Greenup, north on Greenup to Second, west on Second to the Suspension Bridge, to a loop on Front St. in Cincinnati. The cars returned over the bridge to Second, west on Second to Scott, north on Scott to Third, and west on Third to Madison. The Covington Street Railway's carbarn, offices and stables were located in a building measuring 45 feet by 150 feet on the west side of Madison between 12th and 13th.

Destinations and important points served by the line were indicated by large painted panels along the sides of the cars. However, in the days before universal literacy, it was common for a horsecar line to be referred to by the color of paint used on its cars. As the cars of the Covington Street Railway were painted white, it soon became known as the "White Line." Similar type names were bestowed upon the lines of other companies as they began operations.

City regulations governed the new CSR. One rule demanded that cars not exceed a blazing top speed of 6 m.p.h. Another allowed men to get on and off the cars while the vehicle was moving but not "ladies or children," a mandate which would not pass Constitutional muster today.

The ordinance set other conditions including the gauge of the track (five foot, two and one-half inches) and the permissible fare to be charged "within the city limits" (5 cents). The wider-than-standard gauge was chosen so that the Kentucky cars could use the already established horsecar tracks in downtown Cincinnati where service had started in September, 1859.

Campbell County Follows Suit

Newport joined the party in the winter of 1867. Under the terms of a franchise granted by the city to the Newport Street Railway, a horsecar line was built from 11th St. down York St. to Fifth St. and west on Fifth over the Licking River bridge to Covington on Fourth to a connection with the tracks of the Covington Street Railway at Fourth & Greenup. From there, the "Newport and Covington line" used CSR tracks to Greenup & Second Sts. to reach the Suspension Bridge and Cincinnati. Return was via Second to Scott St. to Fourth St. and east on Fourth to the Licking River and Newport.

This line, which commenced operations on December 9, 1867, was single track with "turnouts" or sidings to enable cars going in opposite directions to pass each other. Since the Newport Street Railway cars were predominantly painted blue, the name "Blue Line" was soon adopted by the traveling public.

The first reported accident on the fledgling horsecar lines occurred in 1869. On July 10, the *Cincinnati Enquirer* reported:

"A Newport streetcar, containing 48 passengers, made rather a quick trip from the center of the Ohio River Suspension Bridge to Covington, on Thursday evening, between six and seven o'clock. When the car began to descend the grade, the driver attempted to apply the brake, but the chain with which it is controlled had got tangled up so that the brake would not work, and the car soon gained such rapid headway that all efforts to check it proved unavailing, and it dashed down the bridge at a rate quite alarming to the passengers.

"The driver, who happened on this occasion to be the Superintendent of the Road, stood manfully to his post and

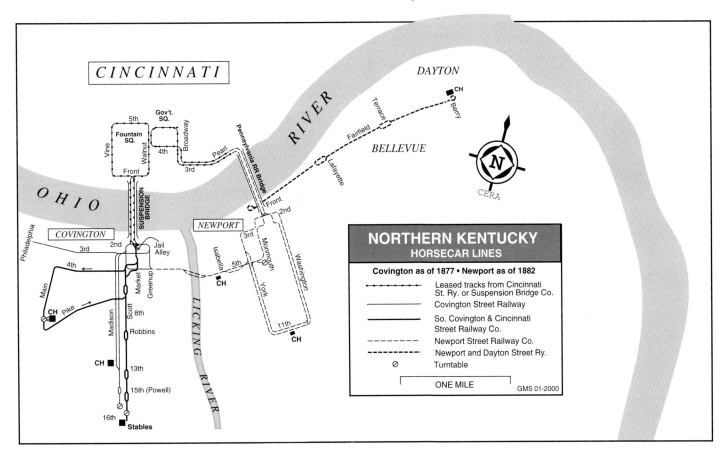

From October, 1877, to February, 1878, the Newport and Dayton Street Railway used a steam dummy **(above)** which, in reality, was a steam locomotive disguised by a wraparound passenger body. But the Newport City Council was not fooled. The Council did not like the noise and smoke the contraption made and banned it from further usage in Newport. A Blue Line car sits on the turntable at Fifth and Monmouth in Newport, **below**. Although retouched, this photograph could date from as early as 1876. Left to right are NSR employees J.D. Maines, John Kaeney, Benjamin Gosney, J. White, and C.R. Garley. *Dayton Centennial booklet, Earl Clark Collection; Special Collections and Archives, University of Kentucky Libraries.*

managed the horses very skillfully, landing the car on the pavement on the south side of Second St. 'right side up with care'. One passenger jumped off while the car was in motion, by which action his pants were badly torn in the seat. This was the only damage that resulted from the runaway."

A Third Railway, a Second Bridge

A third transit line now appeared. The Newport and Dayton Street Railway was incorporated on January 25, 1868, to build from Dayton, through Bellevue, to Newport. In April, 1870, construction was completed between Sixth & Berry in Dayton along Fairfield in Bellevue to the Newport corporation line and service commenced between these points. The year 1870 also saw the company erect a carbarn, a stable and storage buildings at Sixth & Berry in Dayton.

On November 17, 1870, the Newport Common Council granted the Newport and Dayton permission to construct an extension on Main (later Front) from the east corporation line west to Washington. By March, 1871, the horsecar line was in operation over the entire route.

More importantly, Newport's longing for its own bridge to Cincinnati was to be satisfied, thanks to the Pennsylvania Railroad. The PRR incorporated the Newport and Cincinnati Bridge Co. early in 1868 to construct a combined rail and roadway bridge over the Ohio River, at an estimated cost of $1 million to be completed in 1870. It would be located on the line of Butler St. in Cincinnati and Saratoga St. in Newport in order to connect the Pennsylvania's subsidiary Little Miami Railroad with the Louisville, Cincinnati and Lexington Railway, a predecessor of the important Louisville and Nashville.

But there were vexing delays. Construction of the bridge was not completed as scheduled because, in the fall of 1870, the Army Corps of Engineers decided that the almost completed structure posed a hazard to river navigation. The Corps found that the deck was too low for steamboats to safely clear at high water and that the piers were turned two degrees too far in to the current flow of the river thus reducing the opening of the main channel to unacceptable standards. Thus it can be seen that Washington bureaucratic maneuvers are not a new phenomenon.

The extensive (and expensive) changes that the Pennsylvania Railroad had to make to the structure delayed its opening until March, 1872. And then it turned out that street railway investors were not fighting for a place in line even after the Pennsylvania Bridge opened a direct corridor between Newport and Cincinnati. It would be four years before a horsecar line would grace that bridge.

Over in Covington, though, the transit business was bustling. The Madison St. line, operating to Front St. in Cincinnati, obviously filled a need. In the year preceding August 31, 1869, the Covington Street Railway carried more than 600,000 riders. Alas, despite the obvious popularity of the

A retired Newport and Dayton Street Railway horsecar awaits disposition at the back of the Newport Car House on Eleventh St., circa 1893.
Special Collections and Archives, University of Kentucky Libraries.

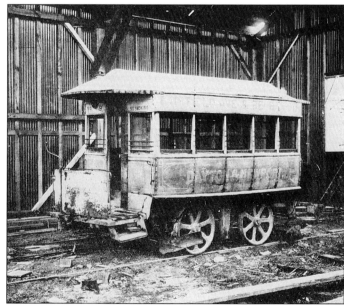

Madison St. line, the rate of investor return must have been dismal, as the CSR could not obtain backing to bid on any of the other four routes offered by the city.

But it did expand in Ohio. On March 20, 1872, the CSR extended its Cincinnati operation north on Vine to Third, then east on Third to Walnut, and then south on Walnut back to Front by leasing the tracks of the Passenger Railroad Co. of Cincinnati. According to *The Ticket*, a newspaper published in Covington between 1875 and 1878, the northern terminus of the Covington Street Railway's Madison St. line was extended to Fountain Square on April 10, 1875. At that time the Cincinnati loop was reversed with the cars going north on Walnut to Fifth, west around the Tyler Davidson Fountain and south on Vine. And, as we shall see, it would share this loop with a new competitor.

A New Competitor

Although the original Covington ordinance of 1864 had set the groundwork for entrepreneurs to bid on a series of proposed routes in that city, the Covington Street Railway had not attempted any further construction by 1874--a full decade of stagnation. Covington officials were delighted when, in early 1874, Edward Fiefield Abbott announced that his new Covington and Cincinnati Street Railway (C&C) had secured financial backing to build Franchise Route No. 4, Main Street. Abbott also secured Council permission to incorporate part of the still unawarded No. 3 Pike St. Route into the new line.

By December, 1874, the C&C started work on modified Route No. 4 which was planned as a single track horsecar line from Fourth & Scott over Fourth to Main, then south on Main to Pike; returning north on Pike to Cooper and back to Scott & Fourth. By ordinance the Covington Street Railway (CSR) was compelled, for a fair rental fee, to allow the C&C to use its trackage from Fourth to and from the Suspension Bridge.

It wasn't going to be that simple. Still smarting over its failure to attract sufficient capital to build the Main St. route and fearing competition, Covington Street Railway obtained an injunction in January, 1875, after convincing a court that the C&C's proposed connections to its tracks at Fourth & Scott and Fourth & Greenup would require some severe curves and present a real danger of derailment.

The injunction, which effectively voided Covington's common trackage ordinance, barred the proposed connections and left the C&C four blocks short of the Suspension Bridge and any prospects for meaningful revenues.

Eager for the new street railway line, the Covington City Council, on January 28, 1875, passed an emergency ordinance allowing the Covington and Cincinnati Street Railway to build a line on Fourth parallel to the CSR's track as far as Market (now Court), to cross the CSR track at that point and to construct a single track on the rather narrow Market as far as Third. The C&C was then authorized to continue through an even narrower alley behind the jail in order to connect with Suspension Bridge Company tracks to Cincinnati.

There was no time to lose. In its anxiety to stake its claim before the CSR could obtain yet another injunction, the C&C started laying rail that very night, completing a short section from the jail alley directly to the Suspension Bridge tracks. The rail

Edward F. Abbott, an 1846 graduate of the U.S. Military Academy with a degree in civil engineering, served as an artillery captain along with Robert E. Lee during the Mexican War in 1847. He resigned in 1856 and migrated to Northern Kentucky. In 1874 he formed the Covington and Cincinnati Street Railway and by 1890 had bought out rival street railway companies in Northern Kentucky.
Earl Clark Collection via John J. Strader, IV

behind the jail was temporarily laid down directly on top of the paving blocks. The C&C also threw down a short section of track across the CSR rails at Fourth and Market.

Construction of the Main Street line continued during the winter and early spring of 1875. A substantial frame and corrugated metal carbarn on the northeast corner of Main & Pike was completed in April. All preliminaries done, the C&C placed into operation its Main Street line on May 24, 1875.

The jail alley right-of-way was so narrow that the company had to put bars on the windows of its cars to keep patrons from leaning out and suffering injury from hitting the sides of the buildings abutting the alley. Later on, in 1882, "Jail Alley" was widened between Second and Third, and along with Market between Third and Fourth, received the more dignified name of Court St.

To alleviate delays on its single track line through Market and Jail Alley, the city allowed the C&C to build, in June, 1875, a single track east through a portion of the space reserved for the town market and south on Scott to connect with its existing trackage. This arrangement meant, in effect, a double track except on the short "Jail Alley" segment.

Interestingly, the 1875 ordinance permitted one rail of the Covington and Cincinnati's track to be laid to the left of, and one rail in the middle of, the CSR's existing track on Scott Street. This created what is known as gauntlet trackage where two sets of tracks overlap but do not utilize the same rails. As a matter of fact, until consolidation in 1883, no tracks of the C&C and the CSR ever connected. The two systems did, however, use leased tracks in common on the Suspension Bridge and in Cincinnati.

Apparently in response to the C&C's penetration of West Covington along Fourth, the Covington Street Railway in 1876 built a short, single-track, one-horsecar line out Third St. as far as

The Green and White Line was the color coding assigned the Newport and Dayton line presumably because it connected in Newport with the White and Green lines which ran on to Cincinnati. The drawing depicts car No. 3 in service during the yuletide season, circa 1885. It seems, however, that the mules are decidedly not cooperating in the spirit of the season! *David Lear Ringo Collection.*

Philadelphia. It did not go to Cincinnati but circled downtown Covington from Third & Philadelphia over Third to Greenup, north to Second, west to Scott, south to Third, and west on Third to the end of the line.

Newport Linked to Cincinnati at Last

With precious little cooperation from the city fathers, Newport's civic pride was restored in late 1875, when the Newport Street Railway announced it would begin construction of a line south from Fifth & York to the Pennsylvania Bridge (otherwise the Newport and Cincinnati Bridge) and on to downtown Cincinnati. But the city decided that the whole idea was illegal.

Construction had progressed down to Third & York by the time the city of Newport sought a restraining order to halt further building, contending that it had not given permission for the extension and the use of its streets. The company insisted that it had been given such powers under its original franchise.

On February 23, 1876, the Campbell County Circuit Court agreed. It ruled in favor of the Newport Street Railway and dissolved the restraining order. Fearing further legal action, the NSR resumed construction as soon as the weather permitted and completed its Cincinnati connection in April, 1876.

The line then extended, according to a 1918 affidavit given by the original construction supervisor:

"...from Fifth and York; north on York to Third (formerly Taylor) street; east on Taylor to Monmouth; north on Monmouth to Second (formerly Eglantine) street to the bridge approach. This was for cars going to Cincinnati. For cars returning from Cincinnati, a line was constructed from the bridge approach to Saratoga street; south to Third; west on Third to Monmouth; south on Monmouth to Fifth, and west on Fifth to York, connecting with the original line at Fifth and York."

On the Cincinnati side, the NSR entered into a rental agreement with the Cincinnati Consolidated Railroad to use its tracks to reach downtown Cincinnati and Government Square. The route from the bridge (and a short connection on Butler) went west to Pearl to Broadway, north on Broadway to Fourth, west on Fourth to Walnut then north on Walnut to Fifth and east on Fifth back to Broadway to Pearl and to the bridge.

The new line took over the tracks of the Newport and Covington line from Fifth & York south to 11th (named Williamson until 1890) and then east to the wye at the carbarn and stables on the southeast corner of 11th & Saratoga. A spur track and turntable was built on the south side of Fifth between York and Monmouth to turn the cars of the Newport and Covington line which became a crosstown shuttle operation between Fifth & Monmouth in Newport and Second & Greenup in Covington. With direct Newport access to the Queen City, it was no longer necessary for the Newport cars to go into Cincinnati via Covington.

At about the time the new York Street line was opened, the Covington Street Railway extended the Madison Street line on single track from 13th out Madison to between 15th and 16th. A turntable was installed in the middle of Madison to reverse the cars.

To better serve expanding east Newport, in May, 1881 the Newport Street Railway started construction on a new line from Cincinnati over the Pennsylvania Bridge east on Second to Washington and south on Washington to 11th. This line was in operation by August, 1881.

Yellow Becomes Green

It was now Covington's turn to get more transit service, and in the process lay the groundwork for its 20th Century transit network. The South Covington and Cincinnati Street Railway Co. was incorporated in January of 1876 to construct a line on Scott from Fourth to 16th. The South Covington and Cincinnati's stock was controlled by the E. F. Abbott group, owners of the Covington and Cincinnati Street Railway.

As was becoming common practice in the industry, the SC&C was formed to insulate Covington and Cincinnati Street Railway from any liability stemming from potential construction accidents or other misadventure.

Without further ado, the Scott Street line opened in July, 1876 with the horsecars patriotically painted in red, soon resulting in the Scott Street line becoming known as the "Red Line". With no need for two corporations, on December 20, 1876, the Covington and Cincinnati Street Railway was merged into the

A Meeting of Doomed Technologies

Two early transit technologies meet in downtown Cincinnati in the frame at **left**. A Newport car on Fifth St. at Government Square, having just turned east from Walnut, passes a Walnut Hills cable car. The United States Post Office and Courthouse Building is in the background. *Earl Clark Collection.*

At the **bottom** of the page is the only known photograph of the South Covington and Cincinnati Street Railway's Scott St. line, known as the Red Line. It commenced service from downtown Covington to 16th St. via Scott in 1877 and was abandoned in 1893 in lieu of a new electric line on Greenup Street. *Kenton Co. Library.*

South Covington and Cincinnati with E. F. Abbott staying on as chief executive until 1892.

The Main Street line cars were originally painted yellow and the company thus was known for a short time as the Yellow Line. But according to a number of accounts, green paint was soon substituted in 1877 for the yellow because of employees of the Covington Street Railway calling out to the South Covington and Cincinnati Street Railway drivers at crossing points that they were too "yaller" to go first.

And so the name "Green Line" was born. It would stick for 95 years.

The Newport and Dayton Street Railway, in 1872, extended its line on Front St. in Newport as far as Monmouth. However, the city of Newport withheld permission to extend N&D cars to Cincinnati via the new bridge. The problem was financial: it seems the Newport and Dayton ran into financial difficulty almost from the start and was continually delinquent in paying its yearly franchise fees to Newport.

In 1877 this line actually tried, for a time, a vehicle known as a steam dummy which essentially was a steam locomotive with a passenger body attached. Two steam dummies served the route from October 22, 1877, to February 2, 1878. However on that date the city of Newport obtained a court order barring the belching steam dummies from entering Newport. For a short time thereafter the N&D hitched horses to the steam dummy at the Newport boundary and hauled it to Front and Monmouth. But this was impractical, and by May of 1878 mulepower ruled again over the entire route.

Consolidation

Competitive pressures now intensified, as they were beginning to do elsewhere. In 1882 the South Covington and Cincinnati Street Railway, led by its president Edward F. Abbott, acquired the Covington Street Railway, operator of the Madison Ave. line, for $172,000. In addition to the Madison Ave. trackage, the SC&C acquired 15 cars, 60 sets of harness, tools for the blacksmith shop, a one horsepower hay cutter, 78 horses and mules, and the CSR's stables.

In 1883 the Newport Street Railway Co., operating the Newport and Covington, York Street, and Washington Ave. lines, was sold to the South Covington and Cincinnati Street Railway for $180,000. As part of the purchase, the SC&C took title to 26 horsecars, 59 horses, 63 mules, carbarns and stables on both the

The Very Model of a Modern Horsecar

The South Covington and Cincinnati received 10 large, 26-foot horsecars in 1887 for the Madison Ave. line. One, No. 9, is shown outside of the Stephenson Car Company's factory in New York City. The cars featured improved springs and a small charcoal heating stove for passenger comfort.   *Smithsonian Collection 72-2834.*

southeast corner of Fifth & Isabella and on the southeast corner of 11th & Saratoga, and a large tract of undeveloped land along the Licking River in the vicinity of 11th & Brighton in Newport. This tract would play a very important role in the future development of public transportation in the Northern Kentucky area.

Subsequent to the 1883 consolidation, the South Covington and Cincinnati constructed some extensions and made other improvements, purchased new horsecars and rebuilt some trackage. The Madison Ave. line, in addition to being double tracked from 12th to 16th, was extended on single track to 20th in 1884. However, no through service was offered south of the double track so it was necessary to change at 16th to a "dinky" (an older 14-passenger car) to reach the Covington city limits at 20th.

As well, the Main Street line was extended east on Fourth to Greenup, thereby allowing the Main Street cars to avoid the Court bottleneck. The Scott St. line, which did not run through to Cincinnati, continued to use Scott to Fourth to Court before turning east through the Covington market and back to Scott. This eased traffic congestion somewhat as the Scott Street line was kept out of the flow of horsecars using Greenup, Second and Scott to and from the Suspension Bridge.

In 1884, the South Covington and Cincinnati rebuilt and enlarged its Newport carbarn and stables. It also rebuilt the roadbed and replaced all old rail, still in place since the construction of the Blue Line in 1867, on York between Fifth and 11th.

Horsecar Technology

Although the horsecars were certainly an improvement over previous forms of transportation, the technology was still primitive. Nevertheless, it could be said that life on the cars was at least cozy. The cars were so narrow that passengers' knees almost touched as they sat facing each other. That is, if they could get a seat. There were no heaters so in cold weather the space between the seats was stuffed with straw for insulation, and there was a lot more of the stuff on the floor.

For a horsecar driver, life was tough by any standard. The platform on which the driver stood while working the horses or mules was exposed. Consequently the driver suffered through the heat of summer and the cold of winter. When fares were to be collected, the driver would tie the lines to the whipstand and come into the car to collect. The horses, of course, knew the way. The driver was responsible for keeping two stubborn horses (or mules) under control at all times. This required considerable skill. The brakes on the horsecars were controlled by a chain mechanism. It took a sturdy driver with bulging biceps to properly operate these brakes, hence their nickname the "Armstrong" brake. The chain frequently got tangled up thereby causing a fair number of runaway situations and accidents. The driver also had to put up with the odor and associated nuisances caused by animal waste. A driver, in the 1880s, worked 12 to 13 hours daily, six days a week, for the princely wage of 16 cents per hour. It wasn't an easy way to make a living.

Draft horses and mules, while not necessarily maltreated, were nonetheless exploited as living capital assets. A poignant and sad reminder of the horse and mule car era on the South Covington and Cincinnati was reported by the *Cincinnati Times Star* in 1890:

> "A faithful old mule, after 20 years of faithful service, lay down on the track while pulling the car up Walnut St. yesterday and died. The mule first slipped on the rail and fell, but managed, after a struggle, to regain his feet, but had scarcely straightened up when he again toppled over, and, after casting a parting glance at his old pard in harness, closed his eyes and quit. 'Heart failure' was the verdict."

Sometimes a horsecar would jump the tracks. On such occasion all male passengers felt obligated to pile out into the elements and help the driver lift the car back into place. Derailments were often caused by a heavy load on the rear platform raising the front wheels of the little cars which measured, depending on the model, between 18 and 24 feet long.

Most Northern Kentucky streets in the 1880s were not paved and pedestrians had to step down to stones laid in street intersections from curb to curb in order to avoid the dirt, mud and sewage.

These stone crossings sorely tested the skill of the horsecar driver who had to stop the car so the rear steps would be precisely adjacent. If they were not, the passengers would have to be on guard lest they step into a sea of mud or sewage upon leaving the car or, vice versa, having to wade out into the mud to board. The three-foot square stone pavers were set in pairs about a foot and a half apart from one side of a street intersection to the other so that people could pass each other while walking across the street. No doubt the passengers marveled at this latest 19th Century convenience.

Horsecar Service in 1883

Horsecar lines in the 1880s were known primarily by their color, and not just in Northern Kentucky.

In an era when literacy was the exception rather than the rule, the fact that the cars of each street railway line were painted in a distinctive color scheme was of no small benefit. In Covington, the Main St. cars, which were painted green, formed the original Green Line. Six cars were scheduled for regular runs and two extra cars ran during the morning and evening rush hours.

For each car, six horses were needed, the animals being changed during the course of the day. This meant that 36 horses were required for regular Green Line service and 10 extra horses were kept in readiness to take the place of any disabled animals and to run the additional rush-hour cars.

The Madison Ave. line, known as the White Line before the 1883 consolidation, saw eight regular cars as well as four morning and afternoon extra cars. In order to distinguish the line from the recently acquired York St. White Line, the Madison Ave. cars were now repainted an orange-tinted cream and so this operation became the Buff Line. A total of 48 horses were required for the regular runs and 14 additional horses were needed to take the place of disabled horses and to haul the extra cars on this Line.

Two regular cars plied Scott St., the so-called Red Line. This route used 12 horses which were stabled at a building on the southwest corner of 17th & Scott. This edifice was too small to also house the cars and they were left out on the street at night. The Third St. line needed only one regular car, whose color scheme is lost to history.

In 1883, the Blue Line still connected lower Covington and Newport. Only two cars were assigned to cover the route between Second & Greenup in Covington and Fifth & Monmouth in Newport.

Newport's York St. and Washington Ave. lines, after the 1883 consolidation, were jointly designated the new White Line. Since the York St. cars ran from Government Square in Cincinnati south on York to 11th and returned to Cincinnati on Washington while the Washington Ave. cars ran the reverse route, the two lines actually formed one continuous belt line. The evidence suggests that the white painted cars, operating from Cincinnati south via York St. to 11th and returning to Cincinnati via Washington, displayed green flags during the day and green lights at night while cars operating south to Newport via Washington to 11th before returning north on York to Cincinnati showed white flags or lights.

The White Line operated a total of 12 regular cars. Additional morning and evening rush-hour service was given, but the records do not tell us how much.

A more complicated color adorned the Newport and Dayton Street Railway cars, which connected with the Washington Ave. and York St. cars at the Pennsylvania Bridge. These reflected the colors of their connecting partners and were appropriately decorated in a white and green checked pattern. No records have survived to indicate the frequency of service on the Newport and Dayton line.

The earlier vehicles were, by and large, replaced by a series of new and improved horsecars built by the John Stephenson Co. of New York from 1883 through 1885. The first horsecars were called "bobtails" because they had no rear platform. They did have a back entrance in the center of the rear of the car flanked by iron rods which one had to grab to climb up into the car. The new and more modern cars had a rear platform and steps on the curb side of the car, which made entering and leaving the cars much easier.

Stephenson re-equipped the South Covington and Cincinnati in 1883, with cars for the York and Main St. lines, with the better of the old horsecars of those two lines being rebuilt with side loading platforms and passed down to the Scott and Third St. lines. The new Stephenson cars were 20 feet long, featured stronger springs for improved riding quality, and had seats for 26 passengers, a far cry from the original rough-riding cars which could seat only 14. Fifteen more Stephenson cars were delivered to the SC&C in 1885.

The Last Independent is Purchased

By 1887 it was obvious that the South Covington and Cincinnati was emerging pre-eminent. In that year the SC&C bought out the remaining independent horsecar line in Northern Kentucky, the Newport and Dayton Street Railway.

For $85,000 the company acquired all the rights and fran-

The year is circa 1887, and this two-horse car is working the Buff Line at 15th & Madison in Covington. The buildings in the background are still extant. Alas, the top-hatted gentleman with cane standing in the background and his fellow onlookers are unidentified. *Kenton County Library.*

chises of the N&D, along with seven cars, one sprinkling car, 35 sets of harnesses, 28 horses, and seven mules. Also purchased was the property at Sixth & Berry which contained the carbarn and stables of the N&D. In short order, the Dayton line was routed over Second St. to the Pennsylvania Bridge and to Cincinnati's Government Square. The SC&C also double tracked the entire line and, in Dayton, extended the route to Third & Benham.

That same year the 10 new 20-foot horsecars already ordered by the N&D from an unknown builder replaced the old N&D "bobtail" cars. With their retirement, the era of the cumbersome end-loading horsecars was ended in Northern Kentucky.

In 1887 the SC&C, apparently satisfied with the cost and durability of the 1883-1885 Stephenson horsecars, ordered 10 more to re-equip the Madison Avenue line. These last horsecars, among the largest ever built in the United States, were some 26 feet long, seated 32 passengers and boasted a small coal burning heat stove for winter use.

It wasn't quite the end of an era, though. The late 1880s also saw one last minor flurry of new horsecar line construction by the South Covington and Cincinnati. It was called the Austinburg line and it was completed in the fall of 1887 as a shuttle connector to the Scott St. line. This route (nicknamed the "Austinburg

Hook" due to its configuration) met the Scott line at 15th, ran east on Powell to Oliver, south on Oliver one block to Rickey, west on Rickey one block to Edward, south on Edward to 17th where it headed due west to Scott.

At the same time, Newport saw the addition of one minor new line, when tracks were built on Central Ave. from 11th to Fifth to connect with the Blue Line.

This expansion, however modest, raised expectations.

With each acquisition or new construction, city councils along the growing system raised a hue and cry for the South Covington to reduce its fares and to institute a uniform 5-cent fare to and from Cincinnati to all points served in Kenton and Campbell Counties. A through ride from Northern Kentucky to Cincinnati prior to the first consolidation cost 12 cents. Of this amount 2 cents was paid as toll for each passenger to the bridge company.

And sure enough, these civic complaints had their effect. In 1882 , the through fare to Cincinnati was reduced to 10 cents, and by the late 1880s, tickets were sold which reduced the fare first to 9 cents cash or three tickets for 25 cents, and subsequently to 7 cents, or four tickets for 25 cents. The local fare remained at 5 cents for intrastate travel. ❏

A Last Glimpse of 2 h.p. Transportation

A White Line horsecar, No. 26, heads south on Vine St. in Cincinnati in the late 1870s after rounding the Tyler Davidson Fountain on Fifth. This landmark was set in the middle of an island called the Esplanade, later named Fountain Square.　　　　　*Earl Clark Collection.*

He Threw His Weight Around

This story made the rounds in the late 1880s. It concerned the South Covington and Cincinnati Street Railway and one Charles B. Simrall, the company's purchasing agent.

Simrall attended a business function one evening in Cincinnati. Afterward he went to the Emery Arcade at Fifth & Vine to catch a car to Covington only to find that the last car had already departed. Knowing that his rank in the company hierarchy was not sufficient for the night manager to order a special car back to Cincinnati just for him, he called the Madison car barn and inquired if they would send a car over for a very large party.

The answer was yes. A car soon arrived with a driver searching in vain for a large group of people and finding only Simrall at the car stop.

When the driver asked Simrall where the large party was, Simrall, who weighed close to 300 pounds, replied, "Am I not a large party?" ◆

Bridge and CN&C Building: Twin Green Line Icons

Perhaps appropriately, near the start of the 20th Century the Green Line's ornate rococo Covington headquarters building provided a dramatic counterpoint to Mr. Roebling's acclaimed Suspension Bridge. The two structures were bound together with the fortunes of the now-bustling transit company. A Green Line Brownell car built in 1893 has just left the Bridge and will shortly make a stop adjacent to the Cincinnati, Newport & Covington headquarters. Another car is behind; a third is on the bridge heading for Cincinnati. *Carl Rekow Collection.*

Electricity and Expansion: 1890-1906

T HE ERA OF THE horse and mule-drawn streetcar was coming to an end. This obsolete technology could not compete with the new electric systems which had begun in places like Richmond, Virginia, as early as 1887.

By 1889, it was clear that the electric streetcar had become a reliable form of transportation. The electric motor did not possess the undependable temperament of the mule, and because it was capable of propelling cars at a greater speed, it ushered in a new era of transportation.

The South Covington and Cincinnati Street Railway Co. began a series of engineering and feasibility studies in 1889. It also knew that any conversion to electricity would require a great deal of new capital. The company, however, was confident that both the technical and financial hurdles for conversion to electric cars could be overcome. Later that year it petitioned the city of Covington for a new ordinance--which was quickly passed--allowing it to erect poles and wires and to convert all horsecar lines to electric operation. The South Covington and Cincinnati also petitioned the city of Cincinnati for a similar ordinance which was granted in February of 1890.

Work started in the summer of 1890 to first convert the heavily used Madison Ave. route (and the Main St. line since it served the carbarn) to electricity. The company had to do more than just erect poles and string wires and order new streetcars. Electric streetcars created certain operating problems. The roadbeds had to be made heavier and more durable, and power from strategically located power stations and substations had to be supplied over an extensive system of "feeders."

Further, the new electric streetcars required the retraining of the horse and mulecar drivers. The entire workforce was transformed because the maintenance and repair of electrically-operated equipment meant that the veterinary surgeon was displaced by the armature winder and the stable boy by the turbine operator in the powerhouse.

In 1890, the company ordered eight streetcar bodies and trucks from its favorite supplier, Stephenson. It ordered motors, controllers and other necessary electrical apparatus to propel the new streetcars from the Short Electric Company of Cleveland.

This last decision was not without subsequent controversy. Short Series motors (two per car at 15 h. p. each) were to be used in the SC&C cars. Further, the cars were to be equipped with two slotted, shoe-like devices (the "Short Sliding Trolley"), each supported on a separate pole, to gather current from two wires spaced 19 inches apart. Both the motors and the shoes would cause trouble.

The eight streetcar bodies along with their trucks were delivered during July of 1890 and the first sets of motors and other electrical equipment arrived in August, 1890. The first eight streetcars were assembled by early September in the South Covington car house by company and contractor personnel.

A New Era

A new era dawned in Northern Kentucky on September 16, 1890, when, according to a next-day account in the *Cincinnati Times-Star*, the first electric streetcar took life in Covington:

> "Midst the sounding of gongs and the lavish display of red fire along the line, the first electric car was run over the lines last night. Although the hour was near 11 o'clock the streets along the route were crowded and a hardy hurrah was given all along the line for the car company. Motor car No. 12 [was started] from the Main St. car-house and taken over Pike St. to Scott to Fourth to Greenup and to the bridge returning by

Newport Gets a Bridge to the 20th Century

The Central or "New" bridge, linking Newport and Cincinnati, is decked out in flags and bunting on October 10, 1892, for the 400th anniversary of the landing of Christopher Columbus in the New World. The ferries are apparently out of work (or will be shortly) due to the start of Green Line service over the bridge to the Queen City which had taken place earlier in the year. A streetcar, heading for Cincinnati, can be spotted just above the twin smokestacks of the ferry nearest to the camera. It is the end of one form of interstate transportation, and the maturation of another. *Cincinnati Museum Center Image Archives, Kenton County Library Collection.*

way of Madison to 15th St. and back to Third and . . . back to the car-house."

The start of the testing program was not without difficulty. Clarence Pebworth, a long-time Green Line employee, related:

"Representatives from the factory were sent to Covington to install the motors and I was delegated to watch their work carefully.

"After several days the electricians proudly announced that the car was ready for operation. The hood switch was 'cut-in' and as the power turned the motors, there was a deafening rumble and grinding that reverberated throughout the building. Sparks were flying from the rails and long streaks of lightning-like flame shot out from under the car. One motor was moving forward and the other was moving backward.

"'Stop it,' thundered one of the electricians, 'STOP IT! Something must be wrong!'

"The other leaped upon the car and in his excitement cut the main feed wire. As the confusion subsided one of the men leaned over to me and knowingly informed me that 'something must be wrong.' I agreed and suggested that we might have the front motor in the rear and the rear motor in the front!

"'Yes sir! Something must be wrong,' continued the electrician, 'I am going to call the factory.'

"The factory superintendent was next on the scene and after the feed wire was spliced together, the hood switch was 'cut-in' once more, with the same result. One motor turned in one direction and the other turned in the opposite direction.

"Instead of cutting the wire, all the superintendent did was take the trolleys off the wires, and the motors stopped immediately, to the amazement of the electrician and myself.

"The men returned to the factory and I, thoroughly disgusted, told the foreman of the barn that I preferred driving a horsecar and I would be unable to learn the operation of the electrical mechanism from the two factory representatives.

"Several days later another pair of men was sent from the factory to install motors properly, and I was sent along to make the trial trip as a conductor.

"We started at the barn on Main near Pike Street and pro-

ceeded down Pike to Second Street. There were no trolley wires yet across the Suspension Bridge so we turned at Second Street and continued our trip to Scott Street. We turned up Scott to Fourth, over Fourth to Main and south on Main to Eighth, where a motor burned out. Horses were needed to tow the car to the barn, where it was repaired.

"I acted as conductor on the next trial trip over the same route. This time, the controller became defective and sputtered and burned, when we were at the corner of Sixth and Main Streets. Again, the car was towed into the barn.

"On subsequent trips, everything worked perfectly, with the exception that the bearings heated up."

On Sunday, September 21, the newly assembled streetcars (Nos. 11-19 less 13) inaugurated revenue service on the Madison Ave. line. But it was only a shuttle service from 15th as far as the Suspension Bridge. No work had yet begun on stringing wire on the bridge because of an ongoing legal dispute between the South Covington and bridge officials over toll charges. Nor had electrification work in Cincinnati been started.

However, the pioneer electric cars, operating at five minute intervals, were "packed the entire day." A back platform on one of the cars collapsed due to an excessive passenger load.

Three weeks later, the *Cincinnati Times-Star* reported:

"The electric cars are now a fixture in Covington and it can also be added the system is a success as far as local traffic is concerned. Some of the motormen are, perhaps, a little rash judging from the rather reckless manner in which cars rush around corners and across streets, but the men will soon learn to get the cars under better control. Although the system in the way of speed, style and comfort is a vast improvement on the old style, yet the real protocol benefit to the public will not be derived until the cars continue the trip to Fountain Square. The thing of dumping people at the entrance to the bridges and compelling them to wait until the mule car comes along, knocks the real benefit out of the new system. It does seem

Newly overhauled 233, built by Brownell in 1893, pauses at **left** in front of the Newport carbarn in 1901 having received new heavy-duty Peckham 7-B trucks. After the photographer has finished with his apparatus, the car will be ready to tackle the extensive private right-of-way of the Ft. Thomas line. Although the conductor is unidentified, the motorman is John M. Ravenscraft.
T.W. Lehmann Collection.

A bit of history is captured in the photo at the **bottom** of the page. Stephenson Car 19 is, on September 21, 1890, about to be the first electric car in revenue service in Covington. The old Post Office and Courthouse Building on the southwest corner of Third & Court in Covington looms in the background. Although the car indicates "Covington and Cincinnati," it would be almost five months before service to the Queen City would begin.
Earl Clark Collection.

the two companies [the street railway and the bridge company] ought to drop their foolishness and arrive at an agreement by which the public could be benefited by this rapid system of reaching either city."

A Delay on the Bridge

By October 27 the project to double track and electrify the Madison Ave. line from 15th to 20th was completed and the streetcar shuttle operation extended. However, since the Suspension Bridge dispute still was not settled, the company erected temporary stables next to the powerhouse in order to feed and house the mules which continued to haul connecting horsecars between Second & Greenup and Fountain Square.

Also delaying electrification to Cincinnati was the federal government. In June, 1890, the South Covington sought permission to place one pole on federal property at Government Square to support overhead wires at the Fifth & Walnut curve. Nobody long remembered what the tiff was about, but after numerous telegrams, letters, and personal visits to Kentucky's congressional delegation, Washington gave its approval on January 2, 1891. The dispute with the Suspension Bridge officials was settled the

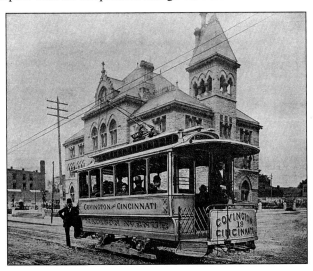

same week and at last the green light was given to complete the electrification of the Madison line. As a result, four more streetcar bodies and trucks were ordered from Stephenson and four sets "of electrical equipments" were requisitioned from Short.

Still, it took weeks to complete the Cincinnati electrification work. Due to heavy Cincinnati traffic, the South Covington's crews were restricted to nighttime hours to erect poles, wires and supporting hardware, and resorted to large barrel fires for illumination of the work sites. At long last, Madison Ave. electric streetcar service from State & Madison to Fountain Square began on February 8, 1891. Two more Stephenson-Short streetcars (Nos. 20 and 21) had been assembled by the start of February with eight of the streetcars providing an eight minute headway; the other two were held in reserve. The last two cars (Nos. 22 and 23) of the second order of four were still uncompleted.

The new electric service was popular. The South Covington reported that, during March, 1891 the Madison line carried 40,000 more people than during the same month in 1890.

Meanwhile the Main St. line experienced a traffic surge as new riders used it to connect with the now electrified Madison Ave. line. It had been planned to electrify the large Madison Ave. horsecars (Stephenson, 1887) for use on the already wired Main St. line but the powerhouse could not generate enough power for regular operation. Instead they were shifted "as is" to the Main Street line and eight new streetcars (Nos. 24-31), with Short electrical apparatus, plus additional generating equipment, were ordered in March. The new generating equipment was up and running by May and, with the delivery of the new cars from Stephenson in June, the Main St. line became a full-time electric operation..

That same month, the new brick carbarn, capable of storing 40-plus streetcars, was completed on the northwest corner of 20th & Madison. The structure measured 140 by 175 feet and the extra space enabled the components of a fourth batch of cars (Nos. 1-10) to be assembled much more rapidly. The best evidence suggests that these cars were built using existing horsecar bodies with Stephenson supplying certain additional parts and Short again contributing the motors and controllers. The SC&C

both of which promised a "smoother ride." The SC&C ordered a number of trucks from Bemis and apparently had a go at fabricating some trucks in-house.

Politicians Push for Competition

Whatever their motives, Newport and Covington lawmakers during the late 1880s repeatedly claimed dissatisfaction with the South Covington and Cincinnati over service levels, quality of equipment and the established 6. 1/4 cents (four tickets for a quarter) through fare to Cincinnati. They especially objected to the 6 1/4 cent fare, claiming that it provided excessive profits to the South Covington's treasury and "discouraged the working man from riding the cars." The alleged rough riding and frequent breakdown record of the SC&C cars, as well as the high fares, were frequently subjects of editorial diatribes in the local newspapers.

As a consequence, both Newport and Covington city councils passed ordinances to encourage new companies to construct and/or operate new street railway routes--if they would agree to charge a 5 cent fare. This began to bear fruit.

Convertible car 234 plies an 1890s unpaved street on the Milldale (now Latonia) line in the frame **below**. The metal window screens kept the passengers from losing limbs on the Suspension Bridge.
Special Collections and Archives, University of Kentucky Libraries.

Covington awarded a 50 year franchise, in 1890, to the Cincinnati, Covington and Rosedale Railway Co. for a route from downtown Covington to suburban Rosedale via new construction from 11th to Russell, to 18th and over to Madison, with the CC&R winning rights to use the South Covington's tracks on Madison from the Suspension Bridge to 11th and from 18th to the Covington corporation line at 20th. The CC&R had previously secured permission from Kenton County officials to construct the

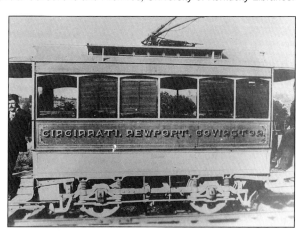

also built a non-powered "trailer closed car," to be pulled by a streetcar, to carry mail and parcels between the Cincinnati and Covington. These cars were in service by the time the Third Street line was converted to electric operation in October.

In response to the criticism by the press and public of the poor riding qualities of the earlier cars, the company announced that they would be fitted with one of two new types of trucks,

Cincinnati's Traction Labyrinth: Fifth & Walnut

Post Office and Custom House, Cincinnati, O. Erected 1874. Cost $5,250,000.

A postcard photo at **right** depicts two early South Covington & Cincinnati open electric cars loading on Cincinnati's Fifth St., having just turned east from Walnut in front of the U. S. Post Office and Courthouse. An eastbound Walnut Hills cable car glides by.
T. W. Lehmann Collection.

In addition to the SC&C's horse and electric car lines from Northern Kentucky, 15 Cincinnati lines also converged on Fifth & Walnut Streets in downtown Cincinnati as indicated by the 1892 diagram at the **bottom** of the page. The intersection was one of the most congested in the U. S. *Street Railway Journal, Earl Clark Collection.*

line from Covington's corporation boundary out Madison and Decoursey to the village of Rosedale.

The CC&R, by ordinance, was also permitted to construct tracks on 12th from Madison west to Hermes to the Covington suburb of Lewisburg, and also to set out east on 11th to Garrard, then south on Garrard to the Covington corporation line to provide a new service to eastern Covington. Finally, CC&R was also awarded a franchise to build east on 12th to the Licking River (to form a crosstown line to Newport) and to extend the Third St. line to Covington's western city limits and to connect with SC&C trackage at both 11th & Madison and Third & Philadelphia in order to gain access to downtown Covington and thence to Cincinnati.

County officials also bestowed on the Covington and Latonia Railroad Co. in 1890 the right to construct a line from the Covington city limits to the village of Milldale and the adjacent Latonia Race Track. A Covington ordinance permitted the C&L to use the South Covington's tracks from downtown Covington to 20th and Madison. The ordinances allowed the new independent companies to use the specified South Covington and Cincinnati trackage upon payment of fair connection and rental fees and granted the upstarts the right to pick up and discharge passengers while on specified South Covington and Cincinnati tracks without limitation.

Also in 1890, the Newport Electric Street Railway Co. (NESR) was formed to build new lines to west Newport, to Ft. Thomas and to Evergreen Cemetery via Monmouth. In 1891 Newport awarded the NESR a 25 year franchise for all three routes including rights to use SC&C trackage on Third, Washington and Tenth. The company said it would begin actual construction in the spring of 1892.

It was the same story in Kenton County, as both the Covington and Latonia Railroad Co. and the

Cincinnati, Covington and Rosedale Railway Co. announced plans to begin construction in the spring of 1892. The CC&R actually initiated survey work for its new line by July, 1892, and began some rough grading by August. By November it had completed almost a mile of grading from 20th south on Madison Ave. and on to private right-of-way as far as the Levassor Estate, just short of the present day intersection of James & 30th.

While all this was going on, the South Covington and Cincinnati was facing a technology crisis.

The SC&C was not at all satisfied with the Short Company's sliding shoe system for collecting electricity from the overhead wire. This was due to it either snagging the wire or falling off

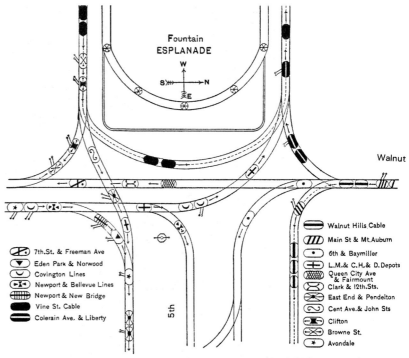

A SEEMING LABYRINTH—CORNER FIFTH AND WALNUT STREETS, CINCINNATI.

We stand on the banks of the Licking River, looking toward the Ohio River. The Central Bridge, linking Newport and Cincinnati, is nearing completion in the **above** 1890 view. In the **inset** photo, a single-truck car heads to Cincinnati on the Central Bridge in 1897. This span carried all Newport Division Green Line electric cars between 1892 and 1897. In that year the Dayton and Ft. Thomas lines were rerouted over the newly rebuilt L&N Bridge which is in the background. *Kenton County Library; Earl Clark Collection via Walter Simpson.*

when a car rounded a curve. Furthermore, the rate of failure of the Short motors was skyrocketing. It was soon apparent that remedial action was an urgent necessity.

For starters, the SC&C installed on the existing cars spring-loaded poles with trolley wheels to gather current from the underside of the double wire. The conversion to spring-loaded poles was completed by Christmas, 1891, and the new current collection system was an immediate success. Over the next couple of years, the SC&C changed (except in Cincinnati) to a one-wire system with ground current return.

Searching for a more reliable traction motor than the one supplied by Short, SC&C Vice President George Bullock, an electrical engineer hired in 1891, ordered two sets each of traction motors in January 1892, from Westinghouse and Thomson-Houston to try them in four of the Stephenson cars. This tale may be apocryphal, but a number of sources claim that Short motors were such poor performers that the term "short-circuit" sprang into the general lexicon to indicate a defective electrical circuit.

Electric Cars Come to Newport

By January of 1892 the South Covington and Cincinnati had 28 miles of track, 30 electric streetcars (Nos. 1-31), one trailer, 47 horsecars, 366 horses and mules, three new competitors, a new current collection system, and a pile of debt.

As a result, the conversion work on the Blue and York Street lines to electric operation was halted that February. The SC&C could not even generate enough cash flow to pay its employees on a timely basis during the early months of 1892, and the stockholders made it known that they hoped to sell the transit system.

Despite this, the South Covington and Cincinnati was able to complete electrification, in May 1892, of the Newport to

Covington Blue Line thanks to a bank loan guaranteed by Newport businessmen, anxious that Newport not miss out on the electric car revolution. The loan also enabled the SC&C to receive the first Laclede cars (Nos. 32-35) equipped with Westinghouse motors.

The Lacledes performed well from the start, and 15 more Westinghouse motored cars were ordered from Laclede (Nos. 36-50). By 1894 Westinghouse motors had replaced the original Short motors on cars 1-31, save the two equipped with Thomson-Houston motors. Every SC&C streetcar delivered between 1892 and 1917 was equipped with Westinghouse motors.

The *Kentucky Post* reported on May 13, 1892:

"The first electric car that ever passed over the streets of Newport successfully made a trial trip at 10:30 a.m. today. It was car 32 of the Green Line...

"Car 32 passed over the Licking Bridge from Covington, up Fifth St. to York, then on down York to the new Newport bridge which it crossed, stopping at Second and Broadway, in Cincinnati."

Newport had joined the revolution.

It should be noted that the reporter states specifically, "Car 32 of the Green Line". However since the Main St. line in Covington was known as the Green Line and this car obviously came from the Covington car barn, it should not be inferred that the entire SC&C was yet known as the "Green Line."

There is no question that all the Laclede cars (Nos. 32-50) delivered in 1892 and all cars subsequently delivered exhibited a predominantly green paint scheme and came equipped with brackets for changeable roof-mounted destination signs, thereby allowing the cars to be operated indiscriminately on all of the SC&C's "electrified" routes. Still, it does not appear that the South Covington and Cincinnati Street Railway actually marketed itself as the Green Line until sometime after 1900.

However, since the local press used the moniker with increasing frequency during the 1890s, the term "Green Line" will be used at times from this point forward to describe the SC&C and its constituent companies.

But we must speak also of other colors. By June the Covington-Newport crosstown line (the Blue Line) was extended

Rare are any views of the Green Line's Monmouth Street tracks, because of their early removal. They were completed in 1894 to carry Evergreen Cemetery cars through Newport's business district. But in 1919 the tracks were abandoned between 5th and 11th. In this 1900-era postcard glimpse, a CN&C car in the distance heads north. *Earl Clark Collection.*

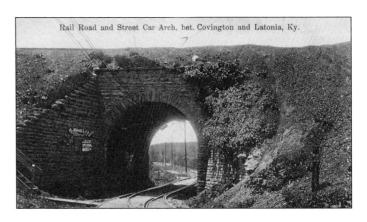

The Rosedale and Milldale (Latonia) lines, both constructed in 1893, burrowed under the L&N Railroad at 30th & James in Covington using a gauntlet track. The tunnel was eventually widened and double-track installed. *Fred Bauer Collection.*

over the Central Bridge to Cincinnati and renamed the "Newport and New Bridge" line.

The Central Bridge, which had opened in August, 1891, between York in Newport and Broadway in Cincinnati, might have seen horsecar service in 1891 but for some differences between the bridge owners and the South Covington over the amount of toll to be charged for the passage of each car. An agreement was finally reached in March, 1892, which assessed the South Covington and Cincinnati a flat 15¢ toll for each car crossing of the bridge, soon dubbed the "New Bridge" by the local press.

This agreement was reached only after engineers, hired by the Green Line, determined that the Pennsylvania Railroad Bridge could not support the heavier electric streetcars. Accordingly, the Central Bridge now held a monopoly on electric streetcar service between Newport and Cincinnati.

The Cleveland Syndicate

Although E. F. Abbott was apparently still in control of the financially troubled SC&C in early 1892, new forces were at work. Among the dignitaries making the first trip on No. 32 was John J. Shipherd, who was in town to examine the Green Line System firsthand on behalf of a group of Cleveland area investors. Indeed, within a few weeks, it was learned that the Cleveland group had negotiated an option to buy the South Covington and Cincinnati Street Railway and had guaranteed a loan for the delivery of the 15 Laclede cars recently ordered.

The Shipherd group also announced plans to buy the stock of the Newport Electric Street Railway and build the NESR's proposed new lines to Ft. Thomas and Evergreen Cemetery as well as to completely rebuild and electrify the SC&C's Dayton and Bellevue, Washington Ave., and Central Ave. horsecar lines. Further, Shipherd promised to institute a new "Belt Line" between York & 11th in Newport and Madison & 12th in Covington over the bridge then being constructed across the Licking River. The fall of 1893 was set as the completion date of all these projects.

For Kenton County, the Cleveland syndicate proposed to buy out the Latonia and Rosedale companies and finish their pro-

Early Days at the Carbarns

Measuring 140 by 175 feet, the 1891 brick Covington carhouse, **above,** could house as many as 40 single-truck cars. The old Dayton and Newport Ry. barn and office building at Sixth & Berry in Dayton is shown at **left** with a track plan **below.** *Special Collections and Archives, University of Kentucky Libraries; Earl Clark Collection.*

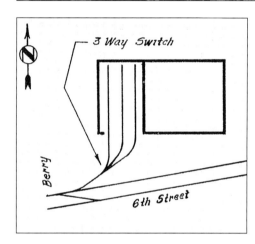

It's February 13, 1893 at the Newport carbarn. Laclede car No. 32, **above,** is about to inaugurate through electric service from 11th and York in Newport to Cincinnati. It appears that No. 15 will follow for the first revenue run once the ceremonial car has departed.
Special Collections and Archives, University of Kentucky Libraries.

---

jected lines as soon as possible. It also proposed to build a new line in central Covington (and to abandon the Banklick horsecar line in the process) and to extend the route of the lightly patronized Third St. shuttle line to the cities of West Covington and Ludlow. The building of a Greenup St. line to replace the Scott St. horsecars was also given top priority--all subject to purchase of the upstart companies and the blessing of Covington city fathers.

There was no question that the Cleveland syndicate had the necessary financial backing to carry out these proposals. In July 1892, The Farmers Loan and Trust Co. of New York City agreed to loan the syndicate's new holding company, the Cincinnati, Newport and Covington Railway Co. (of Ohio), $3 million to acquire all competing companies, to build new lines and upgrade existing ones, in exchange for taking a mortgage covering all the franchise rights, stock and property of the SC&C.

All went smoothly--at first. The Newport Electric Street Railway agreed to the buyout plan in August, 1892, but the Newport City Council made it very clear that all new lines built by the SC&C based on franchises awarded to the Newport

Electric Street Railway would be subject to a franchise duration of 25 years.

On September 20, the South Covington and Cincinnati announced that it had acquired options to purchase the Cincinnati, Covington and Rosedale Railway Co., and the Covington and Latonia Railroad Co. However, the Farmers Loan and Trust promise to the Cincinnati, Newport and Covington Railway Co. and its operating subsidiary, the South Covington and Cincinnati Street Railway Co., to provide new construction money was still contingent upon reaching a comprehensive franchise and fare agreement with Covington city officials.

The city would not approve the transfer of the South Covington's franchises to the proposed new owners without a Green Line agreement to a universal 5 cent fare and complete transfer privileges between the lines. Covington also contended that the Madison Ave. franchise, granted in 1867, was only for 25 years and, without the SC&C's agreement to the above conditions, the city would refuse to extend the term for a like number of years. The city held firm. What would the company do?

Before the Great Bridge Was Strengthened

In the study at **right**, car 44 heads north over a Suspension Bridge that has only two main cables supporting the deck. Thus, the photo was taken prior to the bridge's reconstruction between 1896 and 1898. Until then, electric cars were restricted to a virtual walk of two miles per hour due to the discovery of structural deficiencies which necessitated the severe speed limit. Cincinnati's twin wire overhead system extended a block or so into Covington.

We get a slightly fuzzy circa 1895 look at York St. in Newport **below**. It reveals a Green Line car heading south toward Fifth St. *Both: Earl Clark Collection.*

Breakthrough

Finally, on October 7, 1892, the city of Covington passed an ordinance governing all aspects of street railways and the South Covington and Cincinnati Street Railway Co. accepted the terms two days later. The ordinance set a 5¢ universal fare on all existing streetcar lines and all lines to be built in the future.

The SC&C, in accepting the terms of the ordinance, explicitly agreed to:
• Construct new streetcar lines to central Covington via Russell after the city acquired property to widen that street;
• Build from the end of the Madison line new routes to Latonia and Rosedale

• Rebuild the Third St. line and extend it to West Covington and Ludlow. In addition, the SC&C agreed to build a new double track line on Greenup to 20th (except between 15th and 16th where Greenup was too narrow) and on 20th to Madison and extend the Austinburg line from 17th south on Edwards to the corporation line, then west on private right-of-way to Garrard, north on Garrard to 20th and west on 20th to a new connection at Greenup.

The South Covington and Cincinnati Street Railway Co. was also ordered, by the terms of the ordinance, to abandon within 10 months the tracks on Scott between Fourth and 17th, Banklick between Pike and 15th, 15th between Banklick and Greenup and 17th between Edwards and Scott. The Banklick horsecar line had been built in 1890 and used new track from 15th & Scott to Banklick and down Banklick to Pike where it connected with existing tracks.

As well, the ordinance mandated that the new Greenup streetcar line, as well as the existing Madison Ave. line, run at least every seven minutes from 6:00 a.m. to 6:00 p.m. and not less than every 10 minutes from 6:00 p.m. to midnight. As a result, the SC&C formed a "belt line" using the new 20th Street trackage with the Greenup line cars returning north on Madison and the Madison line cars returning north on Greenup.

In return, the city of Covington recognized the South Covington and Cincinnati Railway Co. as the legal successor to all franchises previously granted by the city of Covington to the Cincinnati, Covington and Rosedale Railway Co. and to the Covington and Latonia Railroad Co. As a result, the SC&C purchased both the Rosedale and Latonia companies. The ordinance was silent, however, on whether the original Madison Ave. franchise, due to the South Covington's buyout in

1883 of the Covington Street Railway, was a perpetual grant or liable to expiration in 25 years.

Why the CN&C Used an Alias

It must be emphasized that, until 1922, the South Covington and Cincinnati Street Railway Co. was the entity that dealt with the outside world on all matters ranging from the acquisition of competing street railways to the purchase of inkwells. This was so in spite of the fact that the holder of all its stock from 1892 onward was the Cincinnati, Newport and Covington Railway Co. (Ohio). The SC&C name also was not very descriptive in view of the company's many lines in Campbell County.

The continued existence of the South Covington and Cincinnati Street Railway was due to the opinion of corporate counsel that the original South Covington and Cincinnati Street Railway's franchises (the Abbott grants) were awarded in perpetuity. Company lawyers felt that since the Newport Street Railway, the Covington Street Railway and the Newport and Dayton Street Railway were acquired by the South Covington and Cincinnati Street Railway without opposition by the cities who originally granted franchises to those companies for a specified number of years, those cities implicitly approved the blending of those franchises into the perpetual grant held by the South Covington and Cincinnati.

Following this line of reasoning, counsel made sure that it was actually the South Covington and Cincinnati Street Railway, with funds advanced by parent CN&C, that actually purchased the Newport Electric Street Railway, the Cincinnati, Covington and Rosedale Railway, and the Covington and Latonia Railroad. Even after 1892, whenever the Green Line formed new subsidiaries to build new lines, the eventual lessee and operator was always the South Covington and Cincinnati Street Railway Company and not the Cincinnati, Newport and Covington Railway Company (Ohio).

Although all photographs from the 1893-1895 period depict the early Green Line streetcars emblazoned with "Cincinnati, Newport, Covington" on their sides, this practice soon was discontinued. Photos from the latter part of the 1890s show no cars painted in such a fashion and it is a matter of speculation whether

On April 8, 1893, Laclede car 41 inaugurated service **(top)** on the recently-constructed Greenup line in Covington, the second of many lines to be opened by the new owners from Cleveland. In the same year, car 60, signed for the newly electrified Dayton line **(upper middle),** pauses in front of the Taylor mansion at Third & Overton in Newport. *Both: Special Collections and Archives, University of Kentucky Libraries.* Caught at Tenth & Washington in Newport, car 72 **(above)** is signed for Inverness (a new suburb, now part of Ft. Thomas), and the military post of Ft. Thomas. The photo possibly dates from the ceremonial opening of the Ft. Thomas line on July 29, 1893. Open car 210 is in the 900 block of Third in Dayton some time before the turn of the century in the photo at **left.** Note the advertisement for the Green Line leased Ludlow Lagoon amusement park and the keystone on the front fender noting that the car served the Pennsylvania Railroad Station in Cincinnati via the L&N Bridge. *Both: Earl Clark Collection.*

A wide radius horse-shoe curve formed part of the almost three miles of private right-of-way linking Newport and the then-unincorporated Highland District. We see it in the 1890s photo at **right.** It now forms part of the Memorial Parkway linking Newport and the city of Ft. Thomas. Prior to 1898, the Ft. Thomas line was double-tracked only to Ft. Thomas and Highland Aves. and single tracked from there past the Ft. Thomas military base to the end of the line. In the postcard view **below,** an early Brownell car heads south past a well known Ft. Thomas landmark, the water tower.
Both:
Earl Clark Collection.

Water Tower and Street Scene, Kentucky Highlands, Fort Thomas, Ky.

the earlier scheme indicated part of the holding company's name or was simply a way of graphically showing the three major cities served.

In any event, by 1900 the Green Line was clearly doing business as the South Covington and Cincinnati Street Railway. A route map published about 1900 is titled "Cincinnati, Newport & Covington Railway Company operated by the South Covington and Cincinnati Street Railway Company." The CN&C reference does not even appear on a similar South Covington and Cincinnati route map of 1910. Even the cornerstone on the Newport car barn, completed in 1899, was engraved "So. Covington and Cincinnati St. R. 1899".

Gradually, this legal hocus-pocus gave way to pragmatism. It would produce, at best, mixed results for the Green Line upon the expiration of certain franchises between 1915 and 1918. Finally the SC&C, as an entity, bowed out in 1922, ending the confusion.

New Streetcars by the Scores

To closely monitor the growth of this new investment by the Cleveland group, Shipherd was appointed president of both the CN&C and the SC&C and took up local residence in October of 1892. Then he got busy. In October, 25 cars were ordered from Brownell for late 1892-early 1893 delivery. Brownell marketed its product as "accelerator cars"--not because of their ability to start up quickly--but due to a patent design of sliding doors at the front and rear of the passenger compartment and longitudinal seating which allegedly accelerated unloading and loading.

Not that this longitudinal seating was popular with Green Line passengers. They didn't like it, and future streetcars were ordered that featured primarily look-ahead seating. Actually, the SC&C received 26 cars (Nos. 51-76) because one had been

Beautiful Scenery, Lagoon Park, Ludlow, Ky.

Everyone took the electric cars to
Lagoon

Some gems from the Carl Rekow and Earl Clark Collections.

Entrance Lagoon Park, Ludlow, Ky.

In the good old summertime of 1897, the Green Line needed up to 50 cars just to serve Ludlow's Lagoon Park, where chills and thrills awaited Northern Kentuckians. Savor these postcard views, such as the one at **upper left** showing the roller coaster overshadowed by the trestle of the City of Cincinnati owned Cincinnati Southern Railway, built in the 1880s from Cincinnati to Chattanooga. The Queen City still receives substantial lease payments every year from the present day Norfolk Southern Railroad for the use of this still vital rail link. The snapshot at **left** portrays the gabled ticket office in 1895. *Ludlow Centennial booklet, Earl Clark Collection; Carl Rekow Collection.*

wrecked during delivery, and it had to be replaced. Then SC&C purchased the crippled car from the insurance company and rebuilt it at the new SC&C carbarn at 20th & Madison.

A new frame and corrugated iron Newport car barn was opened on the north side of 11th between Saratoga and Washington in November of 1892.

The new Cleveland owners also ordered vast amounts of rail, paving materials, ties, copper wire, and other materials for the start of the spring 1893 construction season. In addition, ads were placed in trade journals all across the U. S. for engineers, construction foremen and specialized construction workers.

This was nothing less than one of the larger public works projects ever undertaken in Northern Kentucky, and it perhaps was not duplicated until the rash of expressway building in recent years. Construction work was duly started in the early spring of 1893 on no fewer than five electric railway lines.

In April 1893, the Green Line ordered, according to the *Kentucky Post*, 25 summer or open cars from Brownell. Summer cars were built without side panels and with bench type seats extending the full width of the car. Ingress into a summer car (and egress out of same) was by means of stepping onto a running board which extended the full length of the car body. Summer cars, by virtue of their body wide bench-type seating, had the capacity to seat many extra passengers per car and were particularly valuable for weekend summer excursion traffic.

For some reason, only 20 summer cars (Nos. 200-219) were

delivered. They came without trucks and motors and were used in the summer months by utilizing the trucks and motors removed from closed body streetcars. In late spring the closed car bodies were replaced by a like number of summer car bodies with the procedure being reversed in the fall of the year when inclement weather was expected.

Unfortunately, summer car running boards created safety hazards. By 1894 they were removed and screens were fitted along the sides. An aisle was cut in the middle of the bench seats, reducing seating capacity and lessening any advantage over convertible cars in carrying the crush of summer excursion traffic.

One suspects that close clearances on the bridges to Cincinnati (only one foot in the case of the Suspension Bridge) led to serious injuries to dangling arms and legs and consequent lawsuits, thus ensuring the almost immediate modifications to the cars. Certainly the Green Line never ordered any more summer cars.

A better idea was the "convertible" streetcar. The first such cars, starting with Nos. 220-238, were delivered to the Green Line in the fall of 1893. With open front and rear platforms or vestibules but with enclosed bodies and regular two-across seating separated by an aisle, these cars could be converted to summer "air conditioning" by removing their side panels (including windows and sashes) and installing wire screening in the void. This arrangement prevented passengers from entering or leaving the cars except by the front or rear platforms.

Those wonderful convertible breezers like car 240, which in the frame **above** has rolled to a stop outside the Ludlow Lagoon gates, were a delightful prelude to a day at the park. The poster on the fender promotes another streetcar destination, the Queen City Race Track. The motorman is all business as he glares at the photographer.

Once inside the park, the best way to cool off would be a ride in the steam launch which we see setting out from the shore at **left** with a pretty full load. Again, we spy the high railroad bridge at the top right and a few boaters out for a joyride on Lagoon's lagoon. After an exhilarating day of frivolity, the tired and happy customers would board the cars parked on the Lagoon branch for home. It was, perhaps, a simpler but happier day. *Both: Earl Clark Collection.*

A Tale of Twin Wires

In 1891 an independent street railway line in Cincinnati, the Cincinnati Inclined Plane Co., was sued by the City and Suburban Telegraph Association, the local telephone company. The Inclined Plane Co. had installed the conventional single overhead trolley wire system which used the rails to return the low voltage current to the powerhouse.

The telephone company complained that the Cincinnati Inclined Plane's single wire system caused so much electrical interference that telephones were rendered virtually useless and subscribers were refusing to pay their bills. This, allegedly, was because stray currents from the streetcar rails were seeking--and finding--telephone circuits.

Judge William Howard Taft of the Superior Court of Cincinnati, later to be President of the United States and there-after Chief Justice of the U. S. Supreme Court, ruled in favor of the telephone company and compelled all streetcar companies in Cincinnati to install a twin trolley wire system. For the Green Line, the ruling meant the expense of maintaining both a twin wire system across the bridges, and a second pole on its streetcars for use while on Cincinnati streets.

As streetcar systems went, Cincinnati's was almost unique in the use of two trolleys. Nearly all other systems used the single trolley with rail power return. All Green Line cars operated with two raised poles only from Third & Court in Covington or

Third & York (or Saratoga) in Newport to Cincinnati and back. South of these points, the second wire disappeared. *The Street Railway Journal* of June, 1894, reported that all cars were equipped with a canopy switch to "direct return current to either overhead wire or the return rail."

The cars' conductors were normally responsible for yanking the poles, but during rush-hours, to help reduce delays, men were assigned at Third & Court and Third & York to raise or lower the second trolley pole. A local knee-slapper insisted that when a Green Line employee was asked how he liked his task of raising and lowering trolley poles, he replied: "It has its ups and downs."

1893: a Year of Inaugurals

The York Street line between Cincinnati and 11th & York in Newport via the Central Bridge began electric operation on February 13, 1893. As a consequence, the Newport and New Bridge line reverted to its old name--the Blue Line--and once again plied its old crosstown routing between Newport and Covington only.

The second of the promised lines to be completed was Covington's Greenup route on April 8, 1893. With this, the Scott St. horsecar was discontinued. And as a consequence, the CC&R franchise for a Garrard St. line, which would have run one block parallel to Greenup, became redundant and was repealed. In early 1893, construction of the Russell St. line began, but some

Early-day Green Line emergency service vehicles were apt to be of the one horse or mule power variety. This three person crew appears to be ready to take care of a wire break or other malfunction.
Special Collections and Archives, University of Kentucky Libraries.

residents along Russell obtained an injunction barring any further work claiming that the erection of poles and overhead would degrade property values. By the time the injunction was overturned, the SC&C was in the middle of a financial crisis and a line to central Covington was not built until 1896.

During the first part of 1893 work again commenced toward the villages of Rosedale and Milldale (and its adjacent Latonia Race Track). In Campbell County work was re-started on the Ft. Thomas line and on the reconstruction and electrification of the Bellevue and Dayton line, including new track on Third from Beech to Saratoga. With construction crews stretched thin, the SC&C in June announced that work on the Austinburg and Ludlow lines would be deferred.

There was a lot going on. The electric line to Rosedale via Decoursey, Southern and Huntington was completed on May 27, and the line to Milldale and the Latonia Race Track via Decoursey, 34th, Eugenia and 35th was up and running on August 5. The route to Dayton saw electric car service inaugurated on June 24, and revenue service on the Ft. Thomas line commenced on July 30, 1893.

The company announced in July of 1893 that the Evergreen Cemetery line would not be finished until 1894 due to "slow negotiations with certain property owners in the acquisition of right-of-way parcels." But Green Line officials were silent as to why no work was started on either the conversion of the Washington Ave. line or the construction of the proposed West Newport line.

More urgently, construction of a new powerhouse was started in Newport at Thornton & Lowell. It was designed to supply all of the necessary electric power for the entire system, allowing the eventual closing of the already antiquated power house at Second & Greenup in Covington.

The Spanish-American War of 1898 greatly increased traffic on the Ft. Thomas line and lent impetus to the double tracking of the entire line as demonstrated in this post-war view. Compare this with the Ft. Thomas view on page 29. *Earl Clark Collection.*

The Ft. Thomas Story

The Ft. Thomas line, which opened for business in July, 1893, was a novel and interesting development for the Green Line. A good portion of the this line was built on private right-of-way through a rural area to reach the new U.S. Army base at Ft. Thomas.

In 1804, the United States Army established a post in Newport near the junction of the Licking and Ohio Rivers. The Newport Barracks, as the post became known, served as headquarters for the Army's Sixth Infantry Regiment. Being sited near both rivers on a flood plain, the post was subjected to frequent, and sometimes severe, flooding.

Enter one Samuel Bigstaff, energetic local merchant and real estate broker. Bigstaff was a Confederate cavalry officer who was captured at the battle of Snow Hill and eventually sent to the Newport Barracks as a prisoner of war. After the guns fell silent he stayed in Northern Kentucky, marrying the oldest daughter of prominent Newport attorney F. M. Webster. An attorney turned promoter, Bigstaff acquired thousands of acres of undeveloped land in the Highland District of Campbell County. True to its name, Bigstaff's land was situated on high ground overlooking the lowlands on which Newport and Covington rested. One thing was certain: the Highland District would never fear floods.

Bigstaff approached the War Department in 1887 with a thoughtful proposal. He offered, at below market value, a considerable number of acres of his Highland District property. He extolled the virtues of this land as having unspoiled air, an unpolluted water supply and easy expansion potential. Most importantly, the Army could vacate its antiquated and frequently flooded Newport Barracks post.

Bigstaff offered to improve a one lane dirt road from Newport to the proposed site. In an attempt to make an offer the

War Department could not refuse, he stated that if the Army did relocate to the Highland District, he would also build a street railway line to serve the new post.

Of course Bigstaff's motives were not entirely selfless. If the War Department agreed to his proposal, he correctly reasoned that the remaining land he owned around the base would grow in value as sites for businesses that would supply goods and services to the Army and for off-duty leisure uses. Further, Bigstaff envisioned that the people who supplied the new post or worked in a civilian capacity there would build homes on his nearby land. Bigstaff also expected to make money when they rode his proposed street railway.

In 1887 the War Department accepted Bigstaff's proposal and purchased the agreed tract of land. The U.S. Corps of Engineers immediately started survey work at the new post, provisionally named Ft. Crook.

True to his part of his bargain, Bigstaff rebuilt the old road from Newport in record time. Upon completion, the greatly improved road was named Grand Ave. in honor of the Grand Army of the Republic of the Civil War era. Grand Ave. soon saw numerous contractor wagons carrying construction materials for the new post. In 1890 it was decided to name the post Ft. Thomas to honor Civil War hero Gen. George Thomas.

To build the promised railway from Newport to Ft. Thomas, Bigstaff incorporated the Newport Electric Street Railway in 1890 and became the major stockholder. He secured a franchise from the city of Newport which permitted the NESR to construct a new line from Tenth & Washington out Tenth to the city limits. Upon payment of "fair rental fees," the NESR was authorized to connect with South Covington & Cincinnati tracks at Tenth & Washington for access to downtown Newport and Cincinnati. Bigstaff, always the promoter, had successfully helped attract investor interest in the Central Bridge between Newport and Cincinnati.

In 1890, Bigstaff also founded and became a major stockholder in the Highland Land Co. As a result, the Inverness subdivision was laid out on 250 acres of land around what is now the intersection of Memorial Parkway and North Ft. Thomas Ave. He also founded the Inverness Country Club which sported a nine-hole golf course across from the Newport Waterworks bounded by Southgate Ave., North Ft. Thomas Ave., and the Ft. Thomas streetcar line (now Memorial Parkway). A station and turntable were built at the edge of the club.

By early 1892, the NESR had won approval from Campbell County officials for the necessary right-of-way in the unincorporated Highland District to commence construction. The Ft. Thomas line would not be a "build in the middle of an existing street" construction effort typical of the period. On the contrary, upon leaving Newport, the line was cut into the sides of a series of hills and the topography required the NESR to build two long bridges and four shorter ones to reach the Highland District plateau and Ft. Thomas. With the exception of one 700-foot stretch, the interurban-like Ft. Thomas line faced a 2.5 percent ruling grade for more than two miles from Wilson Rd. to just past Rob Roy.

By the middle of September, 1892, rough grading and considerable bridge support work had been completed. Unfortunately, the cost of the work had greatly exceeded esti-

A Green Line car, **above,** heads for Covington over the newly-reconstructed Suspension Bridge on April 26, 1899. Note that both trolley poles are raised. The second batch of Brownell convertible cars (Nos. 239-253) were delivered in 1895. Judging from the like-new condition of car 249 **below,** it might be on one of its break-in runs on the Milldale (later called Latonia) line. The leather straps hanging down from the ceiling helped standing passengers stay on their feet during sudden stops and starts. *Dan Finfrock Collection; Earl Clark Collection.*

The Green Line opened its office building on the east side of Court between Third and Park Place in 1903. In addition to serving as general offices, the building **(below)** contained a waiting room for passengers. *Special Collections and Archives, University of Kentucky Libraries.*

L. & N. Railroad Bridge, over Ohio River, Cincinnati, Ohio.

A Bridge For All Reasons

The Pennsylvania Railroad (L&N) Bridge was rebuilt and reopened for electric streetcar service on April 4, 1897. As we look from the Cincinnati side, a Newport-bound car is using the shelf-like cantilever extension constructed on the west side of the bridge. The right-of-way for northbound cars to Cincinnati was located between the railroad tracks and the main roadway.
Earl Clark Collection via Fred Veith.

mates. So Bigstaff was undoubtedly relieved when, in late September, he was able to sell the NESR to the new owners of the South Covington and Cincinnati.

Bigstaff stayed on with the SC&C as vice president and general manager until 1896. Still the promoter, Bigstaff also headed a land development company which purchased land along the Ft. Thomas line just outside the Newport and Bellevue city limits. By 1900 the planned village of Bonnie Leslie (now part of Bellevue) boasted more than 40 homes built by Bigstaff's company, and his Cote Brilliant subdivision off Park Avenue (later part of Newport) added 60 more.

Hard Times

In early 1892 the Baird Bros. Construction Co. was awarded a contract to build a new bridge over the Licking River between 12th in Covington and 11th in Newport. During the early part of 1892 work had proceeded smoothly under subcontractor King Iron Co. of Pittsburgh. But then, tragedy: on June 15, 1892, 54 workers were thrown into the Licking River and onto its adjoining banks when the main span collapsed. Twenty-two were killed.

It was not until 1893 that the bridge was rebuilt for electric streetcar operation. And by that time the Green Line was again starting to feel money pressures and decided that the proposed toll per car for using the bridge was entirely too high and plans for the long promised "Belt Line" between Cincinnati, Covington and Newport were shelved.

City officials of both Newport and Covington and the newspapers cried foul. They cited promises made by Shipherd in the summer of 1892 to provide a Belt Line via the upper Licking River bridge. After two years of bad press, the Green Line did, on November 18, 1894, extend certain trips of the York Street line

to 12th & Greenup over newly installed tracks on 11th in Newport from York east over the bridge and on 12th in Covington as far as Greenup. Full Belt Line service was not inaugurated until April 26, 1897, following a series of events soon to be revealed.

If the Green Line thought it was in a squeeze, there was worse to come. The second greatest depression in the history of the United States, now known as the Panic of 1893, created more problems as the cost of capital in 1894 increased significantly. This fallout from the Panic of 1893 caused the Green Line to slow its expansion plans and to curtail some service, defer some maintenance work, and even to lay off some employees during the last half of 1893 and the early winter of 1894.

Moreover, the Green Line deferred construction, in 1894, of proposed Covington lines on Russell and on 12th toward the suburb of Lewisburg. In Newport, the SC&C took no action to construct trackage on Monmouth or to convert either the Central or Washington Ave. horsecar lines to electric.

But all was not bleak. The Green Line did manage to complete, in February of 1894, the Austinburg line extension in eastern Covington, thereby bringing to a close horsecar service in Kenton County; the old trackage on 17th St. was abandoned. The Austinburg line made its way over to Edward (renamed Eastern in 1914), via 15th to Rickey, to Oliver, and south along Edward until it reached the then southern corporation line of Covington. From there the line proceeded west on private right-of-way to Garrard, then north on Garrard to 20th and west on 20th to Greenup.

The Ludlow Line

At last, in September, 1893, the Cincinnati, West Covington and Ludlow Street Railway Co. was incorporated by the owners of the Green Line to construct the promised line to Ludlow.

Reconstruction of the Suspension Bridge between 1896 and 1899 included the addition of a viaduct on the Cincinnati side as far as Second St. which enabled Covington Division Green Line cars to avoid no less than 10 railroad tracks previously crossed at grade. Soon to take advantage of the new viaduct is a southbound Green Line car on Vine at Fourth in Cincinnati. *Earl Clark Collection.*

Ludlow is a downriver Covington suburb, and cars were plying as far as West Covington by July 22, 1894. This was accomplished by routing the line from downtown Covington along the existing Main St. line trackage on Fourth as far as Main and then building a new track on Main north to Third, where double track was constructed west to Crescent and north to Second and the Ludlow Highway. In climbing Ludlow Highway out of the Covington basin, the Ludlow line encountered a 5 percent grade for almost half a mile, and for 700 feet or so, another 5 percent grade coming off the west side of the hill separating Covington and Ludlow.

The old Third St. line trackage from Main to downtown was used for inbound cars, giving the Green Line an equivalent double track line with much less expense. Ludlow Highway work was completed on Elm as far as Adela by August 23, 1894, and

reached the terminus of the line (just inside the adjoining town on Bromley) on November 19, 1894, via Oak.

A small loop was installed in Ludlow, to serve a new amusement park then under construction, which extended south from Oak on Lake and followed Lake as it turned east to Laurel and then north on Deverill back to Oak. A side track for storage of excursion cars was installed on Laurel. A lease dated January 1, 1895 (and signed by Shipherd as president of both companies) turned over to the South Covington and Cincinnati "in perpetuity . . . all of the property, rights and privileges" of the Cincinnati, West Covington and Ludlow.

With the new Ludlow amusement park, the Green Line was on to something. It became common in the 1890s for street railways to build amusement parks to generate business not only from the operation of the park itself but also by transporting the pleasure seekers to it. The Green Line was among the first streetcar companies to realize the win-win advantages of such a park.

Thus it was that in 1894 the company selected a site for the amusement park that straddled the boundary line between Ludlow and Bromley. By the spring of 1895, an artificial lake (or lagoon) for boating was created by damming Pleasant Run Creek and numerous rides including two roller coasters and a miniature train ride, and various ancillary buildings were constructed.

On May 18, 1895 the park, named the Ludlow Lagoon, was opened. The attraction proved very popular and was a money maker for the Green Line System. But it was relatively short-lived. Ludlow Lagoon was leased by the Green Line to concessionaires only until 1918. The park suffered a mortal wound following a July 7, 1915, tornado which devastated the property. World War I delivered the coup-de-grace.

Campbell County Expansion

On the other side of the Licking River, the Evergreen Cemetery line was completed on July 10, 1894. This used the

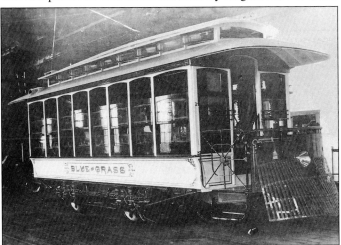

Delivered in 1893 by Brownell, the parlor car *Bluegrass* was available for charter by private parties as evidenced by the 1906 trolley party invitation. The *Bluegrass* soldiered on in charter service until it was scrapped just prior to World War II. *Both, Earl Clark Collection.*

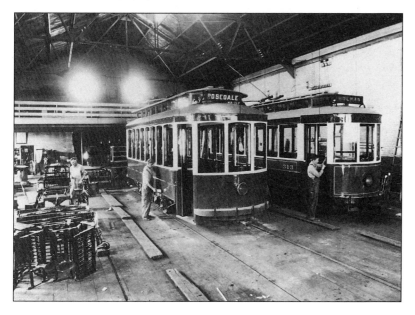

CN&C paint shop employees put the finishing touches on two recently overhauled single-truck cars circa 1915. The car on the left has not yet received its lettering or lining-out. Labor was not that expensive, and in the runup to World War I the Green Line spared no expense to provide the little artistic touches. *Special Collections and Archives, University of Kentucky Libraries.*

tracks of the York Street line to 11th & Monmouth where it angled south on Alexandria Pike to approximately 19th and on to private right-of-way to the newly developed Evergreen Cemetery, today on the southern border of the city of Southgate.

Economic conditions must have improved in 1895 as this was the year the Green Line announced plans to convert the rest of its lines to electric operation. Horsecar service to Cincinnati (and the Green Line's use of the Pennsylvania Bridge) ended when the Washington Ave. horsecar line was converted to electric operation on March 24, 1895, since, as we have seen, the Pennsylvania Bridge could not accommodate the wider or heavier electric streetcars. The electrification of Washington Ave. meant that the Ft. Thomas line had a new direct route via Third to Washington to Tenth instead of the former circuitous routing via York to 11th to Washington and back to Tenth where the original connection had been made in 1893.

On September 7, 1895, electric railway service began to west Newport over new trackage from Third & York over Third to Central, south on Central to Fifth, over existing tracks on Fifth to Patterson, and on new Patterson trackage from Fifth to 11th. As

Snow sweepers like No. 3 were needed to keep the lines open in winter and this one was one of four converted from Stephenson cars between 1895 and 1897. The shop forces must have done their job well as No. 3 poses beside the Newport carbarn just in from a run in 1946! *Earl Clark Collection via Sam Guthrie.*

a result, the parallel Central Ave. "horse" car line was abandoned with mules "Ginger" and "Wildcat" pulling the last car. This unceremoniously ended the era of animal powered public transportation in Northern Kentucky.

Further, on October 10, 1895, the long delayed Monmouth St. trackage in Newport was completed affording the Evergreen Cemetery line a more direct route from 11th & Monmouth to the Central Bridge. To equip the new routes the Green Line took delivery of 15 more 31-foot convertible streetcars (Nos. 239-253) in May and June of 1895.

Dark Clouds--and a White Knight

Expansion or no, the SC&C found itself again backed into a financial corner. By late 1895, the Farmers Loan and Trust Co. was threatening foreclosure on the Green Line properties because the operation was not covering its fixed interest obligations. It became menacingly apparent to the directors of the Green Line that yet another new buyer needed to be found.

Secret negotiations were started with a number of investor groups. Although the streetcar passenger operations of the SC&C were not generating sufficient net revenues to attract any investors, perhaps a couple of byproducts which had been developed by the Green Line just might prove irresistible to investors. Could the tail wag the dog? Green Line directors hoped so.

For example, the company had purchased a large tract of land in Rosedale which it had subdivided for the building of new homes "away from the bustle and bother of city life." These subdivision lot sales did well and, in early 1896, the Rosedale Electric Light Co., a wholly owned subsidiary of the Green Line, generated its first electric power to light the homes of the subdivision and the surrounding area. Not only that, but the Newport powerhouse was selling its excess electricity to homes and businesses in its area and demand was increasing.

Sure enough, the directors' prayers were answered. In 1896 some local investors along with Pittsburgh industrialists Charles and Robert Orr, purchased the Cincinnati, Newport and Covington Railway Co. (of Ohio) and its operating subsidiary, the South Covington and Cincinnati Street Railway Co. (of Kentucky) as well as CN&C's Rosedale Electric Light Co. Two of the major local investors were Charles Fleischmann and his son Julius. Their Fleischmann Yeast Co. was the core around which corporate giant Standard Brands was formed.

The new owners showed they could act promptly by consolidating Rosedale Electric and the non-railway portion of CN&C's electric generation activities in Newport into a newly formed Union Light, Heat and Power Co. ULH&P, over the next few years gained controlling interest in both Suburban Electric and

A single-truck CN&C car on Walnut at Fifth in downtown Cincinnati will turn left and circle Fountain Square before heading south on Vine back to Covington. That's a Cincinnati car following. This is what downtowns looked like in the last decade of the 19th Century.

Wagner-Wright-McNamara Collection.

Covington Gas & Light and was soon furnishing gas and electricity to most areas of Campbell and Kenton Counties.

The new owners soon displayed financial muscle, not to mention their political connections. Appointed to lead both the utility and street railway operations was local banker James C. Ernst, brother of U.S. Senator Richard Ernst, another major new investor. The year 1896 also saw the beginning of renewed transit expansion.

South Covington and Cincinnati Street Railway now announced it would exercise the franchise rights held by its subsidiary Cincinnati, Covington and Rosedale Railway Co. and construct the long-deferred line in central Covington to help relieve traffic congestion on its Madison Ave. line.

Frustrated by the continuing litigation of Russell St. citizens to keep the SC&C from building on their street, the Covington city council amended the original CC&R grant and substituted Holman as the line's main stem. Connecting with existing trackage at 11th & Madison, the new line was constructed on 11th west to Russell, then south on Russell to 12th and west on 12th to Holman and south on Holman to 18th. The new Holman St. line, which essentially ran four blocks west of and parallel to the Madison Ave. trackage, was double track from 18th to 13th but, due to the width of the other streets, was otherwise only a single track line with one turnout (or siding) on Russell. The new line through central Covington was opened on June 28, 1896.

In late 1896 the company also ordered ten more convertible

streetcars (Nos. 254-263) from the St. Louis Car Co. The new streetcars were placed into service in the spring of 1897.

Bridge Problems

Although there is a common adage that "they built them to last in the good old days," it isn't necessarily so. Problems with three separate bridges led to a disruption of the operations of the South Covington and Cincinnati and to the lives and routines of many who lived in northern Kentucky. In May of 1896 it was discovered that the bridge over the lower Licking River could not safely support the weight of the heavier electric cars or even eight-team wagons. Thus, crosstown Blue Line service was discontinued over this bridge on May 24, 1896.

With the bridge closure, the Green Line was faced with the prospect that the owners of the only other Licking River bridge linking Newport and Covington were now in a position to exact whatever toll charges they desired. To head this off, the Licking River bridge between 12th in Covington and 11th in Newport, was purchased in late 1896 and a separate subsidiary, the Licking River Bridge Co., was formed to manage and operate the bridge.

Company auditors figured the $100,000 purchase price of the bridge would be recovered in seven to ten years, thereafter saving the Green Line at least $15,000 a year in car tolls. Furthermore, it made possible a remarkable streetcar operation.

In April of 1897, the Green Line instituted the long promised Belt Line from Fountain Square in Cincinnati to Newport and Covington which ran both clockwise and counterclockwise. The "counter" route used the Suspension Bridge to Covington along Madison to 11th where new trackage took the Belt Line to Greenup for one block to 12th and across the Licking River bridge to Newport. In Campbell County, the route ran

In the summer of 1901, using materials from the recently abandoned Newport barn at 11th & Saratoga, the Green Line constructed a corrugated metal barn on the southwest corner of 20th & Madison in Covington which housed six storage tracks. The "new" barn measured 50 x 190 feet and featured a transfer table to make the task of moving and storing surplus cars easier. We're looking south to the turnoff toward Greenup St. *Special Collections and Archives, University of Kentucky Libraries.*

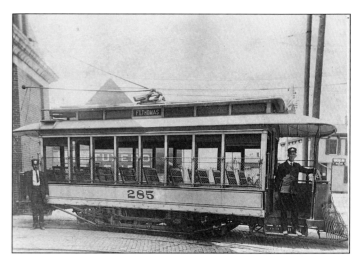

With one of its two poles up, car 285 is captured around 1900 by the snap of the shutter in front of the Newport carbarn. It is from the last order of convertible cars purchased by the Green Line.

T.W. Lehmann Collection.

along 11th to York, then north on York to the Central Bridge and back to Fountain Square.

The clockwise route of the Belt Line used the Central Bridge to start its route through Newport and Covington back to Cincinnati. The Belt Line had to rank as one of the most unique streetcar lines in the United States. For a 5¢ fare, the Belt afforded, in a little over 40 minutes, a streetcar ride in two states, three counties, three cities, over two rivers utilizing three bridges.

A Flawed Masterpiece

The second bridge problem was even more distressing. John Roebling's Suspension Bridge between Cincinnati and Covington was in danger of doing a swan dive into the Ohio River.

This mighty structure, which served as the prototype for Roebling's famed Brooklyn Bridge, possessed serious structural deficiencies which were exacerbated by the heavier electric streetcars and the increasing wagon traffic of the early 1890s. It got so bad that streetcars were restricted to 2 m.p.h. over the bridge.

Fortunately, between 1896 and 1899, engineers were able to direct the reconstruction of the span without any major interruption to streetcar and wagon traffic. To bolster the original support system, the reconstruction included the installation of two additional cables and associated anchorages plus a new system of Pratt stiffening trusses and new wind stays. Also built was a new Cincinnati approach viaduct, completed in 1897, from Second to the Ohio Tower.

The Green Line's annual report for 1897 noted that the new Ohio approach to the Suspension Bridge cut out a block of street running and delays caused by railroad switching moves and "[is] of great benefit to the saving and time and expense in the operation of our cars. With the tracks on the bridge arranged to ensure rapid transit between the two cities, increased receipts and decreased expenses will naturally follow."

Not only did the SC&C benefit, but wagon and pedestrian traffic did too. The virtual rebuilding of the Suspension Bridge more than doubled its allowable loading weight. The capacity of the original structure was 8,400 tons whereas the capacity of the rebuilt bridge was rated at more than 20,000 tons. The traffic on the Suspension Bridge at time of the reconstruction averaged more than 1,200 Green Line streetcars, 1,000 cart and wagon loads, and 6,000 pedestrians a day.

A Monopoly Broken

Ironically, within a month of the other two bridge discoveries, the Pennsylvania Railroad found that its Newport bridge, built in 1872, was also exhibiting some cracks around the main load-bearing members. The decision was made to replace the existing structure and this was carried out in the amazingly short period of six months, from August of 1896 to February of 1897.

James C. Ernst personally visited PRR officials in Pittsburgh to lobby for the Green Line in any reconstruction plans. Although the directors of the Green Line felt that tolls charged by the Central Bridge's owners were excessive, the South Covington and Cincinnati was a captive user since this was the only bridge between Newport and Cincinnati capable of supporting the weight and width of the electric streetcars. That monopoly could be broken if the Pennsylvania Railroad Bridge was rebuilt to accommodate streetcars.

In exchange for an agreed fixed rental price for 20 years, the PRR redesigned the bridge to carry not only heavier railway traffic but also to provide for a new roadway for wagon traffic separate from a right-of-way for Green Line streetcars. A new Newport approach to Third St. was planned to replace the steeply angled Second St. ramp. It was anticipated that the new right-of-way would reduce delays to streetcars caused by slow-moving wagons on the Central Bridge.

A new northbound streetcar track was constructed between the wagon roadway and the railroad track while the southbound streetcar track was placed on a series of supports, on the extreme west side of the bridge with only a guard rail separating the streetcars from a long plunge into the Ohio River in case of a derailment.

In view of all the money it spent, it is noteworthy that the PRR was no longer the prime user of its own bridge. Although the Pennsylvania Railroad Bridge was not sold to the Louisville & Nashville Railroad until 1904, the bridge had been previously used, since the 1880s, primarily by the L&N. Thus the bridge had been commonly referred to, both by the public and the press, as the "L&N Bridge" since that time.

On April 4, 1897, a number of Green Line routes serving Campbell County were duly rerouted over the renovated Pennsylvania (or L&N) Bridge. The company's contract with the Pennsylvania Railroad called for a fixed payment per year regardless of the number of crossings as compared with the contract with the Central Bridge whereby tolls were paid on the basis of a 15 cents per car crossing. In its 1897 annual report, the Green Line stated, "We have effected major savings by virtue of using the new bridge for a majority of our services." To be exact, the Green Line saved $13,578.31 in tolls by virtue of the new arrangement.

Not only were the Ft. Thomas, Dayton and Washington Ave. lines rerouted onto the L&N Bridge in April of 1897, but later in the year the York St. line started using the L&N Bridge thereby leaving the Central Bridge to serve only the Patterson, Evergreen Cemetery (renamed Monmouth St. line shortly thereafter) and Belt Line cars.

The Lagoon Line Balloons!

The Ludlow Lagoon amusement park attracted far more summer passengers than originally anticipated. At peak times during the summer of 1897 as many as 50 cars had to be assigned to the Ludlow-Lagoon car line alone. The Green Line's Annual Report reviewing 1897 indicates that 20 sets of motors and trucks were purchased in June for use on the summer cars (Nos. 200-219) assigned to the Ludlow-Lagoon line. Of significance, this meant that 20 closed cars would not have to be taken out of service.

In its report the Green Line also said it was well pleased with both the versatility and safety of the convertible type streetcar and would purchase no summer cars in the future. The use of the convertible streetcar avoided the costly twice-yearly process of exchanging closed car bodies with summer bodies.

Also as a consequence of the Ludlow Lagoon's popularity, the Covington power plant on the southwest corner of Second & Greenup was not closed during 1897 as originally planned. The increased traffic on the Ludlow-Lagoon line caused the Green Line to make repairs to the Covington powerhouse and keep it open "in order to ensure sufficient electric power for the system."

The Annual Report also states that "as required by the laws of Ohio, all the cars have been fitted with vestibules." The law in question mandated that all cars operating on Ohio streets between November and March be provided with an enclosed front platform or "vestibule" to protect the motorman from the elements. The report notes that the modification "added greatly to the comfort and satisfaction of the motormen, and added...to the efficiency of the service."

Until 1896, all Green Line streetcars had been operated with open front driving platforms year round. There was, by this time, a nationwide movement to enclose the front platforms of streetcars, especially those operating in northern climes.

The Excursion Business

The recreational value of the Green Line's new suburban lines was soon realized. SC&C cars were being ridden in large numbers on weekends and on warm summer evenings to catch the breeze. Keeping cool in hot weather was an art in the early days. Some theaters of the day were also "convertible" with open tops or outdoor facilities. Saloons had beer gardens, and parks were overflowing in mid-summers.

As the 1890s approached the new century, the Green Line happily discovered that ever-increasing numbers were flocking to the newly improved beaches along the Ohio River in Dayton and Bellevue and to Clark's Grove, a Dayton picnic area developed by the German-American Schuetzen Fest Society. Service to the "clean air" parks in the Highland District for picnics and band concerts at Ft. Thomas also was increased on summer weekends.

Ft. Thomas itself created standing loads and there was a need for extra cars for armory boxing matches. Until the matches were over, the cars were brought back to the Newport barn to await their charges, since there was no storage track near the fort.

Two other parks that saw plenty of summer use in the 1890s were located at the end of the Dayton line (Tacoma Park) and near the end of the Rosedale line (Rosedale Park). Tacoma had the usual rides, plus a dog track, dance hall and pool; Rosedale only a pool and small rides such as a miniature train.

Another source of excursion revenue was the Latonia Race Track. It was one of the finest in the country and as many as 45 cars on weekends would grind up Madison Ave. carrying people from the Cincinnati hotels intent on spending their time and money on the spring and fall thoroughbred races. The entrance to the Latonia track was situated near 35th & Eugenia Ave.

The Evergreen cemetery in Southgate (as were Highland and St. Mary's cemeteries after the Lewisburg line was built in 1902) also was a weekend destination in the days when family ties were strong and tradition dictated respect for departed relatives. Memorial Day was an especially busy day for the Southgate car line.

There developed a demand for SC&C cars which groups could charter for excursions to Ft. Thomas, Latonia Race Track, Lagoon Park, and the Bellevue and Dayton beaches on the Ohio River. The more affluent could even charter, when it was not on company business, the *Bluegrass,* a beautifully appointed parlor car built in 1893 by the Brownell Co. It was of the convertible type and featured stylish carpeting, drapes of deep wine color and gold, deep-cushioned wicker chairs and a large cut-glass dome light.

Birthday parties were especially popular and, until the 1930s, the *Bluegrass* carried the well-dressed party-goers to the new suburbs while they sipped pink lemonade, enjoyed cake and ice cream, kept cool by the new fangled "dry ice," and sang along with an accordionist or violinist.

The Green Line Carries the Mail

One activity that added to the profit column in the early days was the transport of mail. Early cars were proudly lettered "U.S. Mail". In 1894 the Green Line started a closed pouch mail service to and from the General Post Office at Fifth & Walnut in Cincinnati connecting to northern Kentucky points. In 1896 the practice of a passenger car hauling a trailer carrying the mail was discontinued due to safety concerns voiced by the City of Covington. The mail henceforth was simply loaded amongst the passengers, albeit in a location where the conductor could keep an eye on it.

By 1900 there were mail routes from Cincinnati to Milldale (Latonia), 6.08 miles; to Dayton, 3.17 miles; and to Ft. Thomas, 7.07 miles. In addition the Green Line carried the mail from the Covington Post Office to Ludlow, 2.62 miles. SC&C mail service to Dayton, Ft. Thomas, and Ludlow was discontinued in 1901, but the Green Line continued closed pouch mail service from Cincinnati to Newport (six trips), to Covington (nine trips), and Latonia (two trips) for almost two additional decades.

Finally, the Green Line's involvement with the U.S. Mail came to an end in 1919. With the ever increasing automobile traffic in downtown Cincinnati, on-street loading of Green Line streetcars in front of the GPO caused delays to both Green Line passengers and vehicular traffic. By now the motor truck was coming into its own, and the Post Office found that off-street dock loading of the more flexible trucks afforded better protection of the mail from both the weather and potential thieves. The last Green Line car to carry mail left for Covington on July 26, 1919.

If there were innovative ways to make money, there were also ways to lose it. Numerous responsibilities were imposed by various franchises which subtracted from the profit column of the SC&C. Generally, they required the company to maintain the street between and to the sides of the rails and this included sprinkling dirt streets in dry weather and snow removal in winter. Many types of "work" cars were kept in reserve to perform such duties plus "line" cars to maintain the wires.

Other work cars included track and ballast cars, tool cars for accidents and derailments, salt and sand cars, and test cars for rail bonds, and an instruction car and a portable substation car. The latter was transported to parts of the system experiencing power shortages during peak traffic.

Also as part of its franchise requirements in Newport and Covington, on-duty firemen and policemen had to be carried free to their assignments. In addition, all Green Line employees were given passes. In those days, most employees lived in the vicinity of the carbarns so they could walk to and from work if they drew an early morning or late night run because owl cars, running all night, were only operated on heavily traveled lines such as Rosedale and Bellevue/Dayton.

Until 1898, the Ft. Thomas line was double tracked only to Highland with single track extending to Ft. Thomas. With the sinking of the *USS Maine* in Havana Harbor on February 15, 1898, Ft. Thomas, home of the U.S. Army's regular Sixth Infantry Regiment, became a beehive of activity. During the ensuing months the Sixth, as well as various volunteer units, "shipped out" from Ft. Thomas via the Green Line for service in Cuba against Spain. The Sixth Regiment fought alongside Teddy Roosevelt and his Rough Riders and participated in the famous charge up San Juan Hill.

The single track segment proved to be a bottleneck and, by August of 1898, the Ft. Thomas line was double tracked to the end of the line. The increased capacity was utilized to transport the victorious Sixth and thousands of well wishers to a gala weekend victory celebration at the post in October, 1898.

Another Look at Ft. Mitchell

In September, 1899, the Green Line's directors gave approval for the formation of a new subsidiary, the Cincinnati, Covington and Erlanger Railway Co. The CC&E was to commence engineering and financial studies of a proposed streetcar line through the Lewisburg section of Covington and on to Ft. Mitchell and Erlanger. The CC&E was immediately leased to the South Covington and Cincinnati in perpetuity, but nothing further happened until 1902.

During 1899 the Green Line carried 14,574,360 passengers, compared to 13,834,546 passengers in 1898. The Kenton County lines carried approximately 8 million riders, with the Campbell

Streetcar in a Rustic Setting

The Green Line featured plenty of private right-of-way. The photographer stands just west of the present intersection of Amsterdam Pike and Montague St. in 1904 in Covington as he captures a southbound Green Line car starting up the 3500 foot, 6.5 percent grade heading to Park Hills. The city may be near, but this looks decidedly rural. *Earl Clark Collection via Jack Doll.*

County lines handling 6.5 million customers. The Central Bridge in 1899 carried but 852,000 Green Line passengers to Cincinnati with the lions' share of the Green Line's Campbell County trips to Cincinnati using the L&N Bridge which, of course, was cheaper for the Green Line to utilize.

Improvements were made to the Newport powerhouse with the installation of 12 American stokers, a new 1,200 horsepower stationary engine and a new 800 kilowatt generator. This expanded electrical generation capacity permitted the closing of the antiquated Covington powerhouse in late 1899.

In 1899 the company received 10 more 31-foot convertible streetcars from the St. Louis Car Co. (Nos. 264-273), each equipped with two more powerful motors (35 h. p. Westinghouse No. 49s) and Peckham 7-B trucks. The cars were delivered in time to handle the peak summer season traffic.

In addition, the company overhauled the 1893 convertible Brownell cars (Nos. 220-238) and fitted nine of them with new Peckham 7-B trucks at an average cost of $479 each. The company also announced that in 1900, the original closed Laclede (Nos. 32-50) and Brownell cars (Nos. 51-76) would be completely renovated to prolong their service lives and would also be refitted with Peckham trucks.

A New Home

Once a streetcar system reached a certain size, it needed a well-equipped maintenance shop. The Green Line had arrived at that point. In February, 1899, construction was started in Newport on a new carhouse and shop complex. The place selected for the new Newport carhouse was at 11th & Brighton with the shops to be erected immediately behind the carbarn at 11th & Lowell and adjacent to the existing powerhouse at Lowell & Thornton.

It really wasn't the Green Line's first choice for a site. The company had decided to utilize the property after attempts to sell it failed, due to its location on the east bank of the Licking River. Potential buyers feared that the land would be subject to severe flooding. This assessment would prove to be all too true during the great flood of 1937.

The city of Newport exempted the Green Line, for five years, from the payment of real estate taxes on the new buildings. Also exempted from taxation was the valuation of all new machinery installed within a five year period.

Completion of the $23,909 carhouse was supposed to be July 1, but owing to delays, it was October 1 before the Green Line occupied the structure. The carhouse (or "carbarn" as it was commonly called) was of brick and iron with a frontage of 90 feet and a depth of 375 feet, having a capacity of 100, 30-foot streetcars. The carbarn covered eight tracks which ran the entire length of the building with pits 60 feet long under each track for inspection and light repairs.

Each pit was supplied with floodlights to aid in looking under the cars, and with steam pipes for the drying out of the cars' undersides. The second floor of the car barn was provided with a room where the crews made out their daily reports and a locker room which contained a first class lavatory supplied with porcelain bathtubs and the "latest sanitary plumbing."

Upon occupation of the new Newport carhouse, the carhouses at Sixth & Berry in Dayton, on the north side of 11th near Saratoga in Newport, and on the northeast corner of Main & Pike in Covington, were abandoned. The Covington and Dayton properties had once been horsecar barns and stables. The previously abandoned horsecar barn on the south side of 11th & Saratoga was torn down and the property leased to the Chesapeake and Ohio Railway. The Green Line System was reorganized into two distinct divisions with all the lines east of the Licking River assigned to the new Newport Division and all of the lines west of the Licking River assigned to the new Covington Division.

The Newport Shops

The new shops also were supposed to be finished by October 1, but the company did not get to occupy them until late

Green Line Shops and a Headquarters for a New Century

The Green Line earned itself a multi-page spread in the *Street Railway Journal* for December 9, 1903. And rightly so, because it had invested a large sum of money in its new Covington headquarters and Newport complex. Please note, however, that the caption regarding the carbarn interior on page 45 is incorrect--it's the Newport barn! Read on for the next 4 pages. ➔

December, 1899. It must have been worth the wait, since these shops contained full facilities for the complete overhaul of the streetcars including motor repair, truck work, and a complete woodworking and paint shop for body work. Soon after the opening of the new Newport shops, in early 1900 major repairs at the Covington carbarn at 20th & Madison ceased. Now, all major repairs and overhauls would be done at the Newport shops.

The machine shop, which measured 60 feet by 175 feet, was located behind the carbarn but separated by Lowell Street. It contained four tracks with pits to facilitate working underneath the cars. Beyond the tracks was a bank of state of the art machine tools, a blacksmith's quarters, a coil winding room and a stock room.

The woodworking shop (opened in 1899) and the paint shop (ready in 1900) were built side by side behind the machine shop. They were connected by an electrically driven transfer table which moved the cars from a track paralleling the machine shop to any of the three tracks which served either the woodworking or paint shops.

At approximately 50,000 mile intervals, the wheels on the streetcars needed to be changed. At such times a streetcar was run into the machine shop where the wheels and axles were removed. Badly worn axles were rebuilt by electric welding. Defective wheels were replaced, and wheels which had developed flat spots were repaired by use of an electric grinding machine. High-speed grinders, located in one of the pits, were brought against the wheels which were smoothed and made round. Both wheels on an axle were ground simultaneously to ensure the same diameter.

Car motors were overhauled at the same time. The motors were removed from the trucks by hydraulic jacks located in the pits and sent to another area of the workshop for the work, including armature repair and new coil winding if necessary. Other electrical and mechanical details such as door mechanisms, controllers, brake rigging, wiring, and trolley bases, were carefully inspected and repaired or renewed as found necessary at that time.

The car was then routed to the woodworking shop where the body could be completely dismantled and inspected. Parts which were rotted, rusted, or judged unfit to withstand four or more years of service were completely renewed. In the case of some

The fender sign says "Cemetery" and that is certainly apt for this Lewisburg car because the line was extended, in 1903, to serve St. John's, St. Mary's, and Highland Cemeteries in what is now Ft. Mitchell.
Earl Clark collection.

of the older cars, this procedure amounted to almost a complete rebuilding of the car body.

A turn-of-the-century streetcar was a marvel of the woodworker's art. The carbodies were made almost completely of wood, and the principal varieties used were ash for corner and window posts, oak for insills and supporting cross members and yellow pine for the side sills. The car floors were replaced with standard yellow pine under the seats but with more durable maple along the aisles. Interior trim, sash, and doors were made from cherry and mahogany. Side and end panels needing replacement were constructed with 5/8 inch yellow pine covered with a heavy gauge steel.

From the woodworking shop the car was transferred to the paint shop where it received a thorough scrubbing inside and out. The interior of the car was revarnished, the floor was repainted, and the window curtains were removed and washed. The outside of the carbody was puttied, primed, smoothed, and finally painted the familiar dark green color with white window and door trim. No less than seven coats of paint were applied to a completely overhauled car.

The window sashes were refinished in another part of the paint shop and were reinstalled after all other parts of the streetcar were thoroughly dry. In some years as many as 25 cars went through the Newport shops.

Into the Twentieth Century

When the 20th century arrived, the Green Line System comprised 52.73 route miles in three counties and two states consisting of 24.11 route miles in Kenton County, 25.87 route miles in Campbell County, and 2.75 route miles in Cincinnati, Ohio.

Although the company was in reasonably good financial shape, an analysis of Green Line's balance sheet for the year ending December 31, 1899, reveals earnings of a little more than 3 percent on investment. That was not a princely return. The commercial bond market of the period was paying higher yields. Thus, in spite of the almost constant political agitation by the Newport and Covington city governments for lower fares on the basis that the company was gouging the public, it is apparent that

TEXT RESUMES ON PAGE 47

IMPROVEMENTS ON A KENTUCKY SYSTEM

The South Covington & Cincinnati Street Railway Company, which owns the Kentucky lines controlled by the Cincinnati, Newport & Covington Light & Traction Company, has been making a number of improvements in its system of late, and additions to its property.

Prominent among these is the erection of the handsome and

complete office building herewith illustrated, which is located on the main street in Covington, Ky., immediately adjoining the City Hall and directly opposite the postoffice. Architecturally, it is in harmony with its surroundings. The structure has 150 ft. front and is 30 ft. deep. It is constructed of Columbus fire-flashed brick laid in red mortar; trimmings of Bedford stone with copper cornice and red tile roof. It is heated by a hot-water system. The first and second floors are supported

HEADQUARTERS OF CINCINNATI, NEWPORT & COVINGTON RAILWAY SYSTEM AT COVINGTON.

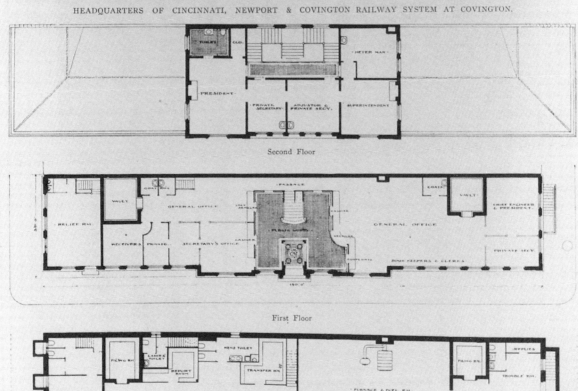

Second Floor

First Floor

Basement

PLANS OF HEADQUARTERS BUILDING

on iron beams throughout. The finish of all woodwork and
furniture is highly polished antique oak. In the center is a
public lobby with marble floor and wainscoating. There are
windows for the receiver, cashier, "complaints" and "lost
articles." An open stairway leads to the second floor. On
either side of the lobby are the general offices with private
offices for the receivers, secretary, chief engineer and relief
association. On the second floor are the offices of the president,
claim adjuster, superintendent and treasurer. In the basement are the trouble room, transfer room, report room, filing
room and a dining room for office employees.

The company has grouped its repair shops and car house on
a site adjoining its power house in Newport, and now has a
very complete lay-out for a road of this size. The arrangement of the buildings is shown in the accompanying plan. The
car house is 90 ft. x 375 ft., has eight tracks extending the
entire length, and holds ninety-six cars. The floor is brick,
and there are brick pits, 60 ft. long, in each track. The roof
is slate and is supported on structural steel trusses with clear
spans. In front between the two large doors is the office of the

CAR HOUSE

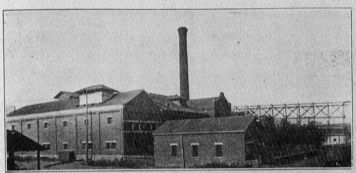

POWER HOUSE AND TRESTLE FOR COAL-CONVEYING SYSTEM

division superintendent. On the second floor is a waiting room,
locker room with individual lockers for the men, reporting
room and reading room, with tables and periodicals, supplied by

well kept up. There is a track at the side of
the building which connects with the machine
shop, paint shop, woodworking shop and
power house in the rear. The dimensions of
the machine shop building are 60 ft. x 176 ft.,
and the construction is similar to that of the
car house. It has four tracks, with pits the
full length. The rear of the building is partitioned off for a blacksmith shop, a store room,
electrical repair shop and office of the master
mechanic and purchasing agent. Up-stairs is
the office of the superintendent and the engineering department of the road. In the basement is a wash room for the men, with tubs
and shower baths. To the rear of the machine
shop are the paint and woodworking shops,
which are each 50 ft. x 110 ft., divided in the center by a fire-
brick wall. There are three tracks in each section, and the
building is made accessible by a transfer table connecting with

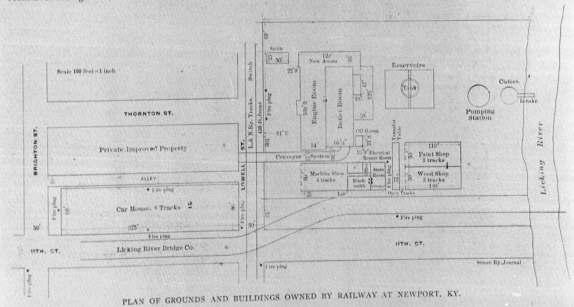

PLAN OF GROUNDS AND BUILDINGS OWNED BY RAILWAY AT NEWPORT, KY.

the company. There is a fireproof oil room on one side of the
building and a lavatory and a bath room for the men. This is
supplied with hot and cold water, and there are both tubs and
shower baths. All the plumbing is first class, and the place is

the tracks at the alley at the side. The machine shop has a
good equipment of tools, including an engine lathe for turning
axles, wheel lathe, boring mill, wheel press, lathes, etc.
The company is receiving a lot of twenty single-truck cars,

designed for both summer and winter service. They are the St. Louis Car Company's semi-convertible type, and are 31 ft. over all, 21-ft. body and 8 ft. wide. The bottom framing has a

NEW CAR OF CINCINNATI, NEWPORT & COVINGTON SYSTEM

sill 7 ins. wide and 6 ins. deep, with a ⅞-in. strip of iron running through it edgewise. The sides are constructed of ⅞-in. poplar panels with no concave. The cars have front end vestibules, closed on one side and open on the other, and the rear end has an open platform. There are fourteen cross-seats, of the St. Louis Car Company's reversible enameled rattan type, and two

brakes, St. Louis sand-boxes and Hunter fenders are included in the equipment.

Thomas Kelch, master mechanic of the shops, has designed several unique devices that have been adopted in the shops and on the road. One of these is a hinged trolley harp, illustrated herewith. By removing a cotter at the side, one arm of the harp may be opened, and the trolley wheel slipped off the bearing. It is claimed that the work of changing a trolley wheel can be done in one-fifth the time required with the ordinary harp. Any style of wheel may be used. The harp fits very close around the wheel, and there is no space for the wire to get between the harp and the wheel. A copper spring carries the current from the wheel to the pole.

For pit work a portable hydraulic jack, shown herewith, is used. This is mounted on four wheels, and it is light enough to be carried from one pit to another by one man. The construction is very simple; the lift portion being made of 3-in. iron pipe, 4 ft. long, while the water tank is of 3-in. pipe, 18 ins. long. The pump is of 1½-in. pipe, 6 ins. long. The table has 18-in. wood rollers, so that an armature may be rolled off easily, and the lift has a capacity of about 1000 lbs.

In pressing off car wheels, without removing the gear, Mr. Kelch uses a pair of cast-iron billets, having one end shaped to

INTERIOR OF CAR HOUSE AT SOUTH COVINGTON

side seats. The interior finish is extra fine cherry. Both the side sashes drop inside the car between the sills. The end sash and the end door sash also drop into pockets. The end inside sash is provided with a screen. Peckham No. 7-D trucks, two Westinghouse motors, a K-10 controller, Westinghouse electric

fit the wheel flange. The accompanying illustration shows this method in operation.

The company has about 150 cars in use, and two Westinghouse No. 49 motors have been adopted as standard equipment for each car. One man and four boys are employed in electrical repair work, and they make all their own armature coils and field coils and do their own controller work, as well as car wiring, etc. Charles Ulrich, who is in charge of the department, has introduced

armature coil cells he uses a simple press, which saves a great deal of time. There is a flat steel plate in which there is a groove the depth of No. 11 Brown & Sharpe gage wire. A hinged arm forms a die to fit the groove, and when stamped down it forms one-half the desired cell. Another lever operates a pair of rollers, which, in passing over the fuller-board, gives

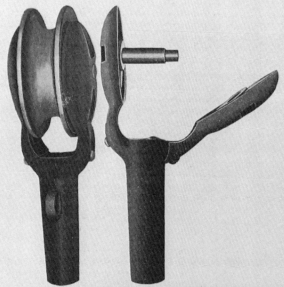

HINGED TROLLEY HARP

HOME-MADE HYDRAULIC PIT JACK

several simple devices of his own invention that assist materially in the work. In winding Westinghouse No. 49 armature field coils he uses the wood form illustrated. This has four adjustable spring clamps, two having straight faces and two curved faces, which press 'the wire down tight and keep it in place during the winding. It is claimed that the device greatly facilitates the work. In forming Westinghouse No. 49 armature coils he uses a brass form made in two sec-

PRESSING OFF WHEELS WITHOUT REMOVING GEARS

it a double crease, thus forming the coil cell.

The management is making extensive improvements in its power station (shown on page 1047), which has been growing piece-meal during the last fifteen years, and several additions have been built during that time. Railway, light and power loads are carried. Four Cleveland Shipbuilding Company's marine type vertical engines, belted to Westinghouse generators, are being taken out, and two Cooper - Corliss cross-com-

FORMS FOR WINDING FIELD COILS AND ARMATURE COILS

tions, having curves exactly the shape of the coil desired. The form is provided with a double hook, operated by one handle, for tightening or loosening the two sections. The hooks are tapered. By throwing the lever forward the two sections of the form are tightened, and by throwing the lever back, both sections are instantly released. In forming fuller-board for

pound condensing engines, of 2600 hp, directly connected to 1650-kw, Westinghouse, 550-volt railway generators are being installed. At present the railway side of the house is short of power, and a 400-kw Westinghouse rotary converter has been installed in the station. The rotary is of the shunt-wound type, and takes current through step-down transformers from a 500-

the owners of the Green Line were not exactly "robber barons" in any classic sense of the term.

While capital matters occupied the company's directors, lesser management had to deal with day-to-day problems. By 1900 the junction at 11th & Madison was extremely congested. To relieve some of the pressure, the Green Line opened, on June 14, 1900, a new single track from 13th & Holman east on 13th to Russell and north on Russell to Robbins and east on Robbins to Madison. This scheme double tracked the rest of Holman St. line and allowed northbound Holman cars to avoid 11th & Madison.

In 1900, St. Louis Car delivered the last 15 "convertible" cars that the Green Line would receive (Nos. 274-288). An early photograph of No. 285 clearly shows the car with an open driving platform. Perhaps one would think that the 1896 law which required streetcars operating in Ohio between October and March to be equipped with closed driving platforms was declared unconstitutional or repealed by that time. Not true; the cars were delivered with fittings and brackets so that an enclosed front and left side panel (complete with windshield and side glass but open on the passenger side) could be quickly and cheaply installed on any car in the fall and removed in the spring. This was done, of course, at the newly opened and well equipped Newport shops. Most other convertible cars were similarly modified.

In the spring of 1901, work was started on a short extension of the Dayton and Bellevue line. The ordinance authorizing the extension provided:

> "The right is hereby granted to the South Covington and Cincinnati Street Railway Company to take up its tracks as now laid on Third avenue, from Clay to Benham streets, and on Clay street, from Sixth avenue to Third avenue, and to relay said tracks as a single track in the center of Third avenue and Clay street, and to continue said single track so laid, so as to form a loop for said railway on and over the following streets: from Third avenue and Benham street, southwardly on Benham to Fifth avenue; thence westwardly on Fifth avenue from Benham street to Main street; thence westwardly on Sixth avenue, from Main street to Clay street; said tracks . . . to connect the tracks of said railway with the present tracks at the corners of Third avenue and Clay street and Sixth avenue and Clay street."

On July 4, 1901, the extension was formally opened amidst hurrah, bands, and fireworks, with the first car appropriately decked out in red, white, and blue bunting.

The Creation of "Transfer Corner"

Covington now started upon a program to revitalize its downtown area. As a part of this 1901 plan, the city desired to abandon the farmers' market between Greenup and Scott and replace it with a street to be named Park Place and to widen Court from Second to Fourth.

The South Covington and Cincinnati owned the entire block on the east side of Court between Third and the market area. In July, 1901, the Green Line ceded to Covington a strip of land 150 feet by 23 feet to enable the city to complete the Court Street widening project. The company also agreed to abandon its tracks on Greenup north of the market area, on Scott north of Third, on Third east of Court, and all of its trackage on Second in exchange for permission to lay tracks on newly constructed Park from both Greenup and Scott and on Court from Park to Second.

This new trackage, which went into service in the fall of 1901, allowed the Green Line's streetcars a more direct approach to the Suspension Bridge. A secondary benefit to Green Line passengers was that all Kenton County lines now met at Third & Court thereby affording a central convenient transfer point soon nicknamed "Transfer Corner."

By 1901 a frame and corrugated metal carbarn, measuring 50 feet by 190 feet, was constructed on the southwest corner of 20th & Madison. The materials came from the recently closed carbarn on 11th near Saratoga in Newport, constructed in 1892. In addition to providing storage space for 30 cars, the new barn allowed parts of the older 1891 barn to be taken out of service for remodeling. The old barn was redesigned with a partial new second floor to accommodate locker and restrooms for the convenience of the Covington Division employees similar to those contained in the recently built car barn in Newport.

The Court St. improvements yielded a splendid new Green Line headquarters. The North American Co., a large owner of midwest gas and electric companies, purchased controlling interest in the Union Light, Heat and Power Co. in late 1901. The Cincinnati, Newport and Covington Railway (of Ohio), its operating subsidiary, the South Covington and Cincinnati Street Railway (of Kentucky), and the Licking River Bridge Co. came formally into the North American fold early in 1902. All were placed under a new holding company, the Cincinnati, Newport and Covington Light and Traction Co. (of New Jersey).

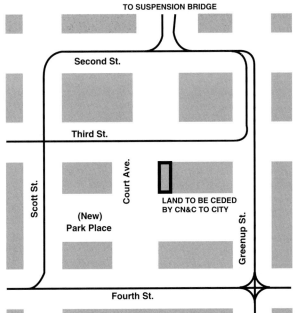

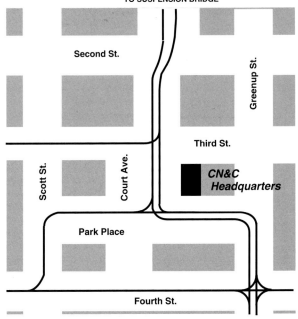

Green Line trackage in downtown Covington was extensively revised in 1901 to create "Transfer Corner."

All this needed a home. A handsome burnt orange brick office building was opened in 1903 on Court between Third and Park to house the general offices of both the South Covington and Cincinnati Street Railway and ULH&P with "CN&C Light and Traction Co." prominently inscribed on the lentil stone over the main doorway. The building would serve as the Green Line's general offices for over 50 years and contained a heated waiting room for the convenience of transferring passengers. The new owners retained James C. Ernst as president.

On to Ft. Mitchell

There would be one more big rail project reaching far into the suburbs. Since the time of the Cleveland Syndicate takeover of the South Covington and Cincinnati in 1892, plans had been announced for the extension of the system to Ft. Mitchell and Erlanger via the southwest Covington suburb of Lewisburg, a former independent village long a part of the City of Covington.

Although one CN&C track map of 1893 showed the proposed extension, a separate subsidiary, the Cincinnati, Covington and Erlanger Railway Co. was not formed until 1899 and construction on the first segment to Lewisburg did not commence until the summer of 1902.

On December 20, 1902, the Green Line inaugurated service to Lewisburg. From Cincinnati the new Lewisburg line followed the southbound Holman line as far as 12th & Holman. From this intersection a new single track route was constructed on 12th west to Hermes where the line turned north on Hermes to Pike and east on Pike to a connection with the existing Main Street line at Pike & Main. The Lewisburg line then utilized the Main Street line's trackage for the return to Cincinnati.

In the next year, the Lewisburg line was extended out Pike and Montague to the Covington city limits and on to private

right-of-way ending at the adjoining Highland and St. Mary's Cemeteries. Upon entering private way at Montague St., southbound cars fought a ruling grade of 6.5 percent over 3350 feet of track until they reached level ground.

This extension of some 2.93 miles (all double tracked except for a 643 foot segment of single track on narrow Montague St. protected by a Nachod block signal system) was opened for revenue service on November 1, 1903 and, although it served an area of rather low population density, it proved to be a generator of important revenue. The SC&C had to assign as many as 12 cars on summer weekends to accommodate those visiting the graves of the departed. Since no loop was constructed and almost all Green Line cars had controls on only one end, a turntable was installed to point the cars back toward Cincinnati.

The Lewisburg extension meant that, due to both the distance from the Newport powerhouse and the steep grade out of the Covington basin, the Green Line had to build its first outlying substation to ensure satisfactory power for the line. Situated directly across from Highland Cemetery, the substation was fed by a newly erected 4500 volt a.c. line from the Newport powerhouse. Two rotary converters transformed the a.c. to 550 volt d.c. traction power.

The company also ordered, in 1902, its first 31-foot "semi-convertible" single truck streetcars from the St. Louis Car Co. (Nos. 289-298). As opposed to the Green Line's convertible cars (Nos. 220-288), where side panels were removed (windows and all) during warm months and wire guards and canvas curtains installed, the "semi-convertible" streetcars were designed so that the window sashes could simply be lowered on guides into the body of the car during warm weather.

All future cars purchased by the SC&C would be of the semi-convertible type but the Green Line and most street railway companies eventually called them simply closed cars.

With the extension of the Lewisburg line to Park Hills and to the Highland and St. Mary's Cemeteries in 1903, the need arose for a substation near the end of the line to boost the voltage. Here we see operator John Cooper in front of the newly opened facility. One of the rotary converters, which changed 13,200 volt alternating current to 550 volt direct current for use by CN&C streetcars, can be glimpsed over the operator's right shoulder. *Kenton County Library.*

To further augment the fleet, the company received 10 more 31-foot single truck cars from St. Louis Car in May of 1903 (Nos. 299-308) with heavy duty Peckham 7-D trucks for use on the soon-to-open "high speed" Lewisburg line extension. The fleet received another increase in April of 1906 when 10 St. Louis single truck cars (Nos. 309-318) arrived. These last 10 streetcars, although identical in body design with Nos. 289-308, were equipped with "improved riding trucks" (Brill Model 21E) for higher speed on the private right-of-way trackage of the Ft. Thomas, Evergreen, and Lewisburg lines.

All 30 cars (Nos. 289-318) were delivered with enclosed front vestibules but with an open rear platform (where passengers entered and the conductor held forth to collect fares) and were not enclosed until the 1920s. The Green Line was apparently well satisfied with the Brill 21E trucks under Nos. 309-318 since all future single truck cars ordered would be so equipped.

Queen City Congestion

Downtown Cincinnati was bustling, and traffic was becoming a problem. This caused a significant change to the Green Line's trackage pattern in Cincinnati in 1903. Prior to that time the streetcars of the Green Line's Newport Division gained access to downtown Cincinnati via Broadway to Fourth to Walnut to Fifth (Government Square) and returned via Fifth to Broadway and south on Broadway to one of the two Newport-Cincinnati bridges then in use.

A 1902 engineering study revealed that congestion at the Fifth & Broadway intersection (also used by numerous Cincinnati streetcars) caused the most serious delays to streetcar service in the entire downtown Cincinnati

area. Consequently, the City of Cincinnati ordered the Green Line to stop using Fifth and Broadway and to turn from Fifth south on Main to Fourth and to use Fourth east to Broadway. The new route meant that new switches at Fifth & Main and Fourth & Main and a new second (eastbound) track on Fourth between Main and Broadway had to be installed. In March 1903 the Green Line commenced operations over the new trackage.

On October 23, 1904, service began on an extension of the Holman line to the city of Central Covington (formerly known as Peaselburg). The extension ran along Holman to 19th, west on 19th to Howell, south on Howell to 21st, east on 21st to Russell and back north on Russell to 19th and west on 19th back to Holman.

Another significant 1904 route extension occurred when the South Covington and Cincinnati built a new line to the southern part of Bellevue. The South Bellevue line left the existing Bellevue and Dayton line at Taylor & Fairfield and proceeded south on Taylor to Walnut, east on Walnut to Washington, south on Washington to Grandview, and east on Grandview to Ward. This loop bridged the Chesapeake and Ohio Railway in two places. The line then continued north on Ward to Center and west on Center back to Taylor and north to Fairfield. The South Bellevue line was completed on November 24, 1904.

Also that year, the Green Line began extensive improvements to the Newport powerhouse at Thornton & Lowell. Its electrical generating output was more than doubled. Although the streetcar company benefited from this reserve power, the additions were made primarily due to increased electricity demands by Newport business and residential customers.

Those electricity demands, yet again, would hugely shape the future of the Green Line. ❏

A track repair project at 3rd & Washington in Newport, circa 1900, reveals the substantial nature of a Green Line streetcar's footing. The company used oak ties and 103 pound rail here; materials that many a railroad superintendent would covet.
Special Collections and Archives, University of Kentucky Libraries.

Green Line Streetcar Routes in 1905

With the completion of the South Bellevue line in 1904, the street railway system of the Green Line had almost reached its zenith. Only two short route additions were constructed after 1904, namely the 1.10 mile Crosstown line via the rebuilt 4th St. Bridge in 1908 and the .79 mile extension of the Lewisburg line in 1910.

Let us take stock of the Green Line empire as it existed in the early 1900s. Excerpts from a Cincinnati area guidebook, published in 1905, describe the routes below. But first, a primer on the development of the small municipalities surrounding Covington. Present street names and cities formed since 1905 are indicated in brackets. Both Austinburg and Lewisburg were annexed by Covington prior to the Civil War. Covington annexed the city of Central Covington in 1906, the city of Latonia in 1909, and the city of West Covington in 1916.

Further, Latonia (the village of Milldale until 1896) annexed Rosedale in 1904. However, to this day, residents of the southern part of Covington are likely to say they are from Latonia or Rosedale instead of Covington, and even the neighborhoods of Austinburg and Lewisburg did not lose all traces of recognition until the 1960s.

COVINGTON ROUTES

All lines enter Cincinnati via the Suspension Bridge to 2nd to Walnut to 5th (Fountain Square) to Vine to 2nd to the bridge except the Belt Line cars which turn at 5th to Government Square before proceeding to Newport.

LUDLOW - From Cincinnati loop - Court - Park Place - Scott - 4th - Main - 3rd - Crescent -2nd - West Covington - Covington and Ludlow highway to Ludlow - to Southern Bridge - Elm -P R W near Adela - West Oak - Bromley loop. Return same route.

LEWISBURG - From Cincinnati loop - Court - Park Place - Scott - 4th - Madison - 11th - Russell - 12th - Hermes - Pike - Montague - P R W [through the present cities of Park Hills and Ft. Mitchell] to Highland Cemetery. Return same to Pike - Madison - 3rd - Court - to Cincinnati.

HOLMAN ST. - From Cincinnati loop - Court - Park Place - Scott - 4th - Madison - 11th - Russell - 12th - Holman - Willow [now 19th] - Howell - Pleasant [now 21st] - Holman [now Russell] - Willow [now 19th] - Holman - 13th -Russell - Robins - Madison - 3rd - Court, to Cincinnati.

LATONIA - Starts from 20th and Madison - P R W - Main [now DeCoursey] to Hamlin [now 34th] - Eugenia - Sandford [now 35th] - Carlisle - P R W through Latonia Race Track -Latonia Ave - Sandford [now 35th]. Return same route.

AUSTINBURG or **EDWARDS ST**. - 15th & Greenup -on 15th to Rickey - Oliver - Edwards [now Eastern] - Corporation line - Garrard - 20th - Greenup -to beginning, transferring passengers to Madison and Greenup lines for Cincinnati.

ROSEDALE - From Cincinnati loop - 3rd & Court - Park Place - Scott - 4th - Madison - P R W through Covington - Main St. [now DeCoursey] Latonia - Southern - Huntington - loop at Rosedale Station and Lake Wolking [now 45th]. Return same route.

MADISON - From Cincinnati loop - Court - Park Place - Scott - 4th - Madison - 20th - Greenup - Park Place - Court - to Cincinnati.

GREENUP ST. - From Cincinnati loop - Court -Park Place - Greenup - 20th - Madison - 3rd -Court - to Cincinnati.

MAIN ST. - From Cincinnati loop - Court - Park Place - Scott - 4th - Main - Pike - Madison -3rd - Court - to Cincinnati.

NEWPORT ROUTES

The Dayton and Bellevue line, the South Bellevue line, the Ft. Thomas line, the Washington Ave. line and the Belt Line cars from Newport enter Cincinnati from the L&N Bridge to Butler to Pearl to Broadway to Fourth to Walnut to 5th (Government Square) to Main to 4th to Broadway and to the L&N Bridge except the Belt Line cars which turn at 5th to Fountain Square before proceeding to Covington.

The Patterson line, the York St. line and the Monmouth St. line cars from Newport enter Cincinnati from the Central Bridge to Broadway and then use the same route as indicated above.

NEWPORT & COVINGTON BELT LINE - In Cincinnati, 5th and Walnut - to Vine - 2nd - Suspension Bridge - Court, Covington - Park Place - Scott - 4th - Madison - 11th - Greenup - 12th - Licking River Bridge - to Newport - 11th - York - 3rd - L&N Bridge - Cincinnati at Pearl & Butler - Broadway - 4th - Walnut - to 5th. Opposite direction, same, except on Main instead of Walnut from 4th to 5th - also on Madison to 3rd to Court in Covington.

PATTERSON - From Cincinnati loop via Central Bridge to Newport - 3rd - Central - 5th - Patterson - 11th - York - Central Bridge to Cincinnati - Broadway - 4th - Walnut - 5th.

YORK ST. - Same as Patterson to Newport -York - 11th - Patterson - 5th - Central - 3rd - York - Central Bridge to Cincinnati.

MONMOUTH ST. - Same as Patterson to Newport - 3rd - Monmouth - past Huber's Garden in Newport on Alexandria Pike - P R W through Southgate - Evergreen Cemetery. Return same route.

BELLEVUE & DAYTON - From Cincinnati loop via L&N Bridge - 3rd in Newport - Beech - Fairfield - Dayton - 6th - Main - 5th - Benham - 3rd - Clay - 6th. Return same route.

SOUTH BELLEVUE - Same as Bellevue & Dayton to Taylor and Fairfield - Taylor - Walnut - Washington - Grandview - Ward - Center - Taylor. Return same route.

WASHINGTON AVE. - Same as South Bellevue to 3rd and Washington - Washington - 10th. Return same route.

FT. THOMAS - Same as Washington, continuing on 10th - Bonnie Leslie - P R W through Highland District [the Highland District surrounding the Ft. Thomas Military Reservation became the city of Ft. Thomas in 1914] to Ft. Thomas. Return same route.

A close examination of the guidebook reveals that the Madison line and the Greenup line actually formed one through-routed or "belt line" operation. The Madison line operated south on Madison Ave., but returned to Cincinnati via 20th to Greenup and north on Greenup and the Greenup line operated south on Greenup but returned to Cincinnati via Madison and 20th.

The guidebook confirms that neither the Austinburg line nor the Latonia line operated as through routes to downtown Covington let alone Cincinnati. The Austinburg or Edwards line was offered as a shuttle from 15th and Greenup clockwise around the Austinburg loop and back to 15th St. via Greenup. The Latonia line also ran as a shuttle, meeting Rosedale, Madison and Greenup line cars at 20th & Madison. ◆

Salad Days on the Green Line . . . a Little Taste

The two men crewing St. Louis Car Co. semi-convertible car 307 appear relaxed and confident as they await another circa 1905 assignment on the Ft. Thomas line. It was indeed a relaxed time, one we can recall here by these souvenirs of another day. At **right,** Junk's Shoe Store has gone all out to celebrate the opening of the Dayton line. *Photo: Earl Clark Collection. Program: C. William Myers Collection; Others: T. W. Lehmann Collection.*

South Covington & Cin'ti St. Ry. Co.

TRANSFER CHECK

FOURTH AND SCOTT
— TO —

Madison Ave. or Greenup St.

Good only on day of date.

TIME CARD—Ft. Thomas and Cincinnati Street Car Line.

Compliments of CHAS. RIEDMATTER'S "BELVEDERE," Ft. Thomas, Ky.

➤ FOR THE SEASON. ❋

		Leaving Ft. Thomas Daily.							Leaving Cin'ti Post Office Daily.			
1	2	3	4	5	6		1	2	3	4	5	6
					5 40					5 54	6 08	6 22
5 51	6 08	6 22	6 36	6 50	7 04		6 36	6 50	7 04	7 18	7 32	7 46
7 18	7 32	7 46	8 00	8 14	8 28		8 00	8 14	8 28	8 42	8 56	9 10
8 42	8 56	9 10	9 24	9 38	9 52		9 24	9 38	9 52	10 06	10 20	10 34
10 06	10 20	10 34	10 48	11 02	11 16		10 48	11 02	11 16	11 30	11 44	11 58
11 30	11 44	11 58	12 12	12 26	12 40		12 12	12 26	12 40	12 54	1 08	1 22
12 54	1 08	1 22	1 36	1 50	2 04		1 36	1 50	2 04	2 18	2 32	2 46
2 18	2 32	2 46	3 00	3 14	3 28		3 00	3 14	3 28	3 42	3 56	4 10
3 42	3 56	4 10	4 24	4 38	4 52		4 24	4 38	4 52	5 06	5 20	5 34
5 06	5 20	5 34	5 48	6 02	6 16		5 48	6 02	6 16	6 30	6 44	6 58
6 30	6 44	6 58	7 12	7 26	7 40		7 12	7 26	7 40	7 54	8 08	8 22
7 54	8 08	8 22	8 36	8 50	9 04		8 36	8 50	9 04	9 18	9 32	9 46
9 18	9 32	9 46	10 00	10 14	10 28		10 00	10 14	10 28	10 42	10 56	11 10
10 42	10 56	11 10	11 24	11 38	11 52		11 38			*12 00		
		12 20			12 42							

★ No. 4 on last trip (12 P. M.) from Cincinnati runs through to Ft. Thomas.

Sunday time, No. 4 first car to Ft. Thomas from Car House.

Edison's Concert Phonograph on free exhibition. Special attention to Wedding parties. All cars stop at the door. Soda Water.

On first trip Cars **1, 2, 3, 6** go to Ft. Thomas from Car House and Cars **4, 5** go to Cin'ti. On last trip in from Ft. Thomas, Cars **2, 4** go to 10th and Washington Ave. only, and Cars **1, 3, 5, 6** go to the L. & N. Bridge.

The Columbia Era: 1907-1929

NO THANKS to its streetcar empire, the Green Line had become a sought-after property. In 1907, Columbia Gas and Electric, a company which pioneered long distance distribution of natural gas by high pressure pipeline, acquired control of the Cincinnati, Newport and Covington Light and Traction Co. (of New Jersey).

CG&E was primarily interested in supplying the customers of CN&C L&T's Union Light, Heat and Power Co. with natural gas. At this time, ULH&P served more than 3000 customers with electricity and about 6000 customers with manufactured gas.

Columbia had little interest in purchasing CN&C Light and Traction's other subsidiary, the Cincinnati, Newport and Covington Railway (of Ohio) and its subsidiary the South Covington and Cincinnati Street Railway (of Kentucky). Although the Green Line carried more than 25 million passengers in 1906, its rate of return was deplorably modest, averaging only 2.5 percent per year between 1903 to 1906.

But it came with the deal, and Columbia couldn't duck it. North American refused to sell ULH&P unless Columbia also agreed to buy all the rest of CN&C Light and Traction assets. As a result, Columbia found itself the owner of a street railway, the only one it would ever own. And there were big doings across the river in 1907, when Columbia acquired the Cincinnati Gas and Electric Co. and placed all its Cincinnati area acquisitions under the control of another Columbia entity, the Union Gas and Electric Co.

Apparently James C. Ernst was well thought of in street railway circles because the new owners retained him as president of the company. He remained in office at the impressive brick and stone building at Third & Court, opened by the CN&C Light and Traction Co. in 1903, until ill health forced him to retire in 1914, at which time W. W. Freeman succeeded him.

However, George M. Abbott, secretary-treasurer since 1890 and son of SC&C founder E. F. Abbott was not retained by the new owners, nor was General Manager Thomas Jenkins. They were succeeded by Polk Lafoon and C. R. McKay.

Covington officials, meantime, were pushing for service enhancements. On July 22, 1907, the Green Line instituted through service to Cincinnati on the Edwards line. At the same time, the Greenup and Madison belt line was unbuckled. The Greenup cars, instead of returning north to Cincinnati on Madison, wyed on the property at 20th & Madison and returned

---

Dixie Terminal: a Bird's Eye View

The opening of the Upper Level of the Dixie Terminal in October of 1921 enabled Covington Division cars to avoid street running in Cincinnati. Looking from the north tower of the Suspension Bridge, we see three northbound cars heading for the terminal and three Kentucky bound cars coming toward the photographer. This off-street terminal and arcade, so useful and ornamental at the same time, was arguably the biggest Green Line improvement of the Roaring 20s. *Earl Clark Collection.*

Kentucky: the Green Line's Touch of Class

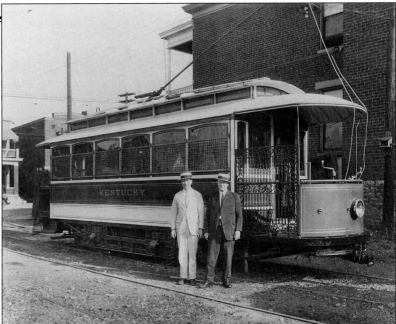

The *Kentucky* was crafted by Green Line shop forces in 1911 from 1892 Brownell passenger car 64 and transformed into a business car for Green Line President James C. Ernst. The *Kentucky* was available for private charters and survives today having been recently restored by the volunteer efforts of the talented maintenance folks at the Transit Authority of Northern Kentucky. Newly appointed General Manager Philip G. Vondersmith and Price Lollard, superintendent of transportation, stand near the front platform. The interior of the car featured curtains, carpeting, wicker furniture, side tables, and ornate lighting fixtures. *Special Collections and Archives, University of Kentucky Libraries.*

---

to Cincinnati eastward on 20th and north on Greenup. The Madison line's cars were wyed in the street at 20th & Madison to return north to Cincinnati on Madison.

The Last Extensions

The bridge over the lower Licking River linking Fourth St. in Covington with Fifth St. in Newport was leased by the Green Line in 1906 and subsequently rebuilt to accommodate streetcars. As a result, the Green Line began, in 1908, a new intercity service between Third & York in Newport and Third & Court in Covington. Thus, the citizens of Newport and Covington were, in effect, provided with two "crosstown" links, the other one being the Belt Line via the upriver Licking River bridge owned by the CN&C.

Through the SC&C's subsidiary, the Cincinnati, Covington and Erlanger Railway, work commenced in 1909 on extending the Lewisburg line from Highland Cemetery over private right-of-way (roughly paralleling the present Dixie Highway) to a loop across from Horsebranch (now Orphanage) Road. The company's new trackage was leased to parent South Covington and Cincinnati in May 1910 and the new segment, less than one mile in length, was opened for revenue service on June 29, 1910.

It would be the Green Line's last streetcar line extension. The CC&E Railway never did get to Erlanger. Independent buses later did.

The Lewisburg route was renamed the Ft. Mitchell line after the area north of Highland Cemetery incorporated as the city of Ft. Mitchell in 1909. Even though the city of South Ft. Mitchell was formed in 1927 to govern the area from south of Highland

Cemetery to just north of Buttermilk Pike, the name of the car line was not again changed. To further confuse present day readers, the cities of Ft. Mitchell and South Ft. Mitchell merged in 1967 to form the larger city of Ft. Mitchell.

More Cars Needed

By 1910, the company was in need of additional streetcars because the passenger count had been slowly but steadily climbing. The 15 or so survivors of the original Stephenson cars (Nos. 1-31) built in 1890-1891 were still needed for rush-hour tripper service and for peak summer weekend excursions. But by now, these older cars were averaging only about 8000 miles between major breakdowns and newer or rebuilt equipment was immediately required to replace them.

The new owners looked at the capabilities of the Newport shops and decided to buy used cars from other companies and rebuild them to an "as new" condition for an estimated 60 percent of the market price for a new car. To test this strategy, in 1911, the South Covington and Cincinnati purchased from the Cincinnati Traction Co. one single-truck car for rebuilding with an option to buy up to 19 more. But it turned out that the cost for rebuilding the car (No. 319) was nearly as much as a new one. So the Green Line ordered from the Cincinnati Car Co. 15 new 31-foot single-truck cars (Nos. 320-334).

A company icon was now created. Earlier in the year, the Newport shops had rebuilt a Brownell streetcar (No. 64) into a parlor car for use by both company officials and public rental. The result was the parlor car *Kentucky*, a rolling celebrity which continued in use until the end of streetcar service in July, 1950.

Convertible car 266 **above** shows its newly-installed enclosed front vestibule mandated by a 1912 city of Covington ordinance to keep the driver's area heated in the winter months. However, it is summer in 1914 and the window panels have been removed from the car. The sign advertising that it serves the Ohio River "bathing beaches" of Bellevue and Dayton indicates an era before the Ohio River dams and pollution. On the other hand, convertible car 267 **below**, in from a 5-Holman rush hour tripper at the Madison Ave. storage yard in 1935, demonstrates its winter look with windows installed. *Earl Clark Collection; Earl Clark.*

In the 1920s the rear platforms on all Green Line single-truck cars also were enclosed, including No. 260 **at right** which also was fitted with double-ended controls for special service during floods and track rebuilding. At the moment, however, it is resting at the Madison Ave. storage yard in Covington. *Eugene Van Dusen, Earl Clark Collection.*

During 1912, the Green Line tried to order 20 more single-truck 31-foot cars from Cincinnati Car, but found that the locally-favored builder could not guarantee prompt delivery due to a backlog of orders. As a result, the Green Line turned one final time to the St. Louis Car Co. for 20 cars--Nos. 100-119, and the remaining 1890 Stephenson cars received their walking papers. At the same time, the less-than-utilitarian 1893 summer cars (Nos. 200-219) were scrapped.

With the delivery of this lot and subsequent orders in 1914 for 20 more single-truck cars and in 1917 for 25 larger double-truck cars, the ever-efficient Green Line shops converted, over the next few years, a number of Laclede and early Brownell cars (Nos. 32-76) to maintenance equipment ranging from sand and salt cars to humble flat cars. However, 25 of them continued in service as passenger cars until the end of World War I and five Laclede and Brownell cars soldiered on in tripper service as late as 1930.

Latonia Demands Through Service

The independent city of Latonia, formerly the village of Milldale, was annexed by the city of Covington in 1909. Almost immediately, the Covington city council complained that its new constituents in Latonia were still without through service to either downtown Covington or to Cincinnati. The Green Line's Latonia route only extended as far north as 20th & Madison.

Local newspapers and Covington politicians also maintained that the Green Line was in violation of the 1892 franchise due to the company's discontinuance of the Madison-Greenup Belt Line in 1907. Not exactly, replied the company. Green Line officials insisted they had extended more frequent service to the Austinburg line, and city officials had given tacit approval to cut the belt line in order to provide enough equipment to meet the demands of the added service to Austinburg. In doing so, the Green Line had "slightly reduced" service to Madison Ave. below 20th.

The city fathers were not buying that. By ordinance of March 27, 1911, they ordered the South Covington and

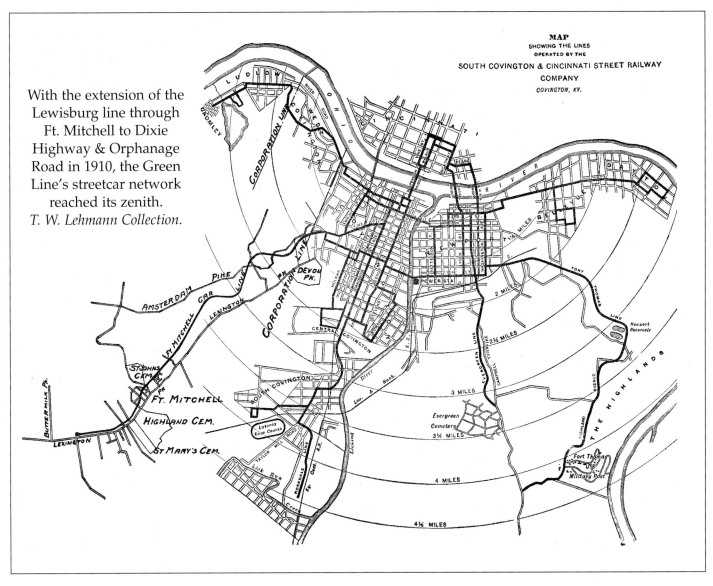

With the extension of the Lewisburg line through Ft. Mitchell to Dixie Highway & Orphanage Road in 1910, the Green Line's streetcar network reached its zenith.
T. W. Lehmann Collection.

Cincinnati to operate a sufficient number of cars to provide direct service from Latonia to, at least, Third & Court. The ordinance mandated thusly:

" . . . That the South Covington and Cincinnati Street Railway Company shall daily from and after the time hereinafter fixed operate a sufficient number of cars from the intersection of Third street and Court avenue in the city of Covington over the tracks of said company on Scott street, Fourth street, Madison avenue, Kruse avenue, Main street, Hamlin street and the intervening streets to and around the loop of said company on Sandford, Carlisle and Latonia avenues to provide and maintain a schedule of cars in each direction over said route of not more than 15 minutes apart between the hours of six o'clock a.m. and 10 o'clock p.m. Said cars shall bear a sign with the word "Latonia" thereon and said sign shall be illuminated during the night time."

Apparently, Covington still was not satisfied with the levels of service on either the Rosedale or Latonia line even after the Green Line complied with the 1911 ordinance. In March, 1913, the city council of Covington ordered certain service frequencies as follows:

" . . . That cars be operated over and upon what is known as the Rosedale line, between the hours of 4:53 A.M. to 10 P.M. at intervals of not more than ten minutes, and between

the hours of 10 P.M. to 12 midnight at intervals of not more than 20 minutes; that cars be operated over and upon what is known as the Latonia line between the hours of 4:53 A.M. and 10 P.M. at intervals of not more than 15 minutes; between the hours of 10 P.M. to 12 midnight at intervals of not more than 30 minutes.

" Cars shall be operated over said Latonia and Rosedale lines between the hours of 12 midnight and 4 A.M. at intervals of not more than one hour."

Politics ruled. With a potential franchise renewal battle coming up in 1917, the Green Line, reluctant to make waves, agreed to the mandated schedule. The Madison Ave. line became largely redundant as a result of the frequent service to downtown imposed on the Latonia line, and survived until 1929 only as a Christmas season Monday and Thursday evening affair.

Accidents and Mishaps

Without doubt, the Cincinnati, Newport & Covington ran a tight ship. Every detail was attended to. Of importance, it suffered few major accidents during electric car days. But there were some.

One occurred on February 15, 1901, about 9:35 a.m. while

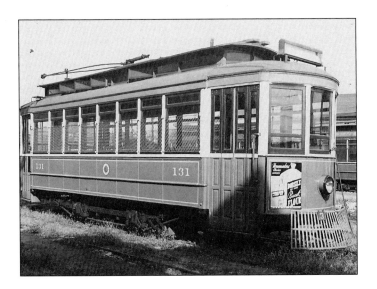

The last single-truck cars purchased by the Green Line (Nos. 120-139) were delivered in 1914. Here, No. 131 basks in the late afternoon sun at the Green Line's yards at 20th & Madison sometime during the mid-1930s. *David McNeil.*

car No. 264, operated by motorman Sewright Yates, was en route to Cincinnati. Yates was slightly behind schedule and was going at full speed when he approached a slight jog in the track on Fairfield Ave. at Taylor's Creek (the former "bottoms" between Bellevue and Newport). On this cold February morning, the car derailed and plunged into the creek. Although many were injured, the car was able to be repaired, despite the description given in the next day's *Enquirer*:

> "One of the most spectacular accidents which has occurred in this vicinity in many a day took place yesterday between Bellevue and Newport. An electric car, every seat of which was filled, jumped the track while crossing Taylor's Bottoms, ran for 20 or 30 feet on the roadway, then plunged down a 40 foot embankment and landed wrong side up in the creek.
>
> "The car was crushed and wrenched until it is a total wreck. The motorman was so badly injured that his death is possible. Most of the passengers were hurt. Many escaped injuries of a serious nature. Others were painfully hurt but not crippled.
>
> "How it happened that there was not appalling loss of life is a mystery. The passengers had an experience which they will recall with shudders until their dying days. No one who went down, down on that dying, plummeting, tumbling car will ever forget it. From the time that the car left the track until it was lying, shattered in the creek bed 40 or more feet below."

Another major accident occurred at the Cincinnati end of Newport's Central Bridge on January 5, 1912. Until stadium work changed street profiles, the Central Bridge approach began at Second & Broadway, Cincinnati. The ramp then made an abrupt turn south to join the superstructure of the bridge. Although a potential trouble spot, thousands of streetcar trips were made past this point without mishap until this fateful day.

It was a Friday evening during a hectic rush hour when motorman Henry Finan was speeding northbound across the bridge to pick up his waiting crowd of homebound passengers standing at Fifth & Walnut in Cincinnati. As the South Bellevue car hit the 80 degree turn on the bridge, it derailed, careened

through the railings, and fell 40 feet to the ground, landing on its top. Luckily, it was lightly loaded with only three passengers, plus the motorman and conductor. All were severely injured with Finan dying the next day. Newly delivered No. 104 is believed to be the car involved since Green Line records show that this car was scrapped in 1912.

The Harris Report

By 1912, downtown Cincinnati had a major traffic congestion problem. It was not caused by a large influx of automobiles, but because practically all the car lines of both the Green Line and the Cincinnati Traction Co. converged on a two block area in downtown Cincinnati. Even before the proliferation of automobiles, a number of consultants had hung out shingles to practice "scientific traffic management." One of them was Ross W. Harris of the University of Wisconsin in Madison.

Cincinnati's Public Service Director hired Harris to make a thorough study of traffic conditions in the Queen City's downtown and to make recommendations to improve both transit service and to relieve the area's congestion.

At the time, all Covington Division Green Line cars entered Cincinnati on the Second St. approach from the Suspension Bridge, proceeded north on Walnut to Fifth, west on Fifth (Fountain Square) to Vine, and south on Vine back to the Second St. approach to the Suspension Bridge. Newport Division cars entered Cincinnati via either the Central Bridge or the L&N Bridge.

The Monmouth, York, and Patterson lines all entered Cincinnati via the Central Bridge, proceeded up Broadway to Fourth, west on Fourth to Walnut, north on Walnut to Fifth and east on Fifth to Main, south on Main to Fourth, east on Fourth back to Broadway, and then south on Broadway to the Central Bridge. The Covington and Newport Belt Line, the Bellevue and Dayton, the South Bellevue, the Ft. Thomas lines (and the Washington rush hour line) entered Cincinnati via the L&N

Wood-slatted seats were the rule on all Green Line streetcars including No. 127, one of the last batch of single-truckers (120-139) built by the Cincinnati Car Co. in 1914. Its mate, No. 131, appears at the top of this page. *Earl Clark Collection.*

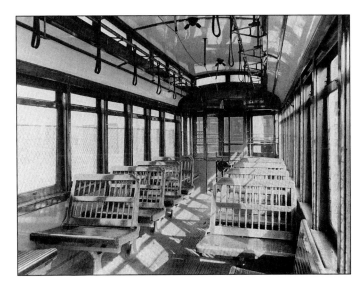

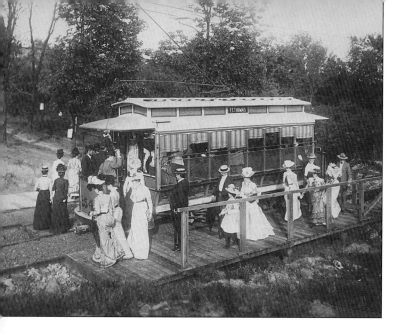

It is Members Day at the Inverness Country Club sometime in the early 1900s and car 254 is holding down a charter to transport members and guests to the club for a day of golf and socializing. This club was located north of Rob Roy Ave. on a wedge-shaped piece of land between the Green Line tracks and North Ft. Thomas Ave. After a fire destroyed the clubhouse in 1913, the membership developed the larger Highland Country Club farther south on Alexandria Pike. *Earl Clark Collection.*

Bridge via Pearl and Butler to Broadway, west on Fourth to Walnut, north on Walnut to Fifth, east on Fifth to Main, south on Main to Fourth, and east on Fourth to Broadway back to Pearl, then to Butler and the L&N Bridge.

This was a prescription for gridlock. Harris' report, presented to city council on August 31, 1912, concluded that service was inadequate largely because there was not enough track capacity in downtown Cincinnati to accommodate all the cars fighting for space there. The report pointed out that during the evening rush hours, 608 streetcars came into the downtown core area to with-

The 1913 flood brought unprecedented misery and property damage to the citizens of Northern Kentucky who lived along the Ohio River. SC&C 54 has gone as far as it can in Dayton at 4th & Benham and has been met by a Green Line rowboat. *Earl Clark Collection.*

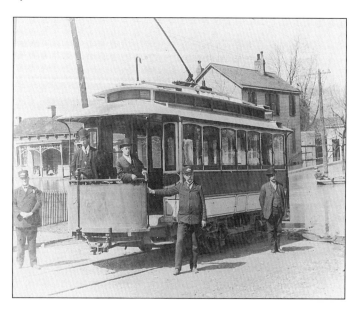

in a block or two of Fountain Square, the renowned Cincinnati landmark, situated between Walnut and Vine on Fifth.

Harris further discovered that 151 Green Line cars used Walnut between Fourth and Fifth during the height (5 to 6 p.m.) of the evening rush. Of those 151 cars, 81 cars of the Covington Division turned left onto Fifth to circle Fountain Square and joined 92 Cincinnati Traction cars also vying for the same piece of track. Harris said this segment of track was 33 percent overutilized, resulting in delays of up to 15 minutes per car. The Green Line's Newport Division cars which turned right at Fifth & Walnut to Government Square also were identified as contributors to Cincinnati's downtown streetcar tangle.

Not everyone was pleased with Harris' recommendations. He wanted all Green Line cars to be barred from Cincinnati streets north of Fourth. He urged that the Latonia and Rosedale cars be turned west at Walnut & Third to Vine and back south with the cars of the remaining Covington Division lines turned west on Fourth at Walnut to Vine and then south toward the Suspension Bridge. Furthermore, he said all Newport Division cars should be sent north on Broadway, west on Fourth, then south on Walnut, and east on Third to Broadway.

This did not sit well with Green Line officials. They protested the recommendations on the basis that their franchise with the city guaranteed their entry into the prime Cincinnati business district along Fifth.

Cincinnati reluctantly agreed that the franchise covering the trackage patterns of the Newport Division routes could not be changed without Green Line concurrence. However, the city found an obscure provision in the franchise concerning the use of Fifth west of Walnut which allowed the Director of Public Utilities to bar Green Line's Covington Division cars from circling Fountain Square. Consequently, from November 1, 1912, all Covington cars were required to use Fourth from Walnut to Vine except rush-hour Latonia and Rosedale cars which were required to turn west at Walnut over Third to Vine.

Fortunately, a better solution to the Green Line's downtown Cincinnati's traffic woes would eventually materialize.

Floods: a Way of Life

Over in Kentucky, in 1913, Covington's Eastern line saw a small modification of its route. New trackage was laid on 15th from Rickey to Eastern and on Eastern to Oliver, and the sharply curved tracks on Rickey and Oliver were abandoned.

To an unusual degree, the Green Line sometimes found itself fighting the furies of nature, forced to heroic exertions to keep intact the mundane business of transporting people.

Due to Northern Kentucky's location in a flood plain, high water from the Ohio River was almost an annual threat. Areas served by the Green Line that were most frequently flooded were: 2nd & Crescent Ave., Covington; lower Broadway in Cincinnati; the "Bottoms" of Cincinnati before the Suspension Bridge was extended to 2nd and 3rd Sts.; 3rd St. in Dayton, Ky.; and Newport's West End. The Green Line provided small boat service in flooded areas and stationed cars on the isolated sections of routes so as to continue service. During World War I, the company decided not to provide the "skiffs" and a public uproar ensued, but the Green Line "navy" never again went into action.

Covington celebrated its centennial in 1914 with great fervor. Here a Green Line car, southbound on Madison, passes under some of the festive decorations.
Kenton County Library.

In 1913, a flood of the Ohio River and its tributaries caused considerable disruption to the Newport Division's operations. All links to Cincinnati from Newport were suspended on March 29 due to the rising waters which caused widespread damage in Newport, Dayton, Bellevue, Ludlow, Covington and Cincinnati. Even after limited service in Campbell County was restored on April 7, it was necessary for some of the motormen and conductors to use boats to get from their homes to the car barn at 11th & Brighton to report for work.

At the time, Green Line officials remarked that the Suspension Bridge stood "impervious" to the flood. Although Ludlow service was discontinued for a time, the Green Line proudly observed that "the Suspension Bridge acted as a fortress to our Covington operations and it is clear the span has won over the greatest flood this area will ever see." Green Line officials ran a good transit property but were not very good prophets, as we shall see in a later chapter.

Sometimes it seemed that the smaller bridges across the smaller Licking River gave more grief than the big ones over the Ohio. In 1914, Columbia engineers found that the bridge of subsidiary Licking River Bridge Co., which spanned the Licking River between 11th in Newport and 12th in Covington, contained serious structural defects. As a consequence, it was necessary in late 1914 to spend $185,000 to repair the bridge.

During the latter months of 1914, officials at times had to restrict streetcar and other traffic on the bridge and to close it for short periods of time, thereby disrupting service on the Belt Line. However, in early 1915 repairs were completed and full service resumed on the Newport and Covington Belt Line, also known as

the Covington and Newport Belt Line, depending on whether the car was starting from Cincinnati through Covington first or through Newport first.

Also in 1914, the Green Line took delivery of its last single-truck, 31-foot hand-braked cars from Cincinnati Car Co. (Nos. 120-139). This delivery enabled the company to retire or convert to work equipment some of the early Laclede and Brownell cars.

Evading Segregation

The Cincinnati, Covington and Erlanger Railway Co. was incorporated in 1899 under Kentucky law as an electric interurban railway and was a wholly owned subsidiary of the South Covington and Cincinnati Street Railway. It was an interurban for a reason.

Since street railways by Kentucky law could not invoke the right of eminent domain (the ability to use court proceedings to take property for right-of-way without an owner's consent) but interurban railways could use such right, the CC&E was able to construct its 1902 and 1910 extensions toward Erlanger fairly readily because property owners knew that if they did not sell parcels of land for CC&E right-of-way voluntarily, a court could determine the fair market value and force a sale.

Upon completion of each new extension of the CC&E, it was immediately leased to the SC&C in perpetuity. Of course, the CC&E had the same board of directors as the South Covington and was operated as a seamless portion of the Green Line System. The Ft. Mitchell line operated regular city-type cars and the universal 5 cent fare applied.

Covington Throws a Party

Another view of Covington's 1914 centennial at **right** shows a northbound Green Line car on Pike about to turn onto Madison among a scattered crowd of celebrating Covingtonians.

In the photograph at the **bottom** of the page, a Holman car heads north at Linden & Holman through the heart of the then largely German-speaking portion of Covington circa 1914. Considerably more than half of the residents subscribed to German language newspapers in 1914 but, due to anti-Kaiser sentiment, by the end of World War I no such newspapers existed. *Both: Kenton County Library.*

The law of unintended consequences now intervened. For the first time, racial segregation reared its head, and the Green Line was caught in the middle. In February, 1916, the South Covington and Cincinnati Street Railway Co. and the CC&E were indicted by a Kenton County grand jury because "a citizen of color was carried in car number 309, a car not equipped with a full length partition separating the races." The Commonwealth's attorney claimed that since the CC&E was chartered as an interurban railroad, it was obliged under Kentucky's separate but equal statute to provide segregated streetcars south of the city of Covington.

Both defendants were found guilty and each fined $500. Green Line management took it all the way to the U. S. Supreme Court, but lost.

The Green Line never did operate partitioned cars on the Ft. Mitchell line or any other line. Instead, legal counsel for the Green Line amended the CC&E's charter from that of an interurban to that of a street railway (where no segregation mandate existed). The net effect in giving up eminent domain rights was to put the final nail in the coffin of any possibility of the CC&E

The reason this photo was taken and the identity of the crew and the little boy are lost to history. But we know we have a fine study of the off-side of car 332, one of 15 built the Cincinnati Car Co. in 1911. We also can see the advertisement for a new on-line subdivision, one of many housing tracts which were developed following the opening of the Ft. Thomas car line, just as Sam Bigstaff predicted. *Carl Rekow Collection.*

being extended to Erlanger. However, it appears that by 1916 the Green Line had decided that further construction to Erlanger was not economically justified and, therefore, eminent domain no longer mattered.

In late 1916, the Green Line ordered 25 double-truck streetcars from the Cincinnati Car Co. These cars (Nos. 500 to 524) were delivered in the first part of 1917, just in time for America's entry into World War I and the eventual doubling of traffic on the Ft. Thomas line due to a newly established draft induction center at Ft. Thomas. These 45-foot long cars had seating for 52 passengers. In addition to the Ft. Thomas line, the big cars were assigned to base service on the Ft. Mitchell and Dayton lines.

Such large cars were a revolution for a system which had

Linden & Holman, Covington, Ky.

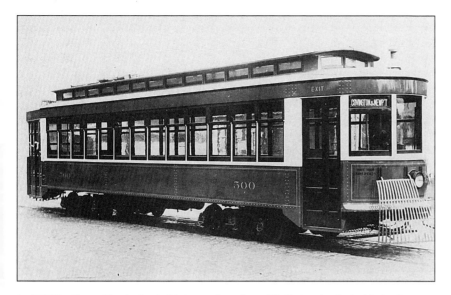

In 1917 the Green Line took a bold step and purchased its first and only double-truck cars. The first of 25, No. 500, poses **above** for its official portrait at the Cincinnati Car Co.
Special Collections and Archives, University of Kentucky Libraries.

We're getting a little ahead of our story, but here's a look at the business end of a 500-series double-truck car as remodeled in 1937. The motorman's cap badge says "conductor", indicating that John Flerlage got his start in the conductor pool many years earlier. And, how about that fingering technique on the controller handle?

The double-truck cars were delivered with slatted wood seats as evidenced **below** by this interior view of No. 503. Nothing fancy, mind you, for the Green Line.
Both: Special Collections and Archives, University of Kentucky Libraries.

nothing but small, single-truckers. They were equipped with air brakes, a first for the Green Line, and four 25 horsepower motors. This addition also brought the system to its pinnacle in terms of carrying capacity; by the end of the year 1917, 201 streetcars were available for passenger service: Nos. 220-334; Nos. 100-139 (less wreck victim 104); Nos. 500-524; and 22 survivors from Nos. 32 to 76.

A Threat to the Green Line

The Cincinnati, Newport and Covington Railway Co., whose stock was purchased by Columbia Gas & Electric in 1907, still did business as the South Covington and Cincinnati Street Railway Co. in 1917. Such a name no longer fit.

Although the SC&C name may have been descriptive immediately after its formation in 1876 when it was operating only between Covington and Cincinnati, the South Covington and Cincinnati's operations had spread far and wide over Northern Kentucky by the end of the century. Yet the South Covington and Cincinnati Street Railway name still appeared on company stationery, tickets, transfers, and promotional brochures.

The reason the name had not changed during this time is simple: fear. President W. W. Freeman, who succeeded Ernst in 1914, and his lawyers were concerned that certain of the franchises granted to the SC&C or predecessor companies acquired by the SC&C in the 1890-1893 period by the city of Covington might not be construed by a court as perpetual. A judge might instead consider them as but 25 year grants, thereby expiring during the years 1916 to 1918.

As may be recalled, in 1864 the City of Covington passed an ordinance permitting companies to bid on franchises of 25 years duration covering six planned horsecar routes in the city. Only one company, the Covington Street Railway, accepted the terms offered by the city and constructed the Madison Ave. line which began operation in 1867.

By 1869, the city fathers of Covington were frustrated by the complete lack of investor interest in bidding on any of the other five designated routes. So, in December of 1869, the city passed an ordinance granting the Covington and Cincinnati Street Railway, an investor group led by Edward F. Abbott, a franchise: ". . . to construct, hold, and operate the Main St. line," and the only provision for a termination of this franchise was "in case of a failure of the grantees to keep their covenants."

The assets and rights of the Covington and Cincinnati Street Railway were conveyed in 1876 to a new corporation, the South Covington and Cincinnati Street Railway subsequent to the construction of the Scott St. horsecar line. A court in 1886 declared the South Covington and Cincinnati's Main St. and Scott St. franchises to be perpetual in duration. In 1883, the South Covington and Cincinnati bought out the Covington Street Railway, operator of the Madison Ave. franchise awarded in 1864. Thereafter, all street railways in the city of Covington were operated under the auspices of the South Covington and Cincinnati Street Railway.

In 1892, the city of Covington declared the old Madison Ave. line franchise expired and proposed putting it up for new bidders. Not so fast, replied the South Covington and Cincinnati. Its position was that since it had perpetual franchise rights, the city couldn't do that. The city thereupon sued the South Covington and Cincinnati Railway in 1892 for a declaratory judgment to determine both parties' rights and obligations.

Then in October, 1892, the SC&C agreed with the City of Covington to improve service on existing lines, to a permanent 5 cent fare and free universal transfer privileges, and to proceed with the construction of the Ludlow, Latonia and Rosedale lines. As a result, the declaratory lawsuit brought by Covington was dismissed. In fact, no decision was ever rendered about whether the Madison Ave. line's franchise was a perpetual grant. Uncertainty continued, but so did the Green Line.

The Political Drums Beat

In today's automobile society it may be hard to imagine that early in the century, public transportation was so vital that it was often the very center of heated, noisy political fights. Politicians rose and fell depending on their zeal to whip the local streetcar company.

A 100-series single-trucker on a Belt Line run crosses the Licking River Bridge linking 11th St. in Newport with 12th St. in Covington. Notice the wood plank roadway surface in this early 1920s photograph.
Special Collections and Archives, University of Kentucky Libraries.

Some Covington politicians in 1916 started making noises to the effect that the 1892 agreement awarding the SC&C a general franchise to operate all streetcar routes in Covington would expire in 1917. The city council announced that it had hired a consultant to study the feasibility of public ownership of all of the streetcar service in Covington or, alternatively, the auctioning of the South Covington and Cincinnati's operating rights to the highest private bidder.

The Green Line cried foul. Its position was that so long as it honored the tenets of the October 1892 ordinance, the South Covington and Cincinnati was the perpetual successor to all franchises awarded by the city. The Green Line claimed it had adhered faithfully to the 1892 agreement. The company

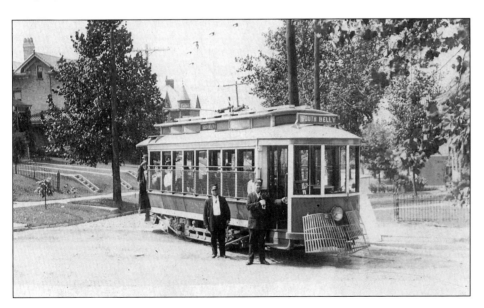

CN&C convertible car 282 lays over at the end of the South Bellevue line at Grandview & Ward. It is prior to the fall of 1921 because of the absence of a route number board on the fender, a feature made mandatory with the opening of the Dixie Terminal due to the quick loading of cars on diverse routings. Conductor John Connor, right, and an unidentified motorman, left, pose for posterity while serving Bellevue's many small subdivisions. These tracts sprang up between 1895 and 1915, and became an attractive semi-suburban development deserving of streetcar service. Soon this car will be on its way back to Cincinnati's Government Square. Little did these folks know that they would be playing cameo roles in a 21st Century history book ! *Larry Fobiano Collection.*

Having seen the Green Line's bridge on the opposite page, we gaze now at the bridge over the Licking River linking Covington's 4th St. with Newport's 5th. The toll house collected fares ranging from 1 cent for those on foot to 15 cents for eight-horse wagons. CN&C service over the rebuilt bridge began in 1908. A crosstown car is in the distance.   *Kenton County Library.*

sor of the South Covington and Cincinnati Street Railway. Since the Covington city fathers approved the purchase of the Covington Street Railway by the South Covington and Cincinnati in 1881 without reservation, the high court ruled that all pre-1892 franchises were perpetual and that the city of Covington reaffirmed the perpetual nature of those franchises by its October, 1892, actions.

It was a great victory for the South Covington and Cincinnati but it came at a price. Among other things, the ruling meant that the Green Line would be saddled forever with another major provision of the 1892 settlement: the lowly 5 cent fare. In the future, the Green Line would have to grimly haggle with the city of Covington for fare increases or take the risk, if it raised fares unilaterally, that Covington could get the 1892 settlement declared null and void.

The First Abandonments

Nobody yet realized it, but as World War I arrived, the North American transit establishment was about to be rocked by a period of wrenching technological change, travail, and decline. Signs now began to appear.

In the case of the Green Line, perhaps it began with some problems with the Newport city government in 1917 and 1918. In 1917, the city of Newport, noticing the increased motor vehicle and truck traffic on Patterson St., decided to replace the brick paving with a heavier asphalt paving. The city demanded that the Green Line pay for the entire cost of repaving Patterson. A shocked Green Line management argued that the street was fine and that the ordinance only required that it work on the portion of the street in between its tracks and to a three foot distance on each side of the tracks when "obvious need for repair was in evidence."

Newport wasn't having that, and in June of 1917, the city went ahead and started repairs on Patterson between Fifth and Sixth Sts. and temporarily removed the track from that portion of the line. When the repaving between Fifth and Sixth St. was completed up to the track portion, the city pointed to the empty gash and instructed the Green Line to relay its tracks and finish the job. The Green Line refused. Instead, it announced the discontinuance of the Patterson line because the city had violated a term of the franchise.

Legal disputes dragged on for a number of years but the city of Newport was not able to prevail. It could not get a court to order the Green Line to reinstall its Patterson St. tracks and thereby the citizens of west Newport along Patterson were deprived of Green Line service until 1936, when the motor bus would provide a solution.

Attention now turned to Monmouth St., an important but narrow downtown Newport thoroughfare. Faced with a tremendous increase in automobile traffic along Monmouth during the

observed that it had kept in place the 5 cent fare for the last 25 years, had kept the tracks and roadbed in Covington in good repair (and, also in good repair, as per the ordinance, a three-foot strip of street on each side of the tracks) and had even improved the frequency of service on all Covington routes. Moreover, it had just ordered 25 double-truck streetcars of the latest technology for delivery in early 1917.

That wasn't enough for Covington. The city refused to back down from its position that the Green Line's franchises would expire in 1917, so in late 1916 the South Covington and Cincinnati Street Railway asked a federal district court for a declaratory judgment to find the 1892 franchise grants as perpetual and to restrain the city from obtaining a new franchisee or operating the property itself.

Covington argued in reply that the grant of 1892 had been awarded for only a 25 year period and that all Covington Street Railway franchises would be subject to new bids in October, 1917. The city also put forth a new argument that it did not even have, under its 1892 charter, the power to make a perpetual grant to a street railway under the Kentucky Constitution and, therefore, no legal franchises could have been awarded by the city in 1892.

In early 1917, the District Court found in favor of the SC&C. The city of Covington appealed, and the case reached the U. S. Supreme Court on March 20, 1918. Less than a month later, on April 15, 1918, the high court decided in favor of the street railway. Modern lawyers will undoubtedly marvel about how quickly the case was decided.

In an opinion written by Justice Oliver Wendell Holmes, that master crafter of reason, the Court held that the city of Covington had indeed granted a perpetual franchise in 1869 to the predeces-

second decade of the century, a number of its merchants complained regularly at Newport City Council meetings that the Green Line's streetcars on Monmouth were driving off "horseless carriages" and hurting business. They proposed that the Green Line Southgate line streetcars be rerouted via 11th to York to relieve traffic congestion on Monmouth.

And so the second major Newport street within 18 months lost its streetcars, this time by fiat of the city. To appease the merchants, in 1918 the city ordered the Southgate line cars off Monmouth by the end of the year. The Green Line, protesting only mildly, apparently figured that the Monmouth St. tracks between Fifth and 11th were in need of replacement anyway, and such expense could be avoided since the York tracks had sufficient capacity to take the added Southgate line traffic.

On January 1, 1919, therefore, the Southgate line was diverted to York and, shortly after, the Green Line took up its southbound track on Monmouth between Third and 11th and both tracks between Fifth and 11th. The Crosstown line continued to use the northbound track on Monmouth from Fifth to Third.

The Alexandria Appendix

In 1910, the Newport and Alexandria Interurban Electric Railway Co. was incorporated by a group of investors not associated with the Green Line. The new company proposed an interurban from Cincinnati, using the tracks of the Green Line's Ft. Thomas route to the end of that line, and then building new tracks from there to the southern Campbell County town of Alexandria.

The Newport and Alexandria was able to secure trackage rights from the Green Line and, after a number of false starts, commenced right-of-way acquisition by 1916. However, it was about this time that doubts about the future of electric interurbans

The Green Line contracted with the Highland Heights Land Co. in 1918 to run a shuttle service from the end of the Ft. Thomas line to Main & Renshaw in Highland Heights over the single track of the stillborn Newport and Alexandria Interurban Electric Railway. Since there was no loop at the Highland Heights end of the line, the company equipped both ends of car No. 61 with controls. *Earl Clark Collection.*

set in because lines to sparsely populated areas like Alexandria (whose 1910 population was only about 1500) were starting to face serious private automobile and motor bus competition.

Investor cold feet, coupled with the entry of the United States into World War I, dried up capital and, by 1918, the Newport and Alexandria had built only 1.3 miles of single track from the end of the Ft. Thomas line along the side of Alexandria Pike to Main St. in Highland Heights and on Main as far as Lincoln. The N&A's nervous investors had had enough.

That year the Green Line acquired the Newport and Alexandria for what amounted to salvage value of materials and instituted a shuttle service from the end of the Ft. Thomas car line loop to Highland Heights. Although the Green Line announced plans to "expand the line to its planned terminus in the future" and "to run through cars to downtown Cincinnati," not even a turning loop was constructed in Highland Heights. As a result, double-ended cars 61, 260 and 319, equipped with trolley poles and motorman's controls on both ends (but without offside doors), were alternately assigned to the Highland Heights Shuttle.

Actually the shuttle was subsidized by the Highland Heights Land Development Co. to showcase a planned subdivision. However, sales were extremely disappointing and the line was abandoned in 1924. Ironically

The CN&C completed the switch to commercially produced electricity in 1921, thereby demoting the Newport powerhouse to a mere substation converting high-voltage a.c. power to 550 volt d.c. for use by the streetcars. At **left** is a diagram showing the schematics of this operation.
T. W. Lehmann Collection.

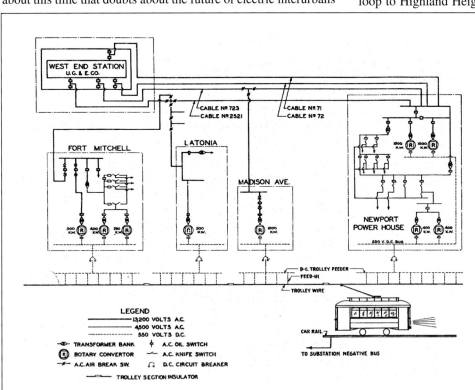

LEGEND
— 13,200 VOLTS A.C.
— 4,500 VOLTS A.C.
---- 550 VOLTS D.C.
TRANSFORMER BANK — A.C. OIL SWITCH
ROTARY CONVERTOR — A.C. KNIFE SWITCH
A.C. AIR BREAK SW. — D.C. CIRCUIT BREAKER
TROLLEY SECTION INSULATOR

WEST END STATION
U.G. & E. CO.

CABLE Nº 723
CABLE Nº 2521
CABLE Nº 71
CABLE Nº 72

FORT MITCHELL

LATONIA

MADISON AVE.

NEWPORT POWER HOUSE

500 K.W. 400 K.W. 750 K.W.
500 K.W.
1000 K.W.
550 V. D.C. BUS

D-C TROLLEY FEEDER
FEED-IN
TROLLEY WIRE

CAR RAIL

TO SUBSTATION NEGATIVE BUS

the largest traffic generator on this line was St. Stephen Cemetery. Today, the sleepy Main St. in Highland Heights where the "dinky" ran, is in a time warp, bypassed and surrounded by postwar suburbia, interstate highways and Northern Kentucky University.

The Streetcar in Everyday Life

For the United States, the expansion of the streetcar network from 1892 into the early 20th century was rapid even for those booming years. The application of electricity to transport completely revolutionized life in the cities and expansion into what had been the tranquil countryside, affording citizens the opportunity to build homes in suburbs away from the smoke and congestion.

It is hard to realize today that the streetcar was the only means of transportation for a majority of Americans through World War I. The streetcar took you to your place of employment or to the downtown shopping areas which were the "malls" of a different era. The streetcar also put a crimp in the legendary practice of marrying the girl next door. You could now go courting farther afield.

The streetcar also served as the major school transportation vehicle during those same decades. Longtime Covington attorney and Ft. Mitchell resident John R. Blakely (whose father Stephens L. Blakely was both founder of the Dixie Traction Co. and later general counsel of the Green Line System for more than 20 years), took the cars to grade school every day from his parents' house in Ft. Mitchell to LaSalette Academy in downtown Covington. Blakely remembers the introduction of the double-truck 500-series cars and shares some cherished memories of his schoolboy days riding the Green Line:

"When classes were out at 3:30 in the afternoon, we walked up to Seventh & Madison and boarded the car--usually a double trucker. Sometimes it was a four wheel dinky and this caused a problem to the operator. A number of us would stand on the rear platform and working in unison would rock the car up and down, front and rear, until ordered to cease and desist or be kicked off. The car would then proceed southwardly on Madison. At the 11th St. intersection, the motorman would open his window and employ a long switch bar. The same thing would happen at 12th & Holman and sometimes at Pike & Hermes in Lewisburg.

"Pike & Hermes is where the boys from Saint John's grade school frequently got on and when they did, that spelled trouble with a capital 'T'. There was no sensible reason for this because, all of us being Catholic, [we] certainly had a community of interest. Nevertheless, each group looked upon the other with a rather cordial hostility.

"As the car left Covington at Montague St., the motorman would set the controls at 'full ahead' for the long up hill haul through Park Hills. In the winter season, when the weather was cold, he would leave his perch, turn his back and commence loading coke into the little heater that stood in front of the car. This is when the fun began and it generally wound up in an altercation between Willis Ruh, a classmate, and a young tough named Fedders whose first name I have forgotten. When they got off at the Altavia Station, order was restored and we rode peaceably enough with the Krumpelman boys to our respective destinations."

Columbia was a big player in energy distribution in Ohio and Northern Kentucky. The Green Line accounted for less than 1 percent of total revenues. This Cincinnati District grid accounted for most revenue and virtually all profit.
T. W. Lehmann Collection.

The Dixie Terminal

From the end of the Civil War, Cincinnati was an important city linking north and south. The opening of the Suspension Bridge in 1866 played a big part. The Queen City liked to identify itself commercially with the burgeoning Land of Dixie. It indulged in grand designs, and in one of them, the Green Line benefited greatly.

In the 1880s the City of Cincinnati got into the railroad business in a big way. It built the Cincinnati Southern Railway, the largest trunk railroad ever funded by a municipal corporation. Constructed over exceedingly rough terrain, it linked Cincinnati with the growing industrial south in the heart of Dixie at Chattanooga. The railroad was eventually leased to the Southern Railway System and, even today, is still an important rail link,

and brings nice returns to the treasury of Cincinnati, which receives millions of dollars a year in rental payments from successor Norfolk Southern Railway.

Other ventures were a little less grand. In the early 1910s, Cincinnati civic leaders Charles P. Taft, A. Clifford Shinkle and Frank J. Jones formed a corporation to build what would be, at the time, Cincinnati's largest indoor shopping arcade and office building on the southwest corner of Fourth & Walnut. The first two floors of the building would be devoted primarily to retail shopping and the remaining eight floors would be leased as commercial office space.

Shinkle, also one of the primary stockholders and president of the company that owned and operated the Suspension Bridge, suggested to his partner Charles P. Taft that an annex to the south of the proposed Fourth & Walnut Building would be ideal as a terminal for the Green Line streetcars from Northern Kentucky. Taft, a large stockholder in Cincinnati Gas and Electric, a company owned by Green Line's parent Columbia Gas & Electric, bought the idea. He quickly secured permission from the

The Green Line *Behind the Scenes*

A look inside the Green Line's two main facilities in Covington and Newport would have impressed any transit professional. Motormen were trained in Covington, and the cars were groomed in Newport. The company was an innovator in the training of new motormen. A formal training program emerged which included the use of a stationary streetcar, a humble forerunner of today's sophisticated aircraft simulators in which pilots are trained prior to their entry into a real cockpit. The training program was the brainchild of longtime Superintendent of Tracks and Buildings William H. Harton, who also served as general manager from 1916 to 1927.

In a special department at the car barns at 20th & Madison, apprentice motormen and conductors were trained in the operation of streetcars. In one area was an instruction board to which a dummy controller and brake were attached. Also in the room was the skeleton of a car, fitted with all regulation appliances. This car is shown in the photo at left.

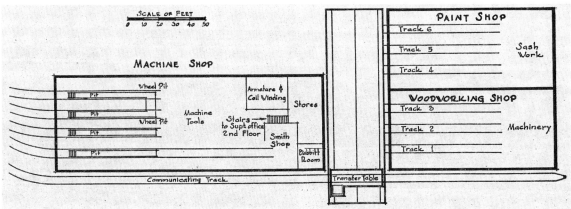

The use of a stationary streetcar, a kind of forerunner of today's aircraft simulator, by the Green Line in 1911 was the talk of the transit community. Plinthed car 67 **(top)** was used for some two decades to train motormen. *Special Collections and Archives, University of Kentucky Libraries.*

The simulator was located at the Covington barns, but let's take a look at the sprawling Newport shops and barn complex, starting with the floor plan **above**. The Green Line had the capability to completely overhaul a streetcar from the trucks up as we can see from this circa 1930 plan. *T. W. Lehmann Collection.*

Extensive repairs were carried out to cars in the Newport shop located immediately behind the Newport carbarn. Sometime before its rebuilding in 1937, car 513 receives attention to one of its trucks in the photo at **near right**. In the frame **beyond**, we peek into the Newport barn during the mid-1920s. The eight track structure accommodated 12, 500-series double-truck cars and as many as 70 single-truckers every night. Pits between the tracks enabled workers to inspect the cars' running gear and to accommodate minor repairs, if these were necessary. If more extensive attention was required, the machine shop (see the track plan) was ready. A track plan of the entire property appears later in this volume. *Both: Special Collections and Archives, University of Kentucky Libraries.*

Columbia board to have plans drawn up for the design of a four story annex to the Fourth & Walnut Building, with the lower two floors to be used by the Green Line and the top two floors to be used for office space.

Final plans called for the Green Line's Covington Division cars to come over the Suspension Bridge and proceed via a ramp over Second and Third directly to the second floor of the proposed annex, thereby enabling the Covington cars to avoid all street running in Cincinnati. Newport Division cars would use the lower street level of the annex with access gained via Third.

The Green Line entered into a long-term lease of the annex in 1917. Cincinnati's Planning Commission was delighted that as many as 70 Covington Division Green Line cars per hour would stay off city streets during the height of the rush hour. Although Newport Division cars would continue to use Cincinnati streets, they would avoid the very congested areas of Fourth and Fifth and the unloading and loading of passengers inside the annex would itself further ease traffic congestion.

With Shinkle's Suspension Bridge linking Cincinnati with the South, his proposal to name the whole project, including the annex, the Dixie Terminal, was approved. Shinkle was also responsible for getting the "Dixie Highway" project (eventually to become U. S. 25) from Michigan to Florida routed over the Suspension Bridge from Cincinnati to Covington and through Kenton County on Lexington Pike. This was soon renamed Dixie Highway.

World War I delayed things briefly, and construction did not begin on the Dixie Terminal until 1919. It was completed in 1921 at a cost of some $3.5 million. The shopping arcade was designed in Italian renaissance style with a sky blue vaulted ceiling over the main shopping area. The ceiling was decorated with alternating brown and cream and blue and cream colored medallions with touches of gold, in low relief, forming a complement or contrast. The arcade was furnished with warm cream marble walls and the shops themselves were framed with pilasters which rose to the vaulted ceiling.

The *Cincinnati Enquirer* called the Dixie Terminal the brightest jewel in Cincinnati's crown. In its day, it was.

Chief Instructor of Motormen and Conductors Clarence Pebworth explained to an apprentice motorman the use of the instruction board. This board acted in connection with a standard controller, and was similar to the electrical equipment installed in a car. By means of small electric lights, the flow of current through the motors was recorded. When the power was increased, the lamps burned with a brighter intensity.

After the new motorman had been thoroughly schooled in the application of power, he then was instructed on the skeleton streetcar. The front vestibule of this car was equipped with all the standard apparatus of a real car, it having seen actual service before being placed in the school, partially dismantled.

The controller, brakes, wheels and motors all were intact. When power was applied, the wheels spun around with all the reality of a moving vehicle. The wheels, however, did not touch the floor, because they were suspended on jacks. When the brake was applied, the wheels would stop. All the mechanism was exposed to the view of the student. Particular emphasis was placed on making "safety stops," which were used in emergencies by applying the brake, sand to the rail, and reversing the motor almost simultaneously. Under this method, a car moving at top speed could be quickly brought to a halt.

A student spent approximately a half-day in the instruction room. When Instructor Pebworth was satisfied that the apprentice had a thorough knowledge of the fundamentals involved in the operation of a car, he assigned the student to a division superintendent. This official in turn assigned him to "road instructors," who in reality were full-fledged motormen.

Road instruction lasted for ten days, during which the learner was shifted to various routes within the division to which he was assigned. The instructor on each route signed a card to the effect that he had charge of the student on that route, and if he had any recommendations regarding the apprentice, he also made them on this card. The chief instructor checked up on the beginner during his ten day road instruction, frequently riding on the cars to see how rapidly the student was learning.

The chief instructor then gave the new man a thorough examination. The trainees were encouraged to ask questions to clear away any uncertainty about the instruction work. Conductors were taught how to properly collect and register fares, punch transfers, make out trip-slips and various reports. Courtesy to passengers, under all conditions, was emphasized here.

Following the passing of an exam by the motorman or conductor, Pebworth indicated on a special form that the student had passed. The student was turned over to the superintendent of the division to which he was assigned, and his name was placed on the "extra board" making the new employee eligible for rush hour or other service. ◆

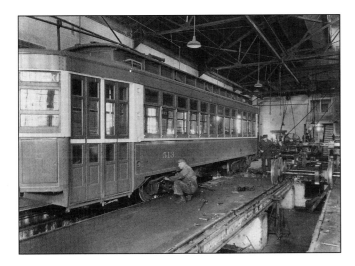

Dixie Terminal . . .

An Italian Renaissance Jewel
In the Green Line's Crown

The 11-story Dixie Terminal building was completed in 1921. **Above** is the shopping arcade structure through which Green Line passengers could pass to the annex and its upper and lower deck loading areas. The arcade **(upper right)** occupied the first floor and balcony. Its vaulted ceiling was elegant, decorated as it was with blue and cream medallions and cream marble walls.The cut-away drawing **below** amply shows how Green Line cars from Covington ramped into the upper level, while just below, Newport cars entered from the street. *All: Special Collections and Archives, University of Kentucky* Libraries.

It's the rush hour **above** on the lower level of the Dixie Terminal, and a big crowd in the background awaits arrival of the proper car, such as this one on Route 12. Turnstiles allowed both streetcar doors to be used for loading passengers. Amazingly, cars were dispatched from both levels about every 45 seconds during peak hours.

In the photo at **right**, we look south from the interior of the upper level soon after its opening. A Rosedale car will soon stop on the east side to unload before pulling around to the loading area. *Both photos: Special Collections and Archives, University of Kentucky Libraries.*

Moving into Dixie Terminal

On Sunday, October 23, 1921, the Green Line's Covington Division cars begin running directly into the upper terminal level via a viaduct from the Suspension Bridge over Second and Third. A month later, on November 27, the Newport Division cars started operating into the lower level via Third St..

The two levels within the Dixie Terminal were similarly arranged. The tracks in each level formed a loop or, to be more precise, a horseshoe. The cars entered the eastern side of the horseshoe, discharged their passengers and proceeded around to the western side to pick up passengers bound for Northern Kentucky. Each horseshoe was 355 feet long and four small or three large cars could be sumultaneously unloaded on one side of a barrier while up to five small or four large cars could board passengers at the same time on the other side.

When inbound passengers alighted from the streetcars at the Dixie Terminal, they simply left the terminal area via an exit only passageway. Northern Kentucky bound passengers dropped their nickels in a set of mechanical turnstiles, or went to a cashier's booth if they needed change, and then proceeded through a cashier-controlled barrier. Since streetcar conductors were not required to handle money in the Dixie Terminal, they could attend solely to the task of rapidly loading passengers.

With the opening of the lower level of the Dixie Terminal, the Green Line discontinued the use of the L&N Bridge, and all Newport Division cars used the Central Bridge to and from Cincinnati. At this time, the Green Line radically altered its Cincinnati trackage patterns.

Starting November 27, 1921, all Newport Division cars operated from the Central Bridge on existing Green Line tracks from Second & Broadway to Pearl, then via new CN&C track west on Pearl to Sycamore, north on Sycamore to Third, and west on Third to the Dixie Terminal. After looping through Dixie Terminal, the cars proceeded east on Third on all-new trackage to Broadway, south on Broadway on the last bit of Cincinnati Traction Co. steel (.037 miles) to Pearl and back on Green Line tracks to the Central Bridge. Thus the Harris recommendation of 1912 to prevent Green Line cars from venturing north of Fourth was realized.

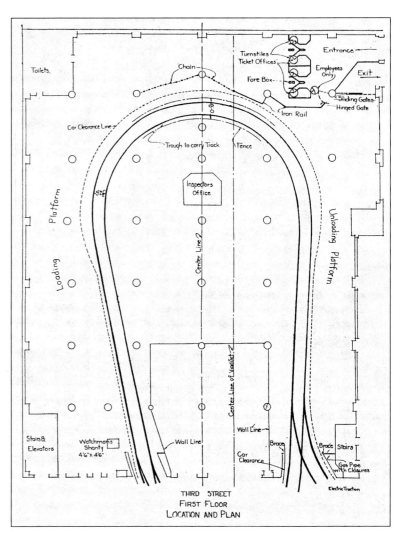

THIRD STREET
FIRST FLOOR
LOCATION AND PLAN

Both floors of Dixie Terminal annex contained 355 feet of track, each in a horseshoe configuration. The arrival area on each level could handle 4 single-truck or 3 double-truck cars whereas the departure area could load as many as five single-truckers or four double-truckers. This is the lower level. *T. W. Lehmann Collection.*

Why did the CN&C decide to give up using the L&N Bridge in November of 1921? The problem was with the bridge itself. It had become an operational bottleneck in 1918 when the Green Line's new double-truck cars (Nos. 500-524), assigned to base service on the Ft. Thomas and Dayton lines, were diverted over the Central Bridge after it was discovered that the L&N Bridge's deck presented such a severe peak that damage was being caused to the undercarriages of the large cars.

Of course, the CN&C's decision to use the Central Bridge exclusively also saved the company the expense of maintaining the tracks on the L&N Bridge and rental payments to the Cincinnati Traction Co. for use of its tracks on Pearl from Butler to Broadway.

The economic benefits of the Dixie Terminal to the Green Line were considerable. Covington Division cars saved an average of 10 minutes per round trip by avoiding Cincinnati surface traffic. Even Newport Division trips saved an average five min-

Until the completion of the Caroline Ave. underpass in 1931, the 6-Rosedale line on Decoursey Pike crossed the L&N Railroad at grade at two different points requiring the conductor to flag his motorman across both sets of tracks. *Fred Bauer Collection.*

A 1920-era Favorite: The *Island Queen*

The stately *Island Queen* entered service between downtown Cincinnati and Coney Island on Memorial Day of 1925. From the foot of Broadway in Cincinnati, a spot served by all Newport Division CN&C streetcars, the Queen carried many Northern Kentuckians eight miles upriver to Coney Island until 1947 when, on September 9, it was destroyed by a tragic fire while docked in Pittsburgh. Twenty crew members perished in the conflagration. *Special Collections and Archives, University of Kentucky Libraries.*

utes by simply being able to unload and load off street. This meant the Green Line could run fewer cars per route with the same service levels. Cutting these minutes off the timecard relegated the later 1893 Brownell cars (Nos. 220 to 238) to primarily race track and peak holiday service only.

A New Corporate Master

In 1922 it was finally time to end the confusion over corporate names. Columbia Gas and Electric dissolved the Cincinnati, Newport and Covington Light and Traction Co. (New Jersey), the Cincinnati, Newport and Covington Railway Co. (Ohio), and its corporate alter ego--the South Covington and Cincinnati Street Railway Co. (Kentucky)--and all three passed into oblivion. Concurrently, a new Cincinnati, Newport and Covington Railway

Co., incorporated in Kentucky, assumed all of the property, rights, franchises and privileges of the South Covington and Cincinnati.

However, the Licking River Bridge Co., although staffed by Green Line employees, remained a separate Columbia owned entity.

With additions to its Newport power station in 1904 and 1906, the Green Line had more than abundant electrical generating capacity to run the streetcar system. As a consequence, excess electricity was sold to its sister corporation, the Union Light, Heat & Power Co., for distribution to Northern Kentucky residents.

By the eve of World War I, the Newport power station was rapidly becoming obsolete as were a number of other power plants run by Columbia Gas & Electric in the Cincinnati area.

The Green Line System Gets Route Numbers

With the opening of the Dixie Terminal, the Green Line numbered each streetcar line for the first time. In addition to the route number designation appearing on maps, transfers, schedules and other printed materials, the Green Line also affixed large white route numerals to both the front and rear of each car in service. This feature was particularly appreciated by passengers at major transfer points and in the dimly lit cavern of the Dixie Terminal. No longer was it so easy to board the wrong car.

The Green Line had reached the zenith of its streetcar operations with the opening of the Dixie Terminal. In a report to the Kentucky Public Utilities Commission, the Green Line detailed the trackage over which each newly numbered route operated in Kentucky as follows:

1 - FT. MITCHELL
Beginning at the approach of the Suspension Bridge, Covington end, Second & Court Ave., south on Court to Park Place, west on Park Place to Scott St., south on Scott to Fourth St., west on Fourth to Madison Ave., south on Madison to 11th St., west on 11th to Russell St., south on Russell to 12th St., west on 12th to Hermes St., north on Hermes to Pike St., west on Pike to Montague

St., south on Montague to the corporation line of the city of Covington. From this point to end of line, cars operate over private right-of-way, returning over same route to city limits at Pike St., east on Pike to Madison Ave., north on Madison to Third St., east on Third to Court Ave., north on Court to point of beginning.

2 - GREENUP
From approach of Suspension Bridge, Second St. and Court Ave., over Court to Park Place, east on Park Place to Greenup St., south on Greenup to 20th St. (formerly State St.), west on 20th to Madison Ave. Cars then return from Madison Ave. & 20th St. over same route to place of beginning. This route is double tracked except between 15th and 16th Sts. on Greenup St.

3 - LUDLOW
Beginning at the Covington end of the Suspension Bridge, south on Court Ave. to Park Place, west on Park Place to Scott St., south on Scott to Fourth St., west on Fourth to Main St., north on Main to Third St., west on Third to Crescent Ave., north on Crescent to Second St., west on Second to Ludlow Hwy., west on Ludlow to Elm St. in the city of Ludlow, west on Elm to Adela St. over private

right-of-way between Elm St. and Adela Ave., west on West Oak St. to Pleasant St. in the city of Bromley, returning over the same route to Third St. & Main St., eastwardly on Third to Court Ave., north on Court to the Suspension Bridge approach.

4 - MAIN

Beginning at the approach of the Suspension Bridge, Covington end, south over Court Ave. to Park Place, west on Park Place to Scott St., south on Scott to Fourth St., west on Fourth to Main St., south on Main to Pike St., east on Pike to Madison Ave., north on Madison to Third St., east on Third to Court Ave., north on Court to the Suspension Bridge approach.

5 - HOLMAN

From approach of Suspension Bridge, Second St. & Court Ave., south on Court to Park Place, west on Park Place to Scott St., south on Scott to Fourth St., west on Fourth to Madison Ave., south on Madison to 11th St., west on 11th to Russell St., south on Russell to 12th St., west on 12th to Holman St., south on Holman to 19th St., west on 19th to Howell St., south on Howell to 21st St., east on 21st to Russell St., North on Russell to 19th St., west on 19th to Holman St. Returning, cars operate north on Holman St. to 13th St., east on 13th to Russell St., north on Russell to Robbins, east on Robbins to Madison Ave., north on Madison to Third St., east on Third to Court St., north on Court to point of beginning.

6 - ROSEDALE

From approach of Suspension Bridge, Second St. & Court Ave., south on Court to Park Place, west on Park Place to Scott St., south on Scott to Fourth St., west on Fourth to Madison Ave., south on Madison to private right-of-way at 26th St. and Madison Ave., entering said private right-of-way bordering James Ave. and the private right-of-way of the L & N Ry. Co., where the streetcar line goes underneath the railway, westwardly on Thirtieth St. to Decoursey Ave., southwardly on Decoursey to Southern Ave., eastwardly on Southern to Huntington Ave., south on Huntington to the end of the line at 46th St., over the loop on private property, returning over same route to Fourth St. & Madison Ave., proceeding northwardly on Madison to Third St., eastwardly over Third to Court Ave., north on Court to point of beginning.

7 - LATONIA

From Second St. and Court Ave., south on Court to Park Place, west on Park Place to Scott St., south on Scott to Fourth St., west on Fourth to Madison Ave., south on Madison to James Ave., paralleling James over private right-of-way to the L & N Bridge, westward on Thirtieth St. to Decoursey Ave., south on Decoursey to 34th St., westward on 34th to Southern Ave., where Beech Ave. intersects same, south on Eugenia Ave. to 35th St., west on 35th to Carlisle Ave., south on Carlisle, forming a loop and connecting with 35th St. and Latonia Ave., returning over same route to Fourth and Madison Ave., where cars proceed north on Madison to Third St., east on Third to Court Ave., north on Court to point of beginning.

8 - EASTERN

From the approach of Suspension Bridge, Second St. & Court Ave., south on Court to Park Place, east on Park Place to Greenup St., south on Greenup to 15th St. (formerly Powell), east on 15th to Eastern Ave. (formerly Edward St.), south on Eastern to Corporation St., west on Corporation to Garrard St., south on Garrard to 20th St. (formerly State), west on 20th to Greenup St., north on Greenup to Park Place, west on Park Place to Court Ave., north on Court to beginning.

9 - BELT LINE

Beginning at the Covington end of the Suspension Bridge and Court Ave., south on Court to Park Place, west on Park Place to Scott St., south on Scott to Fourth St., east on Fourth to Madison Ave., south on Madison to 11th St., east on 11th to Greenup St., south on Greenup to 12th St., east on 12th to the Licking River Bridge, which bridge is controlled and owned by the CN&C, eastwardly over that bridge to 11th & Brighton St., Newport, Ky., east on 11th St. to York St., north on York to Third St. and entrance to the Broadway and Newport Bridge returning over same route until same reaches Fourth & Madison Ave. in Covington, Ky., north on Madison Ave. to Third St., east on Third to Court Ave., north on Court to the Suspension Bridge or place of beginning.

11 - FT. THOMAS

Beginning at Third & York Sts. in the city of Newport, at the entrance of the Broadway and Newport Bridge, east over Third St. to Washington Ave., south on Washington to Tenth St., east over Tenth and Waterworks Rd. to the corporation line near Grand Ave., northeastwardly over private right-of-way to Rob Roy and Mt. Pleasant Ave., known as "Inverness Crossing," westwardly over Dundee Ave. to Elmwood Ave., over North Ft. Thomas Ave. (formerly Mt. Pleasant Ave.) to Highland Ave., over South Ft. Thomas Ave. to the end of the route, near the Alexandria Pike.

12 - BELLEVUE AND DAYTON

Operates from approach of Broadway & Newport Bridge Co. (Central Bridge) at Third & York Sts., Newport, Ky., over a double track as follows, east on Third St. to Beech Ave., south on Beech to Front St., east on Front to the Newport-Bellevue corporate line. In Bellevue, Ky., from the Newport-Bellevue corporation line, through the city of Bellevue, eastward on Fairfield Ave. to the east corporate limits of the city of Bellevue, where same joins the city of Dayton. In Dayton, Ky., from the Bellevue-Dayton corporate line, east on Sixth Ave., which is a continuation of Fairfield Ave. in Dayton, to Clay St., where the double track line ends. Here, a single track loop commences, running eastwardly on Sixth St. to Main St., northwardly on Main to Fifth Ave., eastward on Fifth to Benham St., northwardly on Benham to Third Ave., westward on Third to Clay St., southward on Clay to Sixth Ave., where the single track loop ends, thence cars proceed westward over the double track route to the Central Bridge.

13 - SOUTH BELLEVUE

Beginning at Third & York Sts., Newport, Ky., at the entrance to the Broadway & Newport Bridge, east on Third St. to Beech Ave., north on Beech to Front St., east on Front to the corporation line of the city of Newport, east on Fairfield Ave. (which is a continuation of Front St.) to Taylor Ave. & Fairfield Ave., south on Taylor to Walnut St., east on Walnut to Washington Ave., south on Washington to Grandview Ave., east on Grandview to Ward Ave., north on Ward to Center St., west on Center to Taylor Ave., and continuing over the above described line to the point of beginning at Third & York Sts., Newport, Ky.

15 - SOUTHGATE

Beginning at Third and York Sts., Newport, Ky., at the entrance of the Broadway and Newport Bridge, south on York St. to Fifth & York, continuing south on York from Fifth to 11th & York Sts., eastwardly on 11th to 11th and Monmouth Sts., south on Monmouth to the corporation line of the city of Newport, near 13th St., eastwardly over private right-of-way to end of line.

17 - CROSSTOWN

Beginning at the intersection of Park Place & Greenup St. in the city of Covington, westwardly over Park Place to Scott St., south on Scott to Fourth St., east on Fourth to the Newport & Covington Bridge, over the Licking River, east on Bridge to the Newport approach of said bridge (in Newport, Ky.), southwardly over Brighton St. to Fifth St., eastwardly over Fifth to Monmouth St., northwardly over Monmouth to Third St., westwardly over Third to York St., southwardly over York to the intersection of Fifth & York Sts., westwardly over Fifth to Brighton St., northwardly over Brighton to the Newport & Covington Bridge, westwardly over the Newport & Covington Bridge to Fourth & Greenup Sts., northwardly over Greenup to Park Place, the point of beginning.

For reasons not discovered, the report omitted three Green Line car lines that were also numbered in 1921: 10-Lewisburg, 14-York and 16-Washington. Since all three lines utilized trackage over which one or more full-time routes also operated, perhaps the Green Line felt any mention of these lines to the KPUC unnecessary.

In any event, 10-Lewisburg provided rush hour short turn service on the 1-Ft. Mitchell trackage between the Dixie Terminal and 12th & Hermes. 14-York offered rush hour service between the Dixie Terminal and 11th & Brighton via York, duplicating parts of the 9-Beltline and 15-Southgate lines. 16-Washington covered rush hour service on the inner part of the 11-Ft. Thomas line between the Dixie Terminal and Tenth & Washington.

Between 1921 and 1924, the Green Line also operated the Highland Heights Shuttle between the end of the 11-Ft. Thomas line along Alexandria Pike to Main, and Main to Lincoln. This extremely unprofitable line was discontinued on August 15, 1924 and was never assigned a route number. ◆

A 12-Dayton car advertises the bathing beaches along the Ohio River in both Dayton and Bellevue and a Bellevue semi-pro baseball team. Motorman Manuel Cook (left) who, along with three brothers (William, Samuel, Jake), two brothers-in-law, and five other relatives, gave more than 300 years of service to the Green Line, poses with his unidentified conductor at the end of the Dayton line before returning to Cincinnati.
T. W. Lehmann Collection.

Accordingly, the Union Gas and Electric Co. (another Columbia entity) began construction of the West End power station in 1916. This facility, just west of downtown Cincinnati at Front & Rose, was designed to deliver low cost electricity to the entire Greater Cincinnati area. A building of heroic proportions, 225 feet by 333 feet, was finished in 1917 to house large coal-fired steam turbines which would feed four large generators, each of which was designed to deliver 30,000 kilowatts of electricity.

It was in 1918 that the first of the 30,000 kilowatt turbo generators went on line. A few months later a second unit of the same capacity was put into service. A year later the third 30,000 kilowatt unit was put on line, and in 1923, the West End power station was brought to its full capacity of 120,000 kilowatts with the startup of the fourth 30,000 kilowatt turbogenerator. With the advent of the fourth unit, the Newport power house was essentially closed and feeder lines to CN&C's sub-stations were installed to receive electricity from the West End power station.

Power Arrangements

Alternating current generated by the West End station at 13,200 volts was transmitted to Green Line substations located in Newport, Latonia, Ft. Mitchell

With nary an auto in sight, a CN&C double-truck car holds down an 11-Ft. Thomas run at North Ft. Thomas and Forest Aves. in 1925. Sorry to say we cannot read the fleet number in this low-contrast photo.
Earl Clark Collection.

and Covington. Power was converted to 550 volt direct current at these substations and supplied to the streetcars. The Newport substation was located at the Newport powerhouse and was fed by four 13,200 volt lines from the West End station. The reason for four West End power station lines coming directly to the Newport substation is that it was also the main commercial distributing point in Newport for the Union Light, Heat and Power Co.

The Covington substation, located at Stewart & Madison, and the Latonia substation, located at 35th & Decoursey, were each fed by both a 13,200 volt line of the Union Light, Heat and Power Co. and a feeder from the Newport substation in order to ensure redundancy in case of a fault in one or other of the systems.

The Ft. Mitchell substation, located 500 feet northwest of the present entrance to Highland Cemetery, was originally powered by a 4500 volt line from the Newport substation. The voltage was boosted to 13,200 in 1910. Later, in October of 1929, the Ft. Mitchell substation was also supplied with power from a 13,200 volt line of the Union Light, Heat and Power Co., assuring redundancy in case of a failure from the Newport feed.

All of the equipment in the substations, which converted the 13,200 volt a. c. to 550 volt d. c., was automatic, that is, the substations could be cut in and out of service without any attention from an operator. When the load was light due to only a few cars in service, the Newport substation furnished all the power needed. As more cars came into service and the necessity for additional electricity increased, there was a tendency for the voltage on various parts of the system to lower. At such times, by means of relays and switches, the automatic substations in Ft. Mitchell, Covington and Latonia would spring to life and furnish additional power to the system as long as the voltage remained below that required for efficient service.

Another small portion of the Newport powerhouse remained in service. One 500 horsepower boiler was kept in operation to supply steam heat for the Newport carbarn and shops.

Which came first: the chicken or the egg? In the early part of the 20th century, it was the streetcar that came first, before residential development on the largely rural 1-Ft. Mitchell line. Now the construction of expensive Park Hills homes is in full swing in 1925. A northbound car is about to glide to a halt at the rather nice stone station. Real estate developers made sure that even the lowly car stop had a certain elegance. *Earl Clark Collection.*

Streetcar Technology

Direct current of 550 volts was supplied to the streetcars of the Green Line System and flowed from the trolley wire down the trolley pole to the motorman's controller box located on the front platform. The controller was simply a device for determining the amount of current to the car motors. A slight turn or "notch" of the controller completed an electric circuit between the trolley wire, motors and rail, allowing the current to flow to the motors through a labyrinth of thin, cast-iron "grids" which offered considerable resistance and thereby limited the current to a certain point, affording a smooth start.

As the motorman pulled the controller handle around, a drum switch inside the controller box gradually reduced the resistant grids until full line voltage was sent to the motors, permitting the car to run at top speed.

Each streetcar motor was contained in a watertight housing. The car axle passed through bearings at one end of this housing and the other end rested on springs attached to the truck frame. A large gear on the axle meshed with a pinion on the armature shaft and the motor revolved around the axle at approximately four times the speed of the car wheels. To retard the speed of a streetcar a motorman "notched down" his controller.

Green Line double-truck cars were fitted with four 25 h. p. Westinghouse No. 506 motors while all single-trucked cars from No. 264 on up were delivered with two Westinghouse 35 h. p. No. 49 motors. During the 1920s, cars 254 to 263 were retrofitted with two Westinghouse 35 hp motors (model No. 49) in lieu of their original Westinghouse 25 hp motors (model No. 3) as were six cars in the 220-253 series.

In addition, on those cars equipped with air brakes (double-truck cars 500-524) air pressure was supplied by an air pump driven by a small electric motor. As the pressure dropped, the motor driving a compressor would start up to manufacture compressed air which was stored in a reservoir tank suspended from the car body. A small valve allowed the motorman to admit air under pressure from the reservoir to the brake cylinder allowing the car to be stopped in a smooth and safe manner. The same compressed air was also used to apply sand to the car rails for an emergency stop or when the rails were slippery. A downward pressure on the brake valve actuated the rail sanders.

All of the Green Line's single-truck cars delivered before 1901 were equipped only with primitive hand brakes or what the motorman called "armstrong" brakes. On this type of brake, a chain was wound up on a staff and it was necessary for the motorman to be a strong man to handle the brakes because very little leverage was available and the stopping of a streetcar demanded brute strength in large quantities.

Between 1901 and 1910 the Green Line scrupulously avoided the march of progress. It experimented with various makes and models of more efficient hand brakes. According to a *Street Railway Journal* article in 1903, the CN&C apparently toyed with the idea of air brakes. It reported that St. Louis-built cars 299-308 were being delivered with "Westinghouse electric [sic] brakes." It didn't happen; the Green Line backed away from the idea, as evidenced by St. Louis Car's amended Order 389A which specified hand brakes only.

The Peacock hand brake, manufactured by National Brake of Buffalo, N. Y., was judged to be the most cost-effective and efficient by the Green Line, which placed an order for more than 100 of the appliances in 1911. The older single-truck cars were rapidly refitted with Peacock brakes which allowed, through a series of reduction gears, a man of average stature to safely operate the hand brake. These were now standard equipment on the newer single-truckers.

The Green Line, so progressive in so many ways, never equipped the single-truckers with air brakes.

The Green Line in the Jazz Age

America flexed its economic muscles in the 1920s, perhaps a bit too much, as it turned out. After a short recession following the travails of the World War, prosperity reigned. The Cincinnati, Newport & Covington shared in the boom times, even as it confronted its first real competition from the new bus lines. Let us examine the ways in which the Green Line coped with its everyday responsibilities.

To operate and maintain the Green Line, the company had more than 500 full-time employees. Executive offices for the Green Line were still in the rococo building at Third & Court in Covington. The office housed the president and general manager of the company, the four members of the Purchasing Department, 12 members of the Accounting Department and three private secretaries. (In 1927, W. W. Freeman stepped down and Hubert C. Blackwell was named both president and general manager. Polk Laffoon, secretary-treasurer of the system since 1908, was given the additional title of vice president).

Transportation Department. By far the largest department of the Green Line, in terms of manpower, was the Transportation Department. Heading this up was the superintendent of transportation who was assisted by two division masters and two night barn foremen. To cover the actual day-to-day running of the streetcars required 350 motormen and conductors, 38 barn men (responsible for daily maintenance and cleaning of the cars), eight terminal cashiers, four terminal inspectors, two night cashiers, three terminal watchmen, five outside inspectors, one instructor, two barn clerks and one general clerk. The Transportation Department rostered a total of 419 full-time personnel. In 1929, conductors and motormen, represented by the Amalgamated Association of Street and Electric Railway Employees of America, Division 628, earned 60 cents per hour for a 48 hour week.

Ways and Structures Department. The CN&C was responsible by franchise to maintain the tracks in the streets upon which it operated and to also maintain a certain portion of the street in between and on three feet to each side of the track. The track was maintained by 38 full-time track laborers attached to this department under the direction of an engineer and roadmaster. During the summer months, when track reconstruction projects were greatly expanded, the Green Line employed up to 200 additional laborers.

The Green Line also employed four people who were responsible for maintenance of the company owned bridge over the Licking River between 11th in Newport and 12th in Covington. The bridge was a through truss of 360 feet in length resting on stone piers. Paving on the main span of the bridge in 1929 consisted of four inch creosoted planks with a three inch oak wearing surface. This crew, with the help of outside contractors during the summer months, was also responsible for the maintenance of three smaller bridges on the Ft. Mitchell line and three bridges on the Ft. Thomas line.

Line Department. This department employed 22 men who were to keep the poles, trolley wires and supports in good condition. To service the substations and the rest of the electrical equipment used in converting commercially purchased alternating current to direct current, the **Power Department** employed a total of 17 people. Eleven were assigned to operate and maintain the equipment at the four substations and the other six were responsible for the care and feeding of the one remaining boiler at the Newport powerhouse which supplied steam to the Newport carbarn and repair facility.

Shops Department. Another 45 people were employed here as blacksmiths, machinists, carpenters, painters and motor repairmen at the Newport shops. They were responsible for the periodic reworking of the aging streetcar fleet. Trucks and car motors were overhauled at an interval of every 60,000 to 75,000 car miles. A streetcar was completely overhauled generally every four to six years. In 1929, a record 43 cars were thus dealt with.

Streetcar Confronts Flivver, Loses Face

Although this accident was staged as part of a Green Line safety campaign in 1925, it demonstrates the increasing automobile traffic problem the company was experiencing. A 500-series car is southbound on Madison between Fourth and Fifth and has encountered a jalopy arrogantly pulling out from a sidewalk gasoline station, heedless of the oncoming hulk of the electric car. The motorman, on cue, is suitably shocked at this newfangled interference with streetcars. Allowing gas pumps to be placed at the curb was a practice soon outlawed in Covington. *Special Collections and Archives, University of Kentucky Libraries.*

Track Maintenance Procedures

When new track was to be installed or old track replaced, many problems were encountered. It was necessary that the location of all manholes, sewer basins and water valves be accurately known so that the rails and their supports would clear them when installation was made. The street grade was usually changed so new plans were always necessary.

Orders for switches and crossovers--known as "special work"--had to be placed in advance as these pieces were made to order by a manufacturer from detailed plans. After the special work was fabricated, the manufacturer assembled all the pieces exactly as they were to be installed later. Each part of a switch or crossover was carefully fitted to its neighbor so that the elevation at every point corresponded with the crown and grade of the street as shown on the plans the Green Line submitted to the manufacturer. The assembly was then dismantled for shipment after

numerals were stamped on all the abutting railheads at each joint so as to prevent errors when the pieces were installed by the Green Line track crew.

When rails were to be replaced, evacuation was done by steam shovels and all track tools were operated by compressed air or electricity. The first steps in laying new track were removing the worn out rails, breaking up the pavement and removing the old foundation and ties.

New ties were laid in the trench and rails were fastened to them with screw spikes driven by an electric spike driver. The track was brought up to correct elevation with blocks of wood placed under the ties and the rails aligned.

The rail joints were then prepared for welding. A new welding method was introduced by the Green Line System during the 1920s in which a clay mold was clamped around the joint and a gas flame then applied to preheat the rails and bake the mold over which was placed a graphite crucible containing "Oxalite," the

Taking Care of
TRACKS
on the
Green Line

The growth of Covington and Newport kept the Green Line's track forces hopping. In 1927 an underpass **(above)** was constructed just north of 17th & Madison to eliminate a Chesapeake and Ohio Railway grade crossing. During construction a temporary "shoofly" track was built to allow the Green Line's 6-Rosedale and 7-Latonia lines to continue to use Madison. You can see a streetcar on the shoofly clanking across the C&O tracks as the shutter snaps. Another car is barely visible above the newly-installed railroad deck girder span. In the picture at **right**, Mack truck No. 34 serves the cause by carrying a welding unit. Repairs are being made on a well-used bit of track at Madison & Pike. *Both: Special Collections and Archives, University of Kentucky Libraries.*

trade name for the material used to make the joint. It is interesting to note that the active ingredient of Oxalite was powdered aluminum mixed with a ferrous oxide, a formulation with many similarities to the chemical compound that makes up the fuel used by solid rocket boosters on today's space shuttle.

This mixture was ignited by the use of a small quantity of an ignition powder which caused it to burn fiercely for 35-40 seconds at a temperature of about 5000 degrees Fahrenheit. The molten steel collected in the bottom of the crucible and was admitted to the mold at the proper moment by pulling a clay plug. The steel flowed between the rail ends and around the weld forming a continuous rail surface.

Such a method provided a joint as strong as the rail itself and ensured a smooth and quiet ride. Bolted joints were still used for special work to simplify the work of replacement.

The track was now finished except for its foundation. Concrete, mixed either on the job or delivered ready mixed in trucks, was poured into the trench up to the top of the cross ties and was tamped well under the ties and rail bases. Cars were not run on the completed track until the concrete was thoroughly set and the requisite top paving was completed.

Trackage Changes in the 1920s

In 1926, the CN&C formally abandoned and took up the tracks on Lake and Laurel that had served the defunct Ludlow Lagoon. These tracks, extending only for a little less than a third of a mile, had been unused since the closing of the Ludlow Lagoon Amusement Park. In 1928, CN&C workers salvaged the overhead wire and rail of the ill-fated Highland Heights shuttle, which had ceased operation in 1924.

In conjunction with the C&O Railway elevation project in Covington, a dangerous grade crossing on Madison just north of 17th was eliminated with the completion of a vehicle underpass

The Last Big Track Project Takes Shape

The last major construction project involving Green Line trackage occurred at Latonia in 1931 with the building of the Caroline Ave. underpass, which we see in the illustration at **right**. Here at Rittes Corner, trackwork is being performed to link Southern Ave. to the new underpass. The old track takes the curve, the other heads toward the newly-built grade separation with the L&N. *Special Collections and Archives, University of Kentucky Libraries.*

In the frame at **left**, Green Line workers are using a very hot (5000 degrees) molten metal process to join adjacent railheads to help ensure a smoother ride for streetcar passengers. The man in the business suit smoking the cigar could be the CN&C's official in charge. A stogie was almost a badge of executive office in those days! *Special Collections and Archives, University of Kentucky Libraries.*

in September, 1927. A new underpass at Pike & Russell for road traffic, including CN&C cars, was opened in September of 1928 resulting in a new northbound track for the 5-Holman line on Russell from Robbins to Pike (of 0.231 miles) and the abandonment of the track on Robbins from Russell to Madison (0.199 miles). During the Pike St. underpass construction, the company also rebuilt its connecting track on Pike from Main to Madison.

The last segment of new track laid by the Green Line took place in 1931, but is included here to tell the rest of the streetcar trackage story. The 6-Rosedale route on Decoursey between 34th and Southern crossed, at grade, the busy Louisville & Nashville Railroad at two places.

In 1929, Covington and the L&N began discussions for the construction of an underpass for automobile and streetcar usage on Caroline between 34th and 35th to eliminate the dangerous grade crossings. As a part of the ensuing construction project, the Green Line was permitted to construct new tracks from Southern & Decoursey over Southern and Caroline to connect with the 7-Latonia trackage at 34th. The new underpass was opened for streetcar service on September 21, 1931, and would be the last new street railway trackage constructed in Kentucky.

Changing Times

By the mid 1920s new factors created competition to street railway and interurban electric lines all across the United States. Nothing less than a transportation revolution was taking place. The rapid advancement of automotive technology created an irresistible demand for the paving of roads and streets which, in turn, gave rise to even more private automobile ownership and the creation of the motor bus industry. Consequently, by 1930, almost every Green Line streetcar route faced independent bus company competition.

Independent, because the Green Line moved with extreme caution to respond to this new phenomenon. So did many other streetcar companies.

The rise in both private automobile ownership and competing bus lines was greatly aided by the Federal Good Roads Act of 1916 and the Federal-Aid Highway Act of 1921. These laws funneled millions of tax dollars into highway construction, municipal road paving and widening projects, new underpass and overpass construction, and the installation of traffic control devices. Not a penny went for streetcar construction, of course.

The massive Chesapeake & Ohio Railway grade separation project even affected downtown Covington Green Line trackage. During the 1920s The C&O raised its mainline trackage throughout central Covington which included the construction of an underpass at Pike & Russell. This benefited the 1-Ft. Mitchell, 4-Main, 5-Holman and 10-Lewisburg lines. As part of the project the Green Line upgraded its Pike Street track from Madison to Russell in 1927.
Earl Clark Collection.

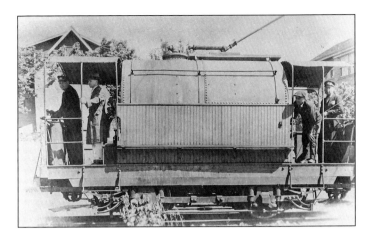

This unnumbered sprinkler car, rebuilt from a passenger car prior to World War I, is engaged in weed control on its private right-of-way near Highlands High School in Ft. Thomas around 1925. Prior to paved roads, earlier Green Line sprinkler cars were mandated by ordinance to wet down the dusty streets over which they operated. *Earl Clark Collection.*

The new competition actually appeared much earlier. But it took a long time for the implications to sink in.

Northern Kentucky's first "motor bus" operation was started by Henry (Bupsey) Neiser around 1910 using what was basically a truck with a canvas top and longitudinal seats. This contraption made two round trips daily from the Hess and Racke General Store in Alexandria, via Cold Spring, Ft. Thomas and Newport to Fourth & Broadway in Cincinnati, carrying all sorts of freight as well as the occasional passenger. The operation succeeded a stagecoach which had been operated since 1880 by the Rardin family.

Sometime in 1911 Philip Gosney started a shuttle service from the end of the Ft. Thomas car line to Alexandria via Cold

In anticipation of the opening of the Dixie Terminal, the viaduct from the Suspension Bridge had been extended from Second to Third Street in Cincinnati in 1919. Sometime later, St. Louis-built single-truck car No. 317 operates over the extension. It's empty of passengers, but the conductor's silhouette can be seen at the rear door. *Earl Clark Collection.*

by J.W. Bentler in 1915. Bentler operated one 30-passenger bus from the end of the streetcar line in Ft. Mitchell south on Lexington Pike (now Dixie Highway) to the adjoining communities of Elsmere and Erlanger.

The combination of hard rubber tires, bench-like seats and the crushed gravel washboard-like surfaces of Lexington Pike and Alexandria Pike did not contribute to the well-being of these pioneer efforts. These factors, coupled with rising fuel prices and parts shortages, pushed all four operations into financial difficulties by the end of World War I.

Both the Neal and Bentler ventures gave up the ghost toward the end of World War I in 1918. The Neiser and Gosney operations barely survived the war. During the 1920s Neiser cut back to what was basically a Cold Spring-Ft. Thomas shuttle operation (with a few morning and evening trips extending to Newport). By 1930 only the shuttle operation remained and the route was sold in 1931 to Paul Schwerling.

Gosney continued to operate shuttle service between Alexandria and the end of the Green Line's Highland Heights shuttle until that line was abandoned in 1924. Apparently Gosney then again operated from Alexandria and Cold Spring to the end of the 11-Ft. Thomas line until the feeder was also acquired by Schwerling in late 1930.

Spring. This operation was possibly supported by the Green Line because Gosney's initial vehicle was an ex-streetcar body mounted on a truck chassis.

In 1912 a C.S. Neal started what was basically a competing line between Grants Lick via Alexandria to a connection with the Green Line in Newport. Neal, using a Schacht panel truck fitted with benches and canvas curtains, made one round trip daily.

The first motor bus operation in Kenton County was formed

Pulling the Pole: a Conductor's Constant Duty

Here is a sight seen hundreds of times daily in Covington and Newport for decades. With 8-Eastern car 326 turning from Court onto Park, its conductor is pulling down the redundant trolley pole now that the car is free of the city of Cincinnati-mandated two-wire system. Double overhead extended to Third & Court in Covington and Third & York in Newport. Although the photograph was taken sometime in the 1930s, use of two wires and two trolley poles in Cincinnati and only one wire and one trolley pole in Northern Kentucky was the rule from 1891 until 1937. This is one of the duties that kept conductors on the single-truck cars for years longer than one would have expected. The double-truck cars did operate with only one pole in Cincinnati after their conversion to one-man. *Earl Clark Collection.*

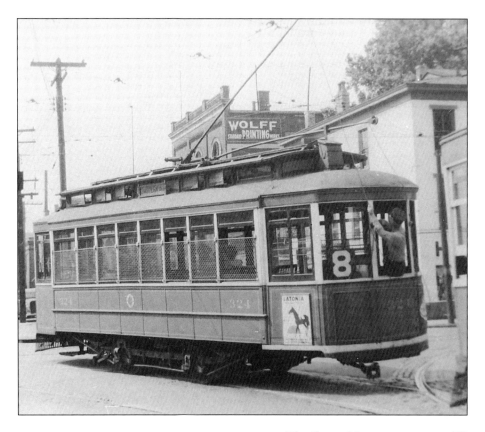

They're Off!
By Streetcar for a Day at the Races

Kentucky is thoroughbred country, and naturally a first-class race track with pari-mutuel betting would attract huge crowds from the greater Cincinnati area. In Louisville the action was at Churchill Downs, site of the famed Kentucky Derby. Filling the need in Green Line territory was the Latonia Jockey Club, located at the end of the CN&C's 7-Latonia line. This facility generated a lot of revenue during the spring and fall racing seasons with as many as 45 extra cars needed to haul the crowds to and from the track. Whereas in earlier years the Lagoon amusement park and the Latonia race track would have been prime traffic generators for the Green Line, now only the race track played that role.
Earl Clark Collection.

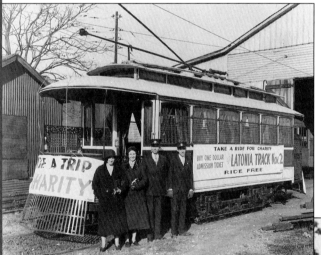

Of course the private car *Kentucky* got into the act. In conjunction with a forerunner of today's United Way, a sign on the parlor car **(above)** promotes a charity day at the Latonia Race Track in 1929. At **right** is a postcard view of car 133 disgorging a big crowd at the gates of the race track, circa 1929. *Special Collections and Archives, University of Kentucky Libraries; Earl Clark Collection.*

The Dixie Traction Co.

With the demise of Bentler's operation, the residents of Erlanger and Elsmere were again without public transportation to get them to Cincinnati (save for a few daily Southern Railway trains), or even to the end of the Green Line's Ft. Mitchell car line. With the paving of Lexington Pike (later Dixie Highway) in August of 1921, new bus service became possible.

In 1922, a group of businessmen led by Kenton County Attorney Stephens Blakely incorporated The Dixie Traction Co. with an initial capitalization of $10,000. Originally the backers contemplated a trackless trolley line, hence the use of the "traction" designation, but cost considerations dictated the use of motor buses. It definitely had nothing to do with electric railroading! Using three Mack AB buses (Nos. 101-103), The Dixie Traction Co., on August 15, 1922 started operations from the end of the Ft. Mitchell streetcar line out Dixie Highway to Elsmere, Erlanger and Florence. The company initially provided service at 30 minute intervals between 7 a.m. and 8 p.m. on weekdays only.

On August 18, 1925, Dixie Traction extended its route north on Dixie Highway through downtown Covington to Cincinnati, offering service seven days a week and also instituted seven-day service on the shuttle route. Three more Mack AB motor buses were acquired in 1925 for the Florence-Cincinnati route (Nos. 104-106).

With the extension of Dixie Traction to Cincinnati, Ryles Auto Bus Service, using a seven-passenger jitney, started a run from Dixie Highway & Buttermilk Pike to Crescent Springs and the Villa Madonna Academy. Ryles' backing appears to have come from Dixie Traction.

The initial investors sold Dixie Traction to Erlanger businessmen F. Walton Dempsey (the local Studebaker dealer) and Arthur Rouse in 1927, and they immediately acquired a small Studebaker 15-passenger bus (No. 107) which was leased to Ryles Auto Bus Service for its Crescent Springs shuttle.

Dempsey was no stranger to the motor transportation busi-

Dixie Traction upgraded its fleet with the purchase of four Studebaker model 99 buses in 1929 including No. 111 depicted here in a factory photograph. Dixie Traction used the Dixie Highway (U. S. 25) to take passengers to Ft. Mitchell, Erlanger, and Florence and directly competed with CN&C's profitable 1-Ft. Mitchell rail line. *Motor Bus Society.*

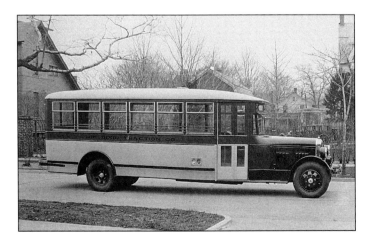

This is probably the first motor bus in Northern Kentucky. In December of 1911, Philip Gosney started a passenger service between Alexandria and the end of CN&C's Ft. Thomas line. The combination of hard rubber tires, a chain drive and an old streetcar body on a primitive chassis (plus snow on the ground) may date the photo to the opening day of this pioneer bus service. *Campbell County Historical Society.*

ness. In 1924, he founded Blue Coach Lines to provide coach service between Cincinnati and Lexington, Ky. By 1929, Blue Coach, utilizing 12, 23- to 27-passenger Studebaker-FitzJohn parlor coaches, was offering 15 round trips daily between Cincinnati and Lexington as well as a number of local trips between Cincinnati-Florence and Carrollton.

In September, 1929, Dempsey sold Blue Coach Lines to Consolidated Coach Corp. in order to concentrate on developing additional Dixie Traction business and running his Erlanger Studebaker dealership. Consolidated's entry into Northern Kentucky came with the acquisition of Red Star Transportation Co., a Blue Coach competitor, in 1926.

In 1931, Consolidated, now operating over two different routes between Cincinnati and Lexington, became Southeastern Greyhound Lines. SEG and the Green Line's paths would cross during World War II when the two companies formed a unique operating arrangement. Of this we shall hear more.

Dixie Traction Expands

Dixie Traction now moved into new territory. In November, 1929, DTC established two new routes from Ft. Thomas to Cincinnati. The Dixie's new routes ran in two directions from Highland Ave. and Ft. Thomas Ave., either west down Highland to Alexandria Pike and north through Newport on Monmouth to Cincinnati, or north on Ft. Thomas Ave. to Waterworks and then via Wilson, Bonnie Leslie, Taylor, Grandview and Lafayette through south Bellevue onto Newport via Sixth to Monmouth and on to Cincinnati. In essence the new Campbell County routes formed a belt line with the Dixie Traction's buses operating outbound on one route and inbound on the other.

Evidence compels the conclusion that the Dixie Traction Company had authority to pick up and discharge intrastate as well as interstate passengers over the entire extent of its Northern Kentucky routes. Thus by 1930 Dixie Traction had become a serious competitor of the Green Line wherever its Kenton or Campbell County routes closely paralleled existing streetcar tracks. Although there are those who recall that some "closed door restrictions" were imposed on The Dixie Traction Company, an Interstate Commerce Commission decision of 1937 states: "Dixie Traction's Kentucky authority authorizes the intrastate transportation of passengers between all points on its lines within Kentucky. It does not have authority, however, to operate intrastate commerce in Ohio or within Cincinnati." Since the Dixie Traction operated for only a few blocks in downtown Cincinnati, this intrastate restriction was of no importance.

Starting in 1928, Dixie Traction upgraded its transit bus fleet with the purchase of three 25-passenger Studebaker model 76 buses equipped with FitzJohn bodies (Nos. 108-110). The year 1929 saw DTC acquire four additional 25-passenger Studebaker-FitzJohn buses (Nos. 111-114). Dixie also purchased three new model 111 Studebaker-FitzJohn 25-passenger buses between 1930 and 1932 (Nos. 115-117). The selection of Studebaker buses for Dixie Traction, in view of F. Walton Dempsey's ownership of the local Studebaker dealership, speaks for itself.

To house Dixie's growing fleet, a new garage to hold 30 buses was built in 1929 on the southeast corner of Dixie & May in Erlanger. In a boundary adjustment, the site was later incorporated into the city of Elsmere but it was always called the "Erlanger Garage." Dixie Traction also picked up five used model 111s between 1933 and 1935 (Nos. 118-122) all probably from Southeastern Greyhound.

Campbell County Bus Lines

Residents of Bellevue and Newport, accustomed to shopping in Newport by taking either the 12-Dayton or 13-South Bellevue streetcar lines to Third & Monmouth and transferring to the 15-Southgate line which served Newport's main retail district on Monmouth, were found to be coming to Newport to shop in much smaller numbers after the removal of the Green Line's tracks from Monmouth St. in June, 1918.

Two Early Independents

Ludlow Transit was a well-managed rival of the Green Line. The suburb was subject to frequent flooding and Ludlow Transit had the advantage of being able to easily detour around blocked streets. In the picture **above**, a 1929 LT Mack AB bus heads off the Suspension Bridge for downtown Covington. There, it will take on more passengers for Ludlow.

By 1930 Central Transit had also dealt itself in as a serious competitor to the Green Line in the Covington area. At the Covington end of the Suspension Bridge in June 1930, Central Transit No. 24 Yellow Coach **(right)** will compete against the 5-Holman car line while **below** Central No. 26, a 25-passenger model Mack AB, is going head-to-head with the Green Line's 6-Rosedale car line. *All: Special Collections and Archives, University of Kentucky Libraries.*

With the rerouting of the 15-Southgate line to York, Bellevue and Dayton shoppers no longer enjoyed "door-to-door" service and had to walk a block west to Monmouth St. and the main Newport shopping area. The shopkeepers, in chasing streetcars away from their doors back in 1918, had outsmarted themselves.

This loss of business led the Monmouth Street Merchants Association in 1919 to form a bus line connecting the cities of Dayton and Bellevue with the main Newport shopping areas on Monmouth between Fifth and Tenth. The new bus line, which ran only during the hours the Newport stores were open, originated in Dayton and proceeded west along Fairfield to the Bellevue city limits, then south on Taylor to Sixth, and west on Sixth to Newport. In Newport the "Merchants Bus" used Sixth to Washington to Fifth, and over Fifth to Monmouth, and south on Monmouth to Tenth.

The service was so successful that the Monmouth Street Merchants Association (formally incorporated in 1922) bought a new White model 50B bus in December of 1927 and added a new White 706M in 1936. This route continued to operate independently for more than five decades, such a long time that few could remember why the line was started in the first place.

Available evidence suggests that Campbell County's first serious Green Line competitor was the Northern Kentucky Transit Co. In 1922 the NKT started service from Dayton through Bellevue (along Fairfield Avenue) and Newport to Cincinnati (via the L&N Bridge) in direct competition with the Green Line's 12-Dayton and 13-South Bellevue streetcar routes.

NKT also offered a rush hour only route from Cincinnati to North Ft. Thomas (via Newport and Sixth to South Bellevue and via Covert Run to N. Ft. Thomas Ave. and Highland Ave.). By 1925, NKT owned five 29-passenger buses offering more than 80

In the Roaring '20s, the CN&C's big 500-series cars continued to do the heavy lifting. Here's the class leader, 500, coming at us off the Licking River Bridge. Note the long-handled switch iron hanging on the front of the car. *Special Collections, University of Kentucky Libraries.*

weekday trips on its Dayton route and 15 weekday trips on its North Ft. Thomas line.

In 1925, Peoples Transit entered the fray by competing against both the Green Line and NKT by starting a bus line from Cincinnati through east Newport on Sixth to Bellevue and then on Taylor to Fairfield and on to Dayton and North Ft. Thomas. In 1930, Peoples Transit acquired NKT and decided to compete with the Green Line only on NKT's original Bellevue-Dayton route and abandoned its Sixth St. route. Peoples, however, did retain a shuttle service from Dayton via Covert Run and N. Ft. Thomas Ave. to Highland Ave., thereby offering connections to both Green Line streetcars and Dixie Traction buses.

Also sometime in late 1922, the Clifton-Patterson Bus Co. started operations between the then independent City of Clifton (now part of south Newport) via Kentucky Drive and the 13th St. Bridge, to Newport via York to 11th to Patterson to 5th. Patterson St. had not been served by public transit since 1917 due to the Green Line's dispute with the city. CPB appears not to have survived the Depression.

Three More Covington Bus Lines

There seemed to be no end to the number of people who wanted to get into the bus business. In 1925, Covington resident Lloyd Ross formed Ross Motor Coaches, Inc. to provide bus service from downtown Covington to the suburb of Rosedale. Ross

The Green Line's portable substation rests beside the Newport woodworking shop in the early 1930s. Though it was not scrapped until 1940, its last regular use was in the summer of 1915 on the Ludlow line to boost line voltage because as many as 50 cars were needed to serve Lagoon Park on weekends. *Sol Korkes, Earl Clark Collection.*

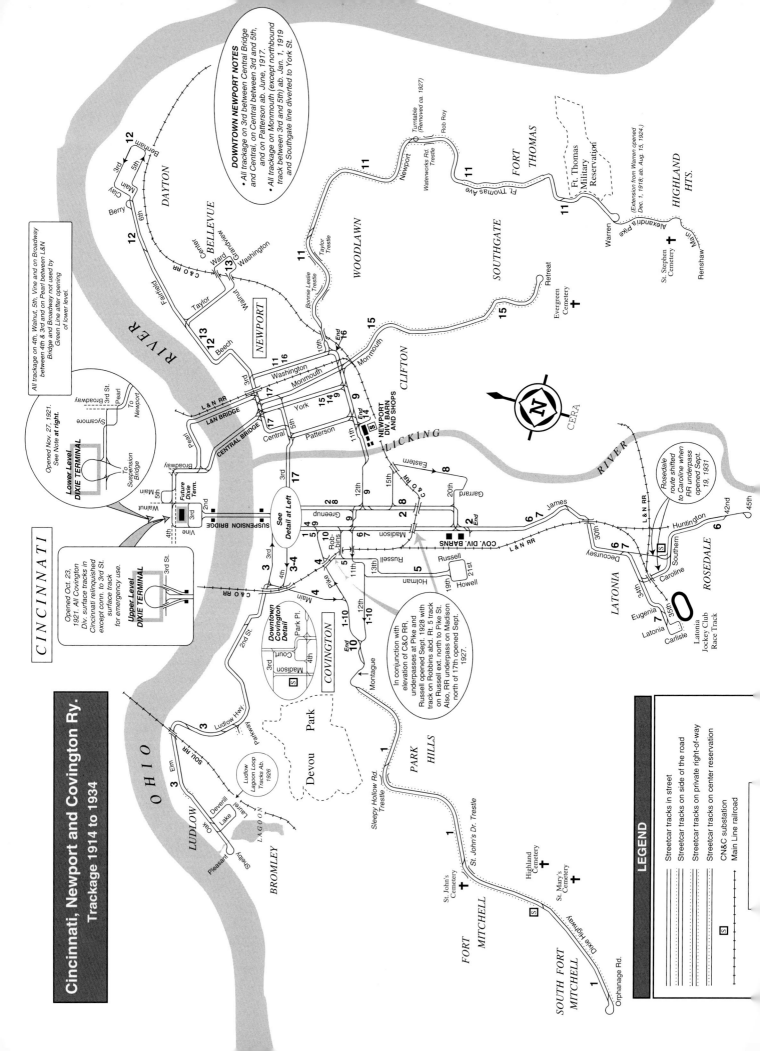

Cincinnati, Newport and Covington Ry.
Trackage 1914 to 1934

CINCINNATI

All trackage on 4th, Walnut, 5th, Vine and on Broadway between 4th & 3rd and on Pearl between L&N Bridge and Broadway not used by Green Line after opening of lower level.

Lower Level DIXIE TERMINAL
Opened Nov. 27, 1921. See Note at right.

Upper Level DIXIE TERMINAL
Opened Oct. 23, 1921. All Covington Div. surface tracks in Cincinnati relinquished except conn. to 3rd St. surface track for emergency use.

DOWNTOWN NEWPORT NOTES
• All trackage on 3rd between Central Bridge and Central, on Central between 3rd and 5th, and on Patterson ab. June, 1917.
• All trackage on Monmouth (except northbound track between 3rd and 5th) ab. Jan. 1, 1919 and Southgate line diverted to York St.

Downtown Covington Detail

In conjunction with elevation of C&O RR, underpasses at Pike and Russell opened Sept. 1928 with track on Robbins abd. Rt. 5 track on Russell ext. north to Pike St. Also, RR underpass on Madison north of 17th opened Sept. 1927.

Ludlow Lagoon Tracks Ab. 1926

Rosedale route shifted to Caroline when RR underpass opened Sept. 19, 1931

(Extension from Warren opened Dec. 1, 1918; ab. Aug. 15, 1924.)

Turntable (Removed ca. 1927)

CERA

LEGEND
Streetcar tracks in street
Streetcar tracks on side of the road
Streetcar tracks on private right-of-way
Streetcar tracks on center reservation
CN&C substation
Main Line railroad

purchased two buses of unknown make and model to equip the initial route which ran from 45th & Huntington in Rosedale to Third & Court in downtown Covington.

Later that year, Ross added service to Latonia, purchased three more buses and extended both routes to downtown Cincinnati, thereby providing competition to the Green Line's 6-Rosedale and 7-Latonia streetcar lines. Both routes must have prospered because Ross acquired three more buses in 1927 and leased a larger building at 26th & Madison to service his eight bus fleet.

In 1929, Central Transit (with Lloyd Ross holding the controlling interest) commenced bus service from Third & Court to central Covington via Russell and Holman, closely duplicating the Green Line's 5-Holman streetcar route. Later, in 1930, Central Transit extended its central Covington route on to Cincinnati and assumed operation of Ross Motor Coaches' Rosedale route. In early 1932, Ross Motor Coaches and Central Transit would receive authority from Cincinnati to use "pull in" slots 16 and 17 on Government Square, thereby affording both entities a bit of off-street loading and layover space.

Buses were here to stay, and the Green Line looked forward to the 1930s with a mixture of fear and hope. But its greatest trial would come not from rubber-tired competition. It would come from the river. ❏

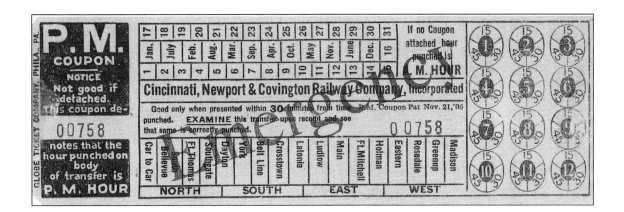

Green Line Mementos of the 1920s

Like so many transit systems, the Green Line went to the Globe Ticket Co. of Philadelphia for its transfers. One from the Roaring 20s appears above. To the **right**, we offer the first page of *Green Line Topics,* one issued in 1922. These appeared in the "Take One" boxes attached to the window stanchions. Finally, the CN&C had an interesting oddball car, 319, which it purchased used from Cincinnati Traction. It is shown with its crew on the HIghland Heights shuttle in 1920. The 319 was given double-end controls for this stub-end assignment. *Photo: Earl Clark Collection. Artifacts: T. W. Lehmann Collection.*

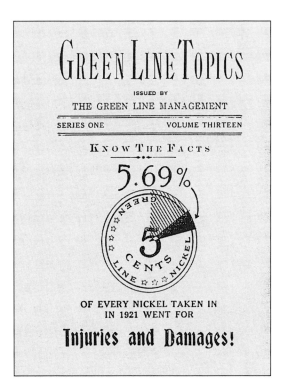

GREEN LINE TOPICS

ISSUED BY
THE GREEN LINE MANAGEMENT

SERIES ONE   VOLUME THIRTEEN

KNOW THE FACTS

5.69%

5 CENTS

OF EVERY NICKEL TAKEN IN
IN 1921 WENT FOR

Injuries and Damages!

A Decade
of Change:
1930-1939

ALTHOUGH THE 20 year period from 1910 to 1930 brought little change to the Green Line, a revolutionary transformation would come in the next 10 years. During that period, most of the system's streetcars would be replaced by motor buses and trolleycoaches. In 1937, five local competing transit companies would be purchased and a number of new transit routes would be established in Newport and Covington. And that's not all.

Streetcar Days in Newport

It is 1932. A photograph is taken from atop the Lawyers Building and more or less sums up the Green Line's role in Northern Kentucky transportation. We look toward Third & York in Newport, its historic character accentuated by parks and classic buildings. In the distance is downtown Cincinnati, where a fair percentage of Newport's residents want to go. We can see that two streetcars, one single-truck, the other double-truck, are in view at Third St. heading for Central Bridge, which can be seen above the trees. Two more streetcars pass on the bridge approach. That's the Ohio River, and behind the spire of St. Paul Episcopal Church we find the *Island Queen* at anchorage, ready for another crowd of holiday-makers. We put out of mind the fact that the Great Depression has settled in; this is a pleasant scene, powerfully evocative of better days in transportation.
The Ferguson Antique Mart via C. William Myers.

At the end of the period, the CN&C would purchase suburban operators Alexandria Bus Co., Cold Spring Bus, The Dixie Traction Co., and Black Diamond Stages in 1940, thereby expanding its scope of operations considerably. But before that, the Green Line would overcome the worst natural disaster in the region's history.

In 1930, the Cincinnati, Newport & Covington Railway Co. was responsible for 14 seven-day-a-week streetcar routes and three Monday to Friday rush-hour only routes. These transported Northern Kentucky citizens to and from Cincinnati and to and from destinations on the south side of the Ohio River. Cincinnati's Northern Kentucky suburbs in 1930 had a population of under 200,000.

All of the Green Line's routes, with the exception of 17-Crosstown, crossed the Kentucky-Ohio state line and ran to and from the Dixie Terminal in Cincinnati.

CN&C committed a total of 62 cars in regular all day base service, 110 cars during the morning rush-hour period, and 134 cars in evening rush-hour service. Two routes, 9-Belt Line and 12-Dayton, provided hourly owl services between the hours of midnight and 5 a.m.

These 17 lines, comprising more than 58 route miles, carried some 29 million passengers in 1929. The Green Line owned and maintained a total of 64.9 miles of track, including 62.2 miles of revenue streetcar trackage and 2.7 miles of carbarn tracks and sidings.

In addition it held trackage rights over 3.6 miles of track in Cincinnati. The Green Line operated 26.1 miles of revenue trackage in Campbell County and 36.1 miles in Kenton County. This empire is listed according to the ownership of trackage in the various political subdivisions of Campbell and Kenton Counties:

Standing on Transfer Corner

On this page we present two August, 1935, cameos of Covington's Transfer Corner and starring a pair of south-bound CN&C single-truck cars. In the frame at **right**, car 296 on the 8-Eastern line is heading for its stop on Court between Third and Park Place. The tracks on the left were used by north-bound cars turning left to access the Suspension Bridge, which dominates the background. **Below**, the photographer moves to the right to catch car 128 on the 7-Latonia line. *Both: Ohio Brass Co., Cincinnati Transit Historical Association Collection.*

Campbell County Trackage

City of Dayton	2.584 Miles
City of Fort Thomas	7.151 Miles
Campbell County	.601 Miles
City of Bellevue	3.700 Miles
City of Southgate	.840 Miles
City of Clifton	1.436 Miles
City of Newport	9.980 Miles
	Total 26.1 Miles

Kenton County Trackage

City of South Fort Mitchell	1.648 Miles
Kenton County	2.603 Miles
City of Fort Mitchell	1.471 Miles
City of Park Hills	1.923 Miles
City of Bromley	.306 Miles
City of Ludlow	3.615 Miles
City of Covington	24.616 Miles
	Total 36.1 Miles

Most of the Green Line's revenue trackage was conventionally set into or to one side of city streets. However, the company also maintained considerable private right-of-way double trackage on three routes: 1-Ft. Mitchell (3.75 miles), 11-Ft. Thomas (2.79 miles), and 15-Southgate (1.31 miles). The CN&C charged a universal 5 cent fare for both intrastate and interstate trips, a fare level that it had maintained since 1892. The Green Line also extended universal transfer privileges for any continuous journey.

More Covington Competitors

Long ago, the Green Line had lost its transit monopoly. As we have seen, a number of entrepreneurial, independent bus lines--some financed on a shoestring--were now snapping at the streetcar company's heels. In addition to the companies examined in the preceding chapter, by 1930 four other bus companies had entered into rivalry with the Green Line in the Covington area.

Some citizen groups had been frustrated for years with disruptions to 3-Ludlow streetcar service caused by frequent spring and fall Ohio River flooding. As a consequence, Ludlow businessmen, headed by Gus Simone, started the Ludlow Transit Lines, Inc. in 1927 to provide motor bus service, with the flexibility to take alternate streets around flooded areas, between Ludlow and Cincinnati. Ludlow Transit rapidly gained a reputation for reliable service with immaculately maintained bus equipment and seriously eroded the number of passengers carried by the CN&C on its 3-Ludlow line.

The year 1930 saw Kathryn Ross, no relation to Lloyd Ross, form two new companies: the Citizens Bus Line, doing business as the "Citizens Blue Line," to provide service from Rosedale to downtown Cincinnati via the Suspension Bridge, and the Merchants Bus Line which ran to and from Cincinnati via the Suspension Bridge to Third & Court in Covington, up Madison to 12th, and over the Licking River to Newport via 11th down Monmouth to Third, and over the Fourth St. Bridge back to Covington. The Citizens Bus Line's Rosedale route provided competition for both Ross Motor Coaches and the Green Line's 6-Rosedale line, and the Merchants Bus Line challenged both the Green Line's 9-Belt Line and 17-Crosstown routes.

Kentucky Motor Coach Co., owned by local businessman Ben Perry, also started operations in the same period. Kentucky Motor Coach ran buses from downtown Cincinnati through central Covington and out Highland Ave. to the newly developing suburbs in the South Hills area of Kenton County.

"Fair" Fare Wars

These were not to be tranquil times. The Great Depression of the early 1930s, the advent of motor bus competition, and the increase in private automobile ownership combined to eliminate the Green Line's profits. CN&C ridership fell from 29 million passengers in 1929 to little more than 24 million in 1930. This decline meant lower revenues and, in 1930, the Green Line incurred a substantial net loss ($108,252.27) for the first time in its history.

To plug this financial black hole was the new job of one Philip Gossler Vondersmith, named as general manager of the CN&C on September 16, 1930. Vondersmith, a 1916 Yale graduate and nephew of one of Columbia's principal stockholders, served under Hubert Blackwell, who remained as president and titular head of the company until 1944. Vondersmith would preside over the day-to-day affairs of the Green Line for the next 20 years. He would prove to be uncannily resourceful.

Following a 1931 net operating loss of $147,713.60, the CN&C decided it must challenge the sacrosanct 5 cent fare, whatever the political consequences. The company entered into negotiations in 1932 with all the political subdivisions it served, seeking permission to raise interstate fares to 7 1/2 cents (based on the purchase of two tokens for 15 cents) or 10 cents cash. From 1892 to 1932 the Green Line had maintained a uniform 5 cent fare. The message was simple: since it was plunging deeper into the red, CN&C could not afford to continue present service levels or properly maintain its cars and tracks based on a fare that had not increased in 40 years.

Not surprisingly, the proposed fare increase was a political non-starter in depressed Northern Kentucky, even though the Green Line had not sought an increase in the 5 cent intrastate fare. One city council after another either turned down or refused to even consider the Green Line proposal.

By March, 1933, it was clear that no city was going to approve a fare increase of any amount. Vondersmith now brought out the legal artillery. Soon, the Green Line sought and obtained an injunction from the U. S. District Court for the Eastern District of Kentucky restraining all Northern Kentucky cities it served from interfering with the collection of a 7 1/2 cent northbound interstate fare. At the same time, following the refusal by the city of Cincinnati to agree to an increased southbound

Competition: the Streetcar's Still on Top

At mid-decade, the battle for the Northern Kentucky transit market raged on. A Peoples Central bus turns south to climb up the ramp to the Suspension Bridge as Green Line car 121 glides into the Dixie Terminal. By 1936, when this photo was taken, Peoples Central and Ross Motor Coaches, both owned by Lloyd Ross, fielded five routes which competed with the Green Line. In the background looms the 376 foot tall Union Central Building completed in 1914. The streetcar is figuratively above it all; motor buses were not allowed into Dixie Terminal, and wouldn't be for years.   *T. W. Lehmann Collection.*

POINTS OF INTEREST IN NORTHERN KENTUCKY AND HOW TO REACH THEM BY STREET CAR

Place	Route	Time from Terminal	Car Stop and Distance from Stop
American Legion Club, Newport	Belt Line No. 9, Southgate No. 15	9 minutes	Sixth & York—½ square
Bathing Beaches, Bellevue	Bellevue & Dayton No. 12	15 "	Van Voast Ave.—2 squares
Bathing Beaches, Dayton	Bellevue & Dayton No. 12	17 "	6th & Walnut—four squares
Bellevue High School	Bellevue & Dayton No. 12	12 "	Fairfield & LaFayette—3 squares
	South Bellevue No. 13	14 "	Taylor & Center—one square
Booth Memorial Hospital, Covington	All Covington Cars	4 "	2nd & Court—2½ squares
Carnegie Library, Covington	Rosedale No.6, Latonia No. 7, Holman No. 5, Ft. Mitchell No. 1, Belt No. 9	10 "	Robbins & Madison—one square
Carnegie Library, Newport	Ft. Thomas No. 11, Bellevue & Dayton No. 12, South Bellevue No. 13	8 "	Fourth & York—one square Third & Monmouth—one square
Covington Chamber of Commerce	Rosedale No. 6, Latonia No. 7, Holman No. 5, Belt No. 9, Ft. Mitchell No. 1	7 "	Seventh & Madison—1 square
Covington Ball Park	Main No. 4	11 "	9th & Main—three squares
Covington Court House	All Covington Cars	4 "	Third & Court Sts.
Covington Post Office	All Covington Cars	4 "	Third & Court Sts.
Covington Reservoir, Ft. Thomas	Ft. Thomas No. 11	33 "	Reservoir
Dayton High School	Bellevue & Dayton No. 12	17 "	Sixth & Walnut—two squares
DeVou Park, Covington	Ft. Mitchell, No. 1	23 "	Park Hills—two squares
Elk's Home, Newport	All Newport Cars	7 "	Third & York
Evergreen Cemetery, Southgate	Southgate No. 15	22 "	End of Car Line
Ft. Mitchell Country Club	Ft. Mitchell No. 1	29 "	Ft. Mitchell Ave.—3 squares
Ft. Thomas Military Post	Ft. Thomas, No. 11	33 "	Military Park
Highland Cemetery, Ft. Mitchell	Ft. Mitchell No. 1	30 "	Highland Cemetery
Highland Country Club, Ft. Thomas	Ft. Thomas No. 11	36 "	Grandview—3 squares
Highlands High School, Ft. Thomas	Ft. Thomas No. 11	27 "	Montrose Ave.
Holmes High School, Covington	Latonia No. 7, Rosedale No. 6	20 "	26th & Madison
Knights of Columbus Hall, Covington	Rosedale No. 6, Latonia No. 7, Ft. Mitchell No. 1, Holman No. 5	11 "	11th & Madison
Knights of Columbus, Newport	All Newport Cars	7 "	Third & York
Knights of Pythias, Newport	Ft. Thomas No. 11	11 "	Seventh & Washington—1 square
LaSalette Academy, Covington	Eastern No. 8, Greenup No. 2	7 "	Seventh & Greenup Sts.
Latonia Race Track (Main Entrance)	Latonia, No. 7	28 "	Race Track
Latonia Race Track (Rear Entrance)	Rosedale No. 6	27 "	Southern & Decoursey—one square
Linden Grove Cemetery, Covington	Holman No. 5	16 "	Linden & Holman, 14th & Holman
Ludlow Baseball Park	Ludlow No. 3	20 "	Oldham Street—one square
Ludlow High School	Ludlow No. 3	22 "	Adelia Ave.
Ludlow Lagoon, Ludlow	Ludlow, No. 3	24 "	Lake Street
Masonic Temple, Covington	All Covington Cars	5 "	Fourth & Scott
Mother of God Cemetery, Covington	Latonia No. 7	27 "	35th and Latonia—3 squares
Newport City Park	All Newport Cars	7 "	Third & York
Newport Commercial & Civic Ass'n	Belt Line No. 9, Southgate No. 15	8 "	Fourth & York—1 square
Newport Court House	Belt Line No. 9, Southgate No. 15	8 "	Fourth & York Sts.
Newport High School	Belt Line No. 9, Southgate No. 15	11 "	Eighth & York—one square
Newport Post Office	Ft. Thomas No. 11	12 "	Eighth & Washington Sts.
Newport Reservoir, Ft. Thomas	Ft. Thomas No. 11	23 "	Reservoir
Notre Dame Academy, Covington	Rosedale No. 6, Latonia No. 7, Holman No. 5, Ft. Mitchell No. 1, Belt No. 9	6 "	Fifth & Madison—one square
Rosedale Swimming Pool	Rosedale No. 6	32 "	End of Line—three squares
Speers Hospital, Dayton	Bellevue & Dayton No. 12	21 "	Fifth & Main Sts.
St. Elizabeth Hospital, Covington	Eastern No. 8	17 "	21st & Eastern
St. Mary's Cathedral, Covington	Rosedale No. 6, Latonia No. 7	12 "	12th & Madison
St. Mary's Cemetery, Ft. Mitchell	Ft. Mitchell No. 1	28 "	Cemetery
St. Paul's Guild Hall, Newport	All Newport Cars	7 "	Third & York
Tacoma Park, Dayton	Bellevue & Dayton No. 12	23 "	Fourth & Benham—2 squares
Twin Oaks Country Club	Rosedale No. 6	28 "	43rd & Huntington—3 squares
WCKY Radio Station, Covington	Rosedale No. 6, Latonia No. 7, Holman No. 5, Ft. Mitchell No. 1, Belt No. 9	7 "	Sixth & Madison
Y. M. C. A. Camp, Rosedale	Rosedale No. 6	32 "	End of Car Line—3 squares

DIXIE TERMINAL

The Dixie Terminal, common terminus in Cincinnati for all Green Line street cars operating across the Ohio River, is located at Fourth and Walnut Streets.

Two floors of the building are occupied by the Green Line. The Newport Division cars use the ground level, entering and leaving via Third Street. Covington Division cars use the second floor level, entering and leaving by inclined ramps off Suspension Bridge.

Conductors collect no fares in the Terminal Building, all being paid to cashiers at the entrance to each terminal before boarding cars.

Routes operating into the Dixie Terminal Building are:

COVINGTON DIVISION

Ft. Mitchell—Number 1
Greenup—Number 2
Ludlow—Number 3
Main—Number 4
Holman—Number 5
Rosedale—Number 6
Latonia—Number 7
Eastern Avenue—Number 8
Covington-Newport (Belt Line)—Number 9
Lewisburg (Rush Hours Only)—Number 10

NEWPORT DIVISION

Newport-Covington (Belt Line)—Number 9
Ft. Thomas—Number 11
Dayton—Number 12
South Bellevue—Number 13
Southgate—Number 15
Washington (Rush Hours Only)—Number 16
York (Rush Hours Only)

———◆———

CROSSTOWN

The Crosstown Line, No. 17, operates between Third and York Streets, Newport, and Third and Court Streets, Covington, providing facilities for direct transportation between Newport and Covington and the transfer of Kentucky passengers between Campbell County and Kenton County routes.

———◆———

BELT LINE

The Covington and Newport Line, No. 9, known as the Belt Line, affords a pleasant ride in two states, three cities, three counties and across two rivers and three bridges in slightly more than half an hour. After leaving the Dixie Terminal in Cincinnati the Belt Line travels through both Newport and Covington. It uses two bridges in crossing the Ohio River twice in one round trip and a third bridge in crossing the Licking River between Covington and Newport.

SCENIC BEAUTY

Northern Kentucky's scenic beauty can be viewed to great advantage from a ride on Ft. Mitchell Line No. 1, Ft. Thomas Line No. 11, or Southgate Line No. 15.

———◆———

FREQUENT SERVICE

Cars operate frequently over all routes, providing convenient service to all points. The approximate time between cars on our regular schedules is as follows:

Eastern Ave.	11 minutes
Greenup	11 minutes
Latonia	11 minutes
Rosedale	11 minutes
Main Street	8 minutes
Ludlow	8 minutes
Holman	10 minutes
Ft. Mitchell	17 minutes
Belt Line	11 minutes
Southgate	11 minutes
Ft. Thomas	12 minutes
South Bellevue	12 minutes
Bellevue & Dayton	8 minutes

During morning and evening rush hours more frequent service is provided, and for special events, such as Latonia Race Track meets, service is greatly augmented, with cars operating as frequently as one every minute from Dixie Terminal.

Where two routes operate over the same streets, cars are so scheduled that time intervals between cars on streets where both lines operate are cut in half. For instance, on Madison Ave., Covington, where both Rosedale and Latonia lines operate, the time between cars is 5½ minutes instead of the regular 11-minute space between cars on any one of the two lines.

———◆———

INFORMATION—Special Cars

Inspectors in the Dixie Terminal Building and at important points along the routes, or any conductor or motorman, will gladly give detailed information about schedules or any other information you may desire.

Arrangements may readily be made for special cars by phoning the office at Third & Court Sts., Covington, HEmlock 2300. In addition to regular cars, two beautifully appointed pullman-type cars, The Kentucky and The Blue Grass, are available for parties.

Public transit was still a vital lifeline in 1932 because only one in seven families in Northern Kentucky owned an automobile. That's why this Green Line brochure was kept by a lot of households in a handy place. The CN&C use of the term "squares" equates to the more common term "block". *T. W. Lehmann Collection.*

The first major conversion from rail to bus on the Green Line was the 15-Southgate. Car 222, from the first batch of convertible cars delivered to the Green Line in 1893, leaves Newport for Cincinnati a few months before buses took over in 1936. The conductor performs the time-honored ritual of raising the second pole to operate over Cincinnati's rare two-wire system. *George Krambles Collection.*

fare of the same amount, the CN&C sought an injunction from the U. S. District Court for the Southern District of Ohio to restrain the city of Cincinnati from preventing its collection of a 10 cent cash fare or a 7 1/2 cent token fare for southbound interstate journeys.

That court, however, refused to grant the Green Line an injunction. Thereupon, on July 9, 1933, the Green Line established a 10 cent northbound cash fare (or a 7 1/2 cent token fare) but could make no changes in the southbound 5 cent fare. Thus, as of that date, the total round trip interstate fare became 12 1/2 cents (if a token was used for the northbound leg to Cincinnati) or 15 cents cash.

A Crazy-Quilt Fare Pattern

It promptly became a legal free-for-all. Aroused Northern Kentucky municipalities appealed the granting of the injunction by the Kentucky federal court and the Green Line appealed the denial of the injunction by the Ohio federal court. After consolidating all the cases, the Sixth Circuit Court of Appeals found, in February of 1934, that municipalities could, in the absence of federal regulation, regulate interstate fares if they had entered into binding franchise agreements for such fares for a definite number of years.

The appellate court found that CN&C's franchise with the city of Cincinnati (running until 1942) mandating a southbound 5 cent interstate fare was valid, as were certain franchises fixing northbound fares over segments of various Green Line routes in Kenton County. No other existing franchise agreements in Kenton County were deemed by the court to be valid and no Campbell County franchises mandating the 5 cent fare were found to be valid.

The Green Line could raise northbound interstate fares across the board on all Campbell County routes and certain streetcar routes in Kenton County, but the Court of Appeals ruled that the Green Line could charge only a 5 cent interstate fare for passengers boarding northbound streetcars on the 1-Ft. Mitchell line between the Covington city line and 12th & Holman, the 5-Holman line on Holman between 18th and Pike or boarding either eastbound or westbound 9-Belt Line streetcars on 12th between Madison and the Licking River.

These route segments were covered by a 5 cent provision in a franchise awarded for a period of 50 years by the city of Covington in 1890 to the Cincinnati, Covington and Rosedale Railway, a company acquired by the Green Line System in 1892. The outer portions of the 3-Ludlow line also were found to be subject to the 5 cent ceiling due to earlier franchise awards by the cities of Ludlow and West Covington to the Cincinnati, West Covington and Ludlow Street Railway Company in 1893. What had been a simple, blanket 5 cent fare was now to become a complicated mess. It was enough to make an accountant cry.

Beating the system now became possible--if you could figure it out. The decision created an anomaly where a prospective Covington passenger could actually be charged a higher interstate fare for boarding a northbound streetcar closer in to Cincinnati than passengers boarding farther out on the lines mentioned above. Depending on the particular car line, knowledgeable riders going to Cincinnati would walk north, east or west a block or two to save money.

The Appeals Court's decision created a hodgepodge of different fares, but what was worse, it denied the Green Line most of the relief it requested. Nevertheless, the judges admitted that the CN&C was not crying financial wolf. In its ruling, the court observed:

Workhorses of the Green Line

On the street or behind the scenes, the Green Line employed a fleet of rail-bound and rubber-tired workhorses (though the vehicles may seem quaint today) to get the maintenance job done. By the mid-1930s, this work was increasingly done by its Mack trucks. The C&O Railway's Licking River bridge forms the backdrop for the **above** lineup of trucks.
Special Collections and Archives, University of Kentucky Libraries.

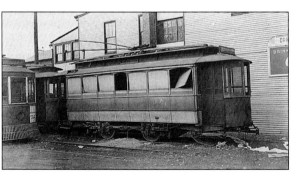

You may not think of a transfer table as a vehicle, but it is. We see at **left** the only known view of the transfer table that connected the main overhaul shop in Newport with the paint and woodworking annexes. Below that at **middle left** is sand car No. 8, converted from passenger car 68, originally built by Brownell in 1893. It came in handy on rainy or snowy days--and it does snow in Northern Kentucky! If the sand car is homely, the vehicle at the **bottom left** of the page is downright ugly. Ugly, but important. If supplies too unwieldy for a work car were to be hauled, this powered flat car filled the bill. These rail cars were needed on the 1-Ft. Mitchell and 11-Ft. Thomas lines because of their long stretches of private right-of-way. Trucks were good enough for the other streetcar lines. *All: Sol Korkes; Phil Lind Collection.*

The January, 1937, flood brought out another Green Line non-revenue vehicle: the testing car. Rebuilt in 1903 from an 1890 Stephenson car, it is shown **above** checking the condition of the little used connecting tracks between the lower and upper levels of Dixie Terminal. The CN&C wanted to use them to divert the Newport-Cincinnati cars away from flooded Central Bridge approaches. Alas, within 24 hours, Covington's rail approaches were flooded out too. *James Gibson Collection.*

"For many years the appellee has charged a 5-cent fare from the Kentucky cities to Cincinnati. It appears in the proofs that 70 percent or more of its traffic originating in these cities is interstate traffic for Cincinnati. It further appears that for several years it has not earned the interest on its bonds, and since January 1, 1930, it has been operating at a substantial loss. It may thus be accepted for the purpose of decision that the 5-cent fare it has heretofore charged is inadequate, and that reasonable rates for such service would not exceed those which it proposes to establish."

It did not take long for Green Line riders in Northern Kentucky to become fed up with this crazy-quilt pattern of fares. Settlements between CN&C and all Northern Kentucky cities were reached in 1935-1936. These resulted in an interstate northbound cash fare of 8 cents or token fare of 6 1/4 cents (by the purchase of four tokens for 25 cents). However, the city of Cincinnati became a holdout to uniform fares by refusing to renegotiate its 1917 agreement, which was not set to expire until 1942. Thus, the Green Line could charge only a 5 cent southbound interstate fare, making the Dixie Terminal a sort of "cut rate" transit store, that is, if you were going in the right direction.

Relief--and More Confusion

In October, 1935, President Franklin D. Roosevelt signed into law the Motor Carriers Regulation Act. This new law, among its other provisions, provided that the Interstate Commerce Commission would have sole authority to regulate the routes and fares of all companies operating motor bus service in interstate commerce.

Suddenly, the Green Line saw hope. After Cincinnati refused the Green Line's request to raise the southbound interstate fare to match the northbound interstate fare of the 6 1/4 cent token or 8 cent cash fare granted by all Northern Kentucky cities, the CN&C applied to the ICC to set a uniform interstate fare tariff. The CN&C anticipated that the Motor Carriers Regulation Act would be construed by the ICC to apply to all the operations of all interstate carriers, even those which operated a mix of bus and streetcar equipment.

However, a hair-splitting decision by the ICC in 1936 did not put an end to the CN&C's agonizing crazy-quilt interstate fare structure. The ICC granted the CN&C's request to standardize its northbound and southbound interstate fares at 6 1/4 cents token or 8 cents cash but only as it pertained to its interstate motor bus routes. The ICC held it did not have authority over interstate transit routes operated by "electrically powered vehicles."

Thus, the city of Cincinnati continued to compel the CN&C to charge only a 5 cent southbound interstate fare on any of its routes operated by streetcars or (later) trolley-coaches. As a result, a passenger wishing to take the CN&C from Cincinnati to Northern Kentucky could now play a game of fare roulette depending solely on what type of transit vehicle he or she boarded.

Meanwhile, in the volatile world of the Northern Kentucky independent bus operators, some consolidation was taking place. In January, 1935, Lloyd Ross bought out all minority interests in Peoples Transit Co. and the Central Transit Co., merging the two entities into Peoples Central Transit Lines Inc. In response, Ben Perry, owner of Kentucky Motor Coach, and Kathryn Ross,

owner of both Citizens and Merchants joined forces, forming Citizens-Merchants Bus Lines. They continued to operate Kentucky Motor Coach as a separate entity.

Then, in late 1935, Lloyd Ross purchased the Celo Bottling Co. plant on Madison for use as a garage to maintain all the buses of Peoples Central and Ross Motor Coaches. Probably due to regulatory or tax reasons, Peoples Central was not formally merged into Ross Motor Coaches.

The Grandfather Clause

The Motor Carriers Regulation Act of 1935 said that no motor carrier could operate in interstate commerce without the approval of the Interstate Commerce Commission, but the Act provided that carriers engaged in interstate motor transport operations prior to October, 1935, automatically qualified as interstate carriers. This meant that The Dixie Traction Co., Lloyd Ross' two companies (Peoples Central and Ross Motor Coaches), Citizens-Merchants Bus Lines, Kentucky Motor Coaches, and Ludlow Transit were all "grandfathered."

There was also some benefit for the Green Line in the new law, which said that no bus companies could establish new competitive interstate routes without applying first to the Interstate Commerce Commission for a certificate of "convenience and necessity." In other words, although a number of competitors had already menaced Green Line System's interstate market share by 1935, in the future new interstate certificates would be hard to come by.

Two other Northern Kentucky bus firms also helped themselves to some of the Green Line's market in the 1930s. One was Black Diamond Stages Inc., founded by Edward Murphy in 1929,

The track diagrams of the Green Line's Covington and Newport divisions on this page and page 95 are adapted from official company records.
T. W. Lehmann Collection.

Covington Division ca. 1935

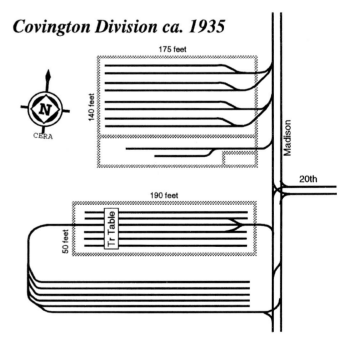

to provide bus service between the villages of Ross, Melbourne, Silver Grove, Brent (all of which boasted a combined population of less than 2000) and Ft. Thomas. Interstate operation between Ross and Cincinnati was inaugurated in February, 1930. The route was officially described as:

Between Ross and Cincinnati via Melbourne, Silver Grove, Brent, Ft. Thomas and Newport, Ky., over River Rd., Ft. Thomas and Grand Aves., Newport city streets (Grand to Tenth, Tenth to Washington and Washington to Third to the L&N Bridge) to Cincinnati.

Black Diamond Stages was restricted by its 1930 Kentucky certificate to interstate only operations, i. e., it could not pick up or discharge passengers in Ft. Thomas, Southgate and Newport unless they were bound for Cincinnati. Black Diamond provided the only service along part of Grand in both Ft. Thomas and Newport and, since it could pick up and discharge passengers on Ft. Thomas Ave. in Ft. Thomas and Washington in Newport bound to or from Cincinnati, BDS was a direct competitor to portions of two CN&C streetcar lines (11 and 16) for passengers bound to and from Cincinnati.

On August 12, 1937, Black Diamond was issued a certificate of public convenience and necessity (MC-588) by the Interstate Commerce Commission. The ICC found that Black Diamond's route predated the Motor Carriers Regulation Act and was entitled to grandfather clause protection. By 1937, Black Diamond owned nine buses and operated 38 round trips daily except Sundays between Ft. Thomas and Cincinnati and six round trips daily except Sundays between Ross and Cincinnati. Sunday service was approximately one-half of the weekday schedule.

The Cold Spring Bus Co.

The Cold Spring Bus Co. was formed in 1931 by local Cold Spring businessman Paul Schwerling following the purchase of the Gosney shuttle from Alexandria and Cold Spring to the end of the Ft. Thomas car line. In addition, Schwerling took in the Neiser Co. which also operated an intrastate route between Cold Spring via then U. S. 27 (now East Alexandria Pike) primarily to the end of the Green Line's 11-Ft. Thomas streetcar line but with a few rush hour trips extending along U. S. 27 in Newport.

In September of 1934, Cold Spring Bus was given authority by the State of Kentucky (certificate No. 50) to extend its route from Ft. Thomas to Third & York in Newport. Cold Spring passengers desiring to go on to Cincinnati had to board a CN&C streetcar at Third & York. Further, certificate No. 50 still prohibited the Cold Spring Bus Co. from competing with the CN&C at any point where a CN&C streetcar line paralleled the new bus route by stating:

"[T]hat no passengers be picked up and then discharged anywhere between the end of the Streetcar Line at Ft. Thomas and their terminal in Newport, Kentucky, but permission is given to the said Cold Spring Bus Company to pick up passengers between Cold Spring, Kentucky and the end of the Streetcar Line to be delivered at points in Newport over their route into Newport, and passengers may be picked up at any point over their route in Newport, or between Newport and the end of the Streetcar Line, to be discharged at points between Cold Spring and the end of the Streetcar Line at Ft. Thomas, Kentucky."

Some of these restrictions would be ignored. Cold Spring Bus, on September 24, 1935, began interstate operations across the Central Bridge into Cincinnati, thus depriving the CN&C of some interstate traffic. Cold Spring Bus, it seemed, had slipped in just under the wire. In 1937, the ICC granted it a certificate of public convenience and necessity (MC-50495) finding that the company had started interstate operations just days prior to the effective date of the Motor Carriers Regulation Act and thus qualified under the Act's grandfather clause.

The total length of the route from Cold Spring to Cincinnati was approximately eight miles. The 1937 population of the Cold Spring District, extending from the southern corporate limits of Ft. Thomas, was about 5000. No other carrier provided a through passenger service between Cold Spring and Cincinnati.

Cold Spring Bus, in 1937, operated one 18-passenger, one 21-passenger, and two 25-passenger buses all built by White. It

Newport Division ca. 1935

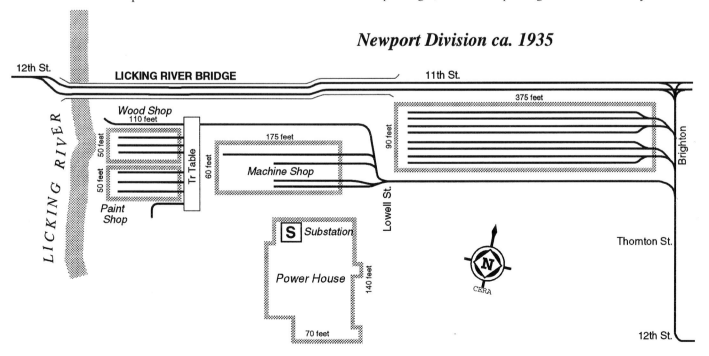

offered 11 interstate round trips per day, Monday to Friday. A half-hourly schedule between Cold Spring and Cincinnati was maintained during the morning and evening rush hours between 6 a.m. and 8:30 a.m. and between 4 p.m. and 6:30 p.m.

Since service was furnished only between Cold Spring and Newport during the other hours of the weekday (and on Saturdays), Cincinnati bound passengers found it necessary to transfer to the Green Line in either Ft. Thomas or Newport during these non-peak periods. Twelve weekday and six Saturday intrastate round trips were operated between Cold Spring and Newport via Ft. Thomas. No Sunday operations were conducted.

A June, 1937, ridership survey revealed 871 passengers boarded the Cold Spring Bus buses between 6 a.m. and 8:30 a.m., of which 75 left the buses in Ft. Thomas, 204 in Newport, and 592 in Cincinnati. During the same week, Cold Spring Bus trans-ported 1056 passengers on its southbound trips between 4 p.m. and 6:30 p.m., with 755 patrons boarding the buses in Cincinnati, 247 in Newport, and 54 in Ft. Thomas, an average of more than 20 passengers per trip.

Cold Spring Bus clearly was a viable competitive carrier.

Fighting for Passengers

Northern Kentucky was now a boiling cauldron of transit competition. Every day there was strife between the bus companies and the Green Line, and the private bus lines were fighting among themselves. Sometimes the companies took to the law courts--and sometimes there were altercations. A *Kentucky Post* story in July, 1936 discloses that Citizens-Merchants Bus Line had filed two suits against Lloyd Ross alleging that, on two sep-

ANOTHER VISIT
to
Dixie
Terminal

Despite acts of man and God, such as depression and floods, Dixie Terminal in the 1930s remained a beehive of activity, a Mecca for traction watchers. The scene at **left** is typical of the afternoon rush hour, when things got very busy on the approach track to the upper deck. We can see two closed single-truckers bracketing a convertible patiently awaiting their turn at the horseshoe track. Note the neon sign directing motorists to the Suspension Bridge. *James Gibson.*

Double truck car 514 loads in the lower level of the Dixie Terminal sometime prior to its rebuilding in 1937 for one man operation as evidenced by the fact that the car still has a chimney on the roof and a narrow front door. Route numbers on Green Line cars first appeared in 1921 in conjunction with the opening of the Dixie Terminal. Also note in the photograph at **right** the route numbers on the back fence (placed above the coffee advertisement) to indicate where cars serving the various routes are supposed to stop for loading. The 13-South Bellevue cars were to pull a bit further forward. *Special Collections and Archives, University of Kentucky Libraries.*

arate occasions, Peoples Central Transit Lines' drivers had rammed into Citizens-Merchants buses in an attempt to arrive first at a downtown Covington corner to pick up passengers.

A January, 1937, *Kentucky Post* article tells how rival bus drivers were cited to police court for racing down a Covington street in another bid to be the first to pick up passengers. Involved yet again were drivers of the Peoples Central Transit Lines and the Citizens-Merchants Bus Line. In court, one bus driver said that the other threatened to "whip me" if he tried to pick up any passengers in Cincinnati.

Newspaper accounts of the 1930s are also replete with stories of fights breaking out in the Third & Court area in Covington and the Third & York neighborhood in Newport between motormen and conductors of the Green Line and bus operators for some of the companies.

It is said by old time veterans of the Green Line that the motormen usually won, because they were "always in training" thanks to muscles built up by use of the manual handbrake on the single-truck streetcars.

A New Low

Green Line ridership in 1935 fell to a low of 20,929,019 passengers. As elsewhere during the Great Depression, people in Northern Kentucky without jobs had less need to travel. The CN&C lost slightly more than half a million dollars that year. In fact, the Green Line was now permanently in the red, losing money in every year from 1930 to 1941. The total deficit for the period was a staggering $5 million.

Yet between 1929 (the last marginally profitable year) and

Looking north from the Suspension Bridge **above**, the company photographer illustrates the approach to the upper level of the Dixie Terminal used by the CN&C's Covington Division cars. Intruding into the picture is a Dixie Traction bus coming up from Third and heading for Florence. *Earl Clark Collection.*

Newport division cars used the streets to access the lower level of Dixie Terminal. 9-Belt Line car 125 **above** has just emerged from the building, while car 122, **right**, on the 13-South Bellevue line has just crossed the intersection of Third & Walnut and is about to duck into the lower level of the building. *Both: Earl Clark Collection.*

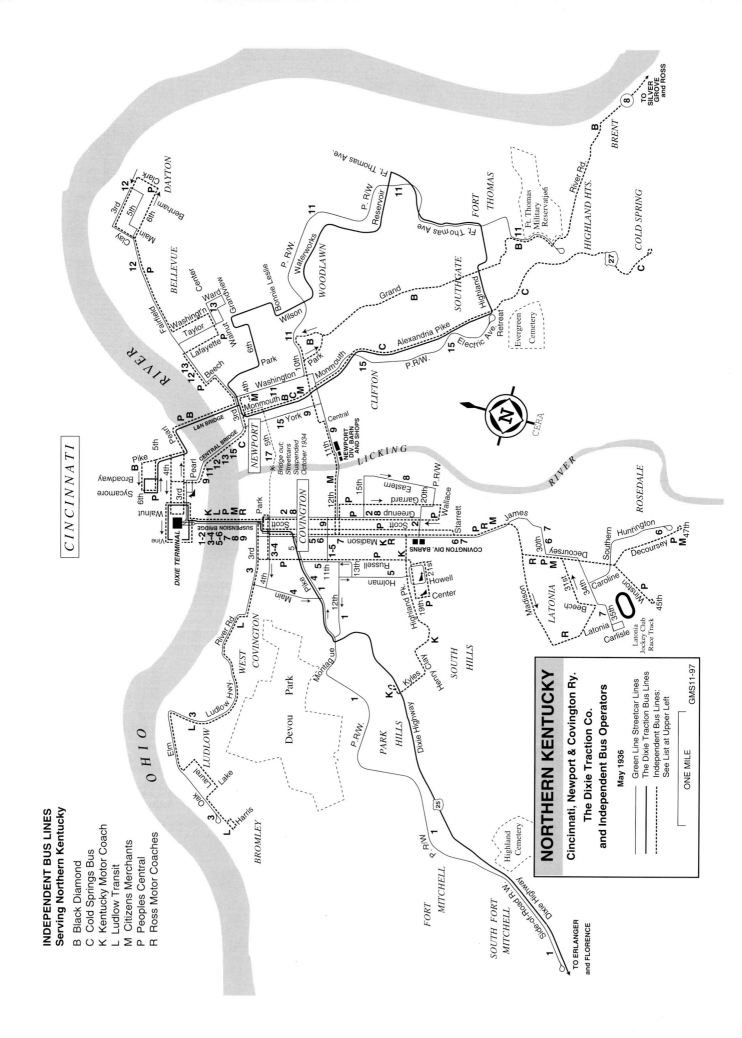

INDEPENDENT BUS LINES
Serving Northern Kentucky

B Black Diamond
C Cold Springs Bus
K Kentucky Motor Coach
L Ludlow Transit
M Citizens Merchants
P Peoples Central
R Ross Motor Coaches

NORTHERN KENTUCKY

Cincinnati, Newport & Covington Ry.
The Dixie Traction Co.
and Independent Bus Operators

May 1936

——— Green Line Streetcar Lines
——— The Dixie Traction Bus Lines
- - - - Independent Bus Lines:
See List at Upper Left

ONE MILE

GMS11-97

1935, only relatively minor service cuts were made. Service had not been seriously cut, as it had in other cities. In April, 1930, the CN&C ran 62 cars in base service over its full-time routes. By April of 1935, the company was still dispatching 60 cars to handle base service. During weekday rush hours in 1935, the Green Line put out an average of 103 streetcars in the morning and 117 in the afternoon, compared to a 1930 average of 110 cars and 130 cars, respectively.

In reality, the moderate cut in the number of rush-hour cars dispatched did not increase headways by more than one or two minutes on most lines because of the abolition of end of line layovers, better scheduling in general and better line supervision. All this contributed to improved car utilization. One device for the relief of motormen (literally) was for an extra-board man to take a car from Third & York or Third & Court to Cincinnati and back, thereby allowing the regular crew to visit the loo and grab a bite of lunch.

Northern Kentuckians were lucky. The Green Line's parents had deep pockets. The reason the CN&C did not resort to draconian service cuts or simply go out of business and turn the market over to its competitors lies in its ownership by Columbia Gas and Electric.

Not only was the CN&C the only street railway owned by Columbia (and thus a minor factor in its overall profit and loss statement), but more significant was Columbia's ownership of the Union Light, Heat and Power Co., the provider of gas and electricity to the very same population served by the Green Line. It is pretty obvious that Columbia suffered the significant losses of the Green Line only because it wanted to maintain intact its lucrative utility business and could do without irate street railway patrons showing up at the state capitol of Frankfort every time it applied for a utility rate hike.

The First Streetcar Replacement

As comforting as this financial stability was in times of economic crisis, the Green Line was not about to overlook

Time has almost expired for streetcars on the 15-Southgate line. We are at Sycamore & Third as No. 267 heads for the Dixie Terminal in Cincinnati on April 20, 1936. The 15-Southgate received motor buses in May of 1936. The route number can be seen prominently displayed on the car's fender. This was one of the Green Line's redeeming idiosyncrasies.
Don McClain, Dave Arganbright Collection.

economies, even if they meant change. An opportunity soon appeared, and it finally put the CN&C in the bus business.

In 1935, the Chesapeake and Ohio Railway and the Louisville & Nashville Railroad started construction in Newport of an underpass, partially financed by the Works Progress Administration, one of President Roosevelt's job-creating alphabet-soup agencies. The underpass was intended to route Monmouth St. between 11th and 15th under the C&O and L&N tracks and eliminate a busy and dangerous grade crossing.

This had long been a traffic bottleneck. The Green Line's 15-Southgate streetcars crossed at grade, on Monmouth between 11th and 12th, both the L&N's single track and the Chesapeake and Ohio's adjoining three track mainline. The rail crossing was protected by gates maintained by the CN&C and by a watchman employed by the street railway.

Excavation work began on February 3, 1936. On that date the Green Line streetcars on the 15-Southgate line from Cincinnati were turned back at 11th & York and substitute shuttle bus service was instituted over a temporary route west on 11th to Central, then south on Central over the narrow bridge (known to Newport natives as the "Wagon Bridge") which spanned the C&O/L&N tracks, and then zigzagging on to Southgate. To equip this shuttle service

A cold, blustery day greeted Green Line and city officials and the good citizens of Newport who, on December 16, 1936, came to celebrate the opening of the Monmouth St. underpass. Mack 61 is driven by Dave Abney. In prior times, Green Line 15-Southgate cars crossed the tracks of both the Chesapeake and Ohio and Louisville & Nashville railroads at grade. *Special Collections and Archives, University of Kentucky Libraries.*

The Green Line   **99**

The Ludlow Transit Inc. was one of the classier independent bus operators which competed with the Green Line. This is a builder's photo of Ludlow's No. 46, a Dodge with a Superior body. We know little else about it. Most of the independents were poorly documented, at least in photos.

Motor Bus Society.

the Green Line purchased from Cincinnati Street Railway four second hand 25-passenger Yellow Coach model Z-29 buses (Nos. 11-14). These were the first buses ever operated by the Green Line System.

Management soon learned to like them. In the spring of 1936, the CN&C obtained permission from both Newport and Southgate authorities to convert the entire 15-Southgate streetcar route to motor coach operation. To do this, the Green Line obtained five model 6-CQ-3S 31-passenger buses from Mack (Nos. 61-65). The rail to rubber conversion of 15-Southgate took place on Sunday, May 24, 1936.

The Newport and Southgate ordinances authorizing the conversion of the 15-Southgate streetcar line to motor coach operation specified a route from Third & York south on York to 11th, east to Monmouth and south on Monmouth (or Alexandria Pike at the Newport corporation line) to Blue Grass, west on Blue Grass to Electric, south on Electric to Ridgeway, west on Ridgeway to Walnut, east on Walnut to Evergreen, south on Evergreen to Temple and east on Temple to Alexandria Pike. The new bus route then returned north on Alexandria Pike toward Newport.

Buses lacked one streetcar advantage: they couldn't use private right-of-way. Unless, of course, it was paved. This was duly accomplished, and the route was slightly modified in September of 1938 with the completion of the paving over of Southgate's abandoned streetcar private way, proceeding from Bluegrass south on a newly extended (and aptly named) Electric Ave. all the way to Temple. The new buses on the 15-Southgate route, however, continued to use the temporary detour from 11th & York via the Wagon Bridge until completion of the Monmouth St. underpass on December 15, 1936.

The CN&C's use of certain Cincinnati streets for its new 15-Southgate bus line was part of a comprehensive city of Cincinnati 1936 restructuring of the routes used by all Northern Kentucky transit companies to gain access to Cincinnati. Because of this, a record exists to tell us exactly how all the Northern Kentucky buses were handled at this time in the big city:

"On and after Sunday, May 24, 1936, Kentucky buses in Cincinnati will operate [by order of the Dept. of Utilities] over the following routes:

Cold Spring Bus Co. and Cincinnati, Newport & Covington Ry. Co. From Central Bridge to Broadway, north on Broadway to Fourth St., west on Fourth St. to Walnut St., south on Walnut St. to Third St., east on Third St. to Broadway, south on Broadway to Central Bridge.

Black Diamond Stages. From L & N Bridge to Pearl St., west on Pearl St. to Broadway, north on Broadway to Sixth St., west on Sixth St. to Sycamore St., south on Sycamore St. to Fifth St., east on Fifth St. to Broadway, south on Broadway to Pearl St., east on Pearl St. to L & N Bridge.

Dixie Traction Co. To and From L & N Bridge - From L & N Bridge to Pearl St., west on Pearl St. to Pike St., north on Pike St. to Fifth St., west on Fifth St. to Broadway, north on Broadway to Sixth St., west on Sixth St. to Sycamore St., south on Sycamore St. to Fifth St., east on Fifth St. to Pike St., south on Pike St. to Pearl St., east on Pearl St. to L & N Bridge.

To and from Suspension Bridge - From Suspension Bridge to Third St., east on Third St. to Main St., north on Main St. to Fourth St., west on Fourth St. to Vine St., south on Vine St. to Third St., east on Third St. to Suspension Bridge.

To and from C & O Bridge - From C & O Bridge to Third St., east on Third St. to John St., north on John St. to Fifth St., east on Fifth St.

The side-wheeler *Island Queen* left from the foot of Broadway, affording CN&C riders access to such attractions as the Coney island amusement park. We see the *Queen* passing under the Suspension Bridge **below**, while in the **lower left** is a 1937 Coney Island excursion ticket for employees of Columbia-owned Union Light, Heat and Power and the CN&C. *W. T. Myers, C. William Myers Collection; T. W. Lehmann Collection.*

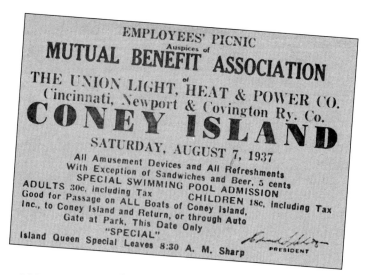

EMPLOYEES' PICNIC

Auspices of

MUTUAL BENEFIT ASSOCIATION

of

THE UNION LIGHT, HEAT & POWER CO.

Cincinnati, Newport & Covington Ry. Co.

CONEY ISLAND

SATURDAY, AUGUST 7, 1937

All Amusement Devices and All Refreshments
With Exception of Sandwiches and Beer, 5 cents
SPECIAL SWIMMING POOL ADMISSION
ADULTS 30c, including Tax   CHILDREN 18c, including Tax
Good for Passage on ALL Boats of Coney Island,
Inc., to Coney Island and Return, or through Auto
Gate at Park, This Date Only

"SPECIAL"

Island Queen Special Leaves 8:30 A. M. Sharp

PRESIDENT

The complex bargain between the Green Line and the city of Newport resulted in three new bus routes, started in May, 1936. They are shown on the map, **above**. To equip them, the Green Line bought five new 25-passenger buses including No. 51, **left**, from Mack. *Photograph: Special Collections and Archives, University of Kentucky Libraries.*

to Vine St., south on Vine St. to Third St., west on Third St. to C & O Bridge.

Citizens-Merchants Bus Line, Kentucky Motor Coach Co., Ludlow Transit Co., Peoples Central Transit Co., Ross Motor Coaches, Inc. From Suspension Bridge to Third St., east on Third St. to Main St., north on Main St. to Fourth St., west on Fourth St. to Vine St., south on Vine St. to Third St., east on Third St. to Suspension Bridge.

Peoples Central Transit (Bellevue-Dayton Route). From L&N Bridge to Pearl St., west on Pearl St. to Pike St., north on Pike to Fourth St., west on Fourth St. to Walnut St., south on Walnut St. to Third St., east on Third St. to Pike St., south on Pike St. to Pearl St., east on Pearl St. to L&N Bridge."

The new motor buses on the 15-Southgate route were barred from using the Green Line's inside loading area in the Dixie Terminal by the building's management "due to the potential of gasoline fumes invading the adjoining office spaces." Therefore,

On April 29, 1937, in exchange for Green Line agreeing to add a 23-Bonnie Leslie bus route, Bellevue city officials allowed the Green Line to convert its 13-South Bellevue streetcar line to motor bus operation. After conversion, an ex-Ross Motor Coaches Mack Model BC is outside the Newport garage ready to go into tripper service.
Special Collections and Archives, University of Kentucky Libraries.

then and later, the Green Line's motor buses were forced to discharge and board passengers in crowded downtown Cincinnati along Walnut between Fourth and Third.

That was another bus disadvantage which would eventually be rectified.

Three New Bus Routes in Newport

As part of the *quid pro quo* in granting the Green Line permission to substitute motor buses for streetcars on the 15-Southgate route, the city of Newport required the CN&C to reinstitute service along Patterson St. in west Newport. As we may remember, the Patterson car line was abandoned in 1917 after a franchise dispute between the Green Line and Newport city officials. Another aim now was to initiate new service to developing areas of south and east Newport.

All this the Green Line agreed to, apparently figuring that the new mandated routes would at least break even and would, of course, save the expense of reinstalling streetcar tracks in the new underpass on Monmouth.

To implement these agreements with Newport, the CN&C, on May 31, 1936, created three new bus routes: 18-Newport East, 19-Newport West, and 20-Newport South, with the latter two routes using the same Cincinnati streets as the recently inaugurated 15-Southgate. The 18-Newport East route also went to Cincinnati but ran via Pike and Pearl to the L&N Bridge (also called the Highway Bridge by this time), to Third & Saratoga, west on Third to Monmouth, north on Monmouth to Sixth, and east on Sixth to Linden, then south on Linden to Eighth, west on Eighth to Maple and south on Maple to Sixth for the return to Cincinnati.

Line 19-Newport West was operated via the Central Bridge to Third & York, east on Third to Monmouth where it turned south to Fifth, west on Fifth to Isabella, then south on Isabella to Ninth and then proceeded west on Ninth to Patterson, north on Patterson to Fifth, and east on Fifth back to Monmouth for the

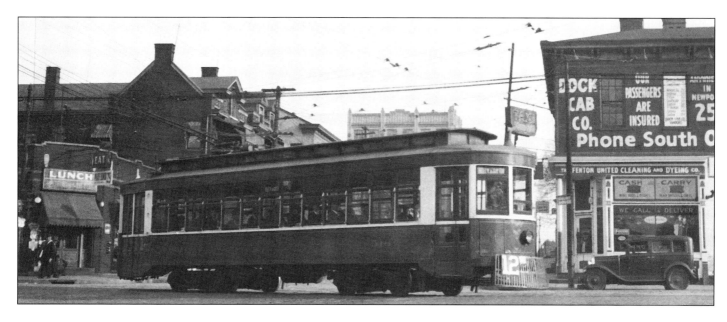

return to Cincinnati. In December, Central Ave. replaced Isabella on the route's southbound trek.

The 20-Newport South route was established to travel the Central Bridge, up York to Sixth, east on Sixth for one block to Monmouth and then south on Monmouth to 16th where it turned west to serve the former city of Clifton, recently annexed by Newport, via 16th to Park to Main to Grandview to Kentucky and Prospect. Of course, 20-Newport South was also subject to the temporary bypass over the "Wagon Bridge" until the opening of the underpass on December 16, 1936.

In May, 1936, the CN&C took delivery of five Mack model 6-CW-3S 25-passenger buses (Nos. 51-55) to cover base service on the three new Newport routes. To house and service its 14 bus fleet, garage space in Newport on Sixth between York and Columbia was leased from the Wiedemann Brewing Co. Until August, 1937, with the completion of a new bus garage behind the Newport Powerhouse, all CN&C buses were serviced at the leased Wiedemann facility.

The Green Line liked its new Mack buses, and the Pennsylvania builder became its favorite coach supplier in the pre-World War II years.

More Bridge Woes

Actually, the 15-Southgate line was not the first Green Line route to lose streetcars forever. The 17-Crosstown streetcar route had been discontinued in 1934 when the bridge (leased by the CN&C in 1906) over the Licking River, linking lower Newport and Covington, was discovered to have a number of fatigued main supports which could no longer bear the weight of even the single-truck streetcars then in service.

Consequently, on October 17, 1934, the 17-Crosstown service was "temporarily suspended." This assessment was true in a sense but when the replacement bridge was opened, a new and expanded 17-Crosstown route would utilize motor buses, not streetcars. And that was not to happen for five long years.

In 1936, the Green Line completed the installation of Johnson fare boxes in all of its streetcars. This introduced to the

CN&C the "pay as you enter" practice which had become commonplace elsewhere at least 15 years previously. Passengers now deposited their fares directly into the device. Since the earliest days of electric service, all of the system's streetcars had used a "pay-within" system with a roving conductor collecting fares directly from the passengers after they boarded the car. The conductor would then note the payment on a rope or foot-operated fare register which would emit a bell-like sound when activated. The Johnson registers put an end to such practice and made fare collecting (and accounting) much easier.

A retired Cincinnati businessman, Frank Barton, tells of the time in 1930 when he and a group of fellow engineering students from the University of Cincinnati boarded a CN&C car at Dixie Terminal to visit the facilities of the Newport Rolling Mill just a block west of Tenth & Patterson. He recounts that:

> "One of my fellow students, a bit of a prankster, thought it great fun to reach over with his foot and operate the fare register. With the conductor otherwise occupied by a concern for a sick passenger, it took him a few minutes to tell the culprit to cease and desist. When he did he noticed that over 55 'fares' had been registered for which no money had been collected. That meant that the conductor would have, by company rule, to make up the difference on the register out of his own pocket. The conductor ordered the motorman to stop the car in mid-block and announced that the car would not move until an additional $2.75 appeared in his hat. A collection was then taken up and only when the necessary funds had been 'donated' by the U.C. group did the car proceed."

Modernizing the Big Cars

More efficient fare collection was one way to fight the Depression; another was to save labor costs. In 1936, the Green Line contracted to have CN&C's 25 double-truck cars (Nos. 500-524) converted at Cincinnati Street Railway's Winton shops to one-man operation. On December 21 of that year the first of the Green Line's remodeled streetcars (No. 508) went into service on the 1-Ft. Mitchell line.

Modifications included the installation of new pneumatical-

Bigger, Better
Big Cars for the
Green Line

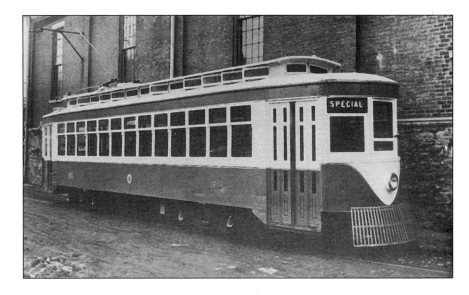

The Green Line's 25 double-truck cars were rebuilt starting in 1936 at Cincinnati Street Railway's Winton Shops for one man operation and lengthened by almost two feet. Prior to that, the cars looked like No. 516 in the 1934 view **opposite**, at Third & York in Newport. At **right**, the first rebuilt car, the 508, gets its official photo taken in December, 1936, at the Newport Shops soon after delivery--and already has a dented side panel!
George Krambles Collection; TANK Archives.

ly controlled double doors at the front of the car and the replacement of the double back doors with a new and narrower exit-only back door. The work resulted in the lengthening of the cars from 45 feet to almost 47 feet and it increased the seating capacity from 52 to 55. Other modifications to the 500s included installation of an electrical heating system in lieu of the original Cooper coke heater.

The new front doors, which were designed to be operated by the motorman, were equipped with a so-called "sensitive edge." This device prevented the door from closing on a passenger since even the slightest of pressure against the door's rubber edge would cause the portal to swing open immediately and prevented the car from proceeding until the doors were completely flush. The total cost, including the installation of Johnson fare boxes, was approximately $4100 per car for a total 25-car expenditure of a little more than $100,000. This was the second major modification of the double truck cars delivered to the Green Line in 1917.

Some years earlier (during 1926-1927) the 500s' motors had been altered in-house to allow an increase in speed to 45 m.p.h. on the private right-of-way sections of the 1-Ft. Mitchell and 11-Ft. Thomas lines. (The 500s also covered, in part, base service requirements on 6-Rosedale and 12-Dayton.) Amazingly, no single-truck streetcars were ever converted by the Green Line to one man operation and continued to be manned by both a motorman and a conductor until the end of their service lives in 1947.

Although the maximum operating speed of a 500-class car now was 45 m.p.h., most observers doubt that this top speed was ever attained in normal service except, perhaps, on some short stretches of the private right-of-way of the Ft. Mitchell line. However, long time Covington attorney John R. Blakely claims to have been the sole passenger when the "unofficial" Green Line streetcar speed record was set in 1934. Blakely relates:

"I paid my nickel and boarded the car at Beechwood Rd. shortly after 6 p.m. northbound to my class at Chase Law School in Cincinnati. Traffic was generally light [inbound] during the supper hour and on that trip I was the only passenger. We traveled through Ft. Mitchell, crossed the trestle over St. John's Rd., proceeded through Barrington Woods and had reached the top of the grade at Decker's Lane when the youth-

ful conductor, apparently by pre-arrangement with the motorman, pulled the trolley.

"We were going at a right smart clip at the time and passed in a blur the stop at Lookout House and the intersection at Ft. Perry, crossed the trestle over Sleepy Hollow Rd. and finally coasted to normal speed somewhere beyond the Altavia Station. As far as I know the speed record was never broken."

The CN&C incurred substantial financial losses in 1933, 1934 and 1935. Fortunately, the 1936 fare increases, plus an increase in ridership (to almost 22 million passengers) as the country started to revive from the Great Depression, contributed to a smaller net loss in 1936. Still, neither the Green Line, nor the citizens of Greater Cincinnati, were prepared for a 1937 event that would bring both company and many of its passengers to the brink of financial disaster.

The Great Flood

Ever since Simon Kenton's band of settlers first populated the area in the late 1700s, Northern Kentuckians were no strangers to the floods caused by the untamed Ohio River and its tributaries. In 1832, 1844, and 1913, the Greater Cincinnati area was hard hit by major Ohio River flooding. Minor Ohio River floods occurred nearly every year, usually without inflicting much damage but causing considerable inconvenience. It seemed, for example, that every spring and fall the 3-Ludlow and 12-Dayton streetcar lines would be out of service anywhere from a few days to a few weeks.

January of 1937 would see the start of the worst natural disaster ever to hit Northern Kentucky. It unfolded like this: on January 18, the Ohio River reached 52 feet or nominal flood stage. The rising waters caused 3-Ludlow service to be withdrawn later that day. The Weather Bureau predicted that the Ohio River would crest at 59 feet on January 20.

However, the Ohio River did not stop rising and by 6 a.m. on January 21 it had reached a depth of 63 feet. Now the Newport Division could no longer operate cars from Newport to Cincinnati because the approaches to both the Central Bridge and L&N Bridge were submerged. Still, there was no panic. Green

TEXT CONTINUES ON PAGE 107

Flood!

The Green Line Fights its Greatest Battle

It started as a mere entertainment for residents of Covington watching car 117, **left,** gingerly treading its way through rising flood waters at Third & Crescent. The Green Line's 3-Ludlow line was susceptible to almost annual flooding but these people could not imagine the terror the river would soon bring to many of them. *Special Collections and Archives, University of Kentucky Libraries.*

But entertainment soon turned to apprehension and finally shock: the Ohio River was rising farther and faster than anyone could understand. Major portions of many Northern Kentucky cities were inundated during the flood's height. The apex was reached on January 27 when the Ohio crested at 79.9 feet. Over several states, the waters took hundreds of lives and caused a billion dollars in damage. These aerial photos tell the story. The **lower picture on page 104** shows the hastily built causeway on the Covington side of the Suspension Bridge, which was the only emergency vehicle lifeline over the Ohio River between near Pittsburgh and Cairo, Illinois. The photo at **upper right** was taken a minute later after the plane had made a half-circle, and shows the causeway from the northwest. Truly, the river has taken temporary possession of the community. *Both: Cincinnati Museum Center Image Archives, Kenton County Library Collection.*

A Changed Green Line Would Emerge in Flood's Wake

Tacoma Park, close to the end of the 12-Dayton line, was almost totally inundated by the Great Flood, as is evident from the photo at **right**. The park's primary attraction was a large swimming pool which survived until the 1970s. *Cincinnati Museum Center Image Archives, Kenton County Library Collection.*

The *Flood . . .*
and its Terrible Aftermath

Limited Green Line service from Cincinnati to Covington resumed on the morning of February 4. The before-dawn scene plays out at **left**. However since the temporary causeway could only be used by motor vehicles, shuttle buses like Mack No. 65 were required. It would be at least a week before through streetcar service to Cincinnati could be restored. *Special Collections and Archives, University of Kentucky Libraries.*

How Do You Deal With the Unimaginable?

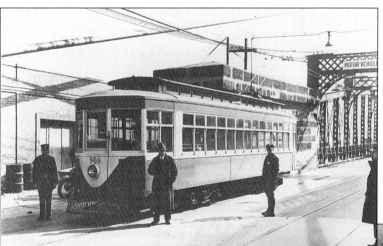

Green Line officials recoiled from the immensity of the unimaginable flooding. But they were determined to put the system back together, as fast as possible. We believe the photograph at **left** depicts the first streetcar to use the Suspension Bridge following its full reopening on February 9. All of the 25 rebuilt double-truck cars were primarily assigned to the CN&C's most profitable lines: 1-Ft. Mitchell, 11-Ft. Thomas and 12-Dayton. *Special Collections and Archives, University of Kentucky Libraries.*

The Green Line's streetcar lines along the low-lying river communities were the last to be restored. This was far from easy, and the conviction that flooding would happen again and again caused management to re-think its loyalty to the steel wheel on the steel rail. In the frame at **right**, a slow-moving Ludlow car cautiously feels its way along Oak Street in Ludlow on March 2, 1937. Although the Ohio River has receded, trapped flood plain water is still visible on the right. Debris can be seen, and it's a sure bet that homeowners along here are mopping up an incredible amount of mud. *Special Collections and Archives, University of Kentucky Libraries.*

Line officials were used to floods of this magnitude. Orders were given to route Campbell County service via the 11th St. Bridge to Madison and through Covington to the Suspension Bridge and on to Cincinnati.

The Weather Bureau predicted around noon on the 21st "a few additional showers" and an Ohio River crest of 64 feet, a serious problem but a level which posed no real threat to the CN&C approach to the Suspension Bridge to Cincinnati, or to its Newport shops and car barn.

But the heavy rains did not subside. By the evening of January 21, the rising water was threatening to cut off the Covington approach to the Suspension Bridge. Quickly, volunteer workers, under the direction of the management of the Suspension Bridge Co., sandbagged approaches to the bridge and built a temporary roadway some 15 feet higher than the normal approach level. As a result, the Green line was able to offer shuttle bus service from Fourth in Covington, where the streetcar lines still in service were terminated, to Cincinnati.

During the evening of January 21, it again rained intensely and the Ohio River rose an unprecedented seven and a half feet during the next 18 hours. This in turn meant that the Licking River in Newport was caught in a backflow from the Ohio and, with Green Line management caught by surprise, the Newport car barn and shops were inundated with eight feet of water.

With dumbfounding speed, some 68 streetcars, all single-truckers, were trapped by the rising Licking River before they could be moved to higher ground. The waters simply had no place to flow except into the low lying areas of Newport and Covington which included the CN&C property in west Newport.

On top of everything else, on Friday, January 22, six inches of snow fell. Even the Green Line shuttle was forced to stop on the evening of Saturday, January 23, when the river reached a level of almost 75 feet. On January 24, the snow was washed into the river by another 24 hour downpour.

At 11 p.m. on January 25 the river crested at an all time high of 79.9 feet. Despite this, the temporary ramp to the Suspension Bridge remained in limited use for emergency vehicles. For more than a week John Roebling's bridge was the only crossing over the Ohio River open for traffic between Steubenville, Ohio and Cairo, Illinois--more than 800 miles. Trucks carrying relief aid from as far away as Michigan and Illinois crossed over it in order to reach stricken cities all along the Ohio River Valley. Flatbed trucks carrying electric generating units for the dark and cold hospitals of Louisville passed over the life line afforded by the Suspension Bridge.

By Wednesday, January 27, the waters of the river started to recede. At 6 a.m. on Thursday, January 28, the level had dropped to 78 feet. By Sunday, January 31, it had receded to 72 feet. Providentially a high pressure area settled over the area during the next week and by 6 a.m. on Friday, February 5, the Great Flood of 1937 was over.

The Flood's Aftermath

In its wake the flood had left little but death, destruction, and financial ruin. In Northern Kentucky alone, the rising waters claimed 22 lives. At the height of the flood, more than 50,000 families were homeless with Ludlow 25 percent under water;

As the floodwaters receded, Green Line officials faced some major street-car curtailments. One doomed route was the 9-Belt Line. Operating in a counter-clockwise fashion in 1938, a Belt Line car heads south on Madison at Seventh. The car would continue on Madison to 11th, use Greenup to 12th and over the bridge to Newport. On February 25, 1939, this line was abandoned.   *Don McClain, Earl Clark Collection.*

Covington and Bellevue 40 percent; Newport 55 percent; Dayton 60 percent; and Brent, Silver Grove and Melbourne were totally flooded. Nobody had ever seen anything like it.

Dazed CN&C officials could only gasp. Flood damage to the Green Line's facilities in Newport, to its rolling stock, and to long stretches of its right-of-way was enormous. Most of the 68 single-truck streetcars trapped within the Newport car barn and shops were declared to be total write-offs. Including lost revenue, the Green Line estimated its flood losses at more than $800,000. How would it cope?

It did so by dipping into those deep pockets. Fortunately the Green Line was financially supported by a healthy parent corporation and immediately started to bounce back. However, in a somewhat ironic twist, a number of its bus competitors were dealt a mortal blow by the Great Flood.

With the exception of the fairly well capitalized Dixie Traction Co. and the Peoples Central/Ross group, most of the bus lines had been barely keeping their heads above water even before the flood. Deprived of passenger revenue by the service disruptions caused by the flood, they soon became unable to pay their drivers or to buy fuel and other supplies. It is worth mentioning that most of the small companies paid their drivers a small base salary plus a "commission," that is, a percentage of the fare receipts they collected during their runs.

Green Line General Manager Philip G. Vondersmith immediately saw opportunity. During the height of the flood, he started negotiations with all competing Northern Kentucky transit systems with the goal of buying them out. Vondersmith correctly reasoned that the flood had rendered some of the companies virtually bankrupt and most of them might sell out cheaply.

Vondersmith also realized that the Green Line had a sudden need for some of the motor coaches these companies owned. Company engineers told him that the rights-of-way of the 2 - Greenup, 3-Ludlow, 8-Eastern, 12-Dayton, and 13-South Bellevue car lines would be out of commission for up to four months. And restoring or finding replacements for the 68 streetcars destroyed during the flood would be virtually impossible.

Wheeling and dealing after the flood, Green Line Chief Vondersmith bought transit companies and their buses. Ludlow Transit had ordered a forward control Ford. It was delivered to the CN&C as its No. 70, and in this picture it heads for its Cincinnati terminal on Walnut. It's on a run it held down for a number of years, 19-Newport West. *James Gibson.*

In short order, the Green Line made offers that the independent transit operators could not refuse. First and foremost, on February 1, 1937, it was announced that Lloyd Ross, owner of Peoples Central Transit Lines and Ross Motor Coaches, which operated 32 buses on five routes, had agreed to sell out for $100,000.

A mere four days later, Ludlow Transit was purchased by the Green Line System for $30,000. Ludlow Transit owned eight buses.

On February 6, the CN&C snapped up Citizens-Merchants and Kentucky Motor Coach for $10,000 each. These purchases netted the Green Line another 18 buses. The fast-moving Vondersmith had acquired five bus companies and 58 buses in six days. His goal was achieved: the Green Line not only absorbed its major competitors but gained some badly needed equipment.

The "New" Green Line Buses

Of course, these 58 buses were hardly prime specimens. Quite a few of them were at or nearing the end of their useful service lives. They were battered and bruised, but they could roll. Most were needed only during the lengthy emergency period fol-

lowing the flood and some, but certainly not all, were disposed of shortly thereafter.

As it happened, 35 of the 58 "Local Lines" buses were retained after the emergency period long enough to be repainted and renumbered into the Green Line scheme. Two ex-Peoples Central Transit 27-passenger Internationals (Nos. 37-38) and six 21- to 24-passenger Kentucky Motor Coach and Ross Motor Coaches Mack ABs (Nos. 20-22 and 27-29) held down rush-hour assignments on CN&C routes 13, 18, 19, 20 and 23. Seven ex-Peoples Central and Citizens Bus Internationals, five 22-passenger (Nos. 15-19), and three 24-passenger units (Nos. 30-32) also stayed around for rush-hour service long enough to be repainted into the current Green Line livery.

Two ex-Peoples Central 29-passenger International buses (Nos. 39-40), two ex-Kentucky Motor Coach 29-passenger Mack BKs (Nos. 41-42) and five ex-Ross Motor Coaches 29-passenger Mack AB and BC buses (Nos. 43-47), were initially assigned to the temporary 12-Dayton bus line as soon as the mud and debris had been cleared from Fairfield Ave. They later saw rush-hour service all over the system. Two ex-Ross Motor Coach model 40 Twin Coaches (Nos. 48 and 49) also filled charter and rush-hour runs. In 1941 No. 49 was sold to the Cincinnati Street Railway (becoming CSR No. 96) whereupon CSR converted it to the open deck sightseeing bus *Losantiville.*

A model 70 Ford 25-passenger bus, ordered by Ludlow Transit in 1936 and delivered directly to the CN&C in March 1937 (No. 70), became a fixture on the 19-Newport West line for a number of years. Four 20- to 24-passenger Fords (Nos. 33-36) and four 22-passenger Mack ABs (Nos. 23-26), all well-maintained by former owner Ludlow Transit, saw rush-hour service all over the Green Line into the early 1940s.

One place where the acquired buses were not needed was on their old independent routes, because these no longer existed. Almost all of them were essentially duplicated by existing Green Line routes and were discontinued. The exception was Kentucky Motor Coach's line from South Hills to Covington which became CN&C route SH-South Hills, its first bus operation in Kenton County.

Starved for reliable buses, the Green Line was able to take immediate March delivery of a Mack demonstrator, a 35-passenger 6-CT-3S (No. 60). A number of Dixie Traction buses were also leased during the February-April emergency period.

The Green Line Dries Out

Service from Covington to Cincinnati was restored at 5:42 a.m. on February 4 with shuttle bus service between Fourth & Madison in Covington (the temporary terminus of all Covington Division streetcars) and Fourth & Walnut in Cincinnati. All of the Newport Division's bus and streetcar lines, with the exception of the 12-Dayton and 13-South Bellevue routes, were back in

Under the watchful eyes of American Legion members, a group of Covington Safety Patrol youngsters, awarded a trip to see the Cincinnati Reds National League baseball team at Crosley Field, boards an ex-Ross Motor Coaches Twin Coach at Post No. 70, Covington. The time: late spring of 1938. One of two model 40s, No. 49 was relegated mostly to charter and special movements.
Special Collections and Archives, University of Kentucky Libraries.

business by February 9, although the 19-Newport West route could not use Patterson St. south of Sixth for two additional weeks.

In Covington, regular streetcar service was restored to Cincinnati on the 1-Ft. Mitchell, 4-Main, 5-Holman, 6-Rosedale, and 7-Latonia lines in fairly short order. However, the 2-Greenup, 3-Ludlow, and 8-Eastern car lines saw substitute bus service for a considerable period of time while the right-of-way was being repaired.

By early March, streetcar service was resumed on the 3-Ludlow route and on April 26 service was restored to east Covington, which had disappeared under the backed-up waters of the Licking River. More precisely, when rail service was resumed, the 2-Greenup line was temporarily discontinued and consolidated with the 8-Eastern route. The demise of the 2-Greenup route was due to a shortage of streetcars. This meant that service on Greenup between 15th and 20th was reduced to a northbound only operation with all the cars using Eastern southbound.

In Campbell County, there was a bigger problem. The Newport Division's 12-Dayton and 13-South Bellevue lines, which closely paralleled the Ohio River, suffered considerable damage. It was late February before even substitute bus service could be furnished along Fairfield Ave. to Dayton. Green Line officials feared it would be mid-summer before streetcar service could be restored on 12-Dayton. They knew this could be done only if enough streetcars were available by that date. And the CN&C had no idea where they would come from.

Gasoline Replaces Electricity

In April, the Green Line proposed to the city of Bellevue a franchise amendment to permanently switch 13-South Bellevue streetcar service to motor coach operation. To sweeten the pot, the company presented a plan to extend service along Taylor Ave. by adding a new bus line (23-Bellevue-Bonnie Leslie) which would alternate trips with 13-South Bellevue and follow the 13 route from Cincinnati to the end of the old streetcar line.

From there it would continue south on Taylor through the formerly independent town of Bonnie Leslie to the Bellevue city limits and a connection with the 11-Ft. Thomas rail line at Wilson Road. This would be a new and useful connection. The plan was accepted by the Bellevue city council and, on April 29, the 13-South Bellevue streetcar line passed into history.

CN&C officials also tried, to no avail, to get the city of Dayton to agree to permanent motor coach substitution for the 12-Dayton line. But Dayton insisted on streetcar service being restored when sufficient equipment was available.

It took a long time. CN&C officials were in the process of making some major decisions. If rail service to Dayton was to be restored, additional streetcars would be needed, and that would mean robbing them from somewhere else.

Dayton finally got its streetcars back on July 11. The Green Line had solved the problem of how.

The First Interstate Trolley-Coach

The 1937 flood helped settle a company debate about future equipment that might have predated the flood. In any event, the Green Line now made a rapid decision to convert 6-Rosedale and 7-Latonia to electric trolley bus operation. Faced with a serious streetcar shortage, in March 1937 the company announced its proposed conversion plans.*

Management ordered 21 trolley-coaches of 40-passenger capacity from the Brill Co. of Philadelphia and entered into a contract to convert the one wire streetcar electrical system to a double-wire system and to extend trolley coach service to new areas in both Rosedale and Latonia.

Plans were also announced to pave a portion of the carbarn at 20th & Madison and to pave the upper level of Dixie Terminal in order to accommodate the rubber tired trolley-coaches.

_____

*Cincinnati had converted one line to trolley-coaches on December 1, 1936. Green Line officials did not have to travel far to see them in action on the 15-Clark St.-Chase Ave. line, and this may have stimulated the debate on the Kentucky side of the river.

On the Eve of Traction Oblivion

As a part of a plan to free up electric cars for the flood-ravaged Dayton line, the CN&C selected the Rosedale and Latonia streetcar lines to be guinea pigs for replacement by trolley-coaches. There had to be a last day for streetcars, and it is duly recorded here. The date is July 10, 1937, and the occasion is Green Line car 324 trundling down Madison Ave. in Covington, on a 6-Rosedale run. Tomorrow will see an electric bus on this schedule.
Don McClain, David McNeil Collection.

John Roebling's suspension bridge survived the 1937 flood without any damage. The bridge's four cables and supporting truss stiffeners are seen up close. Just as important to this part of our story, we behold at **left** a new era for the Green Line: brand-new Brill trolley-coach 602 heading toward us as we stand on the Covington side of the Ohio River. Southbound coach 602 is working the 7-Latonia line, one of two wired up for electric bus operation. This photograph was taken shortly after the start of revenue service in July of 1937. Just as the streetcars had, the trolley-coaches accessed the upper level of the Dixie Terminal via the ramps. *Motor Bus Society.*

Covington's Crowds Hail a New Era: the

Trolley-Coach

Citizens and dignitaries rub shoulders during their inspection of the new Brill trolley coaches in Covington's Park Place on July 10, 1937. Three of them are lined up in front of the CN&C's headquarters in the picture at **right**. The Green Line will kick-off the first interstate service of such vehicles in the United States the next day. *Special Collections and Archives, University of Kentucky Libraries.*

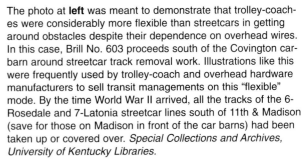

The photo at **left** was meant to demonstrate that trolley-coaches were considerably more flexible than streetcars in getting around obstacles despite their dependence on overhead wires. In this case, Brill No. 603 proceeds south of the Covington car-barn around streetcar track removal work. Illustrations like this were frequently used by trolley-coach and overhead hardware manufacturers to sell transit managements on this "flexible" mode. By the time World War II arrived, all the tracks of the 6-Rosedale and 7-Latonia streetcar lines south of 11th & Madison (save for those on Madison in front of the car barns) had been taken up or covered over. *Special Collections and Archives, University of Kentucky Libraries.*

A target date of July 4, 1937, was set for the conversion of both routes from streetcar to electric bus service.

Why trolley-coaches? There were two primary reasons for using them on the 6-Rosedale and 7-Latonia routes. Had the Green Line selected gasoline buses, a new downtown Cincinnati anchor would have been necessary because only electrically powered vehicles were permitted into Dixie Terminal due to the 1917 lease provision. Since all Covington Division streetcars avoided street running in Cincinnati by using the direct ramp from the Suspension Bridge over Third to the upper level of the Dixie Terminal, any substitute motor bus service would have entailed street running and the resulting delays and expense.

The other reason, of course, is that the Green Line was owned by the Columbia Gas and Electric which was in the business of generating electricity, not refining gasoline.

The 21 Brill trolley-coaches (Nos. 600-620) cost more than $12,000 apiece, and were delivered to the Green Line in June of 1937. Selected drivers were sent for training in May to Indianapolis, where Indianapolis Railways operated trolley coaches. Other operators trained on a practice loop installed on the property at the 20th & Madison car barn. Including the new $60,000 garage at 11th & Lowell in Newport for gasoline bus use, the Green Line spent more than $750,000 in 1937 on transit improvements.

A good portion of this was used to modify the streetcar overhead along both routes into a twin wire trolley-coach configuration, and to construct new overhead for route extensions on both lines. To allow trolley-coach operation to and from Dixie Terminal, the upper level ramps were paved around the rails and safety walls added.

The 6-Rosedale line, instead of proceeding south on its former route at Southern & Caroline, used new wire to reach areas of Rosedale previously served by Ross Motor Coaches. The expanded route, of 1.06 miles, proceeded south via Decoursey to 38th & Church, on Church to 43rd, on 43rd back to Decoursey, on Decoursey to 45th and over that street to the end of the former streetcar line. The 6-Rosedale trolley-coaches utilized the former streetcar route in returning northbound.

The 7-Latonia line, instead of doubling back on the former streetcar route, used new overhead wire to proceed up Latonia to Madison and east on Madison to a new connection at 26th & James. Its extension equaled 1.27 miles.

Streetcar overhead wire was also modified on 11th between Madison and Greenup, on Greenup from 11th to 20th and on 20th between Greenup and Madison for use by electric buses. As a consequence, the Green Line routed all southbound 7-Latonia trolley-coach trips along Greenup except between 4:30 and 6:30 p.m. Monday through Friday, thereby limiting the 2-Greenup streetcar line to the evening rush hours on Monday through Friday.

At 6 a.m., on Sunday, July 11, 1937, the first of the new trolley-coaches entered Dixie Terminal on scheduled service.* That

*Only one other company ever operated interstate trolley-coach service in the U. S. Kansas City Public Service Co. instituted trolley-coaches over one route (46-18th St.-Kansas Ave.) from Kansas City, Mo., to Kansas City, Kansas, on October 4, 1950. Most of its length in Kansas was wiped out on July 14, 1951, by a flood. What remained crossed the state line and continued three blocks into Kansas until 1954. So, what was born of a flood in Kentucky died by a flood in Kansas.

New line truck No. 12, **above**, installs double-wire overhead at CN&C's south car barn in anticipation of the start of trolley coach service in July of 1937. The work crew is identified as, left to right, Carl Lee, James Guffen on the tower, driver John Hardin and James Hendrix, foreman. In the photo at the **bottom** of the page, northbound Rosedale trolley-coach 606 has just passed the John R. Coppin Department Store at Sixth & Madison, Covington's largest retail store in the late 1930s.
Both: Special Collections and Archives, University of Kentucky Libraries.

trip marked the first interstate operation of trolley coach service in the nation. To mark the inaugural of Green Line trolley coach service, all July 11 service on both 6-Rosedale and 7-Latonia was free to the public, with revenue service starting the next day.

Public acceptance of the new service on the 6-Rosedale and 7-Latonia routes exceeded the Green Line's most optimistic predictions. By the end of 1937 six trolley-coaches held down the 6-Rosedale base schedule. Since this route made a round trip in about 60 minutes, and with six coaches in operation on the base schedule, the headway (or interval between buses) was ten minutes. In the morning and evening rush hours, six additional trolley-coaches were placed in tripper service on the No. 6 route, giving the route a headway of five minutes. Four trolley-coaches covered base service on the 7-Latonia and four more were assigned to rush-hour service.

This left the company with only one coach in reserve. In a

With the massive cables of the Suspension Bridge in the foreground, we see at **left** CN&C trolley-coach 611 following a 500-series streetcar into the recently paved upper loop of the Dixie Terminal on May 5, 1939. With conversion to trolley-coaches, the 6-Rosedale route was extended by more than a mile to form a large loop, featuring new southbound overhead on Decoursey Ave. to 45th. In the photo **below**, a Brill returns north at 40th & Huntington past the Kenton County Infirmary on what is now a one-way route. Note that double-wire appears over only the northbound streetcar tracks. *Ohio Brass Co., T.W. Lehmann Collection; Special Collections and Archives, University of Kentucky Libraries.*

pinch, a streetcar could deputize for a trolley-coach between 20th & Madison and the Dixie Terminal and a connecting No. 6 or No. 7 trolley-coach could turn back south. This is because the tracks on Madison between 12th and 20th were left in place to provide car barn access for the streetcars assigned to routes 1, 3, 4 and 5. In an extreme emergency involving the outer end of either the 6 or 7 routes, gasoline buses from the Newport Division could substitute.

The conversion of streetcar lines 6-Rosedale and 7-Latonia to trolley-coach operation and 13-South Bellevue to motor buses, coupled with the retention of the best of the buses acquired in the "Independent Lines" buyout, enabled the CN&C to scrap all of the 68 flood-damaged single-truck cars, including 32 of the remaining 35 cars from Groups C through E (Nos. 220-263), all 20 cars remaining from Groups F and G (Nos. 264-288), and 16 single-trucked cars from Groups H, I and J (Nos. 289-318).

The Suburbs Heard From

In its quest for consolidation, the Green Line had not yet bought everybody out. In 1938, Cold Spring Bus was furnishing 19 round trips daily between Cold Spring and Cincinnati. During 1938, Paul Schwerling incorporated a subsidiary, the Alexandria Bus Co., and proposed to offer through service from Alexandria (some four miles south of Cold Spring) to Cincinnati.

Schwerling, however, was denied a permit to operate direct Alexandria to Cincinnati service by the Interstate Commerce Commission because Blue Ribbon Lines operated thrice daily service between Cincinnati and Alexandria in conjunction with its line haul operation to Ashland, Kentucky. The Alexandria Bus Co. was, however, granted operating authority by Kentucky to operate from Alexandria to Newport pursuant to Kentucky Certificate No. 157. But most trips of the Alexandria Bus Co. ran only from Alexandria to Cold Spring serving as a feeder for Schwerling's Cold Spring Bus Co.

Dixie Traction, the biggest of the independents, had the luck to serve the area's most promising suburbs. And it was prosperous enough to buy brand-new buses. By the end of 1937, Dixie

rostered 25 buses including eight 25-passenger Mack 6-CW-3S models purchased in 1936 and 1937 (Nos. 123-130). The new Macks were primarily assigned to the Erlanger-Florence route with the 25-passenger Studebaker buses acquired from 1928 to 1935 (Nos. 108-122) covering rush-hour runs between Florence and Cincinnati via Elsmere, Erlanger, Lakeside Park, South Ft. Mitchell, Park Hills, and Covington, Kentucky and providing both base and rush-hour service on its Campbell County belt-line operations.

By now the Dixie Highway Corridor was a humming transit market. Dixie Traction offered 62 round trips daily, except Sundays, between Florence and Cincinnati between the hours of 5:10 a.m. and 11:07 p.m., and 26 round trips between Ft. Thomas and Cincinnati between the hours of 6:10 a.m. and 7:25 p.m. The Sunday schedule between Florence and Cincinnati was on a 30 minute basis but no service was maintained on the Sabbath between Ft. Thomas and Cincinnati.

In addition to the services to Northern Kentucky communi-

Bus Mechanics Kept Busy at Newport

By 1938, the Green Line could boast a state-of-the-art bus garage at its Newport complex. From left we find Mack CQ 61, then CW 54 (both with inside-the-window rear destination signs), then we find an ex-Ross Motor Coach Mack BC, an International from one of the independents and another CW. Trolley-coaches were housed and serviced at the Covington division. Streetcars still dominated both venues at this time. *Special Collections and Archives, University of Kentucky Libraries.*

ties provided by Black Diamond, Cold Spring Bus and Dixie Traction, a scattering of suburban service to Northern Kentucky from Cincinnati was also provided by a number of intercity bus companies during the late 1930s. In addition to Blue Ribbon Lines, Southeastern Greyhound Lines provided 12 trips daily between Cincinnati and Florence as part of its route to Lexington via the Dixie Highway but SGL could not pick up or discharge intrastate passengers anywhere between Florence and Cincinnati.

Ohio Greyhound Lines (incorporated into Great Lakes Greyhound Lines [Ind.] in 1941) offered 7 round trips between Cincinnati and Louisville via Florence, but although it lacked pickup and discharge authority authority along Dixie Highway, it could haul passengers (at a premium fare) between Cincinnati and designated stops in South Ft. Mitchell, Erlanger, and Florence.

"Steady As She Goes" in 1938

After the turbulence of 1937, thankfully no major changes or challenges bedeviled the Green Line System in 1938. The Ohio River mercifully remained in its banks and ridership climbed to approximately 24 million passengers.

The Green Line operated 10 streetcar lines, two trolley-coach lines, and six motor bus routes over some 66 route miles. A combination of 120 vehicles of all sorts were required for peak weekday operation for which the Green Line rostered 90 or so streetcars, 45 gasoline motor buses and 21 electric coaches.

It seemed to be the CN&C's intent to squeeze the remaining life out of the buses it acquired from the five transit companies in 1937 because only an ex-Mack demo, a 6-CY-3S (No. 50), was purchased in 1938. Like other properties, Green Line management was ever on the lookout for a good deal on even a single new coach. Traditionally, bus builders shopped their demonstrators around after a year or so on the road. The Green Line was always interested.

During any typical weekday in 1938, CN&C passenger vehicles made 120-plus trips to downtown Cincinnati between 4:30

and 5:30 p.m. The upper level of the Dixie Terminal, serving the Green Line's Covington Division, dispatched no less than 76 streetcars and trolley-coaches during that 60 minute period while the lower level of the Dixie Terminal, from which the motor buses of the Newport Division were barred, was still used between 4:30 and 5:30 p.m. by approximately 25 streetcars serving the 9-Belt Line, 11-Ft. Thomas, 12-Dayton and 16-Washington routes.

Adjacent to the Dixie Terminal, on Walnut, the CN&C dispatched 47 Newport Division buses during the same interval.

Dithering Over a Crosstown Line

The new bridge over the lower Licking River linking Fifth in Newport with Fourth in Covington had opened in July of 1936. Immediately the city fathers in both Newport and Covington began clamoring for a revival of the 17-Crosstown line, albeit with buses since the floor of the new bridge was without tracks.

Fine, said the Green Line. It proposed a new 17-Crosstown bus service crossing both Licking River bridges if both cities would agree to the abandonment of the 9-Belt Line cars which still used the upper Licking River bridge. The CN&C's positive experience with the 15-Southgate line's buses made it clear that the streetcar would not figure in any future expansion plans.

Before a final decision could be reached, the Great Flood of 1937 put the issue on hold. In 1938 the city of Covington agreed to the expanded 17-Crosstown loop line concept using buses. Newport couldn't make up its mind. Time marched on.

Finally, In January of 1939, the city of Newport relented. By ordinance, the CN&C obtained permission for a new bus-served 17-Crosstown route which would replace both the old No. 17 car line plus the 9-Belt Line streetcar. In February the Green Line announced that the 9-Belt Line streetcar line would be discontinued on February 25, 1939, and a new 17-Crosstown bus linking Newport and Covington via both Licking River bridges would begin service.

The 9-Belt Line, running both clockwise and counter-clock-

At first, the cities of Newport and Covington were delighted when the Green Line cobbled together a new 17-Crosstown line to replace the old 9-Belt Line streetcar. After lengthy delay, this happened on February 26, 1939. But then, the cities' happy mood turned sour when equipment like old No. 19, **above,** appeared on the line. The 19 was a 22-passenger International of uncertain vintage which came from the Citizens-Merchants Bus Line. Not so fast, said the city fathers. The CN&C had promised "modern equipment." Where was it? To mollify the councilmen, the Green Line hastily leased from Dixie Traction three one-door 1936 Mack CW's, and assigned them to the Crosstown line. One of them appears **below**. It is CN&C 58, renumbered from Dixie Traction 128, sporting a non-standard Green Line paint scheme. This spelled relief, and everyone was now happy again. *James Gibson; Special Collections and Archives, University of Kentucky Libraries.*

wise from the Dixie Terminal, had served, since October, 1934, as the only crosstown transit link between Newport and Covington. "The Belt" actually crossed the Ohio River twice in one swing through Northern Kentucky. In the counter-clockwise direction, cars left Dixie Terminal's upper level, crossed the Suspension Bridge to Covington, used Madison and 12th, crossed the Licking River to 11th in Newport, went north on York to the Central Bridge, and back to the Dixie Terminal's lower level. Clockwise cars did exactly the reverse.

Riders of the No. 9 route marveled at some unusual streetcar operating practices. Since both 11th and 12th in Covington were quite narrow, company rules required the conductor to get off the car, check for any oppositely bound streetcars or other vehicular traffic, and signal "clear" to the motorman before the car turned onto either 11th or 12th from Greenup.

A rich history defined the route. The German heritage of the

area, for instance, was in evidence. A house on the corner of 12th & Greenup still exhibits a cut stone marker set into the brickwork inscribed "Grunopp," "Twelft," and "1862."

And so on February 26, 1939, 9-Belt Line was replaced by the new 17-Crosstown bus route which operated both clockwise and counter-clockwise loops and basically duplicated the Belt Line's route in Northern Kentucky. However, the new 17 route used the new Licking River Bridge between lower Newport and lower Covington to form its northern loop in lieu of running to Cincinnati as the 9-Belt Line had done.

Following the demise of the No. 9 route, the northbound track on Madison in Covington between 7th and 11th became redundant and was removed. The Green Line also received the blessing of the city to take up both tracks on Madison from 11th to just north of the carbarns at 20th, and this task was accomplished by the fall of 1939. Access to and from the Covington barns for the remaining rail lines 1, 4, 5, 8 and 10 would now be via Greenup and 20th.

Also on February 26, an alteration was made to the 19-Newport West route. The 19 line now extended south on Columbia to 11th, and west on 11th to Patterson.

Two new 31-passenger Mack model 6-CQ-3S buses (Nos. 66-67), delivered in March and assigned to the 18-Newport East line, allowed the release of two 25-passenger Mack 6-CW-3S buses to the 17-Crosstown route. However, a majority of the buses assigned to route 17 were ex-Ludlow Transit Ford buses acquired in the 1937 "Local Lines" buyout.

This proved to be a political mistake. During the latter part of 1939, the governments of both Newport and Covington threatened to revoke the 17-Crosstown franchise on the basis that the CN&C had agreed to provide "modern equipment" in exchange for the cities allowing the substitution of bus service on the revived No. 17 line for 9-Belt Line streetcars.

Already showing evidence of hard service by August of 1938, Brill trolley-coach 603 stops at Third & Court on its way south from Cincinnati's Dixie Terminal.
Special Collections and Archives, University of Kentucky Libraries.

Between July of 1937 and November, 1939, some large 500-series cars were available for base service on the Ludlow route. The slightly water-stained photo at **left** depicts of the end of the loop at Shelby & Pleasant in Bromley. A 500-type has just navigated the balloon loop and starts back to Cincinnati. On November 5, 1939, the Ludlow tracks fell silent, the cars replaced by 10 trolley-coaches from the Green Line's favorite gas bus supplier, Mack. *Earl Clark Collection.*

With the source of its power in the background (the West End Power Plant of Columbia controlled Cincinnati Gas & Electric Co.), CN&C Mack 634, pictured **below**, climbs the steep Ludlow Highway heading out of Covington. *Special Collections and Archives, University of Kentucky Libraries.*

Decidedly, the front-engine Fords did not appear to be very "modern." The Green Line hastily leased from Dixie Traction three model 6-CW-3S 25-passenger Mack buses (Nos. 56-58) in November, 1939 to satisfy both cities.

More Trolley-Coaches

In 1939, the CN&C announced plans to convert the 3-Ludlow streetcar line to trolley-coach operation. Mack, the Green Line's favorite prewar bus supplier, was chosen to provide 10, 40-passenger CR-3S model electric coaches for approximately $12,900 apiece. To cope with the steeper grades of the line, 140 h.p. motors (compared to 125 h.p. motors in the earlier Brills) and dynamic brakes were specified for the new Macks.

They could hardly be safer. In an advertisement the company extolled the virtues of the new coaches with their "silent speed, quick acceleration, and smooth stops." The Green Line proudly informed its customers that the new coaches incorporated no less than three separate braking systems (dynamic, air, and mechanical). The ad also declared that the new coaches would have seats "upholstered in the finest grade of genuine leather."

Conversion of the 3-Ludlow streetcar line proceeded smoothly. The Mack CR-3S trolley coaches (Nos. 630-639) started arriving in late September of that year and were broken in on the 6-Rosedale and 7-Latonia routes.

By late October, work had been completed on both the conversion of the existing route to two wire configuration and a short stretch of new wire which allowed an extension of service further into the adjoining town of Bromley over Shelby, Harris, Boone and Pleasant. The extension, which measured about a third of a mile, caused the new trolley-coaches to display new and revised destination signs reading 3-Ludlow-Bromley.

Finally, on November 5, 1939, the 3-Ludlow streetcar line, completed in large part in 1894 and finished in 1895, gave up the ghost. The conversion of the No. 3 route from streetcar to trolley-coach turned out to be the Green Line's last electric-to-electric conversion.

Suburban Operations Beckon

As the decade neared its end, the Green Line made a sweeping move to widen its own destiny. In June of 1939, news reports revealed that the CN&C had reached "agreements in principle" for the purchase of The Dixie Traction Co. for $200,000 and Black Diamond Stages for $35,000. In October, 1939, the Green

A bobbing single-trucker lurks behind houses on the Route 8-Eastern private right-of-way in August, 1938. *Ed Frank Jr., David McNeal Collection.*

Line announced that Dixie Traction had entered into a side agreement to purchase the Cold Spring Bus Co. and the Alexandria Bus Company for a total of $25,000.

Further, it was learned that most of the suburban routes of Dixie, Cold Spring and Alexandria would be operated under the banner of The Dixie Traction Co. and that Dixie Traction would keep its name as an operating subsidiary of the CN&C. However, Black Diamond Stages would merge into the CN&C and its route from Ross, Ky., to Cincinnati and a portion of the Dixie Traction's Belt Line route via Highland would be integrated into extensions of CN&C's 15-Southgate and 18-Newport East routes.

Since all five of the parties were engaged in interstate commerce, it was necessary for the CN&C to obtain acquisition and route transfer permission from the Interstate Commerce Commission. Here, things did not go smoothly. A number of objections by other transportation companies and community groups were filed protesting the proposed acquisitions. In response, the ICC held hearings in October and November, 1939 but by the end of the year no decision had been reached and the proposed buyouts were still in limbo.

Once again, CN&C discovered that running a complex interstate operation was far from simple. Further, the company was now dealing with two new suburban operations which started up in 1937: Independence Bus Line and High Line Buses.

IBL operated from Independence (population approximately 1000) up Kentucky state highway 17 (Madison Pike) to 3rd & Greenup in Covington during rush-hours and to Madison & Latonia during mid-day. However, IBL could not pick up or discharge passengers within the Covington city limits. With the start of construction in 1940 of the Sohio refinery on the site of the old Latonia Race Track, Newsom Bus Lines instituted service from the Taylor Mill area (population about 1500) along Kentucky route 16 (Winston Ave.) to a connection with the Green Line at Rittes Corner in Latonia. Newsom also ran through to downtown Covington on certain rush-hour trips but could handle no local passengers between Rittes Corner and downtown.

High Line Buses fielded two routes through very thinly populated areas (in those days) of Boone and Kenton counties. One route was operated by HLB from Hebron along Kentucky route 20 to Constance and along Kentucky 8 to the Boone-Kenton county line where it left the Ohio River flood plain and used Amsterdam Road and Highwater Road (hence the company name) to Bromley. High Line purchased Ryles Auto Bus Service and instituted an Erlanger-Crescent Springs-Bromley route operated via Dixie Highway to Buttermilk, Buttermilk to Collins (serving Villa Madonna Academy) and on to Bromley.

This company apparently ran some through trips (perhaps without local rights) along the river from Bromley to Third & Greenup in Covington until 1942 as the telephone directory lists a HLB bus station at that location. Unlike IBL and Newsom, HLB did not survive World War II.

Green Line treated both IBL and Newsom as traffic feeders and thus allies, and it often sold both companies used buses cheaply. HLB was looked upon less favorably.

After the war, two "one-bus" successor companies appeared: Hebron Bus Co. (Hebron to Bromley) and Crescent Springs Bus Co. (Ft. Mitchell-Crescent Springs-Villa Madonna Academy). Both companies were started by former Green Line employees and served as feeders to CN&C routes. It was rumored that both owners were beneficiaries of Green Line startup funds. The CN&C's business strategy was often subtle. ❏

Bus lines ran on paper as well as roads! Here is a small selection of commuter tickets issued during the 1930s by some of the Independent operators: Dixie Traction, **above;** Independence Bus Line at **right** and High Line Buses at **extreme right**. *All: T. W. Lehmann Collection.*

What the steady independent bus line rider needed in Depression Days . . .

Two Poles or One? That is the Question

This 1939 photo shows a southbound single-truck streetcar coming off the Suspension Bridge with two poles up. In less than a minute, one pole will be pulled down for the single-wire Kentucky trackage. We see also Brill trolley-coach 603 heading for Dixie Terminal with, of course, two poles up. By this time, the Green Line's twin wires had been widened to 24 inches (the standard trolley-coach spacing) from the Cincinnati 19-inch regulation for both cars and trolley-coaches. Thus the streetcar poles are slightly splayed, the electric bus poles normal. *Motor Bus Society.*

With the conversion of the 500-series double-truck cars for one-man operation, the use of twin trolley poles in Cincinnati became a major operational headache for the Green Line, which faced two alternatives. Either a full-time pole tender would need to be employed at Third & Court and Third & York or the motorman would have to secure his charge, get off the car and go around to the back to either raise one pole (if heading for Cincinnati) or lower one (if heading south).

Pole-tenders had historically been assigned only during rush hours at those two locations to relieve the conductor of the two-man cars so he could concentrate on collecting fares. During quiet hours, he could simply lean out the back window and accomplish the task himself.

Employing two full-time pole tenders (one each in Covington and Newport) would eat up part of the cost savings of single-manning the 500s. The other alternative would present a safety hazard and cause delays.

What to do? Company lawyers reminded management that the City of Cincinnati's double-pole requirement had ultimately been declared unconstitutional. The CN&C's right-of-way folks advised that it would be relatively inexpensive to bond and ground the few miles of Cincinnati tracks for Green Line cars so that a single pole could be used.

The decision made, ground crews tackled the Suspension Bridge first. By April of 1937 500-series cars to Covington began operating to the upper level of Dixie Terminal using only one pole. It took a little longer before Newport cars began using a single pole but the changeover apparently took place in early 1938. Inexplicably, the Green Line's single-truck two-man cars continued to ply into the Queen City using both poles until the last ones were retired in 1947.

But then, consistency was not exactly at the top of the list for the Green Line, was it? ◆

But the double-truck 500-series cars had been using just one pole on the Covington Division since April, 1937, and from the spring of 1938 on the Newport Division. That is apparent from noting that car 520, **below**, has just pulled out of the lower level of Dixie Terminal onto Third St. with just one pole up. *M. D. McCarter, Tom Taylor Collection.*

Green Line Moves the Troops

World War II was a wild time for the Green Line. While every available streetcar was pressed into service to carry swollen ridership, management had to rely on the motor bus to shoulder much of the increased burden. This was especially true when it came to military charter movements, and because of the role of Ft. Thomas as an Army induction center, there were many. This photo shows how the challenge was met. We see bus 400, the first of 12 Mack CM-3G's of 1940, loading a group of U. S. Army personnel at the Fort, with other buses behind. These larger buses were purchased for the 12-Dayton streetcar conversion, and thus ideal for off-peak charters such as this one. Probably these soldiers were heading for a local technical school, judging from the documents many of them are carrying. Interestingly, streetcars sometimes also were sent to Ft. Thomas to carry soldiers in the off-hours, if the charter was to one of the railroad stations.

Special Collections and Archives, University of Kentucky Libraries.

The Green
Line Goes to
War: 1940-1945

IT WAS THE BEST OF TIMES. It was the worst of times for the Cincinnati, Newport & Covington Railway. Good, because business was better. Not so good, because the system was still losing money and an explosive and expensive labor confrontation was brewing. The year 1940 was certainly a momentous one.

Even though streetcars were still important in the Green Line's scheme of things, buses dominated the headlines now. On February 14, 1940, the Green Line finally received approval from the Interstate Commerce Commission to merge Black Diamond Stages into the CN&C. Along with Black Diamond's operating rights on Kentucky Route 8 and in Ft. Thomas, Southgate and Newport, the Green Line acquired a ragtag assortment of eight Black Diamond buses built by four different manufacturers.

More importantly, the ICC approved the CN&C's purchase of the Dixie Traction with the proviso that it be kept as an independent subsidiary and that there would be absolutely no transfer privileges between CN&C and Dixie Traction routes. However, the Commission did give the Dixie Traction permission to convey certain operating rights to the CN&C outright, namely the portion of Dixie's Belt Line from Tenth & Monmouth in Newport to Ft. Thomas. Dixie Traction's route along Alexandria Pike to Highland Ave. through Southgate to the main Ft. Thomas business district was a logical extension of the CN&C's existing 15-Southgate service.

As we have learned, Black Diamond Stages operated a route from Ross, Ky., through Silver Grove, Melbourne and Brent and up River Road to South Ft. Thomas Ave. and then east along Grand through Ft. Thomas and Southgate to Newport. The CN&C obviously did not buy Black Diamond Stages for its Ross-Ft. Thomas route because the population of Ross, Melbourne, Silver Grove, and Brent did not total more than 1500. However, the Black Diamond's operating rights along Grand from Ft. Thomas to Newport (an area sprouting new subdivisions) was a natural extension for both the Green Line's 15-Southgate and 18-Newport East routes.

New Campbell County Routes

On March 24, 1940, the Green Line System radically altered transit service in Campbell County by beginning five new routes; 15H-Southgate-Highland-Ft. Thomas, 15G-Southgate-Grand-Ft. Thomas, 15R-Southgate-Grand-Ross 18G-Newport East-Grand-Ft. Thomas, and 18R-Newport East-Grand-Ross. The 15G, 15H and 18G routes were designed to provide better and more frequent service to growing residential sections of Newport, Southgate and Ft. Thomas.

It seemed complicated, this remaking of the Green Line route map southeast of Newport. But the riders got used to it and it served the territory well for a number of years.

The new 15H-Southgate-Highland-Ft. Thomas route extended from Fourth & Walnut in Cincinnati and, by following the existing 15-Southgate route, to reach Temple & Highland Ave. The new route then went east on Highland as far as South Ft. Thomas Ave. where the route looped via South Ft. Thomas, St. Nicholas and Trinity before heading back to Cincinnati.

15G-Southgate-Grand-Ft. Thomas duplicated 15H as far as Highland & Grand in Ft. Thomas, where it turned onto Grand to

Rapid growth in the Erlanger-Florence area just prior to World War II prompted Dixie Traction to buy larger buses in 1940 and 1941 in the form of Mack 31-passenger LC-3G's (Nos.131-138). The 136 appears **above**. Parent CN&C purchased seven identical models (Nos.301-307). The purchase of Dixie Traction by the Green Line resulted in lower fares to passengers all along Dixie Highway. Dixie announced the good news in a brochure; we reproduce its cover at **right**.
Special Collections and Archives, University of Kentucky Libraries.

Lower Bus Fares For Dixie Highway Residents Beginning Sunday, May 12

Lower bus fares for residents of the Dixie Highway communities become effective Sunday, May 12, 1940!

Cash fares between most cities and Cincinnati have been lowered, and furthermore, quantity fares are still lower, and may be taken advantage of without as large a cash outlay. The new tokens used for quantity fares are sold four for a quarter.

As an example of the reduced fares, the new cash fare between South Fort Mitchell and Cincinnati is now only ten cents, instead of the former fifteen cent cash or twelve-and-a-half cent token. This new rate applies to all territory north of the end of the car line.

Another example of the reduction is the cash fare from Erlanger to Cincinnati which is now only fifteen cents. This is lower than the former ticket fare.

CHEAPER — EASIER — BETTER

to use the buses

No parking worries or charges. No traffic congestion to fight. Board a Dixie Traction bus at the corner and ride to the center of town. **And you save money, too!** And you'll save even more money now with these new low fares.

The Dixie Traction Company

reach Ft. Thomas using Klanecrest and South Ft. Thomas to return on Grand towards Cincinnati. Both 15G and 15H provided non-rush hour weekday as well as Saturday and Sunday service to Southgate and Ft. Thomas.

However, although 15H also ran during rush hours, 15G was discontinued during rush hours and replaced by yet another new route, 18G-Newport East-Grand-Ft. Thomas. The 18G mirrored the route of the newly extended 18-Newport East line as far as Park & Grand, but then continued out Grand all the way to Klanecrest and South Ft. Thomas Ave. The old 15-Southgate route was now limited to short turn, rush-hour service.

During non-rush hours the new 18-Newport East route oper-

It would be the last summer for "non-essential" charters. Old Peoples Central International No. 17 hauls a group of kids to summer camp in this August 1941 view of Monmouth St. between Eighth and Seventh in Newport. Can we tell what is playing at the "air-cooled" Hipp Theater?
Special Collections and Archives, University of Kentucky Libraries.

ated from Fourth & Walnut in Cincinnati over the Central Bridge to Monmouth to Sixth to Park, to Ninth, to Monroe, to Tenth, to Park, to Grand, to Tenth and back on the same route through east Newport. During rush hours, 18-Newport East trips alternated with 18G-Newport East-Grand-Ft. Thomas trips, both routes using the State Highway Department Bridge (the L&N Bridge) to Third in Newport and over Third to Park and south on Park as far as Grand where the 18-Newport East route terminated.

Service was not abandoned on the former Black Diamond route segment from Ft. Thomas to Ross. Four non-rush hour trips via Southgate and four rush-hour trips via East Newport (designated 15R-Southgate-Grand-Ross and 18R-Newport East-Grand-Ross respectively) were extended on down South Ft. Thomas Ave. to River Rd. and out Kentucky Route 8 to Ross.

Although the Green Line "purchased" the operating rights to part of Dixie Traction's Belt Line, Dixie retained some service from North Ft. Thomas to Cincinnati through East Newport albeit on an altered route. Dixie Traction received permission from the ICC to run a North Ft. Thomas line from a new terminus at N. Ft. Thomas Ave. and Covert Run Road, to eliminate its former route through Bonnie Leslie and Newport via Sixth, and to reroute the line from Ft. Thomas via Waterworks and Wilson to Newport and via Washington and the L&N Bridge to Cincinnati.

This revised North Ft. Thomas route commenced on March

25, 1940, and served primarily as a rush hours only Monday-Friday service, but did offer a few midday Saturday trips for shoppers.

With the institution of Dixie's N. Ft. Thomas route, the Green Line's unremarked and little known Ft. Thomas Shuttle bus line was discontinued. This now redundant route had been absorbed by the Green Line in 1937 as part of the Peoples Central buyout and provided competition for the Dixie Traction Belt Line service. The shuttle used North Ft. Thomas Ave. between Covert Run and Highland and served as a feeder for the 11-Ft. Thomas streetcar line.

In anticipation of operations on the new 15H, 15G and 18G routes, five model 36-S 35-passenger buses from ACF (Nos. 350-354) were delivered to the Green Line in early 1940. Seven 31-passenger Mack model LC-3G buses (Nos. 301-307), delivered

The CN&C tried a different bus builder with an order for five ACF 36-S coaches, like the 353 shown here. They were needed when the Green Line purchased Black Diamond Lines in 1940 and expanded service on the 15-Southgate line.   *Motor Bus Society.*

to the Green Line later in 1940, and one 35-passenger Mack model CO-3G bus (No. 399), also saw considerable service on the new 15G, 15H and 18G routes.

Buses, After All, to Dayton

In one stroke, CN&C now tipped the scales in Newport from rail to bus.

The Green Line announced in early 1940 that gasoline buses were to be substituted for streetcars on the 12-Dayton line as soon as possible. The company cited promises it had made to the city councils of Newport, Bellevue and Dayton to substitute modern bus equipment for the aging streetcars.

Although some double-truck, high capacity 500s were assigned to 12-Dayton base service, it was necessary to use a number of single-truck 100s and 300s during rush hours. These slow, hand-braked cars had a seating capacity of only 32 and the newer of them were approaching 30 years old. Worse, the image was decidedly ancient.

In announcing the switch, the company cited the frequent interruptions to the 12-Dayton line just about every time the Ohio River flooded. For example, at Third & Kenton in Dayton there was a low spot that filled with water, halting car service when the Ohio River reached a stage of 56 feet. In addition the line at Third & Beech in Newport was affected every time there was a flood of over 62 feet.

Whenever the company could not operate streetcars to Dayton, it had to gather gasoline buses from other routes and press them into service. But this was a very difficult and expensive proposition. The floods of 1933 and 1936, in addition to the Great Flood of 1937, had all forced long-term disruptions of the 12-Dayton line.

The company noted that the 12-Dayton streetcar line was one of the Green Line's most heavily patronized lines, carrying more than 2,650,000 passengers in 1939. In the same year, 907,931 paying passengers used the 13-South Bellevue bus line and 479,908 passengers patronized the 23-Bonnie Leslie bus line, both of which duplicated a considerable portion of the 12-Dayton route.

Considering that the 1940 combined population of Bellevue and Dayton was less than 20,000, it is quite apparent that residents of these communities were still very dependent upon public transportation as late as World War II. Buses there would be, but they would have to be big.

CN&C officials, in conjunction with its Columbia overseers, strongly considered replacing the streetcars on 12-Dayton with trolley-coaches in view of the line's heavy traffic volume. However, electric buses were tied to overhead wires, and during the frequent Ohio River floods they would be sidelined due to rising water just as the streetcars had been. Substitute gas buses would still be needed when the waters rose.

Coal on the River Means Power For the Cars

The stern-wheeler *E. D. Kenna* passes under the Suspension Bridge and a 500-series Green Line car while pushing a load of coal toward the West End Power Plant. The Covington skyline is in the background. The coal will do its part in the generating of electricity for the CN&C's streetcars and trolley-coaches. *Cincinnati Museum Center Image Archives, Kenton County Library Collection.*

Therefore, the company ordered 12 heavy-duty 39-passenger Mack model CM-3G buses to replace the streetcars on the Dayton line. The 12 Mack CM-3Gs (Nos. 400-411) cost the Green Line more than $130,000 in total, and were delivered in April of 1940.

On April 28, 1940, streetcar service was discontinued on the 12-Dayton line with double-truck car 514 bringing down the curtain. Officials increased the number of weekday trips to Dayton from 117 when the streetcars held forth to 141 under the new bus schedule. In addition the company improved its owl service (between midnight and 5 a.m.) on this line with a bus every 25 minutes from 12:05 to 1:50 a.m. and then every 45 minutes until 5:15 a.m. This was by far the heaviest Green Line transit line changed from car to motor bus. Officials now watched its performance closely.

Later in the year, buses were substituted for streetcars on the rush hour only 14-York route. However, the tracks on York between Third and 11th remained intact until the summer of 1942 and, apparently, a streetcar or two substituted for an ailing motor coach at times during this period.

Streetcars Get a Death Sentence

Buses did well on the Dayton line, and, for Green Line management, the die was cast. The conversion of the 12-Dayton and 14-York streetcar lines meant that only one Green Line streetcar line, 11-Ft. Thomas (and its short turn 16-Washington), remained in Campbell County. The Newport Division retained for 11-Ft. Thomas service 10, 500-series double-truck cars. The conversions of the 9-Belt Line and 12-Dayton rail lines to buses and the 3-Ludlow streetcar line to trolley-coach operation enabled the CN&C to scrap all but 20 of its remaining single-truck streetcars.

All 14 or so survivors from Groups H through J (Nos. 289-318) were given their walking papers, as were all Group L, M & N cars, except for Group L cars Nos. 321, 323-326 and 15 M and N cars, (Nos. 100-103, 105, 107-109, 121-123, 125, 127, 129, 131).

Plans were also made to convert Covington's 8-Eastern car line to bus operation by January, 1942, which would allow the five remaining Group L single-truck cars to be decommissioned. It was further contemplated that inner-city Covington routes 4-Main and 5-Holman would be changed over to bus operation by December of 1942 allowing the 15 remaining Group M and N 100-series single-truck two-man cars to be retired.

That would leave only the two long suburban rail lines. CN&C management penciled in the 1-Ft. Mitchell and 11-Ft. Thomas for bus replacement "some time in 1944." They could be adequately covered by the 25 Group O double-truck 500-series one-man cars until the final curtain.

But the streetcar death sentence was stayed. World War II intervened and all conversion plans were put on hold. Ridership shot up, and every car that would roll on rails was urgently required. As a result, the five 320-series cars continued in service during World War II, contrary to some reports, as well as 15 of the 100-series and all 25 of the large 500-series cars. Their funeral would be long postponed.

Bargain Fares for Dixie Traction

At the time of the 12-Dayton bus substitution in 1940, Dixie Traction announced that fares would be reduced on its Erlanger-Florence route effective May 12 between Erlanger, Elsmere, Florence, Ft. Mitchell or South Ft. Mitchell and Cincinnati. For example, the new cash fare between South Ft. Mitchell and Cincinnati was reduced to 10 cents from the previous 15 cents

The 8-Eastern line in Covington was slated for motor buses in 1942, but it won a reprieve because of World War II curtailment of domestic vehicle production. Hence the Green Line single-trucker pictured at **right** heads for another load of war workers at Park & Court. *Earl Clark Collection.*

Fresh from the Mack factory in 1941, CN&C bus 361 poses at the **bottom** of the page for a photograph which was used in local area newspaper advertisements extolling the new and progressive Green Line image. That image included a racy stripe which swirled around and surrounded the coach below the windows. Could it have been a foretaste of the Nike swoosh of the 1990s? In any event, it was a roomy bus ideal for World War II crowds. *Special Collections and Archives, University of Kentucky Libraries.*

cash or 12 1/2 cent token rate. Residents of Florence could now get to downtown Cincinnati for only 20 cents, a reduction of 20 percent from what they had been paying.

Ridership improved dramatically. Dixie Traction found that the five remaining 25-passenger Mack 6-CW-3Ss (Nos. 124, 126, 127, 129-130) purchased in 1936 and 1937, augmented by the eight surviving Studebaker-FitzJohn buses (Nos. 113, 115-116, 118-122), could no longer handle the business. So in August, 1940, the company received five 31-passenger Mack model LC-3Gs (Nos. 131-135) at a cost of slightly more than $9000 apiece, for service on the Erlanger-Florence line.

In June of 1940, the Interstate Commerce Commission gave approval for the merger of the Cold Spring Bus Co. (and subsidiary Alexandria Bus Co.) into the Dixie Traction and to the operation of through service from Alexandria to Cincinnati. Accordingly, on July 25, 1940, Dixie Traction assumed the operation of both companies, an event which would contribute to the Green Line System's first major work stoppage later in the year.

Cold Spring Bus boasted relatively modern buses, including a 24-passenger 1938 Yellow Coach model 1204 (renumbered to Dixie Traction 105), a 21-passenger 1938 Yellow Coach model 733 (Dixie Traction No. 104), a 23-passenger 1936 White model 706M (DT No. 103), a 1935 25-passenger White model 702 (DT No. 102) and a 1934 21-passenger World model DA-60 (DT No. 101). Delivery of the new LC-3G Macks (Nos. 131-135) in November, 1940, allowed Dixie Traction to release some of its Mack 6-CW-3S buses for service on its recently purchased line to Cold Spring and to retire Studebaker buses Nos. 113 and 116.

Separate But Not Equal

It should be emphasized that the Dixie Traction, although wholly owned by the Cincinnati, Newport & Covington Railway Co., was conducted between 1940 and 1950 as a completely separate company. In addition to Dixie's buses sporting a different green and yellow paint scheme, free transfers were not permitted between the three Dixie Traction routes (Erlanger, Cold Spring, and North Ft. Thomas) and any CN&C route. And Dixie Traction had a system of zone fares which depended on a passenger's length of travel compared to the CN&C's almost universal flat fare structure.*

Dixie Traction was also distinctive in that it filed route and tariff applications with the ICC independently of the CN&C. Moreover, Dixie Traction operated primarily from its own garage (always called the "Erlanger garage" by the Dixie although the 30-bus capacity structure was actually just across the corporation line in Elsmere at Dixie Highway & May) and its 40 or so hourly employees belonged to a different union, a chapter of the

---

*There was one exception to the CN&C flat fare system. Zone fares were levied on passengers riding past River Road on the eight daily 15R-Southgate-Grand-Ross or 18R-East Newport-Grand-Ross trips along Kentucky Route 8 to Ross.

The Green Line was so proud of its new Mack model LD-3Gs (Nos. 361-365) that it expended the money and effort to rig more than 50 flashbulbs to fire at the same time to produce the 1941 night shot **above** taken outside the Newport Garage. Meanwhile, **below**, the old car tracks are still in place on Madison near Holmes High School as Brill trolley-coach No. 611 heads south. *Both: Special Collections and Archives, University of Kentucky.*

Brotherhood of Railroad Trainmen. For convenience, however, certain Dixie Traction buses, operated in rush-hour service on the Cold Spring and North Ft. Thomas lines, were stabled at the CN&C's Newport garage as a result of the Dixie Traction entering into a service contract with its parent.

Management had reasons for walling off Dixie Traction from the parent company. Trade union suspicions about those reasons now grew rapidly.

The Clouds of War

In May of 1940, the war in Europe took an ominous turn as Germany invaded France. By autumn, Germany had conquered its ancient enemy and was trying to bomb Great Britain into submission. As a response, a new selective service law, which passed by only one vote in the House of Representatives, enabled the United States to start building up its armed forces as the clouds of war pushed ever closer to the U. S. mainland.

The Ft. Thomas military post, which for many years prior to World War I was the home of the famous Sixth Infantry Regiment, was designated in 1940 as a major induction center for the new draftees or "selectees" as they were now called. In October, 1940, the War Department, through its Quartermaster Corps, contracted with the CN&C to supply charter buses to transport selectees and reservists from Northern Kentucky and Southern Ohio train stations to Ft. Thomas for initial processing and to take them back to the railroads for travel to their next assignments.

Further, the Armor School at Ft. Knox, Ky., set up an auxiliary mechanics training unit at Ft.

Thomas. The Quartermaster Corps also selected the CN&C to transport from 150 to 300 soldiers a day to specialized classes at the Cincinnati Automotive School. In one year's time (from October, 1940, through September, 1941) more than 50,000 soldiers were carried on Green Line charters to and from Ft. Thomas.

All this meant that the Green Line was getting an early start on a booming wartime ridership.

CN&C's Anguished Employees

Throughout its long history, the Green Line had been remarkably free of major labor troubles. Management and workers always seemed to get along. But in December, 1940, CN&C employees went on strike. And the amazing thing is that Green Line officials did not see it coming.

Dixie Traction Copes With Record Ridership

The fare reduction on Dixie Traction's main route, coupled with the later gasoline and tire rationing of World War II, forced both Dixie and its parent CN&C to buy more new buses in 1942. These were once again from Mack, 35-passenger model LD-3G models (CN&C Nos. 370-378 and Dixie Nos. 150-152). In the illustration at **right**, Dixie No. 152 waits at the Erlanger Garage for its next call to service. Sister No. 150 on the Erlanger line loads, **below,** on the corner of Fourth & Vine in Cincinnati. Wartime pressures will, in due course, permit Green Line (but not Dixie Traction) motor buses to use the Dixie Terminal, freeing up scarce street space for Cincinnati Street Ry. vehicles. *Both: Special Collections and Archives, University of Kentucky Libraries.*

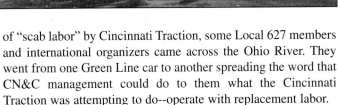

The dispute was not so much over money as over job security. And in some respects the strike was really a union versus union gunfight, with the CN&C caught in the crossfire. It had its roots in the company's efforts to keep Dixie Traction separate, aided and abetted by the ICC.

When it took over, CN&C had recognized Dixie Traction's hourly employees trade union, a chapter of the Brotherhood of Railroad Trainmen. This, coupled with the assignment of the Cold Spring-Alexandria route to the Dixie Traction, left CN&C union members with the uneasy feeling that the Dixie Traction and Cold Spring Bus Co. buyouts would be used by the company as a Trojan horse to "bust" their union, Local 628 of the Amalgamated Association of Street and Electric Railway Employees of America.

Local 628 had been founded in May of 1913, shortly after the international union had organized the operating employees of the neighboring Cincinnati Traction Co. as Local 627. In April, 1913, the Cincinnati Traction employees' demands for wage increases and better working conditions were rejected by the company and the Local 627 membership went on strike in May.

Cincinnati Traction attempted to run cars with strikebreakers, but this was only partially successful. As a result of the use of "scab labor" by Cincinnati Traction, some Local 627 members and international organizers came across the Ohio River. They went from one Green Line car to another spreading the word that CN&C management could do to them what the Cincinnati Traction was attempting to do--operate with replacement labor.

A meeting was held on May 12, 1913, and all but 12 of the eligible 350 motormen, conductors and barn workers voted to join the Amalgamated and became charter members of Local 628. In spite of the problems on the Cincinnati side of the river, Local 628 members received quick recognition by the Green Line and all issues were settled amicably. The agreement called for some revision of schedules, improvements in working conditions and an increase in wages to parity with whatever was eventually agreed to on the Cincinnati side.

Over the years from 1913 to 1940, the collective bargaining process seems to have worked well and the union and the company settled their differences without resort to any job actions on the union's part.

Anatomy of a Dispute

However, new and different forces were at work in 1940. With the Green Line's modification of the double truck cars to one man operation and the retirement of so many two man streetcars in favor of one man buses, some CN&C operating employees had been relegated to only occasional extra board work, and a number of newer hires had been laid off. This could have been borne if all had sacrificed equally.

But they had not. Those working for Dixie Traction, members of a different union, were obviously not being laid off. The more the members of CN&C's Local 628 thought about this, the more upset they became.

They resented the fact that Dixie Traction was kept separate and not merged into CN&C. They saw that many Dixie employees had been on the payroll for shorter periods of time than many Local 628 members had been with the CN&C, but were working regularly while many Local 628 members were not.

Local 628 officials proposed that their members be permitted to bid on regular Dixie Traction runs, thus relegating newer Dixie Traction employees to either extra board or layoff status. To them it seemed clear that the Dixie operators' union, the Brotherhood of Railroad Trainmen, was a "company" union that had been coerced into accepting a lower wage scale by Dixie Traction management. Members of Local 628 feared the company would gradually assign more and more CN&C routes to Dixie Traction in an attempt to lower labor costs. In other words, the Dixie Traction tail would soon be wagging the CN&C dog.

And that would not do. Local 628 would have to act.

A strike authorization was overwhelmingly approved by the membership in August, 1940. However, the members did not immediately go out, but instead carried on a series of negotiations with CN&C management into the late fall. Management assured Local 628 officials that no plans were afoot to expand the Dixie Traction's role in the Northern Kentucky transit picture at the expense of CN&C employees.

But the Green Line seemed to be caught in a labor law tangle. General Manager Vondersmith claimed that, based upon legal advice, the CN&C could not force the BRT local representing Dixie Traction's hourly employees to merge with Local 628 and the CN&C had no choice but to honor the BRT's existing contract with the Dixie Traction, including the lower wage scale. And he did not fail to mention the ICC's role in keeping the two corporations separate.

The union saw this as disingenuous. In November, Local 628 made a new contract proposal that CN&C employees should take over driving the Dixie's Chesapeake and Ohio and L&N contract runs. This was dismissed out of hand by Green Line officials.

Taking on a somewhat autocratic tone, Vondersmith indignantly told Local 628 officials that the CN&C had not made a net operating profit since 1928 and the company simply was not going to agree to any changes in wages, working conditions, or the Green Line's relationship with the Dixie Traction in such troubled financial times.

Strike!

Vondersmith's unwillingness to bend on even the railroad contract runs issue was the straw that broke the camel's back. The union called a strike for December 7, 1940, and, on that morning, set up pickets at both carbarns and effectively shut down the Green Line. The strikers also established pickets at Dixie's Erlanger garage,

At Pearl & Broadway in Cincinnati, a Green Line car has one more block to go before it will turn left at Second to ascend the steep and angled approach to the Central Bridge to Newport. The tracks at the lower right carried Green Line cars to the L&N Bridge until 1921. Thereafter, only Cincinnati Street Railway's line 27 used the trackage. A CSR 100-series car can be seen in the distance. *Earl Clark Collection.*

but were unsuccessful in keeping Dixie Traction's drivers from taking their buses out onto Dixie Highway.

Trouble was not long in coming. By 7:30 a.m. on December 8, Dixie Traction services ran into problems when two Erlanger route buses were disabled in downtown Covington. Two Dixie drivers found that ignition wires had been ripped out of the engine compartments by roving bands of CN&C strikers while buses had stopped to discharge passengers at Third & Court. The strikers also issued verbal threats and, soon after, other Dixie drivers drove their vehicles back to Dixie's garage and went home.

A scheduled meeting set for December 12 by Vondersmith with all the parties gave rise to optimism that the strike would be short lived. However the meeting was unproductive and the strike continued to grind on toward Christmas. Members of Local 627, the Cincinnati Street Railway hourly bargaining group, gave each of their CN&C counterparts a $5 basket of groceries the week before Christmas. And each Local 628 striker received a weekly relief check of $7 ($10 for married members) from the international union.

Not only was the strike going to mean a bleak Christmas for members of Local 628 and their families, but also for many supervisory employees who feared that the Columbia Gas and Electric Corp., tired of a decade of deficits, might just give up the ghost and simply shut down the operation and sell whatever assets or operating rights they could.

David L. Ringo, a young management employee, saw the strike coming and remembers that even as early as October of 1939 when the purchase of the Dixie Traction by the CN&C was announced, the members of Local 628 began worrying about what the sale would mean to their wages and job security in light of the Dixie Traction employees' different union and lower hourly wage. Ringo, who would later become CEO of American Transportation Enterprises (a large transit holding company and the Green Line's eventual parent), agreed with his wife that they

would return the Christmas presents they had already bought for refunds and would start sending out resumes to other transit companies if the strike was not settled by January 1, 1941.

The management-labor impasse had deteriorated into a grim standoff, and it continued into the new year of 1941. The company was unsuccessful in obtaining an injunction to force Local 628 members back to work. Further, the judge ruled that Local 628 members could continue to picket the Dixie Traction garage. The court hearings did air both the concerns of CN&C workers of a Dixie Traction takeover of more of the Green Line routes, and the fears of the Dixie Traction workers if their union was absorbed by Local 628, they would be laid off in favor of Green Line workers who had more seniority.

No matter what happened, one or more of the contending factions would lose.

Resolution

Ringo, who had started with the company in the summer of 1931 as a track laborer between college semesters at the University of Kentucky, had risen to assistant superintendent of transportation by 1940, a position which put him into constant contact with the operating employees. He had sweated up to 16 hours a day side by side with many of the now striking employees after the 1937 flood for more than six months helping to restore full service. He had picked up a case of tuberculosis, resulting in a six month stay in a North Carolina sanitarium.

One thing he knew for sure: top management had grown out of touch with the rank and file. And so on January 5 or 6, 1941, Ringo asked Vondersmith for a chance to meet with the strikers. Much to his amazement, the young manager was given permission by a now distraught Vondersmith to have a go at negotiations.

It was a bitterly cold morning when Ringo met with the Local only two days later. The meeting was in a tent set up by the strikers across from the 20th & Madison carbarn. Proposals for ending the strike were exchanged in the morning session with Ringo agreeing to consult with management and return later that day. When Ringo arrived back at the tent, he saw a meal of cornbread and bean soup being prepared. He saw as well the presence

This Green Line strike is settled, but there is much to do before the cars and buses can roll again. A worker on top of line truck No. 10, **above,** makes some hasty repairs at 3rd & Court in Covington so that streetcar and trolley-coach service can be restored in the early hours of January 14, 1941. It had been the longest walkout in company history. Meanwhile, over on the 11-Ft. Thomas line, it was necessary to clear a month's worth of snow off the tracks. The first rail vehicle to turn a wheel was Brill sweeper No. 6, on January 13, pictured at **bottom left** during a 1939 storm.
Both: Special Collections and Archives, University of Kentucky Libraries.

of union officials from the BRT local. He sensed that the atmosphere had changed for the better and, over the next 12 hours, officials from both unions and Ringo proceeded to take nourishment, to reflect, and to hammer out an agreement.

The pact stated that, although the Dixie Traction would remain as a separate entity with a separate seniority list, laid off or extra board CN&C employees would have a right to bid on any job openings at Dixie Traction prior to the hiring of any new employees. To placate Dixie's BRT union members, a stepped-up pay scale was introduced to give Dixie Traction employees eventual wage parity with CN&C employees. This would happen if Dixie employees would agree to join Local 628 and surrender their BRT charter. Slight increases in the level of medical benefits and certain cost of living adjustments were also negotiated.

The relief was palpable. Peace was at hand. The agreement was quickly and overwhelmingly approved by members of both unions. Green Line employees returned to work on January 14, 1941. Full services on both the CN&C and Dixie Traction were resumed within a couple of days.

It was estimated that the strike caused a loss in revenue of

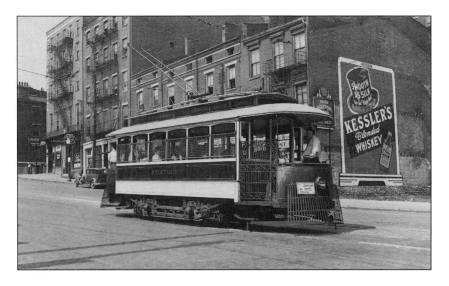

approximately $150,000 to the Green Line and wage losses to the CN&C and Dixie employees of at least $50,000. In May of 1941, the charter of the BRT local was surrendered, leaving Local 628 as the sole bargaining agent for all Green Line and Dixie Traction hourly employees.

And a young and eager David Ringo was on his way.

Gearing up for War

By late 1941, American industrial capacity was running at close to full production. What President Roosevelt had called the Arsenal of Democracy was not only producing war materiel to beef up the weak American armed forces, but was also sending vast amounts of manufactured goods to countries which were resisting Nazi Germany, particularly Great Britain and the Soviet Union.

Humming factories increased the Green Line's passenger ridership in 1941 to a new all-time high. Many more seats were

The most curious transit "system" in Northern Kentucky remained the single-bus operation of the Monmouth St. Merchants Association. Due to wartime gas rationing, the Merchants needed a bigger bus. They got one from White in 1942, a model 782, replacing or supplementing an earlier White 706M. *Motor Bus Society.*

needed, and the CN&C took delivery in 1941 of five 35-passenger Mack model LD-3G buses (Nos. 360-364) and two Mack 40-passenger CM-3G model buses (Nos. 412-413). These deliveries enabled the CN&C to dispose of most of the older buses it had inherited in the 1937 local lines "buyouts" and the 1940 Black Diamond acquisition, so by September of 1941, only 14 "merger" buses were still used in tripper service (Fords Nos. 33-36, Internationals Nos. 37-40, Macks Nos. 44-45 & 47, Ford No. 70, White No. 75 and Mack No. 78).

Five more remained on the property primarily for non-revenue use in transporting workers to streetcar track repair sites (Nos. 16-17, 23-25) while six were converted to service vehicles during the war by the simple expedient of having their passenger bodies removed except for the driver's space (Nos. 26, 29, 30, 32, 72 and 77). Also, one of the Green Line's first buses, a Yellow Coach Z-29 (No. 12), purchased for the 15-Southgate line in 1936, was "sold" to the Dixie Traction in 1941 for conversion and use as a service truck.

Dixie Traction took delivery in 1941 of three more 31-passenger Mack model LC-3G buses (Nos. 136-138) which allowed it to retire Studebaker-FitzJohn buses 115 and 117. Dixie also "sold" three Mack 6-CW-3Ss (Nos. 123, 125, 128) it had leased to the Green Line since 1939 to the CN&C (Nos. 56-58) and "bought" two CN&C 6-CQ-3Ss Nos. 61 and 62 (Dixie Traction Nos. 106 and 107).

CN&C had originally planned to renumber its pre-1940 buses to confirm to the system it devised and implemented in 1940 with respect to new bus purchases (i.e., 20-29 passenger capacity buses in the 200s, 30 to 35 capacity buses in the 300s and 40+ capacity buses in the 400s). But with so many new buses coming in so fast, it was decided to confine the scheme to new purchases only, and the ex-Dixie 6-CW-3Ss (originally assigned CN&C Nos. 210 to 212) were renumbered CN&C Nos. 56 to 58 instead.

On December 7, the Japanese bombed Pearl Harbor and in a fiery instant plunged the U. S. into the cauldron of World War II.

Uncle Sam would now shape the destiny of public and private transportation. In February, 1942, the War Production Board ordered that all production of automobiles, tires, washing machines and other major appliances be discontinued. Due to German U-boat attacks on the east coast and an increased demand by the military for petroleum products, gasoline sales to civilians were soon rationed. And as it became increasingly difficult to obtain spare parts and tires to keep automobiles running, many people simply parked them for the duration of the war. This meant that more and more people had to resort to public transportation to get to their wartime jobs.

Back Into Harness: Castoff Cars and Banished Buses

The enormous World War II passenger loads inflicted unprecedented punishment to Green Line infrastructure. More work equipment was an urgent necessity. Veteran tool car No. 1 was among those pressed back into service. Converted from an 1892 Laclede passenger car, the resurrected contraption in the frame at **left** is loading supplies behind the Newport car barn. The ramp to the 11th Street (Shortway) Bridge is in the background. *T. W. Lehmann Collection.*

Old motor buses played new roles as well. An example is this CN&C conversion of Mack bus No. 77 into a service truck. Ed Voyeye is the man in the picture at **right**.

Photos left and right: Special Collections and Archives, University of Kentucky Libraries.

Line car No. 9, **above**, would have been scrapped if World War II had not come along. Instead, it lasted until 1950.

Like other carriers, the Green Line would see its ridership soar--to a record 33,500,000 passengers in 1942. Ironically, the War Production Board also curtailed the production of transit buses, creating a classic "Catch-22." Transit companies simply could not obtain enough equipment to keep up with demand.

Fortunately, the Green Line had contractual obligations with the War Department to serve Ft. Thomas. Accordingly, the War Production Board allowed Mack to deliver to the Green Line in March, 1942, 10 CM-3Gs (Nos. 414-423), and allocated to the Green Line, in July of 1942, 12 Mack 35-passenger LD-3Gs (CN&C Nos. 370-378 and Dixie Traction Nos. 150-152). These new buses would be the last the Green Line System would receive until the war was over.

During 1942 ridership on the Dixie Traction's Cold Spring-Alexandria route increased a whopping 200 percent. By the end of 1941, old Alexandria Pike (U.S. 27) had been rebuilt and extended through southern Campbell County to Butler in Pendleton County. The new highway made it possible for many full and part time farmers in rural Campbell County to use Dixie Traction to reach wartime production jobs at manufacturing plants in Northern Kentucky and Cincinnati.

Consequently, the 20- to 25-passenger capacity buses inherited by Dixie Traction from the Cold Spring Bus Co. were no longer adequate to handle the crush of new riders. In September,

1942, the CN&C, in another inter-company "sale," transferred to Dixie two more 31-passenger Mack 6-CQ-3S buses (Green Line 64-65 to Dixie 108-109). In turn, Dixie Traction sold one of its White buses (No. 102) to the equipment-starved Independence Bus Co, an important Green Line System feeder, which had a route from southern Kenton County to downtown Covington where it connected with the CN&C.

In early 1943, the Office of Defense Transportation banned all pleasure travel for the duration and decreed that no transit services could be operated primarily for "shoppers or amusement." This edict meant that Green Line could not offer charter service for school outings and such, or provide service to Covington's Devou Park during the 1943 summer concert season. Nor could the Monmouth Street Merchants Association's Dayton-Newport shuttle operate on Saturdays.

Between 1935 and 1942, concerts at Devou Park had generated significant revenue for the Green Line. A number of improvements were made to the park in 1934, including the construction of a band shell under a Works Progress Administration grant. During the following summers, evening concerts were regularly held at Devou featuring both well known local entertainers such as Rosemary Clooney and Andy Williams and nationally recognized big bands led by the likes of Paul Whiteman and Glenn Miller.

With the installation of powerful exhaust fans in the Dixie Terminal in October of 1942, CN&C was allowed to operate motor buses into the structure for the first time. A Newport Division ACF bus has departed the lower level to go east on Third while a Covington Division Brill trolley-coach heads south on the upper level. This was a breakthrough in reducing congestion on downtown Cincinnati streets and saving time and gasoline. *Special Collections and Archives, University of Kentucky Libraries.*

The Green Line provided special bus service to the Devou Park concerts from both Third & York in Newport and Third & Court in Covington. From 10 to 30 buses were routinely needed to transport concertgoers. In addition, since the 1-Ft. Mitchell streetcar line bordered an entrance to Devou Park, extra cars were also seen on this route during concert sessions.

Gas Buses Invade Dixie Terminal

With more and more Kentucky buses pouring into downtown Cincinnati, it became necessary to reconsider their banishment from Dixie Terminal. The war year of 1942 saw both Green Line and Dixie Traction motor buses still loading and unloading passengers on the streets of Cincinnati alongside the Terminal. The Green Line had been barred from operating motor buses into the Dixie Terminal from the start of such service in 1936 but again attempted to get the ban lifted in 1942. Terminal management pointed out that the long-term lease entered into with the CN&C in 1921 covered "electrically powered vehicles" only and contended that bus fumes would permeate into the Terminal's office space and foul the air breathed by its tenants.

But there were other--and more pressing--issues now. By fall, the Cincinnati city manager met with Dixie Terminal Manager Harry Lynch to discuss his refusal to permit CN&C motor buses to enter the Dixie Terminal. With stepped-up streetcar service by the Cincinnati Street Railway on Fourth St. caus-

ing more delay to both CSR and CN&C operations, the city demanded, "for patriotic reasons if for no other reason," that the Dixie Terminal permit, at a minimum, the CN&C's Newport Division motor coach routes to use the Dixie's lower level loop "to lessen delays and thus help conserve energy."

That did the trick. With new-found patriotic fervor (and a commitment from the Green Line to pay for the installation of an exhaust system to vent motor bus fumes), Dixie Terminal officials allowed CN&C motor buses to use the lower level of the structure effective October 27, 1942. Thus, all of CN&C's interstate routes were "under roof" at the Dixie Terminal for the first time since 1936 as follows:

Upper Level (Covington Division)

Route No.	Line	Type Vehicle
1	Ft. Mitchell	Streetcar
2	Greenup*	Streetcar
3	Ludlow	Trolley-Coach
4	Main	Streetcar
5	Holman	Streetcar
6	Rosedale	Trolley-Coach
7	Latonia	Trolley-Coach
8	Eastern	Streetcar
10	Lewisburg*	Streetcar

Lower Level (Newport Division)

Route No.	Line	Type Vehicle
11	Ft. Thomas	Streetcar
12	Dayton	Gas Bus
13	So. Bellevue	Gas Bus
14	York*	Gas Bus
15	Southgate*	Gas Bus
15G	Southgate-Grand¶	Gas Bus
15H	Southgate-Highland	Gas Bus
15R	Southgate-Grand-Ross¶	Gas Bus
16	Washington*	Streetcar
18	Newport East	Gas Bus
18G	Newport East-Grand*	Gas Bus
18R	Npt. East-Grand-Ross*	Gas Bus
19	Newport West	Gas Bus
20	Newport South	Gas Bus
23	Bonnie Leslie	Gas Bus

* Rush-hour service only.
¶ Base service only.

Wartime necessity also forced the resolution of another sorely vexing issue. Thankful for the agreement between CN&C and the Dixie Terminal permitting inside bus loading, the city of Cincinnati permitted the Green Line to raise southbound streetcar and trolley-coach token fares to 6 1/4 cents (or 8 cents cash). Since the ICC had permitted the CN&C since 1936 to collect a 6 1/4 cent southbound token fare on motor bus routes (or 8 cents cash), a uniform fare structure was achieved for the first time in six years.

However, Dixie Terminal Manager Lynch still refused to allow Dixie Traction's three bus routes to use the Dixie Terminal since DTC was not a party to the original lease. As a result, Dixie Traction continued to discharge and receive passengers on its heavy Erlanger-Florence line at Fourth & Vine, and on the North Ft. Thomas and Cold Spring-Alexandria routes at Fourth & Walnut.

A Record Year

World War II saw its turning point in 1943. As for the Green Line System, its resources were stretched to the limit. With the continued ban on automobile production, coupled with tire and gasoline rationing, and with manufacturing plants exceeding 100 percent of capacity, public transit was in demand as never before. The entire system carried a record 37 million transit passengers during the year. It should again be kept in mind that the total population of the three Kentucky counties served by the company was less than 250,000. In addition, Ft. Thomas military charters kept five to 20 motor coaches tied up every weekday.

With gasoline in tight supply, the CN&C utilized streetcars in lieu of motor buses whenever possible to move soldiers to and from Ft. Thomas. The Newport station of the Chesapeake and Ohio Railway, at 11th & Saratoga, was located on non-revenue streetcar trackage linking the 11-Ft. Thomas line at Tenth & Washington with the Newport carbarn. It was frequently used by Green Line cars meeting troop trains.

On a number of occasions, usually during midday, from five to 20 of the high-capacity (55-passenger) 500s were pulled off their regular runs (and 32-passenger single-truck cars substituted) and formed into a "flying squadron" to carry soldiers to or from Ft. Thomas and the C&O station in Newport.

By mid-1943 the Green Line, with more and more employees being drafted into the armed forces and the pool of available male labor nearly non-existent, turned to the unprecedented expedient of hiring females for the operating department. Five women were trained as "temporary" bus operators and, from supervisory reports, performed their duties very successfully. However, with the return of veterans with medical discharges claiming back their old jobs during 1944, the last of the women drivers was released in January 1945.

Ohio's Kentucky Airport

How the Cincinnati airport got uprooted from Ohio and plunked down in a Northern Kentucky pasture is an interesting story which had Green Line fingerprints all over it.

It was in 1943 that workers started construction of the new Greater Cincinnati Airport in Boone County, Ky. By the late 1930s, it became apparent that Cincinnati's Lunken Field had

A Green Line Gathering at the River

The Green Line's World War II charters grew bigger and bigger. Often they were designed to take troops from Ft. Thomas to railroad stations or to technical schools. But this one, photographed in 1942, was delivering these soldiers to the Cincinnati riverfront for a tech school graduation junket aboard the *Island Queen*. We can see the men gathering at the foot of the gangway at lower right. As for the buses, we can identify four Mack CMs in the rear row and in the second row we find the front of an LD at the far left, then ACF 36-S No. 360, another CM and CM 403. Another 36-S starts the front row at left. And there might be more out of the picture. For work or play, the Green Line was at the service of the servicemen.

Special Collections and Archives, University of Kentucky Libraries.

A Streetcar in Search of Passengers

Rumbling down a rain-swept street, double-trucker 519 has just passed the U. S. Army post of Ft. Thomas. Now it is stopped at Ft. Thomas' first shopping area, built in the middle 1890s to serve army personnel and their dependents. The car seems to be devoid of customers at this point, but it's near the end of the line. *Earl Clark Collection via Sam Guthrie.*

become inadequate to handle commercial air traffic. Situated in the eastern part of Cincinnati and adjacent to the Ohio River, Lunken was subject to both periodic flooding and heavy fog.

Level land was scarce on the Ohio side, and entrepreneurs across the river saw opportunity for a lucrative venture. In 1941 a handful of Northern Kentucky businessmen organized to locate potential sites in rural Kenton County for a new airport. They obtained approval of the Kentucky legislature to form a Kenton County Airport Board to develop and manage a "Greater Cincinnati Airport."

As it turned out, the group, which included Green Line General Manager Vondersmith, could not find a suitable site in Kenton County, but did find one in adjacent Boone County. They settled on a parcel located off Mineola Pike which was determined to be one of the least fog prone areas within a 50 mile radius of downtown Cincinnati. And the Boone County site, only 11 miles from Fountain Square in Cincinnati, was a bargain at only $40 an acre and was flat, requiring only minimal grading.

Later that year, the federal government issued, through the Works Progress Administration and the Civil Aeronautics Administration, grants to begin construction. Such federal action came only after the Kentucky legislature approved some unique legislation allowing the Kenton County Airport Board to purchase 930 additional acres in adjacent Boone County and to operate the proposed airport across county lines. Thus it appeared that a new airport in Kentucky for Cincinnati, Ohio would become a reality.

World War II put the plans for the new airport in abeyance. But not for long. In late 1942, a Kentucky congressional delegation led by Sen. Alben W. Barkley and Rep. Brent Spence called upon the White House to authorize construction. Barkley and Spence, both Democrats who were swept into office with FDR during the New Deal, asked the President to give the Army a "gentle push" to develop the site. This he must have done, because the Air Transport Command announced plans in December, 1942, to construct an airfield on the site with four runways, each 5500 feet long, for use as an auxiliary cargo-handling base.

Construction started in April, 1943 on the first two runways. Later in 1944 the Army Air Force also used the facility to practice touch and go landings by bomber crews out of Lockbourne Air Base in Columbus, Ohio. The Army vacated Boone County Field in early 1945, at which time the War Production Board approved construction of a terminal and administration building, and other facilities associated with civilian airport operations.

All this was very nice for Dixie Traction. With the start of construction on the first runways at the future Greater Cincinnati Airport in Boone County in April, 1943, Dixie needed additional buses to carry construction workers from the end of the 1-Ft. Mitchell car line and its own Erlanger route to the airport and tried to place an order for five new buses. Uncle Sam, however, turned a deaf ear to the request for new buses.

The Newport bus garage was busy 7 days a week. The war demanded that every unit be ready at dawn. At **right**, Truman Price steam cleans the engine of Mack 306. *Both: Special Collections and Archives, University of Kentucky Library.*

The Dash of the *Greenhound*

IT IS AN IRON LAW of the urban transit business that much of a transit company's equipment stands idle during a large portion of the weekday with an even larger percentage at liberty on weekends. A transit company typically finds use for most of its equipment only on weekdays between 6 to 9 a.m. and 4 to 7 p.m. It is altogether unproductive.

Numerous Greyhound entities had placed orders for new intercity equipment prior to World War II, but the manufacturers were unable to fill those orders after the government ordered intercity bus, as well as transit bus, production severely curtailed. Especially hard hit was Southeastern Greyhound, which saw a great increase in ridership brought about largely by the new army camps built in its territory.

Furthermore, the states of Kentucky, Tennessee, Alabama and Georgia came to be looked upon as a "reservoir for victory labor" for the defense plants in Ohio, Illinois, Indiana, Michigan and Pennsylvania. Many southerners left their homes in those states to work in war plants in such places as Cincinnati, Akron, Columbus, Cleveland, Toledo and Detroit. They tried to get home on the weekends as often as possible. So did servicemen and women whenever they could obtain leave.

Greyhound did not have nearly enough buses to satisfy the increased demand. It was time for creative thinking, and the general managers of the Southeastern Greyhound, Great Lakes Greyhound and Capital Greyhound approached Green Line management in late 1942. They wondered if the CN&C could furnish drivers and buses to Greyhound during off peak hours and on weekends.

It could indeed. The discussions led to a Green Line contract with Southeastern Greyhound (and verbal agreements with Capitol Greyhound and Great Lakes Greyhound) to put those idle buses to work in Greyhound replacement service. The Green Line agreed to provide 39-passenger buses and drivers for Greyhound service at the rate of 31 cents per mile. Greyhound agreed to bear all fuel, maintenance, taxes and insurance expenses on the CN&C vehicles pinch-hitting for Greyhound.

During 1943 Green Line's transit buses handled Greyhound trips from Cincinnati to Columbus, Knoxville, Indianapolis, Charleston, W. Va., and Louisville, Corbin, Somerset and Lexington, Ky. The Green Line had up to 40 buses in Greyhound service on Saturdays and Sundays, most commonly to Columbus, Lexington or Louisville. Upwards of 20 Green Line buses were also operated in Greyhound service during the week from 9 a.m. to 4 p.m. and 7 p.m. to midnight.

These "Greenhound" runs allowed Greyhound to turn back equipment at, say Lexington, with the CN&C relaying Greyhound passengers on to Cincinnati. Although the service was not particularly profitable for the Green Line per se, it did allow extra-board drivers to supplement their paychecks and contributed to the overall war effort.

In 1943, the Cincinnati, Newport & Covington bus fleet peeled off a grand total of 2,513,962 miles, of which 732,864 miles were operated on behalf of various Greyhound sub-

sidiaries. In 1944, Green Line buses chalked up a total of 2,523,562 miles with almost 700,000 of those miles operated on behalf of Greyhound.

What type of transit buses did the Green Line operate for Greyhound during 1943 and 1944? A review of the mileage records indicates that the company assigned the newest series of heavy duty CM-3G Macks (Nos. 414-423) almost exclusively to Greyhound service. The 10 CMs in question covered 576,114 out of the 700,000 miles operated by the Green Line for Greyhound in 1944. For example, in 1944 Green Line CM-3G No. 414 spent 43,858 miles in Greyhound service out of a grand total of 53,105 miles.

Other Mack CM-3Gs (Nos. 400-413), LD-3Gs (Nos. 360-364 and 370-378) and LC-3Gs (Nos. 301-307) covered most of the remaining miles operated for Greyhound. However, the records reveal that even the Green Line's muzzle loaders (single-door 25-passenger Mack 6-CW-3Ss) occasionally were placed into Greyhound service during holiday weekends.

Green Line operator Hendrix Ravenscraft, who retired after some 40 years of service, frequently drew "Greenhound" assignments during 1943 and 1944. He remembered:

"Those big [model CM-3G] Macks never seriously challenged the speed limit even on trips along the fairly flat routes to Columbus or Lexington. Things really got interesting when a fellow got a trip to Louisville over U. S. 42. The highway was like a roller coaster up and down and with a lot of curves. You spent a lot of time in the lower gears and on the brakes and, thanks to the city bus suspensions, you were sore from head to toe by the time you reached Louisville.

"Upon pulling into the Louisville Greyhound station you felt a real sense of accomplishment but you soon became depressed because you knew you had to take a load of passengers back to Cincy within the hour. A lot of times my bus would connect in Louisville with a trip ready to go to Ft. Knox and I seem to recall that transit buses from the local system often held down those Louisville-Ft. Knox runs. I was sure glad to bid on a regular run in 1944 and escape the 'bite' of the hound."

In late 1944, the Kentucky Division of Motor Transportation filed suit against the Green Line for non-payment of intercity motor carrier seat taxes. Accountants for the Green Line determined that the service was barely covering its own costs and, if the company were forced to pay the additional tax, it would lose money. When it appeared no compromise with the state could be reached, the Green Line pulled the plug. Greyhound was notified that "Greenhound" service would be discontinued on May 1, 1945. But the timing was lucky, because the ban on the building of intercity motor coaches had been lifted in August of 1944, so Greyhound could now look forward to new equipment of its own. ◆

In a stroke of good luck, an employee reported sighting two old ex-CN&C International buses rusting away at a local scrapyard. A delegation was immediately dispatched to investigate and found that the buses in question (ex-CN&C Nos. 74-75) were literally moments away from the cutting torch. These buses were purchased for $250 each (having been sold to the junkyard for $50 apiece!), reconditioned, and renumbered Dixie Traction 90 and 91. They survived in Dixie Traction service until 1946 at which time, amazingly, they were sold to the Newsom Bus Lines for startup service between Covington, Ryland and Visalia in southern Kenton County.

Green Line on its Own

The Public Utilities Holding Company Act of 1935 decreed that gas and electric companies must divest themselves of subsidiaries not directly related to energy production or distribution. Columbia Gas and Electric, the owner of the CN&C and Dixie Traction, was subject to this law. However, with the Cincinnati, Newport & Covington Railway, a perennial money loser until the start of World War II, finding a willing buyer was not to be all that easy.

Finally, in October of 1944, a company called Bayou Inc. (70 percent owned by investment banker Charles Allen of New York and 30 percent by the Lowe Co. with Irving K. Weil of New Orleans as general partner) purchased the CN&C, the Dixie Traction and the Licking River Bridge Co. from Columbia. The purchase price was $1,530,611. The sale was readily approved by the ICC and consummated on October 11, 1944. Interestingly, P. G. Vondersmith, who was also general manager of Union Light, Heat and Power Co. as well as the Green Line System, elected to cast his lot with the newly independent Green Line as both its president and general manager.

Therefore, at the start of 1945, the entire Green Line System was out from under the aegis of Columbia Gas and Electric for the first time since 1907. It was a sobering thought: the Green Line now could no longer look to the almost unlimited financial resources of a benign parent. It would have to make it on its own in a tough business. Perhaps with this in mind it named David Ringo, a future entrepreneur, as its assistant general manager in February, 1945.

Vondersmith thought he knew where he could find some of that needed new revenue. Almost immediately he started negotiations with the Kenton County Airport Board and officials of the airlines planning to use the new Boone County (Greater Cincinnati) Airport. He proposed that Dixie Traction provide scheduled ground transportation and taxi service to and from downtown Cincinnati. This led to good things: the Green Line System would be the exclusive provider of such transportation to the airport for almost 30 years. Unusual for a mere provider of public transit, the Green Line was now in a position to steer itself toward a nice piece of profit.

Above: Pleasant Hill (Ft. Thomas Line).

Below: Bonnie Leslie (Ft. Thomas Line).

In some respects, the Ft. Mitchell and Ft. Thomas car lines were like suburban railways. Over the years, the Green Line, or perhaps neighborhood groups, put up numerous shelters to keep passengers out of the rain (or even snow). Were any two alike?

CAR STOP
A Place to Wait Could be Plain or Fancy
ON THE GREEN LINE

Above: Inverness (Ft. Thomas Line).

Below: Ft. Mitchell Ave.

All photos: Special Collections and Archives, University of Kentucky Libraries.

Almost to the Breaking Point

With gasoline rationing still in effect, Green Line System ridership remained steady in 1944 at 37 million passengers. With unprecedented productivity, the CN&C handled the majority of this throng with only 45 streetcars, 31 trolley-coaches and 65 gas buses.

Although it may be hard to comprehend these numbers today, an average of more than 100,000 people passed through the Dixie Terminal any weekday during the war. Based on a November, 1944, survey, nearly 8000 riders boarded Green Line streetcars and trolley-coaches on the upper level Covington Division every weekday between 5 and 6 p.m. With 65 streetcars

and electric buses using the upper level loop between 5 and 6 p.m., a streetcar or trolley-coach was dispatched every 50 seconds or so. Things were also hectic on the Dixie Terminal's lower level Newport Division as 65 gas buses and eight streetcars trundled around the loop every weekday between 5 and 6 p.m., loading 5500 war-weary souls.

In addition, Dixie Traction's three routes, North Ft. Thomas, Cold Spring-Alexandria, and Erlanger-Florence, and their 25 assigned buses loaded from the streets adjacent to the Dixie Terminal. They took home another 1100 passengers during the same one hour period.

It was quite a performance, to be repeated only three times more, in 1945, 1946 and 1947. After that, all bets were off. ❏

The 1941 streetcar schedule touted 12 minute headways. The 1945 bus schedules were somewhat more complicated, reaching Fort Thomas via different routes from each other and from the Route 11 streetcar line. *T. W. Lehmann Collection.*

Some Wartime Streetcar and Bus Schedule Covers

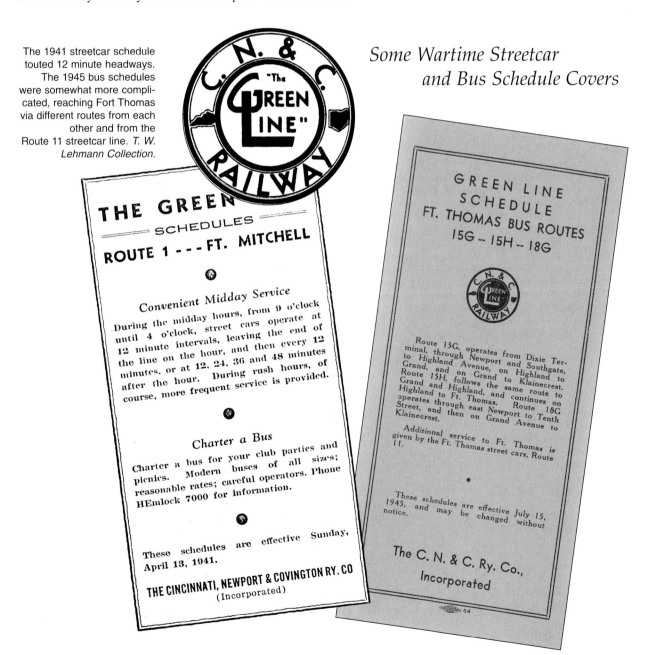

EXPLORING
the
11 *Line*

Ft. Thomas Streetcars Soldier On Under a Delayed Death Sentence

A 4-page ride through 1942-47

Arrows on map show direction of camera by photo number.

DIXIE TERMINAL

3rd St.

1-2 Broadway

Pearl

CINCINNATI

OHIO RIVER

5-6 3rd St.

4

3 Washington

4th St.

Monmouth

York St.

NEWPORT

10th St.

7

11th St.

8

9 P. R/W.

N

CERA

10 Highland

11 Ft. Thomas Ave.

FT. THOMAS

1 CN&C leased a short section of its Cincinnati trackage on Broadway from the Cincinnati Street Railway where CSR No. 393 waits for Green Line 519 to turn from Broadway to Pearl. This July 21, 1947, photo was taken by noted interurban historian David McNeil. There is also a Green Line Mack from the Newport Division edging out of the picture's left margin.
David McNeil.

2 On a snowy day in December, 1944, an inbound Ft. Thomas car, **below,** turns onto Pearl from Broadway. In both photos on this page, a Green Line bus is visible at the left margin. A CN&C Mack follows behind the No. 11 car.
Earl Clark Collection.

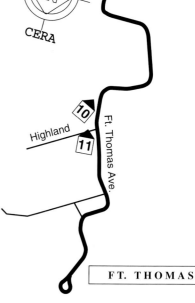

3 Heading downhill along the south ramp of the Central Bridge **(left)**, this 11-Ft. Thomas car will turn left onto Third, proceed east to Washington, then south to Tenth and east to Wilson Road, to the start of 2.79 miles of private right-of-way.
Wiedemann's was a local beer. Its billboard reminds us that at one time every major city had a brewery or two not affiliated with some huge national chain.

Auto Traffic Didn't Seem to be a Problem for Streetcars

4 While still standing at Third & York, the Newport Division's main transfer point **(right)**, we turn the camera eastward. And what do we see but CN&C car 520 heading for Cincinnati while 519 rumbles eastward on Third. It will duck under the Saratoga approach to the L&N bridge in the background before lurching south onto Washington St. and its eventual destination of Ft. Thomas.

5 In the exposure at **left**, an inbound 11-Ft.Thomas car stops for pedestrians at Third & Washington in Newport. When traffic is clear, it will turn left onto Third and set its course for the Central Bridge and Cincinnati. What would we give for traffic-free streets like this nowadays?

All photos this page:
Earl Clark Collection.

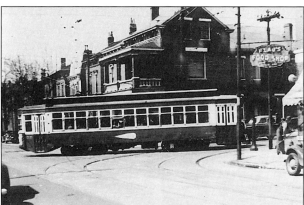

6 Here's a reminder that by the time most of these pictures were taken, a good deal of Newport's Green Line transit service was provided by bus. Still, the star of our show is the 11-Ft. Thomas streetcar. No. 520 turns **(above)** onto Third from Washington. Outbound CN&C Mack 302 heads for the 23-Bonnie Leslie line. *Tom Taylor Collection.*

7 We've moved down Washington to 10th, where the cars turned left toward Fort Thomas. This intersection is rather narrow, making things difficult for the Green Line's almost 47-foot long 500-series cars. We can see in the frame at **left** that the motorman is waiting for an automobile to back up so the big streetcar can safely clear the intersection.
Fred Veith, Earl Clark Collection.

8 Having gained private right-of-way trackage at the Newport city limits, a Green Line car is shown at **left** on the Bonnie Leslie trestle heading for Ft. Thomas. At 160 feet, this was the longest span on the Green Line.
Earl Clark Collection.

Streetcar Adventures Along the Ft. Thomas Line

9 Between Newport and Ft. Thomas, line 11 proceeded over almost three miles of private right-of-way. In the photograph at **left**, CN&C No. 517 heads south over what later became Memorial Highway. We are near Waterworks Road, where the tree growth is lush.

The No. 11 line left private right-of-way just past Highlands High School. Freshly painted No. 522 will now resume street running through the city of Ft. Thomas to the end of the line just short of Alexandria Pike. Look carefully at the study **below** and see the wooden waiting shelter along the tracks near the left margin of the picture. There were some sizable homes along here. **10**

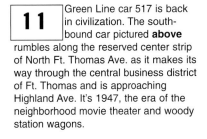

11 Green Line car 517 is back in civilization. The south-bound car pictured **above** rumbles along the reserved center strip of North Ft. Thomas Ave. as it makes its way through the central business district of Ft. Thomas and is approaching Highland Ave. It's 1947, the era of the neighborhood movie theater and woody station wagons.

Top two photos this page:
Earl Clark Collection.
Photo at left: *Earl Clark.*

Hail and Farewell to the Streetcar Era

The death sentence for the Green Line's streetcars, so long stayed, finally took effect in 1950. Cursed with a railway system that was not very modern and not inclined to buck the national trend, the Cincinnati, Newport & Covington Railway tossed in the towel, but did it with panache. There had to be a parade and a jubilation to celebrate a transportation lifestyle that had served so well for so many decades. The appointed day was July 1, 1950, and with the ornate Green Line Covington headquarters serving as a backdrop, the cavalcade is led by the parlor car *Kentucky*, its front platform groaning with dignitaries. Following behind is one of the 500-series double-truckers which had cashed out the 1-Ft. Mitchell line. Bringing up the rear is a lineup of the replacement buses, TDH-3612s from General Motors. Thanks, Green Line, for the memories.

Special Collections and Archives, University of Kentucky Libraries.

Optimism Renewed: 1946-1950

B Y WAR'S END in August of 1945, the Green Line's streetcars were thoroughly spent. Decidedly, they were worn out mechanically, electrically and structurally. The newest of the cars, the 1917 Group O double-truckers rebuilt in 1937 to one-man operation, were approaching 30 years of service.

They had chalked up between 1.5 and 2 million miles apiece. The 20 remaining two-man, single-truck cars from Groups L, M and N had nearly survived 40 winters. Needing major repairs, Nos. 100, 101, 105, 127, 321, and 323 were scrapped by the end of 1945. Replacement of the rest of these veterans, whether by new streetcars, trolley-coaches or motor buses, would be costly.

Green Line officials also faced the problem of deteriorated streetcar trackage. The drafting of a large portion of the Green Line's track maintenance force into the armed services during the war, coupled with the shortage of track repair materials, left a legacy of considerable deferred maintenance. A lot of streetcar trackage was badly in need of repair. The new Green Line owners would face considerable expense if they wanted to bring the track back to prewar standards.

With Columbia Gas and Electric out of the picture, electricity could no longer be purchased cheaply at or near the cost of production to feed the traction motors of Green Line's streetcars and trolley-coaches.

Streetcars and trolley-coaches shared one curse: the inability to reach new subdivisions and new commercial and industrial areas without expensive construction. And so the prewar decision to abandon the residual streetcar network was reaffirmed in 1945.

On the chopping block were routes 1-Ft. Mitchell, 4-Main, 5-Holman, 8-Eastern in Kenton County and 11-Ft. Thomas in Campbell County. But pulling the plug was easier said than done.

The reason was simple. Since most transit companies were unable to obtain new buses during World War II, there was now a pent-up demand for new ones to replace streetcars and buses worn out by the war effort. Although faced with unprecedented large orders for new units, the bus manufacturers could not even start to work until they re-tooled from their World War II defense production. Since there was also a big demand for consumer products ranging from automobiles to refrigerators and toasters, bus builders in 1946 and 1947 had to compete on the spot market for scarce manufacturing materials ranging from sheet steel to nails and screws.

The Green Line, in 1945, had placed an order with its favorite supplier, Mack, for eight model C-41GT, 41-passenger buses. In early 1946, the company also ordered 14 Twin Coach Model 38-S buses, seven for Dixie Traction and seven for the CN&C. All 22 coaches were to be gasoline powered, the company feeling that the diesel engine had yet to prove itself in mass transit service.

Company officials had determined that since the track and roadbed on the 8-Eastern line was in the poorest shape, it would be the first to be converted to bus service. Although the Macks were ordered with Spicer torque converter automatic transmissions, material shortages prevented Spicer from supplying this nicety, so the buses were delivered in March 1946 with manual transmissions as Model C-41Gs, and they became Nos. 430-437.

The new Macks were exhibited at St. Benedict School at 17th & Marilyn on March 27, at Wallace & Eastern on March 28, at 15th & Eastern on March 29, and at 20th & Greenup on March 30. During the afternoon of March 30, the new Mack buses took over route 8. The replacement of streetcars by buses on the 8-Eastern enabled the Green Line to reassign six double-truck 500

Covington's 8-Eastern streetcar line was the first victim of postwar modernization. A short stretch of track on private right-of-way connected the 8 line's trackage on Eastern Ave. with Garrard St. CN&C 515 is caught on film at **right** on March 30, 1946, the last day of car service. Soon after, in a masterpiece of the publicist's art, we see Mack No. 430 (signed for the No. 8 line) at the **bottom** of the page with operator Marvin Black and his 1914 Model-T Ford at Third & Court. Macks 430-437 are showing off their nifty new styling in June of 1946. *David McNeil; Special Collections and Archives, University of Kentucky Libraries.*

series cars to base service on the 4-Main and 5-Holman lines, the last two CN&C bastions of single-truck car operation.

The demise of the 8-Eastern streetcar line meant that seven of the 14 remaining Group L, M, and N cars were consigned to the scrap pile. Surprisingly, the Philadelphia Transportation Co. bought No. 325 for use as a track grinder on its subway and elevated lines. This car, put into service by the CN&C in 1911 and retired on March 30, 1946, had reeled off a million miles in Green Line service. It would be employed by PTC for another 20 years!

The Greater Cincinnati Airport

Green Line officials had high hopes of making some money off the Greater Cincinnati airport purloined from Ohio and placed squarely in its own territory. At war's end Dixie Traction was still running to the still uncompleted airport the shuttle bus service it had started in 1943. This seldom-advertised operation extended from a connection with its Erlanger-Florence route at Commonwealth & Dixie Highway to the airport site.

Although the airlines were still using Lunken Field in eastern Cincinnati, the "Airport Shuttle" route was needed by construction workers working to finish the Administration Building. Unexpectedly, Dixie Traction also discovered that many northern Kentuckians were taking advantage of the bus service to view the ongoing airport construction.

In September, 1946, David L. Ringo, wearing the dual hats of assistant general manager of both Dixie Traction Co. and the CN&C, confirmed that Dixie had contracted with the three major airlines and the Airport Board to carry passengers between downtown Cincinnati hotels and the airport in Boone County when it

opened. In addition, Dixie obtained exclusive rights from the Airport Board to provide incoming passengers with taxi-for-hire service to all points within a 20 mile radius of the airport although Dixie's backhaul "taxi-for-hire" authority was limited to picking up customers in downtown Cincinnati.

Hotel to airport scheduled service was marketed by Dixie Traction under the "Airporter" service mark, and its taxi-for-hire service as "Red Top Limousines" (the CN&C never referred to Red Tops as mere "cabs"). The Red Top fleet initially consisted of five 7-passenger DeSotos, two 7-passenger Buicks and two 5-passenger Plymouths with five 10-passenger stretch Cadillacs modified by Hess and Eisenhart of nearby Cincinnati providing the initial Airporter hotel to airport service. This venerable firm was most noted for its building of Presidential limousines from the Harry S. Truman to the Richard Nixon eras.

In October of 1946, the Airport Division of the Dixie Traction Co. was formed to husband the new limo service. Garage and dispatching facilities for the limousines were established at Court & Plum in downtown Cincinnati. Initially the Dixie Traction limousine service was the responsibility of 14 operators and five supervisors who would double as relief drivers in times of peak demand.

Dixie's airport operation would spring into action coincident with the move of American, Delta and Trans World Airlines from the Lunken Airport to the Greater Cincinnati Airport in January,

Dixie Traction's first postwar equipment consisted of seven Twin Coach 38-S buses, resplendent in their dramatic new body styling and forced air ventilation. Some eight years after the arrival of the new coaches in November of 1946, bus 175, **above**, still holds down an Erlanger run out on Dixie Highway. Concurrent with the arrival of the new coaches, Dixie Traction placed advertisements in the local newspapers, one of which is reproduced at **right**. The parent company, CN&C, also received postwar Twins in two sizes. Although Mack temporarily remained the favored bus supplier, Twin was a runner-up. *Motor Bus Society; T. W. Lehmann Collection.*

1947. The operating schedules of the limousine service called for a running time of 25 minutes from the downtown Cincinnati hotels to the airport.

The Peak Year of 1946

In September, 1946, the Interstate Commerce Commission partially approved a request by the Green Line to increase its basic interstate fare to 10 cents cash (or two tokens for 15 cents). However, since the ICC had held that the fare increase could apply only to routes operated by gas buses, the CN&C decided not to implement yet another crazy-quilt fare scheme.

At last, the first new postwar buses started to show up on Kentucky soil. In November of 1946, Dixie Traction received its seven 36-passenger Twin Coaches (Nos. 170-176). They featured a new ventilation system which forced 15 cubic feet of fresh air a minute per passenger into the bus and contained small additional top windows enabling standees to obtain a "no squat" view of the outside. The buses also boasted seats with footrests and improved lighting. Arriving in the traditional yellow and green of the Dixie Traction Co., the new buses went into service November 17 on the Erlanger-Florence route after an extensive advertising campaign featuring the new equipment was run in the local newspapers.

Nineteen forty-six would be the peak year for transit patronage on the Green Line System. Almost 41 million passengers

A big new batch of Mack buses did in the 11-Ft. Thomas line, a very major rail artery and the last streetcar line in Campbell County's Newport Division. With conversion only weeks away, these 500-series cars sleep away the hours in front of the main Newport shops. Most will soon run out their final miles after 30 years on the job, not needed on the surviving 1-Ft. Mitchell line over in Covington. Each car by this time had run between 1.5 and 2 million miles. *Tom Taylor Collection.*

FIG. 3

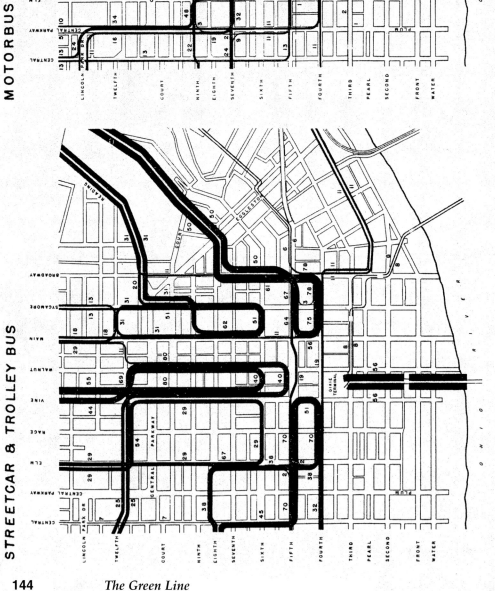

TRANSIT TERMINAL LOOPS

DOWNTOWN CINCINNATI

METROPOLITAN MASTER PLAN

SOURCE OF DATA
1946 RECORDS OF THE CINCINNATI STREET
RAILWAY COMPANY, C. N. & C. RAILWAY AND
THE DIXIE TRACTION COMPANY

VEHICLE VOLUMES
NUMBER INDICATES
AMOUNT FOR MAXIMUM
HOUR 4:45—5:45 PM

CINCINNATI SYSTEM

KENTUCKY SYSTEM

MOTORBUS

STREETCAR & TROLLEY BUS

NORTH

SCALE IN FEET

800   0   800   2400

CITY PLANNING COMMISSION
CINCINNATI OHIO

The end of gasoline rationing and the resumption of automobile production after World War II combined to reduce Green Line ridership and increase waiting time in traffic. That is obvious in this 1947 evening rush hour scene. We are on the ramp leading to the upper level of Dixie Terminal looking east on Third. A new 38-S Twin Coach is on Walnut waiting to make a right turn toward the lower level of the Terminal. A Ft. Thomas streetcar approaches in the distance, while Mack 403 on a 12-Dayton run inches along in the foreground. *Special Collections and Archives, University of Kentucky Libraries.*

used the CN&C and subsidiary Dixie Traction for getting around in Northern Kentucky and to downtown Cincinnati. It would all be downhill from here.

The Big Airport Opens

The new Greater Cincinnati Airport came to life on January 10, 1947, when an American Airlines DC-3 touched down at 9:18 a. m. At 9:20 a. m. the first Delta plane landed. By 9:32 a. m. the first TWA flight had arrived. During the inaugural day, 51

landings and takeoffs were recorded. It was a small beginning for what would become an enormous enterprise.

Dixie Traction common carrier service was expanded that January to include not only additional shuttle trips from Erlanger to the airport but also four through trips from Cincinnati. The new schedule, based on a survey of airline employees and others working at the airport, resulted in both short headway shuttle service and some through trips to Cincinnati during shift change periods as well as 30 minute interval shuttle service during off peak hours.

Only two months after the airport opened, a flap erupted between Dixie Traction and the Kenton County Airport Board which nearly brought the downtown Cincinnati Airporter service to a screeching halt. The contract which the company thought it had reached with the airlines was called into question by the Airport Board, its members claiming that only they could contract for such service. Then they demanded a piece of the action. Shocked, Dixie threatened to withdraw its limo operations.

OPPOSITE: From a traffic survey conducted during a weekday afternoon in August, 1946, we find that Green Line electric vehicles (left side of chart) made 64 trips to Cincinnati between 4:45 and 5:45 p. m. while 85 trips by Green Line and Dixie Traction motor buses were made during the same one-hour period. We can compare this with the density of Cincinnati Street Railway movements during the same time span.

T. W. Lehmann Collection.

Everyone soon calmed down. Dixie Traction and the Kenton County Airport Board successfully reached agreement in mid March. The pact provided that Dixie would pay 3 cents per head on the first 4000 passengers a month hauled to and from the airport; 4 cents each for the next 4000 passengers; 7 cents for the third group of 4000, 12 cents each on those between 12,001 and 17,000 passengers; and 16 cents on those in excess of 17,000. Dixie Traction was not excited. It anticipated that it would haul no more than 10,000 passengers a year in the foreseeable future.

As a matter of fact, Green Line chief P. G. Vondersmith told the Dixie Traction Board in April, 1947, that "it did not appear that there would be a sufficient need for buses of approximately 21-passenger capacity such as those built by the Flxible Company." His crystal ball would turn out to be quite cloudy on this point. Reflecting the Green Line's cautious stance, another 10-passenger 1947 Cadillac limousine, modified by Hess and Eisenhart, was delivered the same month.

Another unique Green Line bus enterprise--the Greenhounds--now made a surprise reappearance. Weekend operation of Green Line buses on lease to Southeastern

THE GREEN LINE ENTERS
the
Air Age

The alpha and the omega of the Dixie Traction Fleet appear at the opening of the Greater Cincinnati Airport in January 1947. Lined up at **left** for inspection are newly-delivered Twin Coach No. 170, a Mack LD-3G (No. 150) built in 1942, a 1936 vintage Yellow Coach Model 1204 (No. 104) acquired from Cold Spring Bus, and a 1935 built International (No. 90). Later, the Green Line would get the idea of posing its Airporter fleet alongside the latest in air transportation. In the photo **opposite**, a brand-new Convair CV-240 of American Airlines dwarfs three equally new Dixie Traction "Red Top" DeSoto taxis and Flxible No. 46. This photo was taken in the summer of 1948.

Meanwhile, the first four-engine air service to the airport was begun by Delta Air Lines in 1947 on its Chicago-Cincinnati-Atlanta and Miami route. A Douglas DC-4 looms at **lower left** behind Dixie Traction's first four Flxible 21-passenger parlor coaches (41-44).
All: Special Collections and Archives, University of Kentucky Libraries.

Greyhound was resumed on July 1, 1947. Again, SEGL's equipment had proved insufficient to meet passenger demand on weekends. As we have seen, the Green Line had suspended such arrangements after it had been sued by the State of Kentucky in 1945 for additional over-the-road use and seat taxes of $120,000 which the state claimed the company owed from 1943 through 1945.

However, in early 1947, the company settled the suit for a mere $14,300. The CN&C again provided "substitution" service for Southeastern Greyhound during major holiday periods until after the 1948 Christmas season by which time Southeastern had finally received sufficient intercity equipment to retire the Greenhound for all time.

Streetcars Exit Campbell County

It was the last act for streetcars in Campbell County on August 23, 1947. The arrival of 20 new C-41GT Macks (Nos. 440-459) meant the end of the 11-Ft. Thomas streetcar line. And the transfer of its double-truck 500s to the Covington Division

The incongruity of photographing some of its oldest transit equipment next to the newest development in air transportation seemed to escape Green Line management, much to our delight. Dixie Traction No. 90, for instance, had a most interesting history. CN&C acquired it in 1940 from Black Diamond Stages but sold it for scrap. Dixie Traction, desperately short of buses, rescued No.90 (and mate) from a scrapyard in May 1943 and reconditioned both for World War II service. It's parked smack in front of the Airport administration building, at **left**. *Special Collections and Archives, University of Kentucky Libraries.*

On the other hand, the Green Line offered some of the newest and most comfortable buses on its Airporter service. A closeup view at **right** of Airporter No. 46 reveals a baggage compartment at the rear, a necessity for serving the downtown Cincinnati hotels. It displays a special "American Airlines" destination sign. *Special Collections and Archives, University of Kentucky Libraries.*

Ft. Thomas Says Goodbye to the Cars

On the very last day of service, CN&C car 521 passes the Ft. Thomas military reservation on its right as it heads for Cincinnati. In the picture at **right**, the large building in the background is the armory, site of many exhibitions over the years prior to World War II ranging from boxing matches to flower shows. *David McNeil.*

spelled the retirement of the remaining single-truck cars still in tripper service on 4-Main and 5-Holman lines. To the scrapyard went Nos. 103, 108, 109, 122, 125, 129, and 131. Surely the endurance of the hand-braked, two-man cars until August 1947 must have constituted the last revenue use of such a type in the United States.

On August 24, the new Macks assumed full-time duty. The new 11-Ft. Thomas bus route involved some changes. First and foremost, the buses operated from Newport via Waterworks to Ft. Thomas and the route was extended on Alexandria as far as Crowell where the city of Ft. Thomas built a new turnaround.

Green Line also inaugurated a new "experimental" 11-Ft. Thomas Limited rush-hour only route. In the evening, these trips made pickup only stops at Third & York, Third & Washington, Sixth & Washington, and Tenth & Washington in Newport, and did not discharge passengers until 10th & Park. The new Limited trips left the Dixie Terminal at 4:42, 5:10, 5:22 and 5:45 p. m. Following a minute later was the 16-Washington tripper service which did local work from Cincinnati on Washington and Tenth to its terminus at Wilson & Glazier. Corresponding morning 11 Limited-16-Washington service also was provided.

Additionally, on August 24, service on the Dixie Traction's North Ft. Thomas route was also increased. Instead of operating in rush hours only, the route now provided hourly service seven days a week (6 a. m. until midnight) as well as more frequent service during rush hours.

The citizens of Ft. Thomas turn out to pay their final respects to streetcar service in their city on August 23, 1947, as the parlor car *Kentucky* leads a 500-series car just west of the intersection of N. Ft. Thomas Avenue and Rob Roy. There's waving and applause, as officials aboard the parlor car wave back.
Special Collections and Archives, University of Kentucky Libraries.

The Green Line in 1947

The new Macks were also assigned to base service on the 12-Dayton line. This was the most heavily patronized CN&C route in Campbell County, and its regular CM-3G Macks were getting to be a little long in the tooth. This was due, in no small part, to their extensive use during World War II on Southeastern Greyhound substitute service.

Along with the introduction of the new C-41GT Macks on 12-Dayton, a new afternoon rush-hour only route was established on December 8, 1947. The new 12-Dayton Limited's buses left the Dixie Terminal at 4:55, 5:05, 5:12, 5:20, 5:30, 5:40 and 5:50 p.m. They made all Cincinnati stops but picked up passengers only at Third & York and Third & Washington in Newport and did not discharge passengers before reaching the Dayton city limits. To fill the gap in local service, a new 22-Fairfield route was added to provide local service for Newport and Bellevue patrons. The 22-Fairfield buses left two minutes after the 12-Limited buses and followed the regular Dayton route but turned at Walnut in Dayton to make a loop over Walnut, to Eighth, to O'Fallon and back to Fairfield.

By March of 1947, the Green Line's Newport Division received its 38-S Twin Coach buses. The new Twins (CN&C Nos. 380-386) were placed into base service on the 13-South Bellevue, 15-Southgate, and 23-South Bellevue-Bonnie Leslie routes.

A month later, the old Newport carbarn, originally opened in 1899, had been remodeled. A new rear door and ramp enabled buses to enter and leave the barn by both the front and rear. A new automatic bus washing facility was also installed in the barn along with new lighting in the old streetcar pits for easier inspection of the new motor buses. The renovations were supervised by newly-appointed General Manager Dave Ringo.

In June of 1947, the first two of the original eight Mack C-

Although the 1-Ft. Mitchell line had a lot of private right-of-way, it also navigated the narrow back streets of Covington. In this view of the aftermath of a winter snow, a Green Line car proceeds west on 12th with the smokestack of the Bavarian Co. brewery in the background.
Earl Clark Collection.

41G buses (431 and 437) were taken out of service for replacement of their manual transmissions with Spicer torque converters. All work was performed in-house with three mechanics taking approximately one week to install the new equipment. All eight buses had received Spicer converters by the fall of 1947.

Much to its delight, Dixie Traction by the end of 1947 found that it had grossly underestimated the number of airport passengers it would carry. So in December, Vondersmith, eating his earlier words, decided to purchase two 21-passenger Flxible coaches at a cost of approximately $9000 each. Dixie also negotiated new contracts for carrying railroad employees between K.C. Junction (16th & Madison, Covington) and the C&O's Stevens yard at Silver Grove and from K.C. Junction to the L&N's Decoursey Yards. This charter contract with the railroads was deemed by the company to be "quite profitable" and caused the transfer of four CN&C Mack LD-3Gs (Nos. 374-377) to Dixie Traction (Nos. 153-156).

At the end of 1947, the Green Line System employed 489 people to operate and maintain 109 motor buses, 31 trolley-coaches, 25 streetcars and 12 airport service vehicles. It carried almost 39,500,000 transit passengers in 1947 and operated 1021 charter trips plus a number of weekend contract trips for Southeastern Greyhound, as well as 20 or so daily contract trips for the L&N and C&O. Clearly, optimism was still justified.

Pull-in and pull-out streetcars used the tracks on Greenup to 20th to access the Covington carbarns following the removal of the rails on Madison from 11th south. In this busy scene, a car from a 5-Holman run is about to turn into the north barn as it passes two Green Line trolley-coaches, circa 1947. Small restaurants and gambling joints are plentiful across the street from the barn. *Earl Clark Collection.*

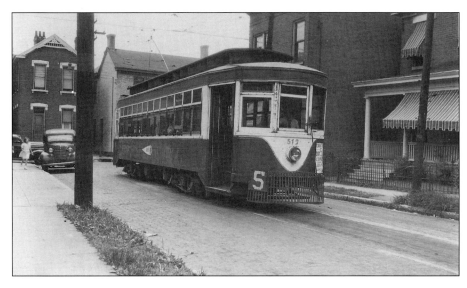

Double-truck car 512 lays over, **above**, at 21st & Howell less than six months before the 5-Holman line was abandoned. In this August, 1947, scene, a little girl urges her mother to hurry, lest the car pull away. That final day came on January 4, 1948, and in the frame at **right** we see veteran Green Liners Taylor Sisson, Dave Webster and Frank Osterman prepare the 515 for its last revenue outing. *Earl Clark Collection; Special Collections and Archives, University of Kentucky Libraries.*

And Then There Was One

In late 1947 the company targeted 4-Main and 5-Holman as the next two streetcar routes for conversion to motor coaches. To replace streetcars on these two inner city Covington routes, the company ordered, in October 1947, 11 model C-36 buses from ACF-Brill. The hope was that the conversion of Routes 4 and 5 could be completed by December 1, before the Christmas shopping season. But the C-36s were not delivered until the end of 1947 because bus production still had not caught up with demand.

So it was on January 3, 1948, that the streetcars of 4-Main and 5-Holman made their final runs. To celebrate the passing of two of the last three streetcar lines in Northern Kentucky, a parade was held on January 3 with the old parlor car *Kentucky* in the lead. On January 4 the new ACF-Brill 36-passenger buses

By now a curiosity, car 125, at the intersection of Pike, Holman & 9th, was the last single-truck, hand-braked, two-man car to operate in regular service in the United States. It made its last 4-Main rush-hour run on August 22, 1947. *Earl Clark Collection.*

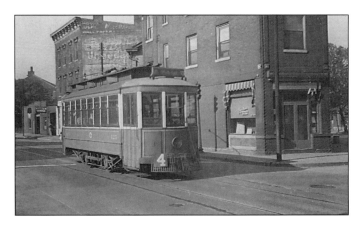

(Nos. 330-340) took over. The CN&C took the opportunity to extend the No. 5 route on Warren between 23rd and 24th and on 24th between Warren and Herman.

With the arrival of the new ACFs, the company announced that its remaining Mack 6-CW-3S 25-passenger buses were for sale. Two were purchased by the Independence Bus Line for service from Third & Greenup in Covington to Independence, Nicholson, and on to Verona and Glencoe--the service to the latter two hamlets being discontinued in the early 1950s. One was sold to Newsom Bus Lines for operation from Third & Greenup to Ryland and Visalia, and one went apparently to the Hebron Bus Co., which ran from the end of the 3-Ludlow line to Hebron.

The Crescent Springs Bus Lines, which extended to Crescent Springs from a connection with Dixie Traction's Erlanger-Florence route, was not a purchaser since it had just acquired an International KB5, nor was the Monmouth Street Merchants Association because it had just received a new Mack C-41GT in 1947 to replace its 1942 White 782. It is interesting that the Merchants always bought factory-new buses, albeit one at a time!

After 56 Years, a Local Fare Hike

In 1948, the CN&C applied to the ICC for an interstate fare of 10 cents cash only on all types of routes including its streetcar and trolley-coach lines which reached Dixie Terminal. The company also asked, in late 1947, the Kentucky Public Service Commission to increase its intrastate fare from 5 cents cash to 10 cents cash or two tokens for 15 cents.

The Green Line explained that in spite of its unprecedented passenger levels, the company had netted only $41,000 in 1945 for a return of less than 1 percent of the value of the company's assets and had fared only a little better in the boom year of 1946. The company argued that, in addition to the ordinary operating expenses that might be incurred by any transit system, its situation was unique in that it paid a considerable rent to the Dixie Terminal for use of that downtown Cincinnati facility and also expended more than $90,000 a year in bridge tolls for operations over the Suspension Bridge.

Moreover, the company predicted that its net income for 1947 would be only $95,000 on a gross income exceeding $2.5 million. In the case of the requested intrastate fare increase, the CN&C pointed out that the 5 cent fare had been in effect since 1892! That turned out to be a successful argument. The Green Line received authority from the Kentucky authorities to boost intrastate fares effective January 11, 1948, thus ending the remarkable 56 year run of the 5 cent fare. The ICC's approval to boost interstate fares on all routes to 10 cents cash only came in November.

Airporter business grew during 1947 and the stretch 10-passenger limousines were sometimes just not big enough to handle the business. Accordingly, in January 1948, Dixie Traction received two 21-passenger Flxible Model 21B1 motor coaches (Nos. 41-42) equipped with comfortable reclining seats and a rear baggage compartment. In March of 1948, two model 21C1, 21-passenger Flxible Airporters (Nos. 43-44) were delivered to Dixie as well as five DeSoto 7-passenger Red Tops.

In July, four 39-passenger Twin Coach model 41-S buses were delivered to the CN&C (Nos. 480-483) for service on 5-Holman. As a result, Holman's ACF-Brill C-36s (Nos. 330-334) were released for base service on 18-Newport East which, in turn, relegated CN&C's older ACF 36-S buses (Nos. 350-354) to tripper service.

At the same time, the Green Line decided it was finally time to try the diesel bus. The company ordered seven GM TDH-4008s (Nos. 190-196) for Dixie Traction. In September, these 39-passenger buses were placed in base service on Dixie's Erlanger-Florence route, to get a workout on one of the system's busiest lines.

Newport Network Reworked

While the basic transit route network in Covington remained remarkably stable at this time, there was constant ferment in Newport as the Green Line coped with growth in the territory

Green Line management finally took the leap into diesel technology in 1948. Dixie Traction 191 is one of seven 39-passenger model TDH-4008s (Nos. 190-196) bought from General Motors. Painted in a yellow and dark green livery, they were a good buy because a majority lasted in Green Line service until 1972! The CN&C would get its first GM diesels in 1950.
Special Collections and Archives, University of Kentucky Libraries.

between downtown and Ft. Thomas. This brought major changes to three routes on October 17.

The rush-hour only 18G-Newport East-Grand line was discontinued and the non-rush-hour 15G-Ft. Thomas-Grand route was re-established as a full time operation through Southgate with the outer part of its route changed. The new 15G route went from Highland to Grand, out Grand to S. Ft. Thomas Ave., north on S. Ft. Thomas Ave. to Highland, and returned to Cincinnati via Highland through Southgate and Newport. The 15H-Ft. Thomas-Highland line was changed to operate through Southgate over Highland Ave. to S. Ft. Thomas Ave., south on S. Ft. Thomas Ave. to Grand and return to Cincinnati via Grand to the intersection of Highland and Grand and thence over Highland through Southgate and Newport.

In effect, the two routes created an outer belt operation in Ft. Thomas with 15H doing the loop clockwise and 15G counterclockwise from 5 a. m. to 1 a. m. seven days a week. Passengers were allowed to board at any place along the loop, even at places

Another One-Off For the Monmouth Merchants

Still fiercely independent, the Monmouth Street Merchants Association in Newport did it again in 1947: bought a single, brand-new, production-line, full-size transit bus. This one was a Mack C-41GT, which had its official portrait taken at the factory just the same as any order placed by a huge transit agency. And here it is.
Motor Bus Society.

One sign that things were returning to normal in Green Line territory after war's end was the more frequent appearance of the parlor car *Kentucky*. Of course, it was not to stay around for long, but for a few bright seasons here it was, taking revelers to a church picnic or maybe even carrying a wedding party! We see the *Kentucky* **below** on August 29, 1948, at 11th & Brighton in Newport. Its two crewmen are busily occupied with their responsibilities. *Cliff Scholes.*

Third & York, Fifth & York, Seventh & York, Tenth & York, and Tenth & Monmouth with the first discharge stop at 16th & Monmouth. The corresponding morning service simply ran "closed door" from 16th & Monmouth to Cincinnati. To supplement this route through central Newport, 14-York St. local service was increased and two new 25-Monmouth St. a. m. and p. m. rush-hour trips were added to run from 16th & Monmouth down Monmouth to Third & York. However, 25-Monmouth St. was soon found to be a poor revenue producer and was discontinued after the 1948 Christmas season.

Additionally, Dixie Traction service to the new Vet Village subdivision east of Cold Spring was also inaugurated on October 25. Its Cold Spring line was extended from U. S. 25 to Doddsworth & Uhl, and 11 trips were scheduled weekdays through to Vet Village (later renamed Crestview) with seven trips being operated on Saturday and five on Sunday.

On November 22, 1948, a reverse loop was established on the 7-Latonia route. During the evening peak period, the 5:05 and 5:25 p. m. runs were served by gasoline powered buses instead of trolley-coaches which enabled the CN&C to operate in the reverse direction on the Latonia loop. As a result, passengers living on the far side of the regular Latonia loop on Madison Pike arrived home a little earlier by not having to make the trip around the entire loop.

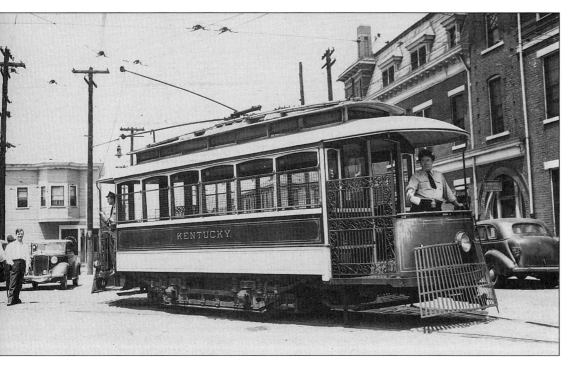

where the vehicle was technically still outbound from Cincinnati, which greatly decreased waiting time and was undoubtedly appreciated during both cold snaps and hot summer days.

To serve the vacated area along Grand north of Highland, the 18-Newport East route was extended up Park to Grand and out Grand as far as Hunteman Lane.

A new 15-Southgate Limited route was also instituted. Four trips during both the a. m. and p. m. peaks were offered. The evening limited service from Cincinnati saw pickup stops at

After World War II, Transit Radio made its appearance in a number of major U. S. metropolitan areas. It seemed like a good idea at the time, made possible by the advent of interference-free FM broadcasting.

On July 10, 1948, the Green Line system made history when FM receivers were turned on in more than 100 motor coaches. The innovation of "music while you ride" marked the first time in history that a whole fleet of buses had been equipped with FM

A Dixie Terminal Moment

Dixie Terminal Covington Division Supervisor Howard Bell was having a busy afternoon on Monday, November 14, 1948, trying to load a vehicle every 45 seconds or so. A turnstile was jamming off and on, and an operator had some trouble getting an 8-Eastern bus restarted, thereby threatening to tie up operations across the Suspension Bridge. The driver was finally able to get the bus in gear and Bell relaxed.

At 6 p.m., two high school girls reported strange sounds in the women's restroom. Bell investigated and found a newborn baby girl in a trash can. The baby was taken to a hospital and found to be normal and healthy. A small trust fund was set up by Green Line employees to help defray the cost of adoption of the baby girl, nicknamed "Dixie Bell," as the mother was never identified.

Bell had never before had quite such a day at the Dixie Terminal, or been honored in quite such a fashion. ◆

receiving sets. Programs were broadcast by station WCTS, the FM affiliate of WKRC in Cincinnati. Featured were popular music, short news summaries, sports news, and commercials. The programs went on the air at 6 a.m. and continued until 7 p.m.

Within two years, a lawsuit complained that passengers were a "captive audience." Following an adverse Supreme Court ruling, transit radio fell silent on June 1, 1953.

Taking Care of Business

As it turned out, 1948 was not a bad year for the Green Line System. It carried more than 35 million transit passengers and, thanks to the fare increases and airport business, it netted a profit of about $125,000. Although 1948 had been an eventful year, 1949 would prove to be a year of very little change. No new equipment was purchased, save for one Flxible Airporter (No. 45).

Perhaps the biggest news in 1949 was in what did not happen. The expected conversion to buses of the system's last streetcar line, 1-Ft. Mitchell, did not take place. The company needed time to train additional mechanics and other maintenance personnel to service the vastly increased bus

CINCINNATI 12¢ EFFECTIVE NEXT MONDAY

CHICAGO 13¢

DETROIT 12½¢

DES MOINES 12½¢

KANSAS CITY 11²/₃¢

WASHINGTON D.C. 11²/₃¢

MINNEAPOLIS 11¢

NO TRANSPORTATION COMPANY IN AMERICA LIKES A FARE INCREASE!

Why, then, are fares being raised in virtually every community? The answer is simple — transit companies including your Green Line, cannot make ends meet when the prices they pay for goods and services continue to go up and up, *and their revenues either go down or do not increase proportionately.*

Fair-minded governmental bodies the nation over, charged with the regulation of public transit companies, have realized these facts and the granting of fare increases is widespread.

● TODAY, Your Green Line is forced to file with the Interstate Commerce Commission, Tariff MP-I.C.C. 17, for the following change in fare structure:

> 10c cash fare between all principal Northern Kentucky cities and Cincinnati. The use of the 7½c token as an interstate fare will be discontinued. This change will become effective November 28, 1948.
> **THERE WILL BE NO CHANGE IN INTRASTATE FARES BETWEEN KENTUCKY CITIES.**

● Here are but a few of the reasons why this move is necessary:

> Gasoline price increase since last November have increased our costs $15,000 annually.
>
> The added 2c Gasoline Tax, which began April 1, 1948 — $18,000 more.
>
> New wage agreements effective November 5, to bring our employee's wages in line with others locally means $113,000 more in 1949 and $168,000 more in 1950.

● The new average of all fares will be slightly less than 9c. This can be contrasted with our over-the-river neighbor where next month's fare increase will mean a fare 33-1/3% higher than ours!

● **Even more to the point is the story of America's 44 cities in our class — 100,000 to 200,000 in population. Average fare: About 9-1/10c — *higher than our average rate* AND NOT ONE OF THESE COMPANIES PAY BRIDGE TOLLS OR TERMINAL RENT AS WE DO — AMOUNTING TO NEARLY A QUARTER-MILLION DOLLARS PER YEAR!**

THE Green Line

THE CINCINNATI, NEWPORT & COVINGTON RAILWAY COMPANY
INCORPORATED

SERVING YOU IN NORTHERN KENTUCKY FOR 81 YEARS

Here's a look into Dixie Traction's own garage, circa 1946. This facility at the Dixie Highway & May in Elsmere really constituted a third major transit facility for the Green Line System. We see, left to right: two Mack model LC-3Gs (Nos.132, 137), a Mack model 6-CQ-3S (No. 111) a new Twin (No. 170), two more Mack CQs (Nos. 110 and 107), and a Mack LD-3G (No. 150). *Special Collections and Archives, University of Kentucky Libraries.*

fleet, and anyway, there were some miles left in the best of the 500-series cars thanks to their 1937 rebuild.

In April, the CN&C's directors approved a gift of the company's property along the abandoned Newport Division Ft. Thomas streetcar line to the state of Kentucky to build a new highway. The donation of the land, which was 90 feet wide and approximately 40 city blocks long, eventually was incorporated into Memorial Parkway which opened for operation between Newport and Ft. Thomas in November of 1953.

The Green Line received permission in May from the Interstate Commerce Commission to sell charter service from

Purchased to replace streetcars on the 4-Main and 5-Holman routes, 11 ACF model C-36 buses (Nos. 330-340) were delivered in December 1947. This one is No. 333. Buying also from Twin, Mack and GM at this time, the Green Line was not placing standardization at the top of its priority list. *Special Collections and Archives, University of Kentucky Libraries.*

various points in Newport and Covington to special events in Cincinnati. This irregular operating authority covered service to special events at Crosley Field, home of the baseball Cincinnati Reds, Coney Island, the Zoo, the Cincinnati Gardens, and football and basketball games at the University of Cincinnati and Xavier University.

It did not take long for this to pay off. On June 1, the company promoted its largest mass charter movement up to that time when 61 CN&C and Dixie Traction buses furnished transportation for several thousand youngsters to Coney Island during Northern Kentucky Parochial School Day. The Green Line also operated a number of School Special services in the Northern Kentucky area. For example, the company ran a trip to and from the Notre Dame and Lasalette Academies in Covington for students who lived in Ft. Thomas and operated a second trip through Bonnie Leslie, Bellevue and Newport to Covington.

Other institutions served by school specials were Holmes High School and John G. Carlisle School in Covington and Highlands High School in Ft. Thomas.

Streetcars in Twilight

Through most of 1949, the remaining handful of faithful Green Line streetcars went about their appointed rounds without any definitive word about their demise.

Finally, in November, the CN&C, in conjunction with Dixie Traction, applied to the Interstate Commerce Commission for permission to abandon its last streetcar lines: 1-Ft. Mitchell and rush-hour only short turn 10-Lewisburg. To demonstrate to the Commission that not one customer anywhere on the entire line would be disadvantaged by the abandonment, the CN&C proposed a complex variety of both new and extended bus routes.

First, it was proposed that the portion of the streetcar line along Dixie Highway in Ft. Mitchell and South Ft. Mitchell be replaced by increasing the frequency on Dixie Traction's existing Erlanger-Florence bus line. To fill the void in the vicinity of Park Hills if the Ft. Mitchell line were abandoned, the CN&C proposed an extension of its 4-Main bus route to that city. This route was to be extended via Montague between Lewis and Amsterdam; Amsterdam between Montague and Sleepy Hollow, and Sleepy Hollow to the junction of Dixie, Old State Road, and Amsterdam. This extension would more or less follow the abandoned rail line through Park Hills, and was to be renamed 4-Main-Park Hills.

To cover for the loss of the car line through the subdivision of Barrington Woods and the Lewisburg area of west Covington, the CN&C proposed that its intrastate SH-South Hills Shuttle route, which ran from the South Hills area of Kenton County down Highland Ave. to downtown Covington, be reincarnated as new 10-Lewisburg-South Hills and 10-Lewisburg-Barrington Wood interstate routes, offering direct access to Cincinnati.

Both variations of the new route were to substitute for the 1-Ft. Mitchell route along 12th in Covington and then to proceed out Dixie Highway to Old State Line Road where new 10-Lewisburg-Barrington Woods trips would turn west to wind through Barrington Woods (to cover for the loss of the car line in this area) before returning to Cincinnati.

The other 50 percent of the new Lewisburg service, 10-Lewisburg-South Hills, would continue out Dixie Highway to Kyles Lane and turn east to provide new service through the newly incorporated city of Ft. Wright and the adjoining South Hills area. One out of every three 5-Holman trips would extend out Highland to fill the void created by the re-routing of the SH-South Hills Shuttle.

Abandonment of the last streetcars would also be the signal to operationally integrate Dixie Traction into the CN&C. Or so the Green Line hoped. It duly petitioned the ICC to approve the blending of the three Dixie Traction routes into the CN&C numbering scheme and to allow universal interstate transfers between Dixie and CN&C lines. At the same time, Green Line management secured the permission of the Dixie Terminal to allow Dixie Traction to use the facility.

On March 16, 1950, the ICC gave the green light to the abandonment of CN&C's 1-Ft. Mitchell streetcar service and approved all of the requested route changes. Inexplicably, as bureaucrats sometimes do, the ICC granted permission for unrestricted transfers between what would become Dixie Traction's

The Green Line's Pennsylvania Connection

Unknown to the vast majority of its Northern Kentucky customers, the Green Line actually persisted in streetcar and interurban service for some time after the Covington abandonment date of July 3, 1950. That's because in May of 1950, Allen & Co., owners of the CN&C and Dixie Traction, acquired the far-off Lehigh Valley Transit Co. and its subsidiaries.

LVT conducted extensive motor bus operations in Eastern Pennsylvania and operated a well-known interurban service between Allentown and Norristown and local and suburban trolley lines radiating from Allentown and Bethlehem. For tax and legal reasons, Allen & Co. made the Lehigh Valley a subsidiary of the CN&C. As a result, legal

title to approximately 60 buses, 30 streetcars and 20 interurban cars passed to the Green Line System.

Until 1949, Lehigh Valley's cars actually reached Philadelphia's 69th Street Terminal via trackage rights on the Philadelphia & Western, which connected with LVT in Norristown. It is just possible that a few Northern Kentuckians had ridden these cars, before they were sold in 1939 and 1940 to LVT by the Cincinnati & Lake Erie. The C&LE was an interurban system extending north from Cumminsville, a northern Cincinnati suburb, to Dayton, Columbus and points north. The so-called "high speed" cars had been built by Cincinnati Car Co.

The Allentown-Norristown interurban was abandoned in 1951, and the Green Line's subsidiary rang down the final curtain on rail service on June 8, 1953 with the abandonment of its Allentown-Bethlehem line. ◆

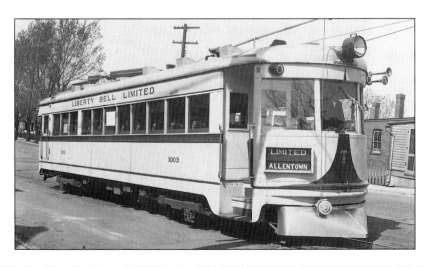

In May of 1950 the owners of the Green Line acquired Pennsylvania's Lehigh Valley Transit Co. and placed it as a subsidiary of the Cincinnati, Newport & Covington Railway. The LVT already had one link with Cincinnati's past. Here is car 1003, one of a group of ex-Cincinnati & Lake Erie interurban cars built by the Cincinnati Car Co. Car 1003 and its mates shuttled between Allentown and Norristown, Pennsylvania, until September of 1951. But the closest it ever actually got to the Green Line was the C&LE's suburban terminus at Cumminsville, a Cincinnati suburb. *Cliff Scholes.*

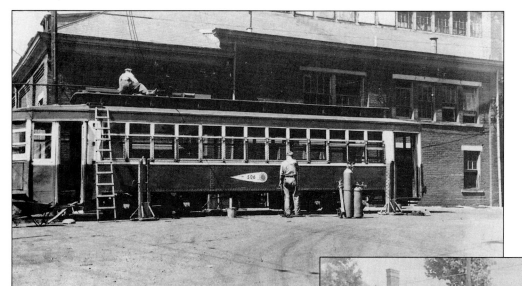

Whether it was needed or not, the Green Line was slow to vanquish Tool Car No. 2. If you look closely at the image at **right**, perhaps you can see the initials " S C & C St. R" on the door of the old-timer. It was converted in 1911, to its tool car configuration. *Sam Guthrie, Earl Clark Collection.*

1-Erlanger-Florence (with the blessing of the ICC, now a numbered route) and existing CN&C lines in Kenton County but denied such privileges between CN&C's lines in Campbell County and Dixie Traction's 21-N. Ft. Thomas and 24-Cold Spring lines.

Deaths in the Family

Employees of the Green Line were shocked and saddened by the premature May 4, 1950, death of Phillip G. Vondersmith, age 54. The company president's death represented a real changing of the old guard coming on the heels of the November 14, 1949 death of Lawrence H. "Perk" Perkins, president and business agent of Local 628 of the Amalgamated Association of Street Electric Railway and Motor Coach Employees Union. Perkins had joined the South Covington and Cincinnati Street Railway in 1913 and served as a streetcar conductor until 1927 when he was granted a leave of absence to become president and business agent of Local 628.

Vondersmith had been named general manager of Union Light Heat and Power Co. in 1929 and general manager of the CN&C in 1930. He became president of the Green Line System in 1944 when the company was sold by Columbia Gas and Electric. As we have noted, Vondersmith was also instrumental in the establishment of the Greater Cincinnati Airport.

David L. Ringo was now propelled to the leadership. He had started with the CN&C as a summer laborer in 1930 while attending the University of Kentucky, and in June was named president of both the CN&C and the Dixie Traction. At 38, Ringo had the distinction of being the youngest chief executive of a major urban transportation system in the United States. He had worked in the Green Line engineering department, as a timekeeper, rodman, mileage clerk and assistant engineer before being transferred to the transportation department. He became general manager in 1947 and a vice president in 1949.

Ringo impressed his peers as an able transit executive, a man who paid close attention to operating detail while at the same time holding a broad vision of where his industry should go in its mortal combat with the automobile.

Colorful Fraud Prevention

He was also an innovator. A small example is instructive. After World War II, Ringo adopted and refined a transfer system to reduce the amount of fraud the Green Line was suffering due to folks taking a trip to downtown Covington or Newport, obtaining a transfer, completing some errands and then going home using the transfer instead of paying a return fare.

Because the Green Line's transfer policy was fairly liberal, abuses were costing more than $50,000 a year. For example, for one fare a passenger could ride from the end of the 3-Ludlow line in Kenton County to the end of the 12-Dayton line in Campbell County--the extreme ends of the system.

The reason the abuse occurred so easily was that most transfers were collected at either Third & Court in Covington or Third & York in Newport, busy junction points where all Green Line routes converged and where the operators had to unload and load

REDESIGNING
The Green Line's
Transfers

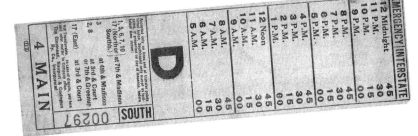

Shown at right (not in color): 4-Main and 1-Ft. Mitchell slips from the 1946-1949 period.

David Ringo's scheme (shown in its modified post-July 1950 form) was as follows:

TRANSFER CONTROL

• All routes from 1 through 17 will use daily dated transfers, and routes from 18 through 24 will use serial dated transfers.

• The serial dated transfer is numerically dated and each number of the transfer will correspond with the day of the month until further notice.

• When travel is exceptionally heavy, as at parades or other unusual days, a special transfer will be used when the daily dated transfers are exhausted.

• These transfers will be punched to indicate the line from which issued.

TRANSFER COLORS

Route	Name	Color
1	Erlanger-Florence	Yellow
3	Ludlow	Pink
4	Main-Park Hills	Pink
5	Holman	Orange
6	Rosedale	Green
7	Latonia	Green
8	Eastern	Purple
10	Lewisburg	Yellow
11	Ft. Thomas	Green
12	Dayton	Yellow
13	South Bellevue	Yellow
15	Southgate	Purple
17	Crosstown (N. on Madison)	White
17	Crosstown (S. on Madison)	Blue
18	East	Green
19	West	Orange
20	South	Purple
21	North Ft. Thomas	Green
23	Bonnie Leslie	Yellow
24	Cold Spring	Purple
	Special	Brown

No interstate transfers can be issued (or collected) to/from 21-N. Ft. Thomas and 24-Cold Spring.

The color of the transfer instantly told the operator whether a passenger was actually on one continuous journey or was trying to double back without paying an additional fare. Soon, losses dropped from $50,000 to less than $3000 a year.

Color coding was particularly valuable to the operator of the 17-Crosstown. And it made life easier for productivity analysts. In an audit conducted on that line during the evening of October 11, 1947, driver Tom McCrann was in service for 498 minutes.

During that time, he made 16 round trips between Covington and Newport, hauling more than 1406 passengers (approximately three full busloads of passengers per round trip) and dispensed or collected 1348 transfers. During his tour of duty he made 512 stops, thus picking up or discharging an average of almost three passengers per stop. ◆

---

passengers in a hurry to keep transit traffic to and from the bridges unclogged.

In response, Ringo developed the color coding of transfers whereby the transfers of each route were printed in a different color. Actually, only eight colors were used as lines operating in the same general area in either Campbell County or Kenton County were assigned a joint color. This could be green for 6-Rosedale and 7-Latonia in Kenton County and yellow for 12-Dayton, 13 South Bellevue and 23-Bonnie Leslie in Campbell County. The entire scheme is explained above.

Modernization at the Margins

In 1950, with the start of the Korean War, Dixie Traction found itself in need of additional motor coach equipment to haul increasing numbers of railroad workers due to increased car loadings on both the C&O and L&N railroads. The CN&C "sold" the other five of its 35-passenger Mack LD-3Gs (Nos. 370-373, 378) to Dixie Traction (which became Nos. 157-161) for this railroad service contract, having previously transferred Nos. 374-377 to Dixie in 1947-1948 (becoming Nos. 153-156).

In September, Dixie was notified for the third time in the last four years that it had won the maintenance efficiency award, awarded annually by *Bus Transportation*, the authoritative transit industry publication. The Cincinnati, Newport & Covington won a similar award in 1946 for being the nation's outstanding transit company among those operating 50 to 100 buses.

In late October, the recently remodeled Newport garage had its "formal" reopening. Originally built in 1937 behind the old Newport power house at Lowell & Thornton, the facility was completely renovated. A new storeroom was created with open face bins and shelves to expedite the handling of parts and supplies. All three entrances to the garage were renovated with each entrance leading to a new hydraulic lift. This enabled Green Line mechanics to safely give the buses a thorough inspection in a more expeditious manner.

Meanwhile, the paint shop and woodworking shops, built in 1899 and located in the back of the old Newport streetcar repair facility, were torn down to make way for the Licking River flood wall project. Nobody wanted a repeat of the 1937 disaster.

The Dixie Terminal received a new coat of paint and an overhaul of the exhaust fans originally installed in 1942. To speed up loading, new directional signs were installed at the entrance of the Terminal to indicate the various destinations in Northern Kentucky which could be reached via buses on either level.

Airporter and Red Top limo business continued to expand, and the company found it necessary to purchase one more seven-passenger DeSoto limousine and another new 21-passenger

The first diesels to wear CN&C paint were 11 General Motors TDH-3612s, shown in this publicity parade actually photographed near the GM Coach plant in Pontiac, Michigan. Though these 36-passenger buses were publicized as "replacements" for the elderly but capacious 1-Ft. Mitchell streetcars, it wasn't that simple. The actual replacement program necessitated the creation or revamping of several bus lines where the 3612s were actually used. Dixie Traction's Dixie Highway line to Florence and Erlanger became route 1 and its bigger buses actually replaced the cars. Anyway, what we see here is the continuation of the paint scheme and "Green Line" speed lettering introduced on the 1948 Twin Coach buses. Now it's 1950, a new decade with new challenges. *Motor Bus Society.*

Flxible coach (No. 46). In 1950, the Green Line System carried a little more than 29 million transit passengers, a fall of more than 10 million from the all-time 1946 high, but a figure which still exceeded pre-World War II levels.

A new decade was starting, and for the Green Line System, the future still looked promising. The truth would prove to be starkly different.

And Then There Were None

After all the talk and planning, the last day of the streetcar in Northern Kentucky was nigh.

In mid-June, 11 General Motors model TDH-3612 diesel buses (Nos. 201-211) arrived on the property sporting the new CN&C white and green paint scheme, complete with the gold striping first seen on the 41-S Twins. The delivery of these 11 buses meant that there were now sufficient new buses to proceed

with the conversion of the 1-Ft. Mitchell streetcar line to motor coach operation.

The coaches, the first diesels to bear the CN&C's initials, were equipped with GMC's hydraulic transmissions, Thermomatic heating, sensitive door edges, single chime passenger signals, stainless steel grab rails and seat backs, and rear destination signs to facilitate loading at the Dixie Terminal. A new split double roll front sign to give more complete destination information to passengers was a feature new to CN&C practice.

The Green Line was not about to let the streetcar era die with a whimper. There would be a proper tribute, a passing of the torch. It all started out on Saturday, July 1, 1950, with a gala parade and appropriate ceremonies in downtown Covington. The CN&C's plush parlor car *Kentucky* and a convoy of new buses then carried a capacity crowd through various cities along the Ft. Mitchell line to mark the bittersweet occasion.

July 1 saw the last full day of streetcar operation in the state

While General Motors was putting the finishing touches on those spiffy new buses, loyal riders of the 1-Ft. Mitchell streetcar line still waited in the weeds for the lurching and lunging cars. It is manifest that the Green Line had not spent much time or treasure attending to the streetcar right-of-way in the countdown to oblivion. That money was being expended on the new buses. Still, there were those who knew deep down that they would miss the big green cars. Perhaps these folks were among them. Or perhaps not. *Cliff Scholes.*

After 83 Years,
IT'S ALL OVER

The clock has just struck midnight. We are about to leave the Dixie Terminal. Can't you hear the wheels screech around that curved track in the upstairs loop? Well, that sound won't be heard again by Green Line commuters! Car 511 will start the Green Line's last timetabled run in the early morning hours of July 2, 1950, and motorman Elmer Denigan will shortly notch out the controller for the last trip, taking perhaps only two points until the Suspension Bridge is gained. Then out to the end of the line and back to the Covington carbarn. This is to be retirement for both the 511 and for Elmer. Retired, too, will be the streetcar era in the state of Kentucky. *Cliff Scholes.*

of Kentucky. The last regularly scheduled service on the Ft. Mitchell line ended at approximately 1 a. m. on the morning of July 2 when car 511 in the hands of motorman Elmer Denigan pulled into the Covington barn. Later, the daylight hours of July 2 saw the last revenue earning streetcars running over the full length of the Ft. Mitchell line with car 518 followed by the parlor car *Kentucky* and tool car No. 2 performing the honors. All three were chartered by a group of streetcar enthusiasts.

But even this wasn't quite the last gasp. The final, final run of a streetcar in Kentucky took place on July 3. About noontime the *Kentucky* was operated from the Covington barn as far as the Park Hills car stop where presentation of the car was made to George Lyon, Covington city manager, for placement in the Behringer-Crawford Museum located in Devou Park. Dave

Webster, retired Green Line operator, was the motorman for the *Kentucky's* last run. Aboard the car were numerous active and retired Green Line officials and employees.

Fenders Garage, a Newport company, handled the moving of the *Kentucky* from Park Hills to the museum. The rear end of the car was hoisted onto a specially constructed dolly and the front end picked up with a heavy duty wrecker and the private car was moved intact to its next resting place.

In 1994 the *Kentucky* was moved to the Transit Authority of Northern Kentucky's facility where TANK employees, on their own time, reversed the ravages of time by restoring the car, from the floor up, to mint condition. It stands today as a splendid reminder of the spirit of the Green Line's streetcar era, ended on that long-ago day in 1950, a half century past. ❏

It Was Now or Never for Green Line Streetcar Fans.

It is 12:35 a. m. on July 2, 1950. The Cincinnati, Newport & Covington's car 511 loads passengers at the Ft. Mitchell loop for the final trip to the Covington barn. It's the last scheduled streetcar in Kentucky, and these celebrants don't want to miss it. The LAST RUN poster on the car's dash says it all, even listing its earlier departure time from Dixie Terminal! Old No. 511 seems to have picked up its share of dents and scars over its three-decade career. *Cliff Scholes.*

FOR GREEN LINE STREETCARS,

it's the

Final Curtain

It was a gala performance, complete with a cast of celebrities. July 1, 1950, was the big day and on the front platform of the *Kentucky* we find none other than Green Line President Dave Ringo at far right, waving to the multitudes. His guest is Cincinnati Street Railway and American Transit Association President Morris Edwards at far left. Motorman William Wharton and Conductor Charles Cummins are in the middle. The last run parade pauses **below** in Park Hills as it winds toward Ft. Mitchell. Motorman Wharton, looking like a Kentucky Colonel complete with beard and mustache and a white duster, frequently operated the Kentucky so costumed and retired after this gig. *Both: Special Collections and Archives, University of Kentucky Libraries.*

Dave Ringo saw to it that the Green Line streetcar era ended not with a whimper, but with a bang. After the funeral cavalcade crossed the river to Cincinnati, it came back and we see **at right** the *Kentucky* rolling merrily along, followed by a 500-series streetcar and a parade of the newest General Motors buses. A trolley-coach heads north for the Dixie Terminal. *Special Collections and Archives, University of Kentucky Libraries.*

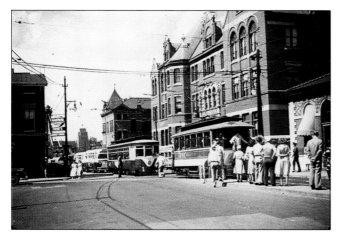

What of the *Kentucky*, Pride of the Green Line?

In the color photo at **left**, the Kentucky and its entourage has proceeded a bit further up the street, reaching the Covington City Hall. The revelry is in full swing. *David McNeil.*

Two days later, it came to this. The *Kentucky* was operated by retired motorman Dave Webster to Park Hills before the electricity was shut off for the last time. From Park Hills, Fenders Garage towed the Kentucky to the Behringer-Crawford Museum in Devou Park for display. We see it mounted on a rubber-tired trailer at **righ**t. Perhaps nobody then could foresee its eventual restoration to its rightful place on the pedestal of historic preservation. *Both: Special Collections and Archives, University of Kentucky Libraries.*

A FAREWELL TOUR OF the 1 Line

We Get a Good Look at the Green Line's Last and Most Colorful Route . . .

1 The last regularly scheduled streetcar to run in Kentucky will shortly leave the Dixie Terminal at 12:05 a. m. on July 2, 1950. The honor goes to car 511 and its motorman, Elmer Dunnigan. Earlier in time we now take an imaginary trip out to Ft. Mitchell which is a composite of trips captured on color and black and white film during the last years of its operation. *Pat Carmody, Cliff Scholes Collection.*

CINCINNATI

OHIO RIVER

DIXIE TERMINAL

3rd St.
4th St.
Main St.
Pike
Montague
Hermes
Greenup
Sleepy Hollow Rd. Trestle
11th St.
12th St.
Holman
Russell
Madison
COVINGTON
LICKING RIVER
CERA
N

St. John's Dr. Trestle
P. R/W

FT. MITCHELL

Dixie Highway

2 George Krambles, noted Chicago transit professional and co-founder of the CERA, visited the Green Line shortly before its streetcar demise. One of the results of his safari with note-book and camera is this June 19, 1950, view of car 507, which has just come off the Suspension Bridge heading for Ft. Mitchell. The bridge's office building is on the right.

George Krambles.

The Case of the Cross-Eyed Trolley-Coach

3 Brill trolley-coach 604 has had its positive pole pulled down by a supervisor to enable streetcar No. 507 of the 1-Ft. Mitchell line to go to the front of the line prior to both vehicles proceeding over the Suspension Bridge in this 1943 rush hour ballet at Third & Court in Covington. Look sharp, and you may be able to see that the poles now resemble crossed sabers! *Earl Clark Collection.*

4 Downtown Covington still looks lively in the 1946 view **below.** A Ft. Mitchell car heads south on Madison as it approaches Pike. Although the inbound cars curve onto Madison here, this car will continue south to 11th, where it will make a right turn. After the abandonment of the 9-Belt Line, only the southbound track remains beyond this point. By the way, Gregory Peck and Jennifer Jones are playing in *Duel in the Sun* at the Liberty Theater. In this era, many folks still went to the movies by transit.   *Earl Clark Collection.*

5 Double trucker 507 is southbound at Madison & Robbins in the 1950 image **above**. It will shortly turn right at 11th and head for Lewisburg and Ft. Mitchell. We can see that there is now only one track in the street and that the car uses the double trolley-coach overhead, drawing positive power from one wire while still using the track for negative return to the substation. "Woody" station wagons are popular in this era. *Pat Carmody, Cliff Scholes Collection.*

Cincinnati, Newport & Covington **6** 521 heads northbound to Cincinnati running on Pike from Montague. It's 1950 and time is running out for Green Line streetcars. *Pat Carmody, Cliff Scholes Collection.*

Ft. Mitchell Cars on Their Appointed Rounds

7 Having left its private right-of-way at the Park Hills-Covington boundary, a northbound 1-Ft. Mitchell car will turn onto Pike from Montague. A close look at the highway signs at the left margin of the picture **(left)** reveals the Dixie Highway, heading off to the left, is the route of U. S. Highways 25 and 42. This artery carries the buses which will replace the streetcar line. *Earl Clark Collection.*

Southbound Ft. Mitchell cars used Twelfth in Covington to Hermes and Hermes for a block to Pike. The private car *Kentucky* is Ft. Mitchell bound in the frame at **right** on a charter . We caught it turning right onto Hermes from 12th in this 1948 vignette. Single track operation is the rule on this part of the route. *Dave Rummel, Phil Lind Collection.* **8**

9 We have now moved further along the route. In the image at **left**, car 521 has just left double track and the private right-of-way in Park Hills and is carefully navigating narrow Montague St. in Covington on its trip to Cincinnati. *Pat Carmody, Cliff Scholes Collection.*

Private Right-of-Way Starts Here

Having already covered more than 650 feet of single track on Montague St. in Covington, a 500-series car is **1 0** about to enter Park Hills on CN&C's double track private right-of-way. The Nachod block signal, which protects the blind single track on Montague, can hardly be seen through the trees at the top left of the photograph at **right**. Interestingly, in addition to negotiating an abrupt turn off the street and encountering a turnout, the streetcar must cope with a sudden steep grade.
Pat Carmody, Cliff Scholes Collection.

1 1 A northbound car has arrived at the Park Hills station. As it pauses for passengers, the motorman charges his car's air reservoir and will not leave until this task is complete. Awaiting him is a 6.5 percent descent down into Covington. Looking at the image **below**, how many people today would have a clue as to why the entire grassy strip in front of the car is called Trolley Park? *Earl Clark Collection.*

12 The weeds will have no streetcars to mow them down after the Ft. Mitchell line is gone. That sad event will happen in just a few months as CN&C car 517 proceeds northbound in Park Hills. In the view at **left**, it has just left the Altavia Road station. In this year of 1950 the neighborhood looks decidedly rural, but hidden in the foliage hereabouts are some very nice residences. *Pat Carmody, Cliff Scholes Collection.*

13 The Green Line's two long suburban routes are noted for some interesting trestles. Car 516 crosses Sleepy Hollow Road Trestle northbound in the illustration **below**. It is about to stop at the sturdy stone Altavia Road station, part of which can be seen. *Pat Carmody, Cliff Scholes Collection.*

14 Rain or shine, winter or summer, the Sleepy Hollow Road Trestle was a picturesque place for street-cars. Snow has fallen on this spectacular scene , captured by *Kentucky Post* photographer Russell Manuel. We see **above** a 500-series car passing over Sleepy Hollow Road on February 25, 1950. *Special Collections and Archives, University of Kentucky Libraries.*

Sleepy Hollow Road Trestle in Sun and Snow

15 Let us now fast-forward to mid-summer, when we find car 518 also on the Sleepy Hollow Road Trestle. Without doubt, the temperature is high and the few folks aboard the car keep cool by raising the windows and leaning elbows out into the breeze. Green Line customers are strangers to mechanical air conditioning, at least aboard their street-cars, trolley-coaches and buses.   *Pat Carmody, Cliff Scholes Collection.*

Heading For Buttermilk Pike

16 Car 506 (**at left**) has found a straight stretch of track to run on as it hurries along near Barrington Woods. It will be on private right-of-way from here all the way to the end of the line. *Dave Rummel, Phil Lind Collection.*

17 It appears that at least a couple of passengers have disembarked from southbound car 517 at the stop shown at **left**. It's the other Park Hills station, just north of the stone one on the other side of the tracks. The year is 1947. *George Krambles.*

The other major trestle on the Ft. Mitchell **18** line is at St. John's. Running just east of the Ft. Mitchell Country Club and St. John's Cemetery, a 500-series car which appears at **right** rides the trestle over St. John's Road. This, however, is no mere photograph. It is a Christmas Card painting created by Don Neumeister on December 10, 1994. The recipient was co-author Earl Clark.

19 Inbound car 515 has left the end-of-the-line loop and the motorman now notches up for a run alongside Dixie Highway. Eventually it will thread through downtown Covington and head across the Suspension Bridge for Cincinnati's Dixie Terminal. This photo dates to June of 1950, not long before the end of service. Buses of the Dixie Traction have served parallel Dixie Highway for decades, and will continue to do so after the electric cars are history.
George Krambles.

20 With a squeal of brakes, a southbound 500-series Ft. Mitchell car **(below)** pulls to a stop at Dixie Highway & Pleasant Ridge Ave. By now the car is almost empty as it will soon arrive at the end of the line. The English tudor styled house in the background is still standing at the time of publication, very well cared for. But depend upon it: Dixie Highway is many times busier! *Earl Clark Collection.*

End of the Ft. Mitchell Line; End of an Era

21 Future Green Line President Dave Ringo's favorite spot on the system was the Ft. Mitchell loop. The photo hung in his office for many years. Car 519 is one of 25 double-truck cars built by Cincinnati Car Co. in 1917. We can see storefronts in the background; as often happened, a shopping center developed around this transit destination. Once called streetcar shopping centers, they now go under the name of strip mall.
David Lear Ringo Collection.

The Ft. Mitchell loop near Buttermilk Pike **22** was usually well groomed.However, in this 1948 photo the grass certainly needs trimming! Nevertheless, the picture at **right** is full of interest: laying over is a double-truck car. A Greyhound 37-PB bus, built by ACF, has appropriately stopped across from the aptly-named Greyhound Grill. The offside of a Dixie Traction coach is captured at the far left margin, and a corner of the Green Line sandbox intrudes into the right edge. Motormen can fill up the sand hoppers of their cars here. *Cliff Scholes.*

GREEN LINE

Flashbacks

Through a Colorful History

Over the years, the Green Line issued a mountain of publication material, ranging from schedules to transfers to maps and advertisements for its myriad enterprises. A postwar route map featured Mack C-41-G 433, delivered in 1946. The inside of the map contained schedules, a listing of points of interest, and of course a plug for the CN&C's convenient charter bus service. We reproduce the cover and part of the inside of the map on this page. A postwar route map will be found in the next chapter. *T. W. Lehmann Collection.*

NIGHT OWL SERVICE

Leave End of Line	ROUTE	Leave Dixie Terminal
12:46CH, 1:05, 1:50, 2:32CH	**3** Ludlow-Bromley (Daily & Sun.)	12:40, 1:25, 2:10
1:00, 1:10CH, 1:29CH, 1:48, 2:30	**3** Ludlow-Bromley (Saturday)	12:40, 1:05, 1:25, 2:10
12:18CH, 12:29CH, 12:40CH, 12:51CH, 1:00, 2:00, 3:00, 4:00, 4:35	**6** Rosedale (Daily)	12:35, 12:55CH, 1:30, 2:30, 3:30, 4:35, 5:12CH
12:18CH, 12:29, 12:40, 12:51, 1:00, 1:35, 1:49CH, 2:00, 2:32CH, 3:00, 4:00, 4:35	**6** Rosedale (Saturday)	12:30CH, 12:35, 1:00CH, 1:10, 1:20, 1:30, 2:05, 2:30, 2:50CH, 3:30, 4:35, 5:12CH
12:18CH, 12:28CH, 12:37CH, 12:48CH, 1:00, 2:00, 3:00, 4:00, 4:35, 5:00	**6** Rosedale (Sunday)	12:35, 1:00CH, 1:30, 2:30, 3:30, 4:30, 5:12CH, 5:30CH
12:07CH, 12:19CH, 12:35, 12:43CH, 1:35, 2:31CH	**7** Latonia (Daily)	1:05, 2:05
12:19CH, 12:40 12:44CH, 1:45, 2:42CH	**7** Latonia (Saturday)	1:05, 2:15
12:01CH, 12:13CH, 12:35, 12:41CH, 1:35, 2:31CH	**7** Latonia (Sunday)	1:05, 2:05
12:43G, 12:55G, 1:05, 2:05, 3:05, 4:05, 5:05	**12** Bellevue-Dayton (Daily)	12:50, 1:35, 2:35, 3:35, 4:35, 5:30G
12:40, 12:55G, 1:05, 1:35, 2:05, 2:25G, 3:05, 4:05, 5:05	**12** Bellevue-Dayton (Saturday)	12:50, 1:10, 1:35, 2:05, 2:35, 3:35, 4:35, 5:30G
12:25G, 12:42G, 1:05, 2:05, 3:05, 4:05, 5:05	**12** Bellevue-Dayton (Sunday)	12:35, 1:35, 2:35, 3:35, 4:35, 5:30G
12:00G, 1:45, 2:45G	**15** Southgate-Ft. Thomas (Daily & Sun.)	1:15, 2:15
12:00G, 1:45, 2:15G, 2:45G	**15** Southgate-Ft. Thomas (Saturday)	1:15, 1:45, 2:15

ERLANGER BUS leaves 4th and Vine at 12, 12:30, 1, 1:30, 2, 2:30.
CH—To Car House. G—To Garage.

Modern transportation systems are constantly on the alert to improve their equipment, facilities and services to the public. The Green Line and the Dixie Traction Company are replacing old equipment with modern streamlined buses just as fast as they can be obtained from the factories. Their slogans: "Go the Green Line Way" and "First Along the ... emphasis to this policy of

FIRST and LAST CARS and COACHES

Leave End of Line First Trip	Last Trip	ROUTE	Leave Dixie Terminal First Trip	Last Trip
5:25 5:50**	12:37CH	**1** Ft. Mitchell	5:55 6:00**	12:05
5:23 5:43**	12:32 12:37* 12:36**	**3** Ludlow-Bromley	5:43 6:03**	12:25
5:40 6:27**	12:46CH	**4** Main Street	5:52 6:38**	12:35
5:40 6:23**	12:21CH	**5** Holman Street	6:00 6:40**	12:02
5:12 5:30**	12:05	**6** Rosedale	5:42 6:00**	12:23
5:36 5:56**	11:56 12:07* 11:55**	**7** Latonia	6:00 6:18**	12:17
5:31 6:02**	11:51	**8** Eastern Avenue	5:47 6:15**	12:05
5:18 6:15**	12:18 1:26CH	**11** Ft. Thomas	5:40 6:25**	12:50
5:33 6:04**	12:25 12:13**	**12** Bellevue-Dayton	5:35 6:25**	12:35
5:36 6:15**	12:27G	**13** South Bellevue	5:54 6:33**	12:10
5:30AP 6:34AP**	12:50AP	**15** Southgate	5:50AP 6:52AP**	12:30AP 12:55AP*
†6:25 6:21* 8:37**	10:58	**15-G** Southgate-Ft. Thomas-Grand	†6:30 5:50* 9:04**	10:32
6:08 6:35* 8:51**	10:45	**15-H** Southgate-Ft. Thomas-Highland	6:35 8:23**	10:45
6:15 6:20* 6:50**	12:10	**18** East Newport	6:30 6:35* 7:10**	12:25
5:36 5:59**	12:22	**19** West Newport	5:49 6:12**	12:35
5:35 6:45**	12:00	**20** South Newport	5:55 7:07**	12:20
6:01 6:33**	12:03G	**23** Bonnie Leslie	6:21 6:51**	11:45
†6:50 Melbourne †7:45 7:40* 10:25**	11:35G	Ross	†9:25 6:48** 9:33**	10:45 Via 15-H

CH—To Car House. G—To Garage. AP—South on Electric Avenue and North on Alexandria Pike. *Saturday. **Sunday. †Route 18-G via East Newport.

CROSSTOWN BUS SERVICE

First bus
Leaves 11th & Brighton— 5:40 Eastbound   6:09 Westbound
                         6:14 " (Sun.)   6:17 " (Sun.)
        3rd & York— 6:25 "   5:51 "
                    6:31 " (Sun.)   6:25 " (Sun.)

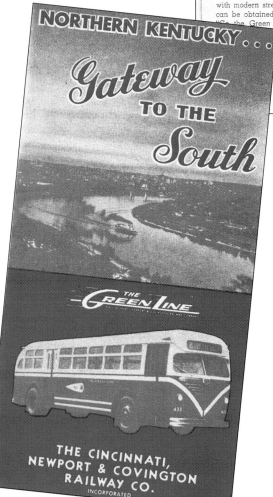

THE CINCINNATI, NEWPORT & COVINGTON RAILWAY CO. INCORPORATED

Dixie Traction had quite a big thing going out at Greater Cincinnati Airport. In addition to its Airporter service, which delivered airline passengers to and from downtown Cincinnati hotels, it offered a "Personal Auto Service at Taxi Rates," its DeSoto chauffeured cars. See at **right** the cover of the limousine brochure. **Below** is a reproduction of a typical Green Line token, shown here oversized. *T. W. Lehmann Collection; Earl Clark Collection.*

The Airport *Chauffered Car*

AT YOUR SERVICE!

Personal Auto Service at Taxi Rates
A Facility of The Dixie Traction Co.

Comparing the Cars

We need at least one color photo comparing the large green cars of the CN&C and the orange cars of the Cincinnati Street Railway, and here it is at **right**. The date is August 8, 1947; the scene is at Pearl & Broadway in Cincinnati, and the characters are CN&C double-trucker 514 and CSR 189, one of 100 low-profile, stylized Peter Witt cars of 1928. Both cars were built by Cincinnati Car Co, the 514 a decade earlier. There's another 100 series car in the distance. Note that the Green Line car uses only one trolley pole, while the CSR car uses two. Note also the "Atomic Bar" at right, undoubtedly the ultimate in dramatic names for a watering hole in the new Nuclear Age. *David McNeil.*

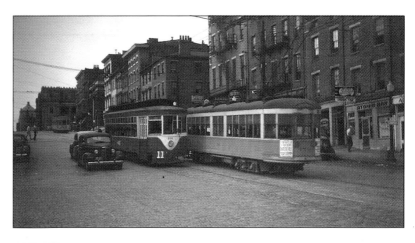

The large 500-series cars briefly held down all runs on the 4-Main route; to be exact, from August 24, 1947, to January 4, 1948 when buses took over. We find car 512 at **left** at Third & Court in Covington. *George Krambles.*

Veteran tool car No. 2 wasn't painted green but was colorful. We see it on 12th St. **above right** in Covington as part of the last railfan excursion, held on July 2, 1950. *Dave Rummel, Phil Lind Collection.*

Here's where we have it all: the Suspension Bridge, the Cincinnati skyline, two of the big Green Line streetcars, the genteel flavor of riverside Covington, and a good perception of the roadway as it dips down to meet the ramp to Mr. Roebling's masterpiece of a bridge. Car 511 coming at us in the frame at **right** holds down a run on the 5-Holman line, and the year is 1947.

George Krambles.

Hand-tinted postcards were a tradition for many years, and the Green Line figured in many. At the turn of the 19th Century a car appears in front of the Green Line headquarters in Covington. The camera has been set up in Park Place, looking down Court St. Not much activity here! *Carl Rekow Collection.*

It's still the turn of the 19th Century as we look north on Madison at 20th St., Covington. The 1891 brick car barn is on the left in this hand-tinted postcard view. The open platform streetcar shares the street with a horse-drawn delivery wagon.
Earl Clark Collection via Fred Bauer.

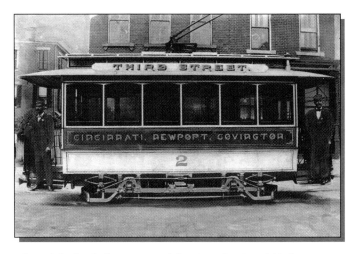

One of the South Covington and Cincinnati's original 30 electric cars, No. 2, is signed for Third Street, a line that was electrified in 1891 and became part of the Ludlow line in 1894. The original photo was hand-tinted by Don Neumeister in 1994. *Earl Clark Collection.*

An eastbound car approaches Sixth & Berry in Dayton. The large building in the background still stands. The Dayton carbarn was just to the right in this hand-tinted view. *Earl Clark Collection.*

A Dayton-bound car heads east on 3rd just beyond Washington Ave. in Newport. The 8 x 10 glass plate camera was placed at the junction with the Ft. Thomas line. *Fred Bauer Collection.*

The "Midway" shopping area across from the Ft. Thomas post **(above)** was so named by the troops after an amusement park of the same name at the 1893 Columbian World's Fair Exposition in Chicago. It was the first commercial establishment in what would become the City of Ft. Thomas. Although certain features like prostitution and untaxed liquor are (presumably) no longer part of the goods and services offered, the Midway remains in much of the same form as in this late 1890s view. *Earl Clark Collection*

A northbound car is about to turn from Pike to Madison as soon as a horse-drawn wagon and a couple of ladies in hoop skirts clear the intersection in the circa 1900 view at **upper right** of downtown Covington. The Motch Jewelers clock on the northwest corner still stands. *Earl Clark Collection.*

After release of a 1912 congestion study focusing on Fifth & Walnut in Cincinnati, the Green Line's Covington cars were ordered to use Fourth St. starting on January 1, 1913. Newport Division cars were unaffected; in the postcard **above** a CN&C car, third in line, has just turned onto Fifth St. from Walnut, a practice that would continue until 1921. A white Cincinnati Traction Co. mail car on the middle track is being loaded in front of the post office. *Earl Clark Collection.*

It appears that the Carew Tower in Cincinnati is about finished, which dates the look at **left** at Pike and Madison to early 1930. The heavy auto traffic means loss of passengers and revenue as well as slower going for the Green Line cars. *Kentucky Historical Society.*

The Green Line in its Dotage

This chapter takes us from the end of streetcars to the end of the Green Line. And toward the windup of operations of the privately-owned Cincinnati, Newport & Covington, many things had changed. Trolley-coaches were long-gone. Headways had widened. But one constant was John Roebling's Suspension Bridge (it's still there!). Even the lower loop of the Dixie Terminal had closed, and all CN&C service to Cincinnati, whether from Covington or Newport, now in 1971 uses the venerable bridge. In that summer, CN&C 314, an ex-San Diego TDH-4512, heads south on a 6-Rosedale assignment. *Richard Segerer.*

Down a Slippery Slope: 1951-1972

THE GREEN LINE was now a much changed property. Streetcars were gone. The bus fleet was being modernized. Automobile use was up. Mass transit use was down. Before the war, it had appeared possible that the electric trolley-coach would be the vehicle of choice for much of the system. Then the diesel bus came into favor. Cost-cutting definitely was in vogue.

Thus the major issue facing Green Line management in 1951 involved the future of trolley-coaches on Routes 3-Ludlow, 6-Rosedale, and 7-Latonia. The 1937 Brill trolley-coaches (Nos. 600-620) and the 1939 Mack electrics (Nos. 630-639) were approaching the end of their useful lives, especially the Macks which suffered from destructive electrolysis due to a design flaw and were literally rusting to pieces.

Would this be reason enough to pull down the 42.64 miles of 2.0 grooved copper wire? Not now, as it turned out. The Korean War was in full swing in late 1950 and early 1951 and there was fear that the "police action" in Korea might blossom into a full fledged world war. The company speculated that such a spread of the conflagration might mean gas rationing and, therefore, decided to hold the line on the trolley-coach network.

But something had to be done about the rusty Macks. And it was. In January, 1951, an order was placed with the Marmon-Herrington Corp. of Indianapolis for five new 44-passenger trol-

ley-coaches. These units (Nos. 651-655) were delivered by rail on April 6 and placed in service shortly thereafter. The choice of Marmon reflected the glowing recommendations of other trolley-coach operators, including the Cincinnati Street Railway. The Macks were all scrapped by the end of 1952.

In May of 1951, the company received permission from Kentucky authorities to raise intrastate fares to 10 cents cash. In July, it won a ruling from the ICC to raise its interstate fares to two tokens for 25 cents, or 15 cents cash, for a one-way fare within the local transportation zone of Northern Kentucky to Cincinnati.

The company had successfully argued that fare increases were necessary following a labor agreement that had been entered into with Local 628 in November of 1950. It called for a starting hourly rate for a coach operator of $1.23 with an hourly wage of $1.54 for all operators with three or more years service. In addition the company pointed out that retirement and medical benefits had been greatly enhanced and that effective November 6, 1951, all employees who had been continuously employed for 20 years would receive three weeks vacation in 1952.

Airporter Service Soars Higher

With increased airport traffic generated by the Korean War, Dixie Traction found it necessary to order three 24-passenger Airporters from Flxible (Nos. 47-49). Further, two more 7-passenger DeSotos were added to the Red Top taxi fleet. From 50 flights a day in 1947, service to the Greater Cincinnati Airport had grown to 138 daily flights by the end of 1950. In 1951, nine Flxible buses and seven DeSoto limos (used for fill-in and Red Top service) made some 29,000 trips to or from the airport. The comfortable Flxibles were also utilized in charter service by the Green Line.

Another consequence of the Korean War was a renewed buildup of activity at the Ft. Thomas Induction Center. For the Green Line it brought a deluge of charter movements to and from area train stations and to meet that challenge an order for 12, 39-passenger TDH-4509s was sent to General Motors.

It soon bounced back. GM advised the Green Line to get in line and to expect a long delay in delivery caused by other Korean War-induced orders. So in a quick jump into the used equipment market, the company was able to purchase three almost new TDH-4509s from Twin Cities Motor Coach, of Benton Harbor, Mich., in November, 1951 (Nos. 251-253). They wore the Twin City paint scheme for more than a year in Northern Kentucky before there was time for a visit to the paint shop. CN&C also was able to purchase four GM TD-4007s (Nos. 212-215) from the Waterloo, Cedar Falls & Northern interurban railway in Waterloo, Iowa, plus a used Twin 38-S (No. 177), believed to be a factory demonstrator, to replace wrecked No. 170.

With the end of streetcar service, the Green Line's infrastructure was greatly simplified. But it still was the owner of a huge hunk of steel--the Licking River Bridge. Said bridge, linking Newport and Covington, now had to be rebuilt. A $175,000 construction contract was awarded in July of 1951 to the Ferro Concrete Construction Co. to undertake the repairs, which put the bridge out of commission from September 17 through November 17, 1951.

The work included ripping up the old wooden floorboards, laying a new reinforced concrete pave-

ment, cleaning and repainting girders, and performing whatever structural strengthening was deemed necessary. By early November, the streetcar rails and the wooden floor had been replaced by a reinforced concrete roadway. The bridge was reopened on November 17. During 1952, a new glass-enclosed toll booth was placed in the center of the span and both new lighting standards and guardrails were installed.

With its rebuilding, the bridge, the third in history to cross the Licking in the vicinity of 11th St. in Newport and 12th St. in Covington, was renamed the Shortway Bridge. This was a marketing ploy. Over the next months an extensive advertising cam-

paign was launched extolling the advantages of using the Shortway Bridge as a shortcut to get to and from Northern Kentucky points. Free passes for a round trip over the "new" bridge were mailed to Northern Kentucky households.

More Trolley-Coaches

If anyone thought the end was in sight for trolley-coaches on the CN&C, they did not reckon on either the tides of war or corporate acquisitions.

The Korean War, now with Communist Chinese involvement, became a bitter stalemate during 1952. Before it was over, the war would result in more than 29.000 American soldiers killed, and more than 100,000 wounded. On the domestic front, shortages of both industrial and consumer products developed and there was again talk of the government imposing gasoline rationing at some point. Would it be the rigors of World War II all over again?

To hedge against potential gasoline shortages, in November 1952, the always prudent Green Line took delivery of six TC-46 ACF-Brill trolley coaches (Nos. 661-666). The purchase of another manufacturer's model in view of the Marmon-Herrington trolley coaches acquired in 1951 raises the question of why the Green Line would not desire some standardization.

The short answer is that Allen and Co., the New York investment bankers that owned the Green Line, had acquired a substantial interest in ACF-Brill in late 1951. Not much more need be said. The CN&C stated that its three trolley coach routes would continue the use of electrically powered equipment for the "foreseeable future." Incidentally, CN&C No. 666 turned out to be the last trolley-coach ever built by Brill. And it was the Green Line's last new electric as well.

Diesels, too, were in urgent demand. Ordered a year earlier, the CN&C's TDH-4509s (Nos. 261-272) finally arrived at the same time and were placed in base service on 5-Holman, 11-Ft. Thomas and 12-Dayton. This permitted the company to retire its pre-World War II Mack LC-3Gs (CN&C Nos. 301-307; Dixie

Laying over on Amsterdam Road in Park Hills is CN&C No. 203 soon after delivery in 1950. The 11 TDH-3612s held down, for more than a decade, runs on the Green Line's shorter, low-density routes such as 4-Main, 10-Lewisburg, 17-Crosstown, 18-Newport East and 20-Newport South. This is one of the buses showcased in the abandonment parade for the Ft. Mitchell streetcars, but the 10-Lewisburg replaced only a portion of it. Bigger buses were needed for the Dixie Highway portion.   *Cliff Scholes.*

Traction Nos. 131-138). The Airporter business continued to hold steady in 1952, and Dixie Traction received three new 24-passenger model 182F1 Flxibles (Nos. 50-52) during the year which enabled the sale to a Mexican concern of two of the original 1948 Flxibles (Nos. 41 and 42).

During the earlier part of 1952, the old powerhouse at Thornton & Lowell Sts. in Newport was remodeled. It was converted into office and work space to house the purchasing department, a parts and materials storeroom, and a combined general office for Newport Division supervisors and office employees.

War brought inflation, and transit was soon caught in another squeeze. This time, in a throwback to the Depression era, fierce opposition developed to throw some roadblocks in the way of increased fares.. On August 1, 1952, the CN&C and Dixie Traction filed an application with the Kentucky Department of Motor Transportation for an intrastate fare hike to a straight 10 cents cash. Without delay, attorneys for the Northern Kentucky Utilities District, which represented 19 cities and communities in Northern Kentucky, objected to the fare increase and forced numerous hearings to be held in which more than 1,600 pages of testimony was taken.

But unlike Depression days, the protests were to no avail. The Department of Motor Transport refused the NKUD's demand to suspend the increase and the new fare was placed in effect on November 9, 1952. The fare boost, helped by

The impetus for the purchase of the new Marmon-Herrington trolley-coaches was the fact that the 1939 Macks were wearing out. The 1937 Brills, on the other hand, were doing a little better. Yet for various reasons the Green Line was a little nervous about giving up on electricity. Due to structural fatigue, the Macks (Nos. 630-639) were replaced by the end of 1952. No. 631 awaits a tripper run at **left** on 6-Rosedale behind the Covington barn.   *Pat Carmody, Cliff Scholes Photos.*

With a background flanked by the massive C&O Railway bridge on the left and the Suspension Bridge on the right, we view downtown Covington looking north from Madison Ave. & 11th St. The southbound streetcar track is still in place (it begins to curve west on 11th at the bottom of the photo) but the streetcars are gone. As the newest transit vehicle in the picture appears to be a Green Line Marmon-Herrington trolley-coach built in 1951, the logical date is the late fall of 1951 or early spring of 1952. You'll probably have to take our word that the southbound Marmon is in the picture; it's nosing into the curb about four blocks north of 11th. *Special Collections and Archives, University of Kentucky*

increased Airporter business, offset the fact that CN&C transit vehicles carried only 25,214,412 passengers during 1952, a 5.6 percent decrease from the previous year, and this enabled the Green Line System to turn a modest profit of almost $60,000.

Awards and Other Accomplishments

With the memory of its turn-of-the-century single-truck streetcars still fresh, it is remarkable how the Green Line embraced the air age with such born-again fervor. The reason had everything to do with the bottom line and the Green Line's role in promoting the Greater Cincinnati airport.

Briefly, the Green Line even wanted to take to the skies itself. It applied to the Civil Aeronautics Board for permission to operate helicopters between the airport and downtown Cincinnati and suburban points, but changed its mind when confronted with the stupendous costs of such a pioneering venture.

In February of 1953, Delta Air Lines introduced new Convair 340 twin-prop airliner service to Cincinnati. In conjunction with the inauguration of the new $6 million airliners, January 19, 1953, saw businessmen, travel agents, and public officials transported by five Dixie Traction Airporter Flxibles to the airport. All the guests were given a short demonstration flight on the Convair 340, which a reporter for one of the local newspapers described as "the fanciest ship in the skies today," and a bird's-eye view of the Ohio Valley and Kentucky countryside. The *Kentucky Post* also commented that "Dixie Traction's coaches were almost as brand-spanking clean as Delta's new birds."

That observation reflected the high maintenance and operational standards of the Green Line set by President Dave Ringo and General Manager James S. Osborne in the postwar period. Between 1946 and 1960, Superintendent of Operations Joe V. Garvey and Superintendent of Equipment Harold Grenert collected no less than 11 first place awards in its class from the

American Transit Association for CN&C's maintenance or passenger service standards. As well, the weekly house organ, *The GreenLiner*, edited by Cam Coffman and Charles Lee, was the 1953 winner of the ATA competition as the best in-house publication by a transit company with less than 1000 employees.

The Green Line outdid itself on May 20, 1953. In conjunction with Parochial School Day, the company ran a record total of 140 charter trips to Cincinnati's well-known amusement park, Coney Island. No less than 74 buses from the CN&C and Dixie Traction made a morning trip to Coney Island, and 66 motor coaches were assigned to pick up the students after their day at the park. In addition to the Coney Island trips, the Green Line ran nine charters to Crosley Field for the School Patrol Day and two charter trips to Union Terminal in Cincinnati.

The top man was pleased. "The charter trips on May 20 were the largest yet and were performed without slip-up, breakdown or other difficulty. My compliments to all those involved for a job well done," said David Ringo in a memo.

A Crack in the Dike

Despite hopeful predictions from some industry officials that the decline in transit patronage would level out in 1952, the Green Line found that its own ridership for all of 1952 continued to erode at about 6 percent. With fewer coins tinkling through its fareboxes, the CN&C and Dixie Traction in February of 1953 asked the ICC for a rate increase.

Requested was a hike of 1 1/4 cents on base token fares and the add-on fare increased to 10 cents for passengers bound for the outlying areas of Erlanger and Cold Spring, and to 20 cents for travel to Florence, Alexandria and Ross. The CN&C also petitioned the ICC to allow it to merge with the Dixie Traction Co. This was no afterthought. Management had obviously been aiming at this money-saving goal for some time.

A 1 1/4 cent increase in token fares between Northern

Pleased with the performance of the 25 General Motors diesel buses purchased since 1948, the Green Line again looked toward Michigan in 1952 and ordered 12 more 39-passenger TDH-4509s (Nos.261-272) . Unit 271 is pictured in 1952. These larger buses were more suited for the major lines. *Special Collections and Archives, University of Kentucky Libraries.*

Kentucky points and Cincinnati was formally approved by the Interstate Commerce Commission on July 3, 1953. The ICC order permitted the Green Line to charge 55 cents for four tokens for interstate travel in place of the previous 50 cents for four tokens, with the 15 cent cash fare remaining unchanged. A 5 cent suburban zone fare raise was also approved. The change went into effect on Monday, July 6. The Commission found that the new rates were "just and reasonable" and were caused by the continuing increases in operating costs and the decreasing level of ridership.

In conjunction with the new rates, the first major reduction in Green Line System scheduled route miles took place. Most routes saw slightly increased headways on Saturdays and Sundays, and some early morning and late night weekday trips were eliminated. All rush-hour limited trips on the 12-Dayton

Covington Learns to Live Without Streetcars

The Green Line lost no time making the streetcar tracks disappear on Court St. in Covington. In this 1951 scene on Court St., Dixie Traction 193, a TDH-4008, heads south toward Florence as a CN&C 17-Crosstown bus, a postwar ACF C-36 in from Newport, edges into the intersection. This photo is dominated by the Covington City Hall that, until its demolition in 1970, occupied the northeast corner of Court & Third. *Kenton County Library.*

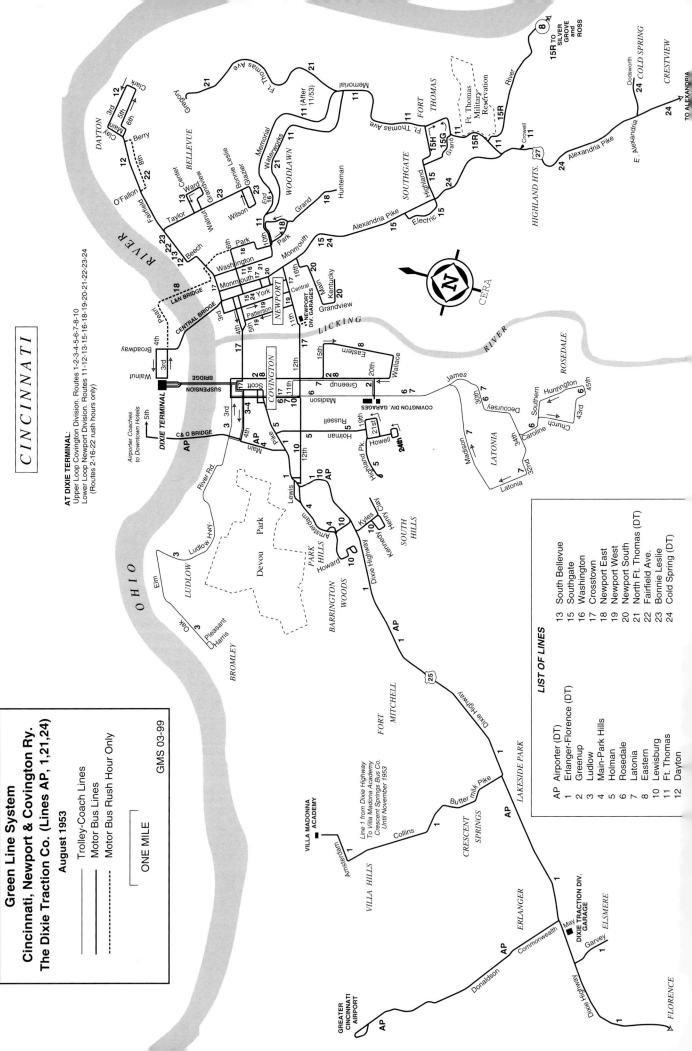

NORTHERN KENTUCKY

Green Line System
Cincinnati, Newport & Covington Ry.
The Dixie Traction Co. (Lines AP, 1,21,24)

August 1953

—— Trolley-Coach Lines
—— Motor Bus Lines
- - - Motor Bus Rush Hour Only

ONE MILE

GMS 03-99

CINCINNATI

AT DIXIE TERMINAL:
Upper Loop Covington Division: Routes 1-2-3-4-5-6-7-8-10
Lower Loop Newport Division: Routes 11-12-13-15-16-18-19-20-21-22-23-24
(Routes 2-16-22 rush hours only)

LIST OF LINES

AP	Airporter (DT)	13	South Bellevue
1	Erlanger-Florence (DT)	15	Southgate
2	Greenup	16	Washington
3	Ludlow	17	Crosstown
4	Main-Park Hills	18	Newport East
5	Holman	19	Newport West
6	Rosedale	20	Newport South
7	Latonia	21	North Ft. Thomas (DT)
8	Eastern	22	Fairfield Ave.
10	Lewisburg	23	Bonnie Leslie
11	Ft. Thomas	24	Cold Spring (DT)
12	Dayton		

Line 1 from Dixie Highway
To Villa Madonna Academy
Crescent Springs Bus Co.
Until November 1953

Airporter Coaches
to Downtown Hotels

CERA

and 15-Southgate routes were discontinued, as was service on corresponding short turn routes 22-Fairfield and 14-York. And the 13-South Bellevue and 23-Bonnie Leslie routes were combined on Saturday and Sunday. Total route miles decreased by 7 percent as a result of these cuts.

And the ICC agreed to rule on the requested merger of the CN&C and Dixie Traction.

Crescent Springs Bus Co. Purchased

The Green Line now turned its attention to expanding its routes into newly developing subdivisions fanning out from Dixie Highway. In 1953, Dixie Traction purchased the Crescent Springs Bus Line, which operated between a connection with 1-Erlanger-Florence in South Ft. Mitchell and Crescent Springs, paying $9000 for its operating rights and $3100 for its only bus, an International model KB5 (never used by Dixie Traction). On November 16, Dixie Traction instituted service between Crescent Springs and South Ft. Mitchell but, by late 1954, through trips were operating to Cincinnati during rush-hours.

Dixie Traction also purchased another 24-passenger Flxible Airporter (No. 53) for $13,974, the amount financed by the People's Liberty Bank and Trust Co. of Covington over five years at a whopping (for the time) 4 percent interest rate.

On November 15, 11-Ft. Thomas buses, which had been operated temporarily on Waterworks Rd. since the discontinuance of the streetcar line on August 23, 1947, began using the new Memorial Highway. It extended from Wilson Road in Bellevue to Waterworks Rd. in Ft.

Downtown in the Early 1950s: Still Full of Life

Downtown Covington was still a vibrant shopping area in the early 1950s as a Dixie Traction TD-4008, in the image **above**, crosses Madison on Sixth and a Marmon-Herrington trolley-coach heads away from us for Cincinnati.

Shortly after the end of streetcar service, a TDH-4509 on the 5-Holman line going eastbound on Pike, is about to turn left onto Madison in the picture at **left**. The streetcar tracks are still in place in downtown Covington. *Both: Special Collections and Archives, University of Kentucky Libraries.*

THE LAST ROUNDUP
for the
Independent
Bus Lines

The Green Line regarded the post World War II small but scrappy local entrepreneurs as friends who basically fed traffic to the large company along its routes. The very last independent bus company purchased by the CN&C was Crescent Springs Bus Line in 1953. Signed for the Crescent Springs shuttle is Twin 381, which we see at **right** going through the Newport washer. *Special Collections and Archives, University of Kentucky Libraries.*

The Independence Bus Line continued to hang around until the end of the Green Line. Loading around the corner from CN&C headquarters at 3rd & Greenup in Covington is an Independence Bus Lines Studebaker, **above**, which will soon depart for its namesake town. It has a school bus body. *Dave Arganbright Collection.*

The Hebron Bus Co. provided service from the end of the 3-Ludlow-Bromley line until it gave up the ghost in 1955. Half of the entire fleet, a Dodge of uncertain vintage and diminutive size, is captured on film in the 1951 scene at **left**. *Dave Arganbright Collection.*

Thomas primarily over the old 11-Ft. Thomas streetcar right of way. Following discontinuance of the rail line in 1947, the CN&C had deeded its right-of-way to the State of Kentucky for the new highway, so in effect the buses had now reclaimed the old streetcar route .

The First 40-Footers

Buses were getting bigger, and the Green Line thought they would be needed for its heaviest route. In March, 1954, the system received its first 40-foot long, 102 inch wide buses, to wit: eight General Motors TDH-5105s (Nos. 501-508) for service on 1-Erlanger-Florence. The TDH-5105s were purchased by Dixie Traction but were delivered in CN&C paint because the ICC had tentatively approved the merger of Dixie Traction and its parent pending a year-end financial review and final hearing. The ICC did end the ban on free transfers between CN&C and Dixie Traction's routes in Campbell County.

The CN&C also received four TDH-4512s (Nos. 273-276) from General Motors in 1954. All the new buses featured air suspension, full length ceiling grab rails and a new pressure ventilating system.

A new paint booth was added to the southwest corner of the 1937 Newport bus garage in May, 1954. The old paint and woodworking shop was torn down to make way for the Newport flood wall. The new paint facility, which was constructed of concrete block, featured both downdraft ventilation and an automatic blower system which started whenever the paint sprayer was turned on. Dixie Traction TD-4008 No. 194 was the first customer for the new paint shop and was turned out in the Cincinnati, Newport and Covington Railway's livery of green, gold and white.

Drastic Changes

As 1953 merged into 1954, it was menacingly apparent that the Green Line's ridership was in a nosedive. The figures were hard to believe, but they were all too true. From 1950 to 1952, the decline averaged about 6.5 percent. In 1953 the overall decrease was almost 8 percent, and the plunge from July 1, 1953 to the end of the year was 11.5 percent.

Americans loved their automobiles as never before. Statistics released by the Covington-Kenton County Chamber of Commerce offer some explanation as to why the Green Line System had lost almost half its ridership between 1946 and 1954. According to the report, in August, 1953, auto traffic on the C&O

Marmon-Herrington trolley-coach 655 helped hold down base service on the well-patronized 6-Rosedale route until sold to the Johnstown Traction Co. of Pennsylvania in 1958.   *Dave Arganbright Collection.*

and Suspension Bridges had skyrocketed to 41,000 vehicles a day from 18,000 vehicles in 1938. The report said the jamming of the downtown streets by the added thousands of automobiles put the Green Line System in jeopardy along with the old established merchants in the downtown Covington core area.

That was blunt language. The report cited the tremendous increase in suburban residential housing starts. It tallied a flight to the suburbs caused by racial block busting, new road building, and construction of more suburban shopping centers. This, it predicted, would mortally wound downtown business areas and mass transit in Northern Kentucky.

The Green Line knew all about this first hand. Tragically, first five months of 1954 saw a 13 percent loss in ridership which, if the trend continued to the end of the year, meant that the company would lose about $300,000. This could not be borne. Stern measures would have to be taken to offset the losses in revenue.

Accordingly, the Green Line filed a new tariff with the ICC requesting the approval of a 15 cent cash fare and the elimination of the 13 3/4 cent token (actually, four tokens for 55 cents) and it urgently renewed its plea to merge the CN&C and Dixie Traction.

And that was not the half of it. The company also decided to

Twin Coaches played a diminishing role in Green Line operations as the 1950s unfolded. One of them, CN&C 384, a 1947 Twin 38-S, emerges at **upper right** from the lower level of Dixie Terminal in 1951.
Dave Arganbright Collection.

The Green Line's first 40-foot long buses were ordered by Dixie Traction but delivered in parent CN&C's paint scheme in March of 1954. The eight GM TDH-5105s (Nos. 501-508) were assigned to all-day duty on the 1-Erlanger-Florence route. No. 504 is shown at **right**.
Special Collections and Archives, University of Kentucky Libraries.

consolidate the operations of the Covington and Newport divisions for greater operating efficiency (and raising cash) by converting the old Newport machine shop into an additional bus servicing facility and selling the Covington barns and property at 20th & Madison. Notice was also given that the company's offices at Third & Court in Covington would be vacated and all CN&C offices would be relocated in the old Newport powerhouse after it was enlarged for additional office space.

After three-quarters of a century, there would no longer be any fixed transit facilities in Covington.

While that thought was sinking in, on June 10, 1954, significant service cuts were made. The remaining 11-Ft. Thomas Limited. and 16-Washington (local) trips were discontinued. The 18-Newport East and the 21-North Ft. Thomas routes were combined during non-rush-hour periods on weekdays and all day on Saturdays and Sundays. The newly combined 18/21-Newport East-North Ft. Thomas route ran from the Central Bridge over Sixth St. and up Park then out Waterworks Rd. in north Ft. Thomas to Gregory Lane. This meant that Green Line patrons along Grand as far as Hunteman Lane were served only during rush-hours when both routes reverted to their former status.

Also, the 13-South Bellevue and 23-Bonnie Leslie routes, previously combined during non rush-hours weekday periods and on Saturdays and Sundays, lost their separate identities. Other service changes which reduced the number of route miles operated were more subtle. The company trimmed an early run here and a late run there from weekday schedules and reduced Sunday service on a number of routes. The effect was to reduce route miles operated by approximately 8 percent.

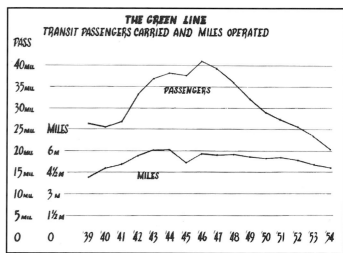

THE GREEN LINE
TRANSIT PASSENGERS CARRIED AND MILES OPERATED

A familiar sight to passengers was the bank of turnstiles in the Dixie Terminal. After no fare increases for more than 40 years, the sign above the turn-stiles changed frequently in the 1950s and 1960s to reflect ever increasing fares. The interstate fare shown was in effect from July 1951 to July 1953. By 1954, as we see in the graph at **right**, it was evident that people were deserting public transit in ever increasing numbers and the Green Line was no exception. From an all time 1946 high of 41 million passengers, the CN&C saw its ridership sink to 20 million folks by 1954 as the American love affair with the automobile grew ever more intense. *Special Collections and Archives, University of Kentucky Libraries; T.W. Lehmann Collection.*

With the Korean War over and Brill exiting the manufacture of electric vehicles, there seemed to be no further reason to maintain trolley-coaches as a protected species. On the other hand, there was no urgent reason to completely do away with them in 1954.

It may not have been the end, but it was the beginning of the end. For efficiency, the 7-Latonia route was converted to motor bus operation in December of 1954. This meant that the 11 recently acquired trolley-coaches, along with five recently over-hauled 1937 Brill trolley-coaches (including Nos. 607 and 617), would be sufficient to provide service on 3-Ludlow and 6 - Rosedale.

American Transportation Enterprises decided in 1955 to paint the buses of each of its companies in a standard aluminum coat with a horizontal green stripe, in honor of its first acquisition, the Green Line. The idea allowed ATE to transfer vehicles from property to property easily and cost much less to apply than the old CN&C scheme. This recently-dieselized Mack 454 emerges from the Newport paint shop sporting the new ATE look. *Special Collections and Archives, University of Kentucky Libraries.*

A telling example of the erosion of transit ridership can be found in a 1954 anecdote. A passenger boarded a 15-Southgate bus to go to Newport after telling the operator about her car breaking down. When the lady dropped only a nickel into the fare box, the operator told her the correct fare (15 cents) and the passenger asked "Well when did the fare go up from a nickel?" The reply: "January 11, 1948."

The Covington Property is Sold

The old Newport streetcar machine shop, built by the South Covington and Cincinnati Street Railway in 1899, was ready for

The decline in ridership had its effect on bus assignments. Fewer were needed to fill the schedules. By 1954, the Green Line's 11 ACF model C-36 buses built in 1947 and the ex-Waterloo TD-4007s (manufactured in 1945) had been relegated to rush-hour only service. In October of 1954, they wait their cue at the Newport carbarn along with a number of well-worn C-41-GT Macks. *Special Collections and Archives, University of Kentucky Libraries.*

The sale of the Covington carbarns put increased pressure on the Green Line's Newport complex. Here's a 1955 bird's eye view of it. Looking northwest, the 1899 carbarn is at the lower right with the former streetcar main shop immediately behind. To the left of the old shops is the powerhouse with the bus garage behind. The Transit Authority of Northern Kentucky (TANK) occupied the premises until 1982. The Licking River, spanned by the Green Line owned Shortway Bridge, separates Covington (top of photograph) from Newport. *Special Collections and Archives, University of Kentucky Libraries.*

buses in late 1954 at which time all Covington Division motor buses were transferred to Newport. Temporarily, the Covington carbarn would still care for trolley-coaches. Four lanes were constructed in the old Newport shop, two for fueling and greasing, one for inspection, and the fourth for the washing and interior cleaning of the buses. Two service and inspection pits were added and a new concrete floor installed.

In February, 1955, the Covington Division's trolley-coach operations were also moved to Newport, enabling the Green Line to sell, for $200,000, the property at 20th & Madison in Covington. The move to Newport, not incidentally, caused the construction of the last new trolley overhead in Kentucky. It was necessary to erect new overhead in Covington on 12th between Madison and Wheeler and on Wheeler between 12th and the

Licking River Bridge in Covington, and across the Licking River Bridge to the Newport garage complex.

A former Dixie Traction bus became the centerpiece of a *Cincinnati Enquirer* feature in 1954. Dixie Traction No. 133, a 1940 Mack LC-3G, was reported to be the most widely traveled city-type bus in the country. Sold in 1952 to Robert J. Woeber, a Cincinnati Realtor, the bus was converted into a rolling home complete with stove, sink, refrigerator and bedroom and had completed a 7,000 mile trek that took it to Los Angeles, Sacramento, Yosemite and Rocky Mountain National Park with a side trip to Mexico.

In November, 1954, the Green Line also put into operation a new mobile, radio-telephone communication system. An antennae was located on the top of a Covington water tower at 26th St.

Five of the 1937 Brill trolley-coaches were given extensive overhauls for continued use in tripper service on CN&C's 3-Ludlow and 6-Rosedale lines. Brill No. 617 is looking remarkably good for her age in the 1955 portrait at **left**. At the **bottom** of the page, we view among other things the relocated trolley-coach facilities at the Newport Division. Ready for the afternoon rush is a diverse assembly of CN&C transit vehicles in August, 1956. The scene was shot from the Short Way Bridge and gives a good view of the yellow glazed brick garage completed in 1937. *Both: Special Collections and Archives, University of Kentucky Libraries.*

and enabled supervisors in roving cars to maintain contact with the dispatcher from a communication headquarters located at the Newport garage. Twenty-five mobile units, seven supervisors' automobiles and one service truck were equipped by Cincinnati Bell Telephone. The new communications system was designed primarily for use during the hazardous winter months when salt and sand trucks were dispatched to critical locations with the least possible delay, and to report the breakdown of buses or their re-routing due to blockage by fire or emergency equipment. The call letters of the new Green Line station was KII681. Almost immediately station KII681 became "Yippee Kiyea 681" to all who used the channel.

Increased air traffic required Dixie Traction early in 1954 to purchase two 24-passenger Flxible model 182B1 Airporters (Nos. 54-55), one 1954 Cadillac seven-passenger Red Top lim-

ousine and two five-passenger Red Top Pontiac taxis. The larger 29-passenger Flxibles (Nos. 56-57) were bought that fall.

The successful management of a business in secular decline is an art form. The Green Line seemed to be pulling it off. The steps taken to reduce transit route miles (and ICC approval for a fare increase) allowed the CN&C to eke out a profit of $24,000 in 1954 despite the fact that ridership plummeted to an all time post World War II low to slightly more than 20 million passengers. This was a record 12.3% drop.

The Dixie Traction is No More

One of the most unusually-named bus companies in the U. S. now passed into history. In March, 1955, the Dixie Traction Co. was formally merged into the Cincinnati, Newport &

Covington Railway following final approval by the ICC. On March 15, Stephens Blakely, general counsel for the Green Line and one of the original incorporators of Dixie Traction in 1922, had the painful duty of being the omega as well as the alpha by filing Dixie Traction's dissolution papers with the Kentucky Secretary of State.

In June of 1955, Allen and Co. created a new holding company for its transit properties called American Transportation Enterprises, Inc., and both the CN&C and Lehigh Valley were folded into the new entity. ATE also acquired the capital stock of the Licking River Bridge Co. outright as a shareholder dividend.

Much, much more would be heard from ATE.

An unusual event happened early on Sunday, June 12, 1955. The Chesapeake and Ohio Railway's crack passenger train, the *George Washington*, jumped the tracks in Newport and stranded some 335 passengers a few miles short of their Cincinnati destination. Green Line supervisor Lonnie Coates sprang into action, but was concerned that it would take quite some time to find operators for nine chartered buses.

However, in 21 short minutes, nine operators showed up for service and took nine buses out to the derailment site. Soon the passengers were on their way to their final destination at Cincinnati Union Terminal without great delay. As a passing note about the changing face of transportation in the United States, it is instructive that this passenger train was carrying 335 passengers, the equivalent of one jumbo jet today.

Two weeks later, on June 27, the transit company suffered its own misfortune when the former Dixie Traction garage in Elsmere was destroyed by fire. The blaze, which broke out at approximately 5:20 p.m., quickly spread through the building and destroyed GM TDH-5105 (No. 503), Twin Coach 38-S (No. 172) and a Flxible Airporter (believed to be No. 49).

Garage worker Malcolm Stewart, who was refueling No. 172 when gas or fumes exploded, suffered only minor facial burns and was released from St. Elizabeth Hospital in Covington the next day. Along with the building and the three buses, valuable tools, company records and a number of fare boxes were destroyed. President Ringo announced that the loss would total more than $100,000.

Clinging to Profit

At first, the Green Line had taken a cautious attitude toward the diesel-powered bus. But by 1955 the company had been thoroughly won over, and it started installing GM diesel engines in its 20, 1947-vintage Mack C-41-GT gasoline powered buses (Nos. 440-459). By the end of the year, eight of the Macks had diesel engines, 10 more were converted in 1956 and the remaining two in 1957. The Mack C-41-Gs (Nos. 430-437), purchased in 1946, were not converted.

In 1955, the CN&C added another Mack C-41GT to its roster thanks to the Monmouth Street Merchants Association which decided that its "big gasoline powered Mack" was uneconomical for its Dayton to Newport shoppers shuttle. Thereupon, the MSMA sold its 1947 C-41GT to the CN&C for $3600. The MSMA stuck to its longstanding policy of buying factory fresh buses with the delivery of a General Motors TDH-3714. The ex-MSMA Mack (renumbered CN&C 438) was dieselized in 1959, using the engine from wreck victim No. 449, and it remained in Green Line service until 1968.

Suburban bus service from Hebron and Constance ended at midnight on October 29, 1955, when the Hebron Bus Co., which connected with CN&C 3-Ludlow trolley-coaches in Bromley,

THE GREEN LINE'S
New and Improved

Newport
Division

With the sale of the Covington carbarns for commercial development in 1955, Covington Division buses moved over to Newport as soon as the old car shop, **left,** was converted to a motor and trolley-coach repair facility. *Special Collections and Archives, University of Kentucky Libraries.*

Two ACF C-36 buses and a Marmon trolley-coach are on the newly installed lifts in the old car shop in June of 1955. We see them in the cameo shot at **left.** The poor reliability of the ACFs in Green Line service made them candidates for early disposal. *Special Collections and Archives, University of Kentucky Libraries.*

For the Green Line, Good Housekeeping Is Good Business

"Good Housekeeping is Good Sense", says a sign hanging in the Newport garage in 1956. From its spotless appearance it seems that the message is being heeded. The sign still exists at Transit Authority of Northern Kentucky's well-kept maintenance facility in Ft. Wright (and is still heeded). In the 1956 photo **above** we see a Mack, a Twin, and two General Motors coaches. *TANK Archives.*

Part of the powerhouse was converted in 1955 to a washing facility. We're watching a TDH-3612 going through the mechanical washer in the image at **right,** while a TDH-4509 receives some hands-on attention. *Special Collections and Archives, University of Kentucky Libraries.*

Mack Loses its Starring Role

The 1950s saw a severe shakeout in the ranks of bus builders. Among the victims was Mack, once the Green Line's favorite bus supplier. In fact the CN&C had not bought from the Allentown, Pa., manufacturer since 1947; General Motors was now getting the orders. Consigned to tripper service by 1954 were the pre-war Mack CM-3Gs such as the 417 in an austere aluminum, white and green livery, while No. 407 is still in the old "cat whiskers" paint scheme as the two vehicles await rush hour assignments beside the Newport garage. *Special Collections and Archives, University of Kentucky Libraries.*

gave up the ghost. Charles Webster, owner and operator, would say only that low ridership made it impossible for him to continue operations..

At the end of 1955, the CN&C was still serving 32 cities, towns and communities in Campbell, Kenton and Boone Counties via 24 routes while racking up a daily mileage total of some 14,800 miles. The company employed 411 persons, including 247 bus drivers. The remainder of the work force was composed of 82 maintenance men, 22 clerical personnel, 45 supervisors and managers, and 10 cashiers and collectors. The Green Line also had 92 pensioners on its books, several of whom had completed 50 years of service with the company.

As to equipment, the Green Line rostered some 120 diesel and gasoline buses and 18 trolley-coaches. Serving the Greater Cincinnati Airport in Boone County were 12 Flxible Airporter coaches of 24- and 29-passenger capacity and 16 Red Top taxis seating either five or seven passengers. CN&C's Airporter business remained steady in 1955; Green Line transit ridership declined by only 6 percent and, with the June, 1954, cost reduction measures in force for a full year, the CN&C showed a profit of some $60,000. There was some satisfaction in that.

Good Financial Tidings

There had to come a time when the Cincinnati, Newport & Covington Railway decided it was no longer a railway. The year 1956 was it.

There was, in fact, a general face lifting. American Transportation Enterprises decided to adopt a standard paint scheme for all its transportation subsidiaries. As a cost reduction move, the elaborate green, gold and white Green Line livery was replaced with an all-over aluminum paint scheme broken by a horizontal green band or line in recognition of ATE's first acquisition. The first CN&C (and ATE) bus to receive the new image was a TD-4008, No. 192. And the Green Line's name was now the Cincinnati, Newport & Covington Transportation Co.

Another Northern Kentucky independent bus route bit the dust when, on April 6, 1956, service between Third & Greenup Sts. in Covington and the town of Visalia was discontinued by Newsom Bus Lines. Newsom said that each trip carried fewer than three passengers. The Department of Motor Transportation at Frankfort concurred in Newsom's sad story and ordered the operational certificate for the route canceled. Significantly only

The Green Line opened a new paint shop beside Newport garage in May 1954 and Dixie Traction No. 194 was the first customer, receiving a fresh version of the white, green, and gold scheme reserved for transit vehicles operating in base service. It may be possible to see that the bus, although technically a Dixie Traction asset, includes the "Green Line" speed lettering along its side, under the third and fourth windows. *Special Collections and Archives, University of Kentucky Libraries.*

one person filed a protest with the state agency against the abandonment of the line, a Lula Cook of Newport. She owned a summer home in Visalia and did not know how to drive.

Green Line President David L. Ringo was promoted to executive vice president of American Transportation Enterprises in 1956. James S. Osborne took over as CN&C president.

The Green Line in 1956 earned a record profit of $163,519 despite the fact that transit ridership had fallen off by almost 8 percent. It happened because the ICC had permitted an interstate fare increase from 15 cents to 20 cents cash (or two tokens for 35 cents), and also because diesel buses really saved money. A slight increase in Airporter traffic also helped. Three more 29-passenger Flxibles (Nos. 58-60) were purchased for this service.

And the amazing thing is that, although a few Saturday and Sunday cuts were made in November of 1956, service levels still roughly equaled 1935 when the population was much more transit-dependent. For example, the evening rush-hour in 1956 saw the CN&C dispatch 99 buses in transit service compared to 117 streetcars and buses in 1935. This meant that, among other things, during morning rush-hours, both 6-Rosedale and 12 - Dayton passengers could still catch a bus along the outer parts of both routes as often as every 7 minutes.

It was a good year, at least financially speaking. But the unrelenting decline in ridership cannot have given much cheer to Ringo & Co.

The Wires Come Down

The tail that wagged to dog was the Green Line's vestigial trolley-coach network of a mere two lines. The 16 electric coaches were lost in a sea of 120 diesel and gasoline transit buses. Could there possibly be any further reason to keep the wires up?

That was the question confronting Ringo prior to his assuming overall management of all of ATE's transit holdings as he contemplated the 3-Ludlow and 6-Rosedale routes. In the summer of 1957, Ringo had to re-examine the Green Line's long range plans

regarding the United States' first and only remaining interstate trolley-coach operation.

Plans had been developed in 1954 to keep trolley-coach service going until 1964. At that time the 1951 Marmon-Herringtons (Nos. 651-655) and the 1952 ACF Brills (Nos. 661-666) would be fully depreciated and ripe for replacement. The five 1937 Brills, selected from the best of the original lot of 21 and extensively overhauled in 1954, would not last that long. The CN&C had planned to purchase some motor buses in 1960 to replace the Brills.

Trolley-coach miles represented 14 percent of the total revenue miles operated by Green Line transit vehicles in 1957. The 3-Ludlow route needed only three trolley-coaches to cover base service and two more electrics during peak hours. The 6-Rosedale line scheduled four trolley-coaches in base service and another three during rush-hours. The 11 trolley-coaches delivered in 1951 and 1952 covered all base service on the two routes and accounted for almost 90 percent of the total revenue trolley-coach miles with a road availability of near 97 percent. One thing you could say about the electrics--they were dependable.

Nevertheless, the decision was crystal clear: Thumbs down.

A combination of factors combined to spell out an early demise for the Green Line's trolley-coach operations. In a July, 1957, memo, Ringo reported to ATE's owners these cold facts:

"1. Construction of the Third St. Distributor in Cincinnati, particularly the Suspension Bridge approaches and ramps leading into the Dixie Terminal Building will present many problems and increase costs for trolley-coach operation during the next three-year period. These costs, principally for overhead relocations, may or may not be borne by the City of Cincinnati and the State of Ohio.

"2. Proposed construction of a new bridge over the Ohio River west of the C & O Bridge as part of the new interstate highway system will affect trolley-coach routing on the Ludlow Line and will necessitate extensive relocation of overhead construction. It is impossible to prepare estimates at this time due to the fact that the Highway Department has not finalized its plans.

"3. Status of the present trolley-coach fleet consisting of 16 vehicles: 5 Marmon-Herrington trolley-coaches purchased in 1951; 6 ACF-Brill trolley-coaches purchased in 1952; and 5 Brill trolley-coaches purchased in 1939 [sic]. If conversion is delayed until 1965, as presently planned, it will be necessary to replace the five 1939 [sic] Brill trolley coaches in 1960. As shown in Exhibit No. 3, this replacement would be made with 5 used gasoline buses purchased at an estimated price of $10,500.

"4. The company's present earnings position is such that advantage may be taken of the tax savings in the last five months of 1957 and during the year 1958. In fact, the total tax savings from the write-off of the trolley-coach property in 1957

And the Last Shall Be Last

It would be difficult to say goodbye to the Cincinnati, Newport & Covington's trolley-coaches without paying tribute to the very last ACF-Brill electric coach delivered to any property, the Green Line's No. 666. As it turned out, it was the last one that the CN&C bought. This color study finds the 666 at the corner of Park & Scott in downtown Covington in 1954, signed for the 6-Rosedale line. Note that this stretch of Park Place is extra-wide, leaving room for the head-in "farmer parking" we used to see in cities large and small. *Pat Carmody, Cliff Scholes Collection.*

and 1958 alone more than offsets the cash outlay necessary to accomplish the conversion. Salvage and savings from operating expenses will produce more than $88,000 in addition by the end of 1958."

In other words, the Green Line could not afford not to get rid of trolley-coaches.

Ringo proposed replacing the seven electric buses that covered the base schedules of the 3-Ludlow and 6-Rosedale routes with seven new General Motors TDH-4512s at a cost of $22,000 each. In addition, Ringo suggested that five used ACF C-36 gasoline buses could be purchased from ATE's Harrisburg Railways at a nominal cost and that any remaining buses needed to cover rush-hour could be provided from the Green Line's present motor bus pool. As it turned out, the Green Line did not need the Harrisburg vehicles because the Green Line's peak requirements dropped to 112 motor buses leaving 18 spare buses.

ATE's eastern owners, Allen & Co., quickly agreed. To put this plan in effect, seven new TDH-4512s (Nos. 277-283) were ordered from General Motors and delivered in March of 1958. And so it is recorded that, on March 17, 1958, Green Line operator E.A. Klinghorn completed the last interstate trolley-coach run in the United States when Brill No. 664 turned into the Newport

garage after its final assignment on the 6-Rosedale route.

The Marmons and the newer Brills were sold to the Johnstown Traction Co. in Pennsylvania, where they replaced PCC cars. They ran there for a number of years before being resold to Mexico City, where some of them endured until 1990!

Down but not out, the Green Line's Marmons and newest ACF-Brill trolley-coaches are loaded onto flat cars at Cincinnati's Court Street yard and shipped to Johnstown, Pa., where they ran until 1968. The lucky 11 then were sold to Mexico City where they logged in 20 more years of service. *Special Collections and Archives, University of Kentucky Libraries.*

American Transportation Enterprises:

PARLAYING THE GREEN LINE
into a

Transit Empire

DAVID LEAR RINGO
Up from the ranks to nationwide transit leadership.

The Green Line was now the senior member of the American Transportation Enterprises conglomerate, and its transit ridership in 1957 declined by about 9 percent. However, some judicious service cuts which reduced route miles but caused little real inconvenience to a majority of the riders, contributed to making 1957 the Green Line's second most profitable post World War II year. In fact, the CN&C proved to be the most profitable of ATE's transit properties that year. Let's examine the income statements supplied to the Interstate Commerce Commission to see how it stacked up:

	CN&C	Lehigh Valley Transit	Delaware Coach	Harrisburg Railway
1956 Results: (000) omitted.				
Gross operating revenues	$3,280	$2,834	$2,424	$2,037
Net income before taxes	$383	$72	$70	$388
Net income after taxes	$164	$8	($15)	$199
Operating ratio (percent)	88.4	96.8	103.3	89.4
1957 Results (000) omitted.				
Gross operating revenues	$3,257	$2,426	$2,464	$1,903
Net income before taxes	$313	$48	$134	$219
Net income after taxes	$136	($6)	$31	$100
Operating ratio (percent)	89.8	97.6	91.6	91.9

NOTE: Parentheses indicate a deficit.

In 1957, the Allen family selected Ringo to run the entire American Transportation Enterprises operation. At its zenith (say, 1960), ATE controlled 12 transit operations, three charter outfits, one small intercity operation and one tourist attraction. At this time ATE owned more than 1600 buses and employed more than 5000 persons at the following properties:

Transit Operations
Akron Transportation Co. (Akron, Oh.)
Baton Rouge Transit Co. (Baton Rouge, La.)
Cincinnati, Newport, and Covington Transportation Co. (Newport, Ky.)
Delaware Coach Co. (Wilmington, Del.)
Harrisburg Railways Co. (Harrisburg, Pa.)
Lehigh Valley Transit Co. (Allentown and Easton, Pa.)
Nashville Transit Co. (Nashville, Tenn.)
Omaha Transit Co. (Omaha, Nebr.)
Southern Coach Lines, Inc. (Chattanooga, Tenn.)
Virginia Transit Co., Inc. (Norfolk and Richmond, Va.)
Wilkes-Barre Transit Corp. (Wilkes-Barre, Penn.)
Youngstown Transit Co. (Youngstown, Oh.)

Charter Operations
Atwood's Transport Lines, Inc. (D. C.)
Keystone Charter Service, Inc. (Harrisburg, Pa.)
Penn Stages, Inc. (Allentown, Pa.)

Intercity Operations
Delaware Bus Co. (Wilmington, Del.)

Tourist Attraction
Lookout Mountain Inclined Plane (Chattanooga, Tenn.)

Additionally, ATE became substantial minority stockholders in both the Dallas Transit Co. and the Cincinnati Transit Co. and owned the Short Way Bridge linking Newport and Covington. ATE's owners, Allen & Co., through its holdings in American Diversified Enterprises and American Realty Enterprises, also had extensive interests in non-transportation related fields.

Dave Ringo now had nationwide responsibilities. The next few years would sorely test the conciliation and executive talents he first exhibited so long ago battling war, flood and labor strife. ◆

Airporters Bring Joy
to the Green Line
Bottom Line

CINCINNATI SUBURBAN
AND
HAMILTON
AIR CONDITIONED
Airporter

MARCH 14, 1971

FROM

HAMILTON
EATON INN
HOLIDAY INN
(Hamilton)
HOWARD JOHNSON'S
MOTOR
LODGE
(North)
MARRIOTT
INN
HOLIDAY INN
(North)
IMPERIAL
DRAKE MOTEL
CAROUSEL INN
NORTH PLAZA MOTEL
SWIFTON CENTER
(Airline Ticket Office)
HOLIDAY
(Downtown)
75

**FREE
PARKING**

**TO
GREATER CINCINNATI
AIRPORT**

As the Green Line's Airporter service grew by leaps and bounds, bigger buses were called for. By the late 1950s, the 24- and 29-passenger Flxible "Airporters" lacked adequate seating capacity during certain peak times. Hence, CN&C rostered a stable of 38- to 41-passenger GM parlor coaches starting with four model PD-4104s (Nos. 63-66) including No. 64 shown at **upper left.** The earlier standard was the 24-passenger Flxible, exemplified by No. 53 at the immediate **left.** This is a 1953 model. A typical schedule folder emphasized the frequent service by air conditioned equipment. *Both photos: Special Collections and Archives, University of Kentucky Libraries; Schedule, T. W. Lehmann Collection.*

Airporters: From Strength to Strength

For the Green Line, there was invariably one cheerful line in the income statement. Airporter service continued to churn out good profits. By 1959, it was clear that the 24- and 29-passenger Flxibles had insufficient capacity at certain times to handle the passenger loadings to and from the Greater Cincinnati Airport. Thus, in 1959, four GMC PD-4104s with reclining seats for 41 passengers and air conditioning were delivered in Airporter livery to relieve weekday overcrowding.

Originally delivered as CN&C Nos. 91-94 as a part of some ATE numbering scheme, the PD-4104s were quickly renumbered to CN&C Nos. 63-66.

One advantage in the creation of American Transportation Enterprises was a grander economy of scale in the purchase and management of rolling stock. The year 1959 saw the purchase by ATE about 50 or so 1947 Twin-Coach 41-S gasoline buses from Niagara Frontier Transit of Buffalo. The best 43 or so of these buses were overhauled at the Harrisburg Railway shops (with help from CN&C personnel) with the remaining seven cannibalized for parts.

Eighteen of the overhauled units stayed at Harrisburg Railway, two went to Wilkes-Barre Transit, and 23 were sent to the Green Line (as its Nos. 460-479, 484-486) in late 1959 and

1960 for rush-hour duties. The rebuilt Twins spelled the demise of the Green Line's remaining prewar CM-3G Macks (Nos. 164, 165, 412-423) and LD-3G Macks (Nos. 151, 153, 154 and 156). Unfortunately, Buffalo's severe winters apparently had been very hard on the Twins and, even with the best efforts of CN&C mechanics, these veterans had a very high road failure record.

Although transit ridership continued to decline on most Green Line routes to a little bit more than 14 million riders by the end of 1959, here too there was one bright spot. Business continued to grow on the 1-Erlanger-Florence route as more and more subdivisions were constructed along the line in both Kenton and Boone Counties. Therefore, in early 1960, the CN&C ordered for Route 1 service seven "new look" 40 foot, 102 inch wide, 51-passenger capacity TDH-5301s from General Motors.

Thus the Green Line was an early user of this new image bus with its huge expanse of windshield and "go faster" side windows. Bus fans immediately dubbed the 5301s "fishbowls" because of all that glass. They were delivered in May of 1960. As a result, the Green Line's older 40-foot TDH-5105s (Nos. 501-508 minus No. 503 destroyed in the Elsmere garage fire in 1955) were transferred to ATE's Virginia Transit Co. Prior to the arrival of CN&C's own TDH-5301s (Nos. 551-557), the Green Line leased a TDH-5301 from Cincinnati Transit in March (No. 403) to give Green Line operators and mechanics some familiarity

Two Studies in Silver and Green

The simplified silver and green color scheme was the order of the day by the early 1960s. General Motors TDH-4509 No. 264 in the image at **right** approaches the barn at 11th & Brighton after running afternoon tripper service. And at the **bottom** of the page we behold one of the last ex-Niagara Frontier Transit 41-S model Twin Coach units entering Covington at 12th St., having used the company owned Short Way Bridge to fill a rush hour run on 6-Rosedale. Both color photos were taken in July of 1963. It is interesting that, after using speed lettering two decades previously, the Green Line has reverted to the old-fashioned but sturdy railroad Roman as the style for fleet numbers.
Both: Eddie Gibbs, Don Hess Collection.

with the new design and to make sure the new model would take the tight Dixie Terminal curves.

To complement the Green Lines' "new look" 40-foot TDH-5301s, similarly designed but shorter (35 foot) General Motors TDH-4517s (Nos. 701-705) arrived on the property later in 1960, for service on 6-Rosedale. All 12 new buses were state-of-the-art, with full air suspension, tinted glass, the larger windows, new bright interiors, fluorescent lights and a much improved heating system.

A Major Disruption

On January 2, 1961, work began in demolition and reconstruction of the outbound ramp from Dixie Terminal to the Suspension Bridge. This work, forecast in David Ringo's trolleycoach memo, was necessary to allow the building of Cincinnati's Ft. Washington Expressway, designed to connect Interstate highways 75 and 71, both also in their early stages of construction.

Inbound ramp changes followed with all work being completed in record time by April 19, 1961.

However, those four months wreaked havoc with the Green Line's operation into Cincinnati when access to the Covington Division's upper loop in the Dixie Terminal was cut. Routes 1 through 10 had to use Cincinnati surface streets, causing greatly extended turnaround times. To cope, the Green Line needed every available transit bus during rush-hours and even resorted to enticing retired drivers back into harness during the four month emergency.

From this point, the Green Line equipment story becomes ever more complicated, because of ATE's ability to shuffle buses among its many properties.

For instance, five one-year-old TDH-4517s and five over-hauled TDH-4512s (dating to 1953) were transferred in 1961 from Harrisburg Railways (to become Nos. 706-710; 284-288) for use on the Green Line's most heavily patronized Campbell County routes. Prior to going into service on the 11-Ft. Thomas and 12-Dayton routes, two of the "new" TDH-4517s were displayed at places along both routes, and the Green Line gave free rides on the new buses prior to their formal July 8 introduction into service. With the arrival of the these GMs, 10 diesel C-41GTs (Nos. 450-459) were transferred to another ATE entity.

On January 22, 1961, bus fares were increased by 2 1/2 cents. Thus, the base intrastate fare became 20 cents cash or two tokens for 35 cents, while passengers crossing the Ohio River had to pay a straight 20 cent cash fare. The new higher fares, coupled with the construction interruptions, drove transit passengers to their automobiles in such numbers that monthly ridership in June, 1961, was a full 10 percent less than it had been in December of 1960.

Caught in the classic downward spiral, General Manager James S. Osborne imposed a new round of service cuts in July. Sunday service was eliminated on 10-Barrington Woods-South Hills. And the 2-Greenup afternoon-only rush-hour route was discon-

The advent of Interstate Highway 75 offered an opportunity that the Green Line could not refuse. Here is GM New Look TDH-5301 coach 557 crossing the Short Way Bridge to fill an express run on the 1-Erlanger Florence line. Note the red destination sign, complete with a small I-75 medallion.
Eddie Gibbs, Don Hess Collection.

tinued. Also, routes 19 and 20 (Newport West and South) were combined on Saturday and Sunday. Sunday service intervals on all routes were also stretched with weekday late night service trimmed on most routes.

A Cause for Optimism

And yet . . . was there a ray of hope? The Green Line achieved some financial stability in 1962 as ridership declined only 6 percent. At the year's end tally, the Green Line found it had carried 11,428,397 transit riders. The Airporter service remained profitable as it had done in every year except in the recession of 1958.

At the end of 1962, the CN&C still employed 290 people, stabled 105 transit buses, 12 Airporter coaches and 14 Red Top taxis. The Airporter fleet had been upgraded with the purchase of new General Motors PD-4104s (Nos. 67-68) in 1960 and PD-4106s (Nos. 69-70) in 1961. The eight other Airporter coaches in the fleet included four PD-4104s (Nos. 63-66), two Flxible model 218GM1s (Nos. 61-62) and two Flxible model 218F1s (Nos. 59-60). A PD-4106 (No. 69) was traded to ATE's Delaware Coach Co. in 1963 for a PD-4104 (also renumbered CN&C 69).

Green Line's transit fleet of 105 buses held down 46 base and 92 rush-hour assignments. Base service requirements were easily covered by the 64 GM diesels (7 TD-4008s, 11 TDH-3612s, 13 TDH-4509s, 16 TDH-4512s, 10 TDH-4517s and 7 TDH-5301s). Supplementing the GM diesels in tripper service were 10 diesel Mack C-41GTs and 31 gasoline powered buses consisting of eight C-41G Macks and 23 Twin Coach 41-S models. An eclectic fleet, this.

The Impact of I-75

Slowly it took shape: a huge river of pavement from Cincinnati, grinding its way to the southwest, ousting homes, businesses and humans from its path. Interstate Highway 75 was

opened between Cincinnati and U.S. 42 in Florence in October, 1963. It was a superhighway which would promote automobile use, but at the same time present a potential for faster transit. The Green Line was ready with a new express service via I-75 to myriad Kenton and Boone County points on its 1-Erlanger-Florence route.

The opening of the expressway, which was also only a short distance from the Greater Cincinnati Airport's front door, also created new opportunities for the CN&C's Airporter service because I-75 cut some 10 minutes off the running time between the airport and downtown Cincinnati. Airporter ridership increased after the opening of I-75, and weekday headways were cut from 20 to 15 minutes between 7 a.m. and approximately 9 p.m.

Interstate 75 was also extended north from Cincinnati, spurring the Green Line to obtain permission from the ICC in 1963 to extend its Airporter franchise deep into Ohio. This service was operated on half-hour intervals between the airport and motels along I-75 as far north as suburban Sharonville, Ohio. In 1964, every third Sharonville trip was extended along Ohio Route 4 as far as Hamilton, fully 40 miles from the airport.

Later, with the completion of Interstate 71 to the northeast part of Cincinnati and Hamilton County, Airporter service was extended in that direction. The CN&C ultimately offered hourly Airporter service from the airport along I-71 all the way to near Mason, Ohio.

While this heady expansion of Airporter service might have been good news for CN&C management, the accountants were not happy at all with what was happening to the rest of the system.

During 1963, Green Line transit ridership declined by only 4 percent, but wage hikes put the CN&C into the deficit column. New General Manager Richard Bennett had his hands full trying to stop a new flow of red ink. June of 1963 saw the erosion of midday base service frequencies on most routes as well as far fewer weekday late night trips. Saturday and Sunday trips were also cut. Service was significantly reduced on the 17-Crosstown route which had offered since 1939 a 15-minute headway on both

For more than 50 years, the Monmouth St. Merchants Association ran its shoppers shuttle from Dayton and Bellevue. This TDH-3714 was purchased in 1955, and it was the last of a string of coaches used by the Merchants over the years. It has just pulled into the Newport Division for servicing on July 20, 1963. *Eddie Gibbs, Don Hess Collection.*

Elderly Bus Ambles Along Music Row

One of the ACF C-36 buses of 1947 vintage lumbers down Cincinnati's Fourth St. in 1958. The venerable vehicle will turn on Walnut to Third to get to Dixie Terminal. This block might be called Music Row; the Symphony box office is on the right, under the Steinway sign, and behind the Wurlitzer name. On the left is the Willis Music Co. Could this bus be a golden oldie in harmony with its surroundings?
T. W. Lehmann Collection.

clockwise and counter-clockwise loops through the hearts of Newport and Covington. This service was reduced to 30 minute frequency Monday-Saturday with Sunday service eliminated except between 10 a.m. and 6 p.m.

At the same time, 19-Newport West and 20-Newport South were permanently combined into one route. This new routing resulted in slightly increased running times for customers in South Newport or West Newport, depending on which way the service loop ran on a particular alternate trip.

In 1963, Local 628 of the Amalgamated Transit Union celebrated its 50th anniversary. President James V. Cummins, who held the post for some 34 years between 1958 and 1992, com-mented "that over the years of understanding, the union and the company have settled their differences by working together." That said a lot about the statesmanship of both parties in a time of general labor unrest and downward business pressure on privately-owned transit companies. Motormen earned 23 cents an hour in 1913; operators $2.39 in 1963.

The Central Bridge Facelift

For more than four months in 1964, Newport-Cincinnati Green Line passengers had to make their trek via Covington. On June 4, work started on a construction site adjacent to the Central Bridge linking Newport and the Queen City. Because of this, all Campbell County CN&C motor coaches were routed to Covington via the lower Licking River Bridge and then on the Suspension Bridge to Cincinnati. Thus Campbell County passengers found themselves, for the first time, using the upper loop of the Dixie Terminal and rubbing elbows with passengers from Kenton and Boone Counties.

The Central Bridge was reopened on October 16, 1964. In conjunction with the reopening, the company announced new schedules which contained some sweeping revisions. For example, the 10-Lewisburg-South Hills route was eliminated and

Was it an attempt to boost declining ridership in the late 1960s--this door-to-door service? Not really. What we view here is a situation where a Green Line bus lost braking control and plowed into a house at 1310 Fourth Ave. in Dayton on June 23, 1969. No one was hurt but the structure was heavily damaged. No. 292, an ex-Virginia Transit TDH-4512, built by GM in 1953 and acquired in 1964 from that other ATE property, did the honors. In spite of this incident, the CN&C won numerous safety awards from local governmental and industry groups many times during the decade. *Kenton County Library.*

certain trips of the 4-Main-Park Hills route were extended across Dixie Highway to serve the South Hills area. The new combined route became known as 4/10-Main-Park Hill-South Hills.

Further, the 24-Cold Spring route was taken off Alexandria Pike between South Ft. Thomas Ave. and Grand Ave. and changed to use South Ft. Thomas, Grand and Highland. Since the new 24-Southgate-Cold Spring route now furnished almost all weekday base service as well as all Saturday and Sunday trips, only a few short turn rush-hour tripper runs as far as Burney Lane & Grand and up Highland Ave. to Ft. Thomas Ave. kept the old 15-Southgate designation alive. Furthermore, the 17-Crosstown route was truncated to a short shuttle between 3rd & York and 3rd & Court via the 4th St. Bridge.

With other service cutbacks, the Green Line needed only 40 buses for base weekday service and 82 in the rush hours. Contrasted with 1949 service levels of 75 base and 140 peak, the CN&C had become only a shadow of its former robust self.

varying periods of time during 1965, due to serious engine, drive train or electrical problems with many of the Twins received the year before. It appears that each Akron-bound Twin assumed the fleet number (and probably the license plate) of the ailing Twin it replaced, making compilation of a definitive record of such usage near to impossible.

More Bad News on the Doorstep

It was getting to be a hauntingly sad refrain. In 1964, Green Line passenger counts slid to a new record low of 10,080,000, with operating expenses again outstripping revenue. The year 1965 exhibited yet another example of the vicious circle in which the transit industry carried fewer passengers, therefore needed another fare increase, which resulted then in another drop in passengers, which led to yet another fare increase, and so on and on.

On May 1, 1965, the Green Line increased its interstate fare

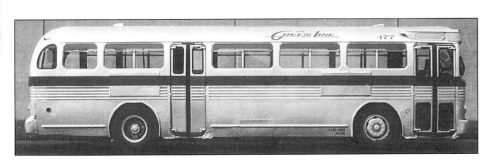

Gas Buses Return From the Dead

The Green Line got rid of the last of its gasoline-powered buses in 1963--or thought it had. Here is an April, 1962, side and front "mug shot" of No. 477, the last ex-Niagara Frontier Transit Twin to receive extensive attention before the whole lot was put out to pasture. As it turned out, the bean counters miscalculated, and now there was a shortage. So ATE sent in 10-plus gasoline engined 41-S Twins in 1964-65 from Southern Coach Lines of Chattanooga to help out in tripper service. The comings and goings of buses among ATE properties in this period made for a most confusing situation. *T. W. Lehmann Collection.*

This cloud had a small silver lining. During 1963 and 1964, the Green Line retired all its remaining gasoline engined buses, consisting of the unreliable ex-Niagara Frontier 41-S Twins and the eight veteran gasoline C-41-G Macks. In their place the Green Line received five diesel C-41-GTs from Akron Transportation (CN&C Nos. 434-437, 439), seven TDH-4512s from VTC in Norfolk (Nos. 289-295) and one ex-Triboro Coach Co. of New York City TDH-5301 to replace wrecked No. 552.

With these transactions, the CN&C had "dieselized." Or had it? The company soon realized it had cut its requirements too close to the bone and occasionally found it did not have enough vehicles to fill rush-hour demands. So lo and behold, no sooner had the Green Line divested itself of its last gasoline engined bus, than ATE sent ten gasoline engined Southern Coach Lines (of Chattanooga) 41-S Twins to Newport in late 1964 for tripper service (becoming Nos. 470-479). Spare Twin Coach parts probably were not a problem as a number of derelict ex-NFT 41-S Twins remained on the back lot of the Newport facility. Indeed, a number of these were also returned to service.

Confusingly, a number of other Southern Coach Twins destined for service on ATE's Akron Transportation Co. were intercepted on their way north and pressed into Green Line service for

to 25 cents cash or two tokens for 45 cents and abolished the use of two tokens for 35 cents for intrastate fares and set the new intrastate fare at a cash only figure of 20 cents. With unrelenting inflation showing no signs of abatement, ICC permission was getting to be a foregone conclusion.

The transfer, in 1966, of four TDH-4512s (Nos. 296-299) from Youngstown Transit Co. and the purchase of ten TDH-4512s (Nos. 300-309) from Chicago and Calumet District Transit and Columbus Transit marked the end of gasoline powered bus transit in Northern Kentucky. This time it was really true. Some of the ex-Southern Coach Line Twins remained parked for many years at the end of the Green Line's property in Newport adjacent to the floodwall, awaiting a call from a buyer that never came.

Two more years of discouragement now ensued: 1965 and 1966 saw ridership decline by a steady 8 percent. A shell-shocked Green Line had to answer with some drastic measures. On February 5, 1967, significant cutbacks in Saturday and Sunday service were made on all lines.

Weekend service was completely eliminated on 21-Newport East-North Ft. Thomas, 4-Main-Park Hills-South Hills, 13-South Bellevue-Bonnie Leslie, and 19-Newport West-Newport South. In addition the 6-Rosedale and 7-Latonia routes were combined

Dark Shadows at Dixie Terminal

Inky black shadows and massive concrete lend a sense of impending doom to the scene **above**. Indeed, the lower transit level of the once-magnificent Dixie Terminal is about to be converted to a parking garage. CN&C 312 leaves the lower level of the Terminal sometime during the early fall of 1969. But still going strong in 1971 is the Airporter service and in the frame **below** GM PD-4104 No. 66, delivered in 1959, is turning onto Fifth from Race in Cincinnati and will soon make a stop at the recently refurbished art deco Omni Netherland Plaza Hotel. *Both: Richard Segerer.*

after 7 p.m. on weekdays and all day on Saturday and Sunday.

When the new service reductions were added up, the CN&C needed to field only 28 buses for weekday base service, 68 during rush hours and 12 buses to cover Sunday service. On July 23, 1967, both interstate and intrastate fares were again increased.

Ironically, it was the Interstate Highway which now provided a bright spot in the dark cloud of service reductions. On the 1-Erlanger-Florence route a couple of new rush-hour expressway runs were added, and base service to and from Florence actually improved from 20 minute to 15 minute intervals. The 1-Erlanger-Florence route was obviously still profitable inasmuch as ATE allowed the Green Line to purchase its first air-conditioned transit buses (TDH-5303s Nos. 558-564) to re-equip the route. Four TDH-3714s from ATE's Nashville Transit Co. (becoming Nos. 215-218) also came north to the Green Line in 1967.

Again the Airporter service turned in a profit. In 1966, the company took delivery of two new GMC PD-4107 coaches (Nos. 71-72) and leased two more PD-4107s from ATE owned Atwood's Transport Lines in Washington, D. C. (Nos. 103-104). In addition, to cover some lesser patronized Airporter runs, the CN&C purchased six 12-passenger Checker Aerobuses (Nos. 90-95). The Green Line also still fielded 20 or so Red Top taxis.

Amazingly, in 1967 the Independence Bus Line was still running 10 trips every workday between Independence and Covington (and six on Saturday) and its subsidiary Taylor Mill Bus Co.-- which had replaced the onetime Newsom service-- offered six trips (Monday through Saturday) between Taylor Mill and 3rd & Greenup. Both operations continued until the advent of the Transit Authority of Northern Kentucky.

In 1968, the Green Line received ten additional TDH-4512s (Nos. 310-319) from San Diego Transit and Metropolitan Tulsa Transit. These coaches replaced the remaining dieselized Mack C-41 units.

Hanging On: 1968-1970

No significant reductions in Green Line service occurred in 1968. However, new General Manager Robert B. Shaffer and Transit Division Manager Lonnie Coats had their hands full as ridership continued to decline by another 750,000 and the company lost money for the fifth straight year. In order to improve operational efficiency a bit, and to reduce a rash of recent robberies of bus operators, an exact fare system was instituted on August 31, 1968. After that, drivers no longer made change.

The Cincinnati Reds are in first place as TDH-4512 No. 284, a handmedown from Harrisburg Railways, passes Riverfront Stadium in August, 1972, just 90 days or so before the 105-year old Green Line will become extinct. Big parking lots, not transit facilities, were in vogue at football and baseball's new trophy stadiums, and Cincinnati was no exception. Believe it or not, the stadium was to be torn down by 2003 for a newer one!   *Richard Segerer.*

In November, 1968, the base interstate fare was raised to 28 1/2 cents (available in a strip of tickets for $2.85) or 30 cents cash. Outer suburban zone fares were correspondingly increased with the fare to Florence set at 35 cents and to Alexandria at 45 cents. The intrastate fare was also fixed at 30 cents cash or 10 tickets for $2.60.

With route miles cut to the bone already, there were no major service cuts in 1969 either. The only equipment delivered to the Green Line was six GMC PD-4107s (Nos. 106-111) from various ATE properties for Airporter service and four used TDH-4512s (Nos. 319-322) from Cleveland Transit. ATE, with its large and diverse properties, was a continuing wheeler and dealer in used buses.

On November 6, 1969, due to work on the Central Bridge, all Campbell County routes were again rerouted over Fourth in Newport to Fourth in Covington to Court and north across the Suspension Bridge to the upper level of the Dixie Terminal. This time the Green Line permanently abandoned the lower loop of the Terminal, which had originally opened for Campbell County streetcar traffic in November, 1921. Also, with the rerouting of all of the Campbell County routes over Fourth St. to Covington, the 17-Crosstown route was discontinued because with all the Newport routes going to and from Covington, it was superfluous.

However, a strange new 17-Crosstown-Stevens-Ross route

now emerged. It seems that Dixie Traction had operated since the 1930s a contract service for C&O Railroad employees from KC Junction (16th & Madison) in Covington through Newport via 11th with stops in Southgate and Ft. Thomas, to C&O's Stevens Yard at Silver Grove. On November 7, the Green Line, in conjunction with the C&O, kicked off the new No. 17 route which ran during weekdays on more or less an hourly basis from 7 a.m. to 11 p.m. and less frequently on the weekends. During the week, four of the Stevens rush-hour trips were extended to Ross.

The schedule for this route contained the following notation: "This route is being subsidized by the Chesapeake and Ohio Railway Company as a convenience for their employees, and as a community service to the citizens in the area served. This service is not self supporting and therefore cannot be continued without the support of the C&O Railway Company." But it actually continued to run until the end of the Green Line's days in November of 1972.

Nothing could disguise the fact that things were going from bad to worse. Across the nation, privately-owned transit was crumbling. Recognizing this, during the late 1960s, ATE began disposing of its operating properties one by one. In an interesting turn of events in 1970, parent American Diversified Enterprises dissolved ATE, returned the operating assets of the Green Line back to the dormant Cincinnati, Newport &

A Green Line Bus Soldiers On . . . But for How Long?

Crossing over Ft. Washington Way, the Interstate 75-Interstate 71 highway connector, CN&C No. 707 departs the Dixie Terminal from the upper level for Dayton in this July 1970 scene of downtown Cincinnati. This coach is the 45-passenger version of the General Motors "new look" bus, and was transferred to the Green Line from the affiliated Harrisburg Railways. After the CN&C became a cog in the ATE machine, keeping track of the intra-company bus transfers became a dizzying exercise. *Richard Segerer.*

Covington Transportation Co., and transferred the Green Line's realty assets (i.e., the Newport Garage property) to subsidiary American Realty Enterprises.

By 1971, it was altogether remarkable that the Green Line was running any service at all, let alone the level of service it did. Weekday base service still saw 28 buses in operation with 68 buses on the streets during rush-hours. To those who took a good look, the end for the Green Line was in sight. Expenses were far outstripping revenues and, since no further service reductions could reasonably be made, the investment bankers who owned the Green Line were threatening outright abandonment of Northern Kentucky transit service.

End of the Green Line

As early as 1960 it had become clear to many observers that privately owned transit had no future. The companies were not public utilities in the accepted sense because they had no stand-by guarantees if their revenues failed to match expenses, nor did they have any prospects for obtaining government subsidies to continue to operate in the areas they served. The ongoing federal and state mania for building new expressways and highways encouraged Americans to forsake public transport and embrace their automobiles. Gridlock and smog alerts were not yet universal, and where they happened, they were ignored.

But this was not ignored by ATE's David Ringo. In 1963, members of the American Transit Association, led by the ATE chief executive, met with representatives of city governments, labor and other interested parties to form the Urban Passenger Transportation Association which lobbied for federal transit aid.

This brought almost immediate results. As part of his "Great Society" program, President Lyndon B. Johnson signed the Urban Mass Transportation Act into law on July 9, 1964, which provided a firm base for a future granting of transit subsidies.

The Urban Mass Transit program was placed under the direction of the Department of Housing and Urban Development. In 1965 the Department of Transportation was established to conduct research and report to Congress on where mass transit fund-

ing could best be used. The DOT in turn formed the Urban Mass Transportation Administration (UMTA) which took control from HUD of all transit programs on July 1, 1968.

After belatedly realizing that the Green Line could become extinct, community officials began exploring the possibility of a publicly owned successor. Under the then existing federal legislation, funds became available through UMTA to assist communities in the purchase and operation of privately held transit companies. UMTA required the formation of a public transit authority and local public financial participation before any federal subsidies could be provided for a private system takeover. Thus, in June of 1971, by the action of the fiscal courts in Boone, Campbell and Kenton Counties, the Transit Authority of Northern Kentucky was created.

Deferred maintenance had reduced the available Green Line transit fleet. It was made perfectly clear that the company's banker owners were not going to throw good money after bad for new equipment or even improve fleet maintenance to keep even a skeleton service going. In March 1972, the Green Line announced that it would terminate all public transit service as of November 4, 1972, to put an end to almost a decade of unprofitable operations. Its profitable Airporter and taxi services continued under CN&C ownership until the whole operation was sold in November, 1974.

In June, a bond issue for funding the proposed Transit Authority of Northern Kentucky was authorized by all three county governments to be placed on the November ballot. In October, the Cincinnati, Newport and Covington Transportation Co. forfeited its state operating license.

At midnight on Saturday, November 4, 1972, the last Green Line transit bus rolled into the Newport garage. There was no ceremony, no drama, to mark its passage. The few employees coming off duty simply closed the doors and went home. The CN&C, this venerable and always faithful workhorse of public transit, had given up the good fight and expired.

Northern Kentuckians awoke the next morning to the absence of public transit for the first time in 105 years. Within a few days, the world would find out if anyone cared. ❏

Portrait of a Dying Institution

As it did when the very first jaunty little White Line horsecar crossed, John Roebling's cherished Suspension Bridge looks down on a Green Line that is now in its death throes. The gloomy weather of March, 1972, matches the mood of CN&C passengers and employees. They have just heard that the notices of abandonment of service, effective November 4, have been posted. Here, bus 309 climbs the ramp to Dixie Terminal with the city of Covington and the Suspension Bridge in the fog-laden background. In the bleakness of despair and disbelief, the future of transit in Northern Kentucky is an unanswered question. *TANK Archives.*

Clock, Bus and Fog: a Hint of Hope

It is now 1982, a new era for Northern Kentucky public transportation, which survived in the form of the Transit Authority of Northern Kentucky. The Motch Jewelry clock, a Covington landmark since the 1890s, stands sentinel at Madison & Pike as a southbound TANK bus on a 7-Latonia run pierces the fog of a March morning. The fog, which permeated the portrait on the previous page, is still with us. But it will lift, to reveal a resurgent transit environment, a regeneration of the economies of Newport, Covington and especially the suburbs, a renewal of optimism. By century's end, the movers and shakers will even be talking of light rail crossing the Ohio River to keep company with Mr. Roebling's Suspension Bridge. *Richard Pridemore,* Kentucky Post, *Kenton County Library.*

TANK: A
New Beginning
1972-2000

THE VERDICT WAS NOT LONG in coming. On November 7, 1972, the voters approved a $5.4 million public transit operating bond issue with Kenton County residents contributing $3.1 million, Campbell County folks $1.9 million, and Boone County citizens $400,000. It was a renewal of faith.

The two-thirds vote needed to pass the operating levy proved to be no obstacle; the issue passed, in all three counties, by margins of more than 70 percent. Thus, the Transit Authority of Northern Kentucky was born, and the citizens again had an alternative to the automobile.

Like the phoenix, public transportation in Northern Kentucky rose from the ashes from the Green Line's demise the very day after the passage of the bond issue. As a matter of fact, as soon as it appeared that the bond issue would pass in all three counties, preparations were made to get the buses rolling the next morning. The newly appointed TANK board, working with Dave Ringo and others, arranged during the night for liability and workman's compensation insurance, and made credit agreements for fuel and tires.

Arrangements were made with owners of the defunct Green Line to lease 58 or so buses along with the Newport storage and maintenance facilities. In addition, during the night former Green Line drivers and mechanics were notified that their services would be needed as early as the next morning.

If the new management team at TANK had a decidedly familiar look, it was because the TANK board entered into an agreement with a group called ATE Management and Service Co., Inc. (ATEMS), formed by none other than former American Transportation Enterprises CEO David Ringo.

Other public transit boards throughout the country also recognized that the old American Transportation Enterprises' managers were highly qualified and demanding of strict standards of performance. They, too, hired ATEMS to run their day-to-day operations.

The most immediate problem facing TANK was the lack of enough operable buses to put on the road. The ex-Green Line buses still sitting in the Newport barn, with the exception of the eight GM TDH-5303s purchased in 1967, averaged about 18 years of age and suffered from deferred maintenance. So to ensure a big enough fleet of operable buses to meet basic schedules, TANK immediately purchased 20, 51-passenger General Motors TDH-5105s from the Kansas City Area Transit Authority.

Perhaps to put a little distance from the Green Line image, the 20 "new" buses, built in 1956 and 1957, were painted aluminum but with the mid-line green stripe replaced by an orange stripe when they arrived before Christmas. Former CN&C vehicles also saw their green stripe exchanged for an orange one.

It's Now the "Rainbow Line"

In the next 24 months, TANK initiated some major changes. The basic fare was reduced to 25 cents and service headways on many routes were improved to achieve a phased increase of 44 percent more service mileage. In addition, passenger shelters were placed at many boarding locations and an information center was established to provide to the public continuous schedule and route information.

In 1973 TANK developed new branches of route 1-Erlanger-Florence to serve the rapidly developing areas of southern Kenton

and Boone counties and established a new 9-Independence route to reach another rapidly developing area around Taylor Mill and Independence in southeast Kenton County. Certain 24-Alexandria runs were extended to Grants Lick in extreme southern Campbell County.

New equipment soon became a priority. In 1975, armed with a capital grant from the federal government, TANK purchased 74 AM General 41-passenger air conditioned transit buses (Nos. 1902-1975). The new AMGs allowed TANK to put out to pasture the majority of the ex-Green Line buses except the relatively new (and air conditioned) TDH-5303s originally purchased by the Green Line in 1968 and the better of the ex-Kansas City TDH-5105s. These were needed for base and rush-hour service respectively on the still heavily patronized 1-Erlanger-Florence route.

Of course, there had to be a new image. The delivery of the new buses gave TANK its desired new look; they arrived in an overall white paint scheme with diagonal red, yellow and blue stripes amidships representing the unity of Campbell, Kenton and Boone counties. The ex-Green Line TDH-5303s (Nos. 558-564) also received the new "rainbow" livery.

In Campbell County, TANK separated Route 15-Southgate from 24-Cold Spring-Alexandria and redesignated the Southgate route 16-Grand Towers with increased service along both Highland and Grand to Ft. Thomas. Further, express runs were reinstituted on 11-Ft. Thomas, 12-Dayton and 24-Cold Spring-Alexandria.

Also arriving in 1975 were four smaller 25-passenger buses from Highway Products Inc. for use on certain routes where the level of ridership did not warrant the assignment of a larger capacity bus. However, these units did not last long in regular service. The agency salvaged them by installing a large side door and a wheelchair lift for the start, in 1978, of TANK's Regional Area Mobility Program ("RAMP") to accommodate those riders who cannot use

To supplement the aging ex-Green Line fleet, TANK purchased 20, 51-passenger buses from the Kansas City Transit Authority in late 1972. One of them, the 804, stands in front of the Newport garage in the **top** photo. TANK's first paint scheme was a simple modification of the Green Line's livery in which the green stripe was replaced by orange. **Above**, an ex-KC bus loads patrons in the Dixie Terminal's upper level in the summer of 1973. Check out both the zone signs which indicate where particular routes boarded and the Sonny and Cher look: long hair, bell bottom slacks and, on the men, sideburns. *TANK Archives; T. W. Lehmann Collection.*

Fresh Replacements for the Weary and Wounded Warriors

TANK finally came of age in 1975, with the delivery of its first new buses. And there were a lot of them, without doubt the largest single purchase of transit vehicles in Northern Kentucky history. Arriving were 74 air-conditioned AM General buses (Nos.1902-1975). We see here the road warriors--victor and vanquished. The victorious AMGs are so new that some have not even received road numbers and the vanquished ex-CN&C and ex-Kansas City buses, in various stages of disrepair, will make only one more trip . . . to the junk yard. *TANK Archives.*

conventional public transit. TANK now operates 12 RAMP vans.

TANK also devised, in 1975, a 10-Visalia route along the Licking River on the Kenton County side, but poor patronage doomed it to expire in January 1976.

Thanks to all these changes plus the OPEC oil crisis, which led to spot gasoline shortages and higher prices, TANK carried 5,731,517 passengers in 1976, almost doubling the number of riders carried in Green Line's last full year of operation in 1971. This encouraged the agency to seek additional public funding.

But the voters proved to be fickle. In November, 1976, they rejected a sales tax increase of one quarter-percent for additional transit operating funds. Faced with an enormous increase in the price of diesel fuel, TANK was forced to raise its basic fare to 40 cents in 1977 and to curtail week night and weekend service by about 50 percent. Predictably, this caused ridership in 1977, 1978, and 1979 to remain stagnant.

TANK in the Eighties

TANK now discovered, as the Green Line had known, that the demand for transit is elastic. Raise fares, lose customers. But seeing no choice, in July 1980 management raised basic fares to 50 cents and, with gasoline prices for the family auto stabilizing, transit ridership saw a downturn. In 1981 ridership slipped to 4,945,000 passengers.

However, in 1981, TANK was able to secure an UMTA grant from Washington to replace the old, cramped, and inefficient ex-Green Line maintenance and storage facility in Newport. A new TANK office and a maintenance facility was constructed on Madison Pike in Ft. Wright, and dedicated on November 20, 1982 by general manager Stephen L. Morris with former general managers Dean Hetrick and John Williams in attendance.

The system also took delivery, in 1981, of 10, 51-passenger

The passengers on TANK's AM General bus 1945 are probably glad they are not compelled to drive during this slippery Covington December evening in 1979. Assigned to the premier 1-Erlanger-Florence route, the bus is carefully making its icy way north on Madison Ave. toward Cincinnati. Can't you feel the shivers down your spine? *Kenton County Library.*

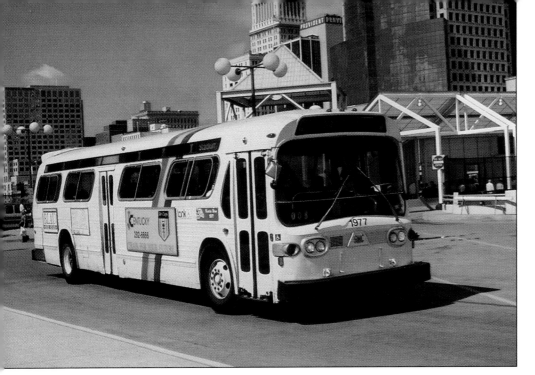

TANK Gives the 'New Look' Bus a Second Wind

The Transit Authority of Northern Kentucky acquired, in 1981, ten 51-passenger T8H-5307A air conditioned buses (Nos. 1976-1985, built by GM of Canada) for its 1-Erlanger-Florence suburban operation. Here the 1977 is caught on a charter at Riverfront Stadium on September 27, 1992. All were taken out of service in 1998 with No. 1980 being donated by TANK to the Cincinnati Transit Historical Association, a local preservation group. *Don Hess.*

T8H-5307A air conditioned buses (Nos. 1976-1985) from GM of Canada for route 1 Erlanger-Florence. With delivery of the new buses, the TANK fleet was completely air conditioned because the remaining ex-Kansas City buses were retired. Further, in 1983, TANK purchased 10, 39-passenger buses from Gillig (Nos. 1986-1995). This gave TANK a fleet of 95 buses, all under eight years of age.

Nationally, public transportation took a back seat as the Ronald Reagan administration gradually reduced the amount of aid to mass transit in the mid-1980s. In a squeeze, TANK had to raise its basic fare, first, to 60 cents and eventually to 75 cents. And so, despite a combination of clean, well kept equipment, convenient schedules and the establishment of numerous park and ride locations, TANK's ridership slipped to around the 4 million level by 1989.

By 1988, the AM General buses of 1975 vintage were starting to exhibit a high rate of road failure. In other cities they had not lasted even this long. TANK management, drivers and maintenance workers were now hard pressed to field enough buses to cover rush-hour requirements. Fortunately, TANK's application for some of the increasingly scarce Federal grant money was approved and this was used to buy 27 buses of 38-passenger capacity from Gillig (Nos. 949-975). This enabled the agency to consign the worst of the AMGs to the scrap heap.

There also was some modest route expansion in 1988. A new service was launched to the newly opened St. Elizabeth South Hospital in suburban Kenton County. Seven trips a day were scheduled on the new 33-St. Elizabeth South route designed to run primarily at shift change times to carry hospital workers to and from downtown Covington.

Renewal in the Nineties

Bus ridership dropped to under 4 million in 1990, putting it close to the all-time Green Line low. As a result, TANK revised, during 1991, the schedules of most routes. Pruned was weekday mid-day service with several routes losing all trips after 7 p.m. and many others a trip or two after 7 p.m. Further, it was necessary to discontinue all Saturday and Sunday service on many routes.

In 1992, the agency bought 13 more 37-passenger buses from Gillig (Nos. 936-948). Then in late 1992 and early 1993, TANK received 23 Flxible 37-passenger buses (Nos. 1913-1935) and 10, 44-passenger buses from Flxible (Nos. 1996-2005). This enabled TANK General Manager Mark Donaghy and Director of Maintenance Paul Clayton to put out of their misery almost all of the remaining AM General buses originally purchased in 1975.

Five AMG buses, however, soldiered on in rush-hour service until early 1995. Finally, with the delivery from Gillig of six 38-passenger (Nos. 1907-1912) and 10, 44-passenger (Nos. 2006-2015) buses, time ran out for the AMGs when, on March 21, 1995, No. 1903 made its final trip. However, No. 1930 was spared from the scrapyard, taken to the garage, and restored by

In 1995, TANK initiated a new 2X-Airport Express route primarily to transport workers to and from the growing Greater Cincinnati-Northern Kentucky International Airport and downtown Cincinnati. TANK 1997, a 1992 40-foot Flxible, awaits a shift change at the airport. *James Rodecker.*

The onetime Dixie Traction 21-North Ft. Thomas route was discontinued on February 16, 1996, with Gillig No. 961 bringing down the curtain. Thirty-five foot Gilligs, such as this one, formed the backbone of TANK's fleet in the 1990s. *James Rodecker.*

the talented TANK maintenance staff. Eventually No. 1901 (ex-1930) emerged showroom new and is used for historical events and community relations purposes.

By 1995 it was time for a mighty TANK counter attack on the ridership malaise that had gripped the territory. Many tactics were tried. No idea was overlooked to entice folks out of their cars. For starters, a new route 2X-Airport Express was instituted between downtown Cincinnati and the Northern Kentucky-Greater Cincinnati International Airport with the schedule primarily aimed at shift change times at the airport.

Another new route begun during the year was 10-Cross County. This would be the first crosstown route in Northern Kentucky since the demise of the old Green Line 17-Crosstown in the late 1960s. Operating from the Village Green Shopping Center via U. S. 27 to Northern Kentucky University and on via I-275, to Taylor Mill, the Latonia Shopping Center and terminating at Florence Mall, the service started at 10 a.m. and ended about 8 p.m. Monday through Friday only. Alas, although the 2X route proved to be a winner, ridership never developed on 10-Cross County and it was quietly discontinued during 1996.

There was a nagging thought at TANK headquarters in 1995 that the jumble of suburban express routes branching off the 1-Erlanger-Florence and 24-Cold Spring-Alexandria trunks was too complicated for potential riders to grasp. And yet this was promising territory for transit.

The answer was to simplify. This is what the planners came up with: The 1A-Villa Hills rush-hour route via I-75 was given its own route number (17X-Villa Hills), 1B-Edgewood via I-75 became 18X-Edgewood, 1C-Hallam Beechgrove via I-75 became 19X-Beechgrove. Two new Boone County weekday rush-hour services via I-75 were also established: 32X-Burlington and 22X-Walton. Also, the rush-hour only service that branched off of 30X-Independence Express at Hands Pike was redesignated 31-Hands Pike. Certain 1-Erlanger-Florence trips continued to operate via I-75 during rush hours as 1X-Florence Limited and were not assigned a new route number.

In Campbell County, base and rush-hour express service trips on route 24, whether to just Cold Spring-Crestview or on to

Alexandria or even to Grants Lick, had been all lumped under the one route number. To remedy this, TANK redesignated this trunk route as follows: 24-Cold Spring-Crestview (and rush-hour express service via I-471 as 24X), 25-Alexandria (and 25X via I-471) and 26-Grants Lick (plus 26X via I-471). Also, the 27X express service to Moock Rd. was rerouted via Alexandria Pike..

Not given a separate route number but continued were certain 11X-Ft. Thomas and 12X-Dayton express trips which also used I-471 for part of their runs.

Dixie Terminal Closed

It was a blow, and it came at short notice. In late September, 1996, the Transit Authority of Northern Kentucky was notified that its tenancy in the Dixie Terminal would be terminated on October 18. TANK and its predecessor Green Line had used the off-street structure as its primary Cincinnati terminus since 1921.

At 12:45 a.m. on October 18, Flxible bus 2004, covering the last evening run on 1-Erlanger-Florence, pulled into Dixie

October 18, 1996, was the grand finale for Dixie Terminal, ending 75 years of use by the Green Line and TANK as their primary Cincinnati terminus. Flxible No. 2004 awaits the signal by TANK General Manager Mark Donaghy to end a very long and colorful era. *James Rodecker.*

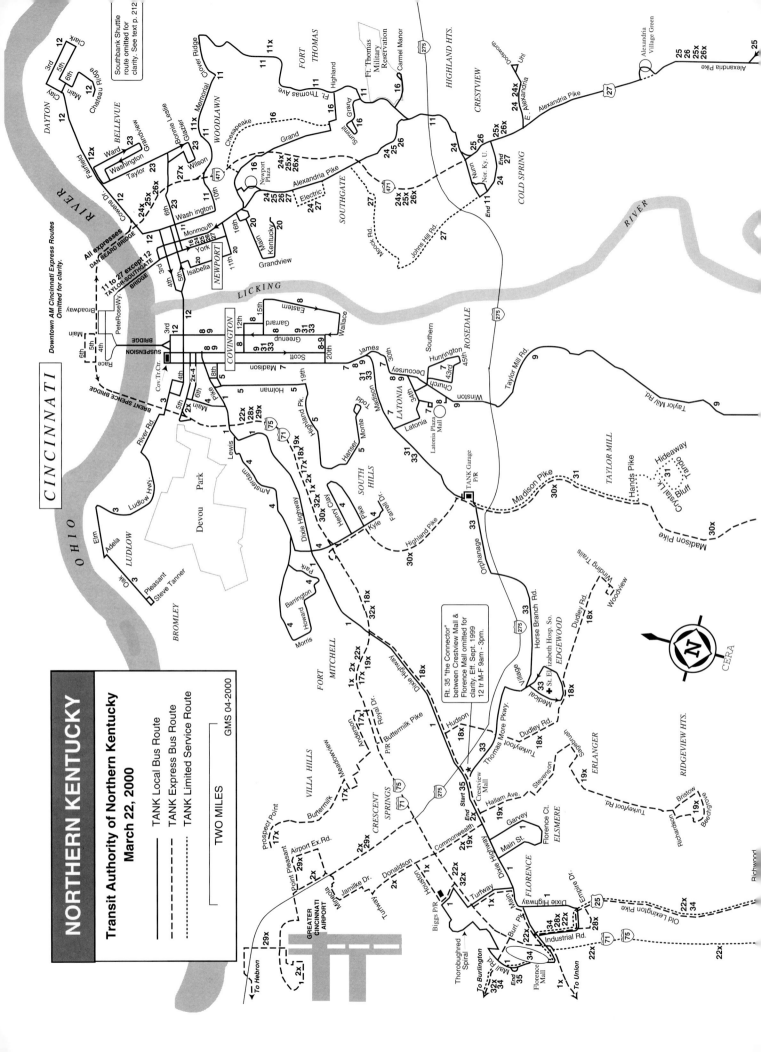

PINCHED FOR SPACE,

TANK gets a

Garage Upgrade

In New Ft. Wright Maintenance Facility

AM General bus 1921, pictured **above**, awaits its next assignment adjacent to the old Cincinnati, Newport & Covington powerhouse in Newport. The move of TANK to a new office and maintenance facility in Ft. Wright is only months away. There is quite a contrast between the very modern bus and the industrial gothic of the ancient building. Thanks to federal funding, TANK was able to move into a state-of-the-art transit maintenance and storage facility with plenty of elbow room on Madison Pike in Ft. Wright in 1982. A panoramic view, taken from the bluff above, appears **below**.   *Both: TANK Archives.*

Terminal. Operator Missy Stone drove the bus around to the loading area where recently retired operations director Bob Mason took over the wheel and, after seeing to the loading of the final passengers, TANK general manager Mark Donaghy stepped aboard and a long era in Northern Kentucky transit came to an end.

History now reeled backward. Once again, Cincinnati's downtown streets would be packed with local Northern Kentucky buses. With the closing of the Dixie Terminal, Campbell County buses, except 12-Dayton which continued to operate via Covington (and thus function as a "crosstown" line), were routed across the new Taylor-Southgate Bridge to Fourth to Main to Fifth to Broadway and back to the bridge. Kenton/Boone County buses were routed north from the Suspension Bridge to Main to Fourth to Race and back to the bridge.

Express buses using the freeway, though, had been loading downtown for some time. Most TANK express trips had used Cincinnati surface streets (Main, Sixth and Race) since 1984, via either the I-75 or I-471 bridges and they continued to operate as before. At the peak of afternoon rush-hours in 1996, TANK had 92 buses on the road as well as seven special needs vans in "RAMP" door-to-door service.

And there was good news in 1996. Ridership increased by 2.5 percent, marking the first such gain since 1989.

TANK Turns 25

On November 11, 1997, TANK celebrated its 25th anniversary of service to Northern Kentucky by staging an open house at its Ft. Wright facility. Guided tours were conducted and numerous displays covered topics from how TANK helps ease traffic congestion while lessening pollution and how mobility impaired

Bus ridership for 1997 remained steady with about 4 million riders. Additionally, in late 1997-early 1998, TANK took delivery of 10 new 35-foot Gillig units (nos. 2016-2025).

In the bubbling economic prosperity of the 1990s, there was a strong gentrification movement along the Ohio River and downtowns of Covington, Newport and Bellevue. Fortunately, these areas had not become derelict as had happened in so many river towns. There was, decidedly, an upbeat atmosphere. Business perked up, restaurant/entertainment districts flowered, trendy condominiums were built.

This was a heaven-sent opportunity for an innovative new transit approach. Sure enough, May 6, 1998, saw the beginning of the Southbank Shuttle, a new bus link between the downtown business districts of Cincinnati, Covington, Newport, and Bellevue.

Actually two routes were created, with one operating from Cincinnati counter-clockwise, going through Covington first, and the other route winding its way clockwise first through Newport and Bellevue. The routes were designed to join the downtown Cincinnati retail and restaurant district, the Newport shopping and entertainment district and Riverboat Row as well as the Covington Landing area and Covington's Mainstrasse Village.

The Southbank Shuttle was conceived by TANK with Southbank Partners, a public-private group, providing marketing

citizens could utilize lift-equipped transit buses to an explanation of TANK's weekly and monthly passes.

Unveiled for the first time, on bus No. 1921, was the new TANK paint scheme incorporating green and blue horizontal stripes (the green recognizing the heritage of its predecessor Green Line?) and a new TANK logo. Also shown with pride was the venerable parlor car *Kentucky*, renovated by Authority employees on their own time, and restored AMG No. 1901 - the only surviving example of the first new buses (74 in all) bought by the then fledgling agency in 1975.

Although TANK lost the use of Cincinnati's Dixie Terminal in 1996, the opening of the Riverside Transit Center somewhat lessened the blow. The "Covington Transit Center," as it is commonly called, not only provides covered shelter for Kenton and Boone County passengers transferring from one TANK route to another, but with the institution of through routing of many Campbell County trips, the CTC also serves the needs of many Campbell County passengers. Gillig 942 enters the new Riverfront Transit Center at Third & Madison shortly after its opening in 1998. *Terry W. Lehmann.*

19th Century Suspension Bridge Adapts to 21st Century Transportation

With the landmark Roebling Suspension Bridge and the Cincinnati skyline for counterpoint in the background **above**, a Flxible in TANK's new paint scheme heads for Covington in November of 1999. What an eclectic mix of architecture! *Terry W. Lehmann.*

And here's the latest in small bus design for those special transit jobs. In the image at **right**, an Orion II, painted for the successful Southbank Shuttle, a new crosstown route, enters Covington. In April, 2000, the route received newly designed low-floor Gillig buses. *Terry W. Lehmann.*

support. TANK originally assigned eight specially painted Orion II 22-seat buses, part of a group of 12 such buses (Nos. 301-312) purchased from the Central Florida Regional Transit Authority and overhauled by TANK. The other four Orion IIs were painted in TANK livery (Nos. 301, 309, 311, and 312) and assigned to relief duty on the lightly patronized routes. Six new Orion IIs (Nos. 313-318) were delivered in late 1998.

Initially, operations were scheduled between 10 a. m. to 10 p. m. on Sunday through Thursday and to 1 a. m. on Friday and Saturday nights. The headways were 20 minutes from Sunday through Thursday and 15 minutes on Friday and Saturday. Executive Transportation of Newport was selected to supply the drivers and to lease and maintain the shuttle buses.

To further encourage ridership the fare was set at a low 25 cents and hotels and restaurants in the Northern Kentucky area were encouraged to buy bus tokens to give to patrons to entice them to use the service. Alan Bernstein of Southbank partners explained that the routes were designed to persuade both tourists and locals to leave their cars on the perimeters of the downtown districts while visiting one or more tourist venues on either side of the river.

Covington Transit Center

As had been done in many cities, TANK built a central transit station. The indoor facility was located in downtown Covington east of Madison Ave. between Second and Third. Opened on July 25, 1998, the Riverfront Transit Center was designed to serve as TANK's major transfer point in order to speed up operations, replace the former main transfer locations in congested downtown Cincinnati and at Third & Madison in Covington, and to afford TANK's transferring passengers a place to make connections out of the elements. Almost immediately the new facility was nicknamed the Covington Transit Center by the press and by TANK itself.

In conjunction with the CTC opening, TANK radically changed its local service patterns by through routing almost all of them from Campbell County through Cincinnati to Kenton County or visa versa. For example, a 3-Ludlow trip to Cincinnati might well leave the Queen City as a 16-Grand Towers bus bound for Campbell County.

In fact the schedules of all inbound and outbound Campbell County trips (including both local and express) were recast to designate the Covington Transit Center

Celebrating the 1999 SORTA-TANK operating agreement in front of Queen City Metro bus 901 are Charles Schroer, general counsel; General Manager Paul Jablonski and board member Edward Babbit while TANK bus 1916 forms the backdrop for TANK board chairperson Ronald R. Stormer, board members Charles R. "Chuck" Peters, John R. "Jack" Kinsella, Mary Fisher, General Manager Mark Donaghy and General Counsel David Schneider. Not present were TANK board members Juanita Mills, Glenn Gunning, Don McMillian, Vivian Llambi, Robert Boswell and Secretary-Treasurer David L. Anneken. *TANK Archives.*

as their first or last stop--not downtown Cincinnati as before.

What is more, almost all Kenton/Boone County express service schedules were modified to reflect the CTC as their last morning rush-hour stop or their first evening stop. All Kenton County local service trips include a stop at the CTC on their way to and from Cincinnati via the Suspension Bridge.

Other major TANK developments effective July 25 included the start of a new "crosstown" service, the 34-Walton-Burlington Connector, designed to join two growing areas of Boone County with three trips a day via the Florence Mall. Joining route 34 were express routes 28X-Empire Drive (connecting Cincinnati and the area south of Florence) and 29X-Hebron Express (joining Cincinnati and the rapidly growing area northwest of the

As appropriate for the millennium, Flxible bus 2000 (actually delivered in 1992) and signed for line 32X-(Burlington) Oakbrook, is discovered in a corner of the TANK Ft. Wright property. It wears a semi-overall advertising livery, including a sign for "Dixie Chili." *G. Mac Sebree.*

Honoring His Eminence

TANK forces restored AM General coach 1901 for the historical collection. This bus represents the 74 units which arrived in 1975 to rescue the fledgling transit agency from a severe shortage of serviceable buses. Rehabilitation took a lot of work, since the AM General proved to be a troublesome breed. Interestingly, there was no number 1901 originally. The series started at 1902, so in dealing with the restoration, old coach 1930 was refurbished and renumbered to 1901. The inset photo shows that these buses carried nameplates above the front door to honor famous Kentucky Derby winners. *His Eminence* won the 1901 Derby.

Large picture: G. Mac Sebree. Inset: Terry W. Lehmann.

Greater Cincinnati Airport)--both being new routes with three a. m. and three p. m. rush-hour trips.

On the downside, Saturday and Sunday service was discontinued entirely on the 33-St. Elizabeth South line and Saturday service became a thing of the past on the 23-South Bellevue route, a line with a long Green Line history.

On the Way Back Up

For calendar year 1999 TANK ridership jumped more than 10 percent. As a result, the Authority racked up more than 4 million boardings for the first time in nearly a decade. General Manager Mark Donaghy credited the increase in ridership to I-75 reconstruction in Kenton County, the high parking prices in downtown Cincinnati, and TANK's continuing efforts to operate, during rush-hours, 324 route miles which covered almost every nook and cranny of its tri-county area. The fact that TANK was keeping equipment in first class condition helped, and Donaghy also praised the agency's safety-conscious and friendly drivers.

Also contributing to its new popularity was a $1 million federal grant to enable TANK to reduce its one-way fare on regular routes from 75 cents to 50 cents during June, July, and August. This infusion of money was meant to encourage commuters to use buses to help reduce air pollution in the Cincinnati basin. And starting June 1, 1999, the Southbank Shuttle began operating at 6 a. m. (instead of 10 a. m.) to attract people staying in downtown hotels to use the shuttle instead of driving.

In June of 1999 TANK spokesperson Gina Douthat announced that the Southbank Shuttle carried, in its first year, more than 7000 passengers per month, twice the number originally forecast. Then in October Assistant General Manager James Seibert confirmed that the operation and maintenance of the shuttle would be taken over by TANK and that larger capacity buses would be used at peak times.

Carl Ward, owner of Executive Charter and operator of the Southbank Shuttle, said his company was not equipped to operate bigger equipment. The takeover by TANK in November

delighted Local 628, still representing Northern Kentucky transit workers. Its members had been concerned in 1998 when Executive Charter was given the assignment.

The low-floor era came to TANK in April, 2000, when the agency received delivery of 12, 40-foot low floor buses from Gillig (Nos. 2101-2112) including four painted in the distinctive blue Southbank Shuttle livery. Director of Maintenance Don Neltner said that delivery in late fall, of 15 more low-floor Gilligs (Nos. 2113-2127) allowed all of the older 1988 Gilligs to be removed from service but some were stored, and not disposed of, in case of increasing ridership.

Hands Across the River

The new millennium may bring some very interesting developments. Cincinnati and the Northern Kentucky cities have long since become one seamless conurbation, an economic powerhouse with an increasing need for political cooperation. And yet mobility has not been greatly improved even with the miles and miles of freeways.

In March 1999, TANK and SORTA (Cincinnati's Southwest Ohio Regional Transit Authority) took a first step toward a possible unified regional transit authority by signing a "Cooperative Interlocal Agreement." The first benefits included TANK's adoption and support of a new $7 million SORTA radio dispatch and bus management system.

Through its operating company, Queen City Metro, SORTA

Transit Twins Bonded by the Great Bridge

The Ohio-Kentucky-Indiana Regional Council of Governments has pushed a coordinated transit network for Cincinnati and Northern Kentucky. In 1999 TANK and SORTA (Queen City Metro) entered into a comprehensive cooperation agreement as symbolized by TANK Flxible 1999 cheek-by-jowl with Queen City Metro Gillig 861, with John Roebling's great Suspension Bridge (no doubt) looking on approvingly. Whether or not the light rail scheme comes to fruition, there certainly will be bus coordination, to the benefit of all. *Don Meier via Dave Etienne and Dave Warning of Queen City Metro.*

operated 425 buses (and 40 vans for the mobility impaired) in 1999 while TANK stabled 117 transit buses and 12 RAMP vans. TANK and SORTA had already linked up in the early 1990s by offering a joint monthly pass and later opened a joint sales office in downtown Cincinnati.

Commenting on the new agreement, Paul Jablonski, Metro general manager, had this to say: "It's not a merger, but it's as close to a merger as you can get and still maintain a separate identity." In the long term, the flexible agreement could allow a TANK/SORTA (Metro) combination to manage multiple transit systems all over the region. Under the agreement, the two agencies will help advocate regional transit policies and work jointly to obtain local, state and federal funding. They will look at combining some routes with some Metro buses traveling into Northern Kentucky and vise-versa.

Added TANK's Mark Donaghy: "I think the new agreement gives us the ability to do everything from buying pencils together to managing a rail system jointly if and when that time comes."

Back to the Future

That mention of rail was not accidental. High on the agenda of collaboration between TANK and Cincinnati Metro is this item: the possible return of urban rail to Cincinnati and Northern Kentucky. After half a century, could it really happen?

TANK and SORTA are determined that the answer shall be yes. They formally agreed to jointly manage preliminary engineering studies for a proposed light rail line from Kings Island north of the Queen City, along I-71 to downtown Cincinnati, and on across the Ohio River to Covington and the Greater Cincinnati/Northern Kentucky International Airport.

It would cost $743 million, and start near downtown Covington, cross the Ohio River on a new bridge parallel to the CSX railroad bridge, serve the downtown Cincinnati sports stadiums, extend through downtown streets and head northeast through a tunnel and then along its own right-of-way to Blue Ash.

Later there could be extensions on both ends--in Kentucky, to the Greater Cincinnati Airport.

This project is the brainchild of the Ohio-Kentucky-Indiana Regional Council of Governments. The LRT option emerged the winner after considering busways and highway widening. While preliminary engineering is already under way, voters, in 2001 or 2002, will be asked to decide whether to approve some kind of a tax for the local share of funding. National experience has been that less than half of the new light rail schemes have received voter approval, although both Denver and Seattle have scored recent successes with the electorate. One way or another, one or two new cities a year are added to the light rail list.

If the voters bless this project, final design could begin with a view to beginning construction in 2002-2003, so that the initial segment could open sometime in 2008. And who knows, perhaps the cars will be painted green. ❏

As a part of the light rail plan, an underground bus station would be built under Second St. and Ft. Washington Way, near the two stadiums. LRT trains would use a street-level station above. *A computer model by Todd Channer, David Tharp and Robert Valentine of Parsons Brinckerhoff.*

A Plan for
Light Rail

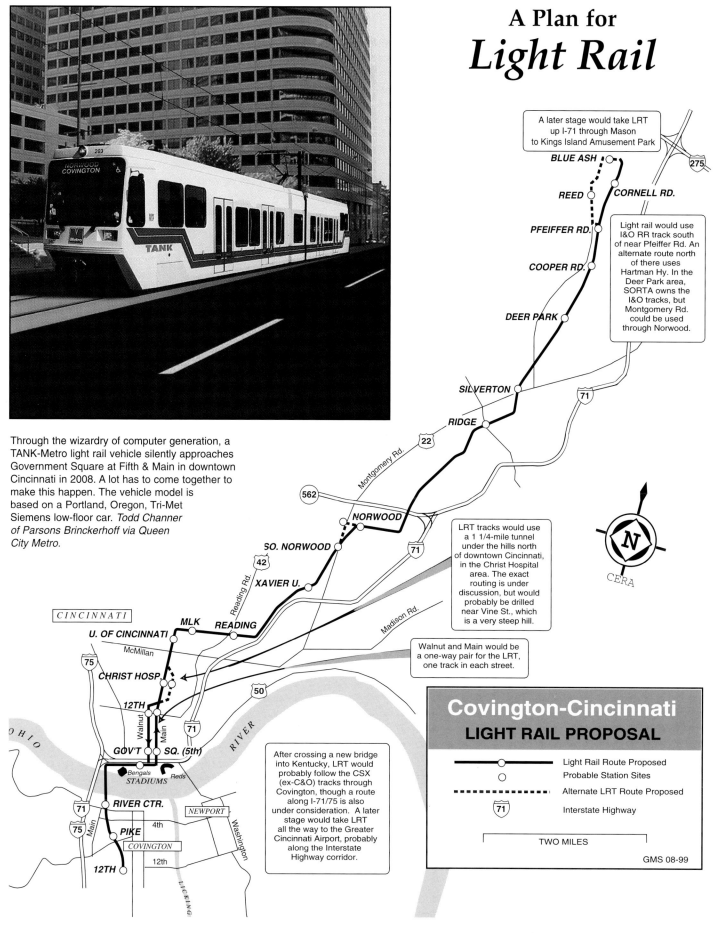

Through the wizardry of computer generation, a TANK-Metro light rail vehicle silently approaches Government Square at Fifth & Main in downtown Cincinnati in 2008. A lot has to come together to make this happen. The vehicle model is based on a Portland, Oregon, Tri-Met Siemens low-floor car. *Todd Channer of Parsons Brinckerhoff via Queen City Metro.*

A later stage would take LRT up I-71 through Mason to Kings Island Amusement Park

Light rail would use I&O RR track south of near Pfeiffer Rd. An alternate route north of there uses Hartman Hy. In the Deer Park area, SORTA owns the I&O tracks, but Montgomery Rd. could be used through Norwood.

BLUE ASH

REED   CORNELL RD.

PFEIFFER RD.

COOPER RD.

DEER PARK

SILVERTON

RIDGE

Montgomery Rd.

LRT tracks would use a 1 1/4-mile tunnel under the hills north of downtown Cincinnati, in the Christ Hospital area. The exact routing is under discussion, but would probably be drilled near Vine St., which is a very steep hill.

NORWOOD

SO. NORWOOD

Reading Rd.

XAVIER U.

CINCINNATI

MLK   READING

U. OF CINCINNATI

McMillan

Madison Rd.

Walnut and Main would be a one-way pair for the LRT, one track in each street.

CHRIST HOSP.

12TH

Walnut

Main

GOV'T   SQ. (5th)

Bengals
STADIUMS   *Reds*

RIVER CTR.

NEWPORT

PIKE

4th

COVINGTON

12th

12TH

OHIO

RIVER

LICKING

After crossing a new bridge into Kentucky, LRT would probably follow the CSX (ex-C&O) tracks through Covington, though a route along I-71/75 is also under consideration. A later stage would take LRT all the way to the Greater Cincinnati Airport, probably along the Interstate Highway corridor.

N
CERA

Covington-Cincinnati
LIGHT RAIL PROPOSAL

——○——	Light Rail Route Proposed
○	Probable Station Sites
▪▪▪▪▪	Alternate LRT Route Proposed
71	Interstate Highway

TWO MILES

GMS 08-99

Spirit
OF THE
Green
Line

Lives on
In (of all places)
LONDON

More than half a century ago, the Spirit of the Green Line was perhaps captured in this photograph: ever faithful streetcar backed up by the distinctive Cincinnati, Newport & Covington Railway headquarters building in Covington. That was the essence. That was before the big paradox: a local transportation enterprise in decline, but a nationwide transit empire building up. Now that paradox has seen a world-wide transit conglomerate whose roots were planted firmly in fertile Northern Kentucky soil. And there is this twist of fate: long thought to be dead and buried, the Green Line still lives . . . at least in spirit.   *Earl Clark.*

Ringo Saw Opportunity in All Those New Transit Agencies

Transit conglomerates have been around for a long time. National City Lines naturally springs to mind. The Fitzgerald brothers parlayed a dinky bus line in frozen Northern Minnesota into an empire encompassing dozens of cities, including some very large ones such as Baltimore, Philadelphia and Los Angeles. Even earlier, the electric utility industry controlled transit systems both major and minor, until Congress engineered a shotgun divorce.

But the story of how such a modest undertaking as Northern Kentucky's Green Line came to slice off a formidable chunk of the transit industry for itself first as an owner and later as a hired management firm is a fascinating tale of ups and downs, expected success, unexpected twists and turns, exceptional savvy--and maybe a little luck.

It started with David Ringo, who became a kind of local folk hero after soothing the bitter 1940 strike and went on to steer the entire company safely through crisis and tumult. He was not an unambitious man, and his American Transportation Enterprises was quite a profitable undertaking until the early 1960s. As related in Chapter 7, Ringo was named to head the entire ATE organization in 1957, encompassing a dozen mid-size transit companies and several charter bus operations.

Industry leaders saw by 1965 that public transit could not survive without public subsidy help. The Allen family, owners

of ATE, well knew this and refused to throw any additional dollars into the game. Waiting to see what would happen, the owners folded ATE into American Diversified Enterprises.

Ringo and his managers figured they would soon be out of a job. But they loved the business, so they pooled their knowledge and experience and hung out a shingle to manage any and all public transit agencies that might be interested. ATE owners had no objection to Ringo forming such a business, and even allowed him to use the ATE initials as long as Ringo agreed to spend 50 percent of his time in the sale and liquidation of ATE's remaining transportation assets.

Thus on January 1, 1970, ATE Management and Service Co., Inc. (ATEMS) was open for business, based in Cincinnati. Ironically, it started with a five-year contract to manage all of ATE's transit companies with a mandate to sell or shut them down by the end of 1974.

But cracking the public transit agency market proved to be difficult at first. Two larger transit chains had been in operation for several years, picking off most of the early business. Soon, though, the customers appeared when public authorities in Duluth, Baltimore, Peoria and Minneapolis-St. Paul signed up with ATEMS within a year.

Denver came aboard in 1971, and by 1980 Ringo's group had contracts with no less than 45 public transit agencies in the

U. S. including Green Line successor TANK and Queen City Metro, across the river in Cincinnati. This must have been eminently satisfying to David Ringo.

Philip J. Ringo succeeded his father as ATEMS president as the company moved into the 1980s. In 1986, ATEMS was sold to Ryder Systems Inc. of Miami for $10 million. At that time ATEMS was involved with some 52 transit properties. It was made a part of Ryder's Leasing and Service Division which had a fleet of more than 100,000 vehicles which included some 2000 leased-out school and transit buses.

Under Ryder, the business thrived over the next decade with many ex-ATEMS people in key positions. By 1998 the Ryder Public Transportation Service generated revenue of $582 million by running buses for more than 475 school systems in 26 states, and furnishing management and/or maintenance service for three score public transit systems, including TANK.

Just how well Ryder PTS had prospered was evident in July, 1999, when First Group plc, a British company led by Chairman Moir Lockhead, purchased that segment from Ryder for $940 million in cash. First Group was a success story in itself. It was formed in 1995 with the merger of two British bus companies and by century's end owned and operated more than 9000 buses in the U. K. and another 700 in Hong Kong. On top of this, it operated three privatized railways in Great Britain, and held a majority stake in Bristol International Airport.

The Ryder sale allowed First Group to enter the U. S. pub-

lic sector transportation market with a subsidiary called First Transit Inc. All this dizzying corporate development out of the thankless business of transporting people was enough to boggle the mind. But not the mind of David L. Ringo, thriving in his 80s and living in retirement in Florida. He was honored by First Transit Senior Vice President Rich Clair for "his vision and outstanding leadership of ATE." This accolade was given to Ringo during the 1999 American Public Transit Association convention in Orlando.

Ringo must have been bemused by an ultimate irony in all this: the Green Line back in America!

No, not the old Northern Kentucky Green Line. But it so happens that First Group operates a number of London suburban bus routes which carry the brand name of the Green Line. These routes have been around for decades under that name, once under the aegis of London Transport. Back in 1949 the London Transport Board exchanged some good-natured banter with Ringo at the Cincinnati, Newport & Covington Railway about who stole the name from whom. The larger purpose was to promote (via CN&C's *GreenLiner* employee newsletter) a tide of Christmas toys and candies for the children of London, still scarcely recovered from World War II.

Since First Group as of 2000 holds the management contract at TANK, by an ever-so-slight stretch of the imagination, the Green Line can be said to have gone full circle. And by the way, we had the name first! ◆

The Green Line, Second Time Around

Just as it did years ago when it was an offshoot of London Transport, Great Britain's Green Line fills a major transit role in the London suburbs and First Group operates part of the service. This Volvo B10M parlor bus has paused at Windsor on a London-Windsor working in June of 1999. Famed Windsor Castle, part-time home of the Royal Family, is nearby. *Terry W. Lehmann.*

Over the years, the Green Line and successor TANK kept the printing presses busy with tickets, transfers, schedules, announcements, and, of course, *The GreenLiner* house organ. On some of the next pages we present a selection.

The Licking River Bridge Co. issued auto, truck and pedestrian tickets in various colors and denominations.

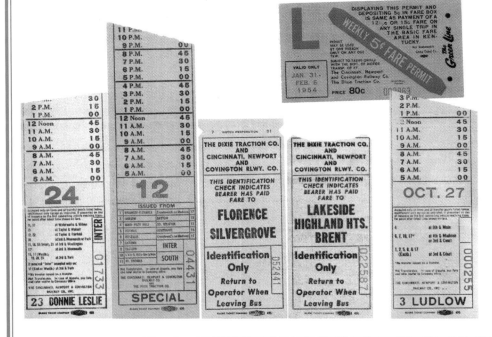

The Christmas, 1949, edition of *The GreenLiner* featured not only line art of both a Twin Coach and a General Motors bus, but carried the names of each and every Green Line employee. The names covered four pages; we show you the cover only, **above**.

As mentioned elsewhere in this book, the Green Line issued transfers in a number of different colors in order to control usage. At **left** is a selection from the mid 1950s. Also displayed is a "weekly 5-cent fare permit," a short-lived experiment whereby one purchased a pass for 80 cents a week and paid only a nickel a ride. This one was valid from January 31 through February 5, 1954.

All: T. W. Lehmann Collection.

Some Green Line Historical Paper

When you think about it, you realize that the Green Line was a transit system of unusual complexity. This is shown in the myriad forms of fare receipts both interstate and intrastate, identification slips, transfers, and so forth, necessitated by the fact that the system crossed the Ohio-Kentucky state line. For much of its life, the Green Line was cursed with diverse tariffs mandated by local, state and federal authorities with conflicting agendas. Two interstate fare receipts (including a 5 cent one issued during a franchise dispute in the 1930s) are reproduced at **right** in black print with buff and purple backgrounds. The cover of TANK's 1996 route map shown **below** captures the vintage and modern architectural aspects of Northern Kentucky today.

The Crosley Field ticket, **above**, is yet another product from that transit industry stalwart, Globe Ticket Co. of Philadelphia. **Below** is the colorful patch that drivers for the Green Line's varied services wore on their uniform sleeve. *Above and left: T. W. Lehmann Collection. Below: Phil Lind Collection.*

Appendix A

Cincinnati, Newport & Covington Railway Co.
Transit Operations: January 1930
Vehicle Requirements and Headways in Minutes

	M-F AM Rush	M-F PM Rush	M-F Mid-Day	Sat. 8am-8pm	Sun. 8am-8pm
COVINGTON DIVISION (All streetcars)					
1 Ft. Mitchell, (12.45)*	6 (12")	8 (9")	4 (18")	4 (18")	6 (12")
2 Greenup, (4.91)	6 (6")	6 (6")	3 (12")	3 (12")	3 (12")
3 Ludlow, (8.84)	12 (4")	15 (3")	6 (9")	6 (9")	6 (9")
4 Main, (3.55)	5 (6")	7 (3")	3 (9")	3 (9")	3 (9")
5 Holman, (5.82)	7 (6")	8 (5")	4 (12")	4 (12")	4 (12")
6 Rosedale, (9.84)	9 (8")	11 (6")	6 (12")	6 (12")	6 (12")
7 Latonia, (8.96)	5 (12")	6 (10")	5 (12")	5 (12")	4 (15")
8 Eastern, (5.32)	4 (10")	7 (5")	3 (12")	3 (12")	3 (12")
10 Lewisburg, (4.51)	1 (30")	3 (10")	-	-	-
Covington Totals	**55**	**71**	**34**	**34**	**35**
NEWPORT DIVISION (All streetcars)					
9 Belt Line (clockwise), (9.04)	3 (12")	3 (12")	3 (12")	3 (12")	2 (18")
9 Belt Line (counter-clockwise), (9.03)	3 (12")	3 (12")	3 (12")	3 (12")	2 (18")
11 Ft. Thomas, (13.62)	12 (7")	14 (6")	6 (15")	6 (15")	6 (15")
12 Dayton, (7.41)	13 (5")	18 (3")	7 (8")	7 (8")	7 (8")
13 So. Bellevue, (5.77)	8 (6")	9 (5")	3 (15")	3 (15")	3 (15")
14 York, (4.38)	6 (6")	3 (12")	-	-	-
15 Southgate, (6.79)	8 (6")	10 (5")	4 (12")	4 (12")	4 (12")
16 Washington, (3.81)	-	1 (2 trips)	-	-	-
17 Crosstown, (2.20)	2 (10")	2 (10")	2 (10")	2 (10")	2 (10")
Newport Totals	**55**	**63**	**28**	**28**	**26**
TOTAL CARS IN SERVICE	**110**	**134**	**62**	**62**	**61**

*Note: round trip mileage shown after name of line.

The 8-Eastern line was hard-hit by the Great Flood of 1937, but was put back into service afterward. Between June of 1940 and March of 1946, 500-series cars were used for base service. In this picture, one of the class, car 506, is near the end of the line at Greenup & 15th in Covington. *David McNeil.*

Appendix B

Cincinnati, Newport & Covington Railway Co.
Transit Operations: November 1944
Vehicle Requirements and Headways in Minutes

	M-F AM Rush	M-F PM Rush	M-F Mid-Day	Sat. 8am-8pm	Sun. 8am-6pm
COVINGTON DIVISION (All streetcars unless otherwise noted)					
1 Ft. Mitchell, (12.45) *Note A*	6 (10")	8 (9")	5 (12")	5 (12")	6 (10")
2 Greenup, (4.99)	-	3 (10")	-	-	-
3 Ludlow, (9.25), *trolley-coach*	10 (4")	11 (3")	4 (10")	4 (10")	3 (15")
4 Main, (3.55)	3 (8")	3 (8")	2 (12")	2 (12")	2 (12")
5 Holman, (5.74)	4 (9")	6 (6")	3 (13")	3 (13")	2 (20")
6 Rosedale, (10.20), *trolley-coach*	14 (4")	15 (4") *Note B*	6 (10")	6 (10")	5 (12")
7 Latonia, (9.66), *trolley-coach*	6 (10")	6 (10")	5 (10")	5 (10")	4 (12")
8 Eastern, (5.32)	5 (8")	4 (10")	3 (11")	3 (11")	3 (11")
10 Lewisburg, (4.51)	1 (2 trips)	1 (2 trips)	-	-	-
SH South Hills, (8.03), *motor bus*	1 (40")	1 (40")	-	-	-
Covington Totals	**50**	**58**	**28**	**28**	**25**
NEWPORT DIVISION (All motor buses unless otherwise noted)					
11 Ft. Thomas, (13.62), *streetcar*	8 (10")	9 (8")	5 (14")	5 (14")	4 (18")
12 Dayton, (7.78)	9 (6")	12 (4")	5 (12")	5 (12")	5 (12")
13 So. Bellevue, (5.96)	3 (12")	5 (12")	2 (30")	2 (30")	2 (30")
15G Southgate-Grand, (10.46), *note C*	-	-	2 (15")	2 (15")	2 (15")
15H Southgt-Highland, (10.03) *note C*	4 (8")	4 (8")	2 (15")	2 (15")	2 (15")
15 Southgate, (6.89)	3 (8")	4 (8")	-	-	-
15R Grand-Ross, (26.21)	-	-	1 (4 trips)	1 (4 trips)	1 (3 trips)
17 Crosstown (No. on Madison), (3.90)	2 (15")	2 (15")	2 (15")	2 (15")	2 (15")
17 Crosstown (So. on Madison), (3.97)	2 (15")	2 (15")	2 (15")	2 (15")	2 (15")
18 Newport East, (5.26)	-	-	1 (40")	1 (40")	1 (40")
18R Grand-Ross, (25.64)	1 (2 trips)	1 (2 trips)	-	-	-
18G East-Grand, (10.64)	6 (10")	6 (10")	-	-	-
19 Newport West, (4.33)	4 (6")	5 (5")	2 (13")	3 (12")	3 (12")
20 Newport South, (6.80)	3 20")	3 (20")	1 (45")	2 (45")	2 (45")
23 Bonnie Leslie, (6.89)	3 (20")	3 (18")	1 (40")	2 (30")	1 (60")
Newport Totals	**48**	**56**	**26**	**29**	**27**
Military/Greyhound charters/Misc.	11 (n.a.)	10 (n.a.)	10 (n.a.)	Note D	Note D
TOTAL VEHICLES IN SERVICE	**109**	**124**	**64**	**57**	**52**

Note A: round trip mileage shown after name of line.
Note B: includes one assigned motor bus.
Note C: Headways cover combined main portion of routes.
Note D: No Saturday or Sunday data has been found.
No data has been located for Dixie Traction vehicle requirements or headways for this period.

A delectable steel engraving of a pair of electric cars adorns the Cincinnati, Newport and Covington Railway Company stock certificate, **above**. This caption is flanked by the cover of 1946 Dixie Traction bus schedules for the Florence-Erlanger and Cold Spring-Alexandria lines. The Green Line gave both Twin Coach and Mack some publicity in the form of pictures of buses 170 and 136, respectively. And finally, a nod to the curious independent, one-bus Monmouth Street Merchants Association. **Below** is an October 27, 1938, bus schedule. Only participating merchants could redeem 2 cent off tickets.
All: T. W. Lehmann Collection.

Appendix C

Cincinnati, Newport & Covington Transportation Co.
Transit and Airport Operations: August 1956
Vehicle Requirements and Headways in Minutes

	M-F AM Rush	M-F PM Rush	M-F Mid-Day	Sat. 8am-8pm	Sun. 8am-6pm
KENTON-BOONE COUNTY (All motor buses unless otherwise noted)					
1 Erlanger-Florence, (24.11) *Note A*	12 (10")	12 (10")	6 (20")	6 (20")	4 (35")
1 Ft. Mitchell-Crescent Sprs., (18.40)	2 (25")	2 (25")	1 (25")#	1 (25")#	-
3 Ludlow, (9.25), *trolley-coach*	5 (10")	5 (10")	3 (20")	3 (20")	2 (30")
4 Main-Park Hills, (7.20)	4 (10")	4 (10")	2 (20")	2 (20")	1 (35")
4 Main-Barrington Woods, (8.45)	2 (20")	2 (20")	1 (45")	1 (45")	1 (45")
5 Holman, (6.72)	5 (10")	6 (8")	3 (15")	3 (15")	2 (20")
6 Rosedale, (10.20), *trolley-coach*	6 (10")	7 (8")	4 (15")	4 (15")	3 (20")
7 Latonia, (9.40)	5 (12")	5 (12")	3 (20")	3 (20")	2 (30")
8 Eastern, (5.46)	4 (10")	4 (10")	2 (20")	2 (20")	1 (45")
10 Lewisburg-South Hills, (9.15)	4 (15")	4 (15")	2 (30")	2 (30")	1 (60")
Kenton-Boone County Totals	**49**	**51**	**27**	**27**	**17**
#Shuttle					
CAMPBELL COUNTY (All motor buses)					
11 Ft. Thomas, (14.76)	7 (8")	7 (8")	4 (15")	3 (20")	3 (20")
12 Dayton, (7.78)	9 (8")	9 (8")	5 (12")	4 (15")	3 (20")
13-23 So. Bellev.-Bonnie Leslie, (7.77)	4 (15")	4 (15")	2 (25")	2 (25")	2 (25")
15G Southgate-Grand, (10.64)	9 (8")	9 (8")	5 (12")	4 (18")	4 (18")
15H Southgt-Highland, (10.22) *note B*	Incl. in 15G	Incl. in 15G	Incl. in 15G	Incl. in 15G	Incl. in 15G
15R Southgate-Ross, (26.64) *note C*	- (2 trips)	- (2 trips)	- (1 trip)	- (2 trips)	-
17 Crosstown (No. on Madison), (3.90)	2 (15")	2 (15")	2 (15")	2 (15")	1 (30")
17 Crosstown (So. on Madison), (3.97)	2 (15")	2 (15")	2 (15")	2 (15")	1 (30")
18 Newport East, (5.26)	2 (15")	2 (15")	-	-	-
18-21 East N. Ft. Thomas, (7.97)	-	-	1 (60")	1 (60")	1 (60")
21 North Ft. Thomas, (7.62)	3 (15")	3 (15")	-	-	-
19 Newport West, (4.62)	2 (15")	2 (15")	1 (30")	1 (30")	1 (30")
20 Newport South, (6.80)	2 (20")	2 (20")	1 (40")	1 (40")	1 (40")
24 Cold Spring-Alexandria, (27.42)	8 (10")	8 (10")	3 (25")	3 (25")	2 (40")
Campbell County Totals	**50**	**50**	**26**	**23**	**19**
RAILROAD CONTRACT SERVICE					
Stevens (C&O Railway), (24.95)	3 (45")	3 (45")	3 (45")	2 (60")	2 (60")
Decoursey (L&N Railroad), (10.50)	2 (30")	2 (30")	2 (30")	1 (60")	1 (60")
TOTAL VEHICLES IN SERVICE	**104**	**106**	**58**	**53**	**39**
AIRPORTER SERVICE					
Downtown, (25.94) *Parlor coaches*	-	-	10 (8-10")	7 (15")	7 (15")

Note A: round trip mileage shown after name of line.
Note B: Headways combined over main portion of route
Note C: Certain trips of either 15G or 15H extended to Ross..

Cincinnati, Newport & Covington Transportation Co.
Transit and Airport Operations: April 1971
Vehicle Requirements and Headways in Minutes

	M-F AM Rush	M-F PM Rush	M-F Mid-Day	Sat. 8am-8pm	Sun. 8am-6pm
KENTON-BOONE COUNTY					
1 Erlanger-Florence, (25.35) *Note A*	7 (10")	7 (10")	5 (20")	4 (25")	2 (50")
1 Erlanger-Garvey, (20.10)	4 (12")	4 (12")	-	-	-
1A Ft. Mitchell-Crescent Sprs., (21.15)	1 (30")	1 (30")	-	-	-
1X Interstate 75 Express, (26.50)	6 (5-8")	6 (5-8")	-	-	-
3 Ludlow, (9.45)	4 (12")	4 (12")	2 (25")	2 (25")	1 (50")
4 Main-South Hills, (10.30)	4 (10-15")	4 (10-12")	1 (60")	1 (60")	-
5 Holman, (6.72)	4 1/2 (12")	4 1/2 (12")	2 (25")	2 (25")	1 1/2 (40")
6 Rosedale, (10.20)	6 (10")	6 (10")	4 (15")	2 (35")	2 (35")
7 Latonia, (9.40)	4 (15")	4 (15")	2 (30")	2 (35")	2 (35")
8 Eastern, (5.75)	2 1/2 (12")	2 1/2 (12")	1 (30")	1 (30")	1/2 (50")
Kenton-Boone County Totals	**43**	**43**	**17**	**14**	**9**
CAMPBELL COUNTY					
11 Ft. Thomas, (14.76)	4 (12")	4 (12")	2 1/2 (20-30")	2 (30")	1 (70")
12 Dayton, (7.78)	5 (10")	5 (10")	2 1/2 (20")	2 (30")	2 (30")
13-23 So. Bellev.-Bonnie Leslie, (7.77)	2 (25")	2 (25")	1/2 (90")	1/2 (90")	-
15-24 Southg.-CS-Alexandria, (27.15)	5 (15")	5 (15")	3 (25")	3 (25")	1 (90")
15 Southgate-Highland, (10.65)	2 (12")	2 (12")	-	-	-
15 Southgate-Birney, (10.95)	2 (12")	2 (12)	-	-	-
17 Crosstown-Stevens, (24.00)	1 (80")	1 (80")	1 (80")	1 (80")	1 (80")
19-20 Newport West-South, (9.65)	2 (30")	2 (30")	1/2 (60")	1/2 (60")	-
21 North Ft. Thomas-E. Npt., (8.35)	2 (30")	2 (30")	-	-	-
Campbell County Totals	**25**	**25**	**11**	**9**	**5**
TOTAL VEHICLES IN SERVICE	**68**	**68**	**28**	**23**	**14**
AIRPORTER SERVICE (Parlor coaches)					
Downtown, (26.30)	-	-	6 (20")	4 (30")	6 (20")
I-75-Sharonville, Ohio, (47.50) *Note B*	-	-	2 1/2 (30")	1 (60")	2 1/2 (30")
I-75-Hamilton, Ohio, (80.00) *Note B*	-	-	2 1/2 (60")	-	2 1/2 (60")
I-71-Mason, Ohio, (75.50) *Note B*	-	-	2 (75")	-	2 (75")
Total Airporters			**13**	**5**	**13**

Note A: round trip mileage shown after name of line.
Note B: Sunday service started at noon.

Appendix E

The Transit Authority of Northern Kentucky
Transit Operations: August 1996
Vehicle Requirements and Headways in Minutes

	Type of Equipment Assigned	M-F AM Rush	M-F PM Rush	M-F Mid-Day	Sat 8am-8pm	Sun 8am-6pm
KENTON-BOONE COUNTY	35-foot buses Except:					
1 Erlanger-Florence (34.50) *Note A*	All 40-footers	7 (15")	7 (15")	5 (22")	4 (30")	3 (40")
1X Express via I-75 (32.20)	2 40-footers	6 (10")	6 (10")	-	-	-
2X Airport Express (42.10)	2 40-footers	2 (30")	2 (30")	2 (30")	1.5 (50")	1.5 (50")
3 Ludlow-Bromley (10.10)	-	2 (30")	2 (30")	1 (55")	1 (60")	1 (60")
4 Main-Park Hills (13.80)	-	2 (30")	2 (30")	-	-	-
5 Holman-Ft. Wright (7.60)	-	3 (20")	3 (20")	1.5 (40")	1.5 (40")	1 (50")
6 Rosedale (11.50)	-	2 (20")	2 (20")	3 (30")	2 (40")	1 (60")
7 Latonia (10.30)	-	2 (20")	2 (20")	Combined with above mid-day, Sat. & Sun.		
8 Eastern-Latonia (11.50)	-	2 (30")	2 (30")	1.5 (40")	1.5 (40")	.5 (60")
9 Taylor Mill-Independence (37.40)	-	4 (5 trips)	4 (5 trips)	1.5 (60")	1.5 (60")	-
17X Villa Hills via I-75 (27.10)	1 40-footer AM	3 (4 trips)	3 (4 trips)	-	-	-
18X Edgewood via I-75 (15.60)	-	2 (3 trips)	3 (3 trips)	-	-	-
19X Beechgrove via I-75 (27.40)	-	3 (4 trips)	3 (4 trips)	-	-	-
22X Walton (52.10)	-	3 (3 trips)	3 (3 trips)	-	-	-
30X Madison Pike-Indep. (37.80)	-	2 (3 trips)	2 (3 trips)	-	-	-
31 Hands Pike (23.60)	-	3 (3 trips)	3 (3 trips)	-	-	-
32X Burlington via I-75 (41.30)	-	4 (5 trips)	4 (5 trips)	-	-	-
33 St. Eliz. Hospital South (16.20)	-	1 (2 trips)	1 (2 trips)	1.5 (45")	1 (45")	1 (3 trips)
School specials		5	6	4	-	-
Kenton-Boone Totals		**58**	**60**	**21**	**14**	**9**
CAMPBELL COUNTY						
11 Ft. Thomas (26.20)	-	5 (20")	5 (20")	2.5 (45")	2 (45")	1 (60")
12 Dayton (10.40)	-	4 (20")	4 (20")	2.5 (30")	2 (45")	1 (60")
16 Grand Towers (20.30)	-	2 (45")	2 (45")	1 (70")	1 (60")	1 (6 trips)
20 South Newport (9.30)	-	2 (20")	2 (20")	-	-	-
23 So. Bellevue-Bonnie Leslie (5.30)	-	2 (30")	2 (30")	1 (60")	1 (60")	-
24 Cold Spring-CV (23.30)	-	4 (25")	4 (25")	3.5 (40")	3 (40")	2 (50")
24X Express via I-471 (26.50)	-	2 (2 trips)	2 (2 trips)	-	-	-
25 Alexandria (36.10)	2 40-footers PM	2 (2 trips)	2 (2 trips)	1.5 (2 trips)	1 (5 trips)	-
25X Express via I-471 (35.20)	-	2 (2 trips)	2 (2 trips)	-	-	-
26 Grants Lick (41.70)	-	2 (2 trips)	2 (2 trips)	1 (2 trips)	1 (6 trips)	-
26X Express via I-471 (47.90)	All 40-footers	3 (3 trips)	3 (3 trips)	-	-	-
27 Moock Road (27.00)	-	2 (2 trips)	2 (2 trips)	-	-	-
Campbell County Totals		**32**	**32**	**13**	**11**	**5**
TOTAL BUSES IN SERVICE		**90**	**92**	**34**	**25**	**14**
Regional Area Mobility Program ("RAMP" vans)		**6**	**7**	**7**	**2**	**2**

Note A: Official TANK route miles are calculated by the agency by totalling all of the alternative branches of the outer portions of the route. Any specific round trip mileage over a route could result in less mileage than indicated.

Appendix **F**

Streetcars Of The Green Line 1890-1950
(South Covington and Cincinnati Street Railway Co. 1890-1922)
(Cincinnati, Newport and Covington Railway Co. 1922-1950)

(1) Revenue Equipment

Fleet Nos.	Builder	Model	Group	Length	Seats	Built	Remarks
11-31	Stephenson/Short	Closed-ST		26'	25	1890-91	
1-10	Stephenson/Short	Closed-ST		26'	25	1891	1-31 assembled at SC&C carbarn. There was no car 13. (1-10 from horsecar bodies).
32-50	Laclede	Closed-ST	A	30'	29	1892	Laclede Car Co. order #265
51-76	Brownell	Closed-ST	B	30'6"	29	1892-93	61 converted to double end control 1918
200-219	Brownell	Open-ST		33'	45	1893	
220-238	Brownell	Convertible-ST	C	31'	32	1893	
"Bluegrass"	Brownell	Parlor-ST		31'	14	1893	Parlor Car
239-253	Brownell	Convertible-ST	D	31'	32	1895	
254-263	Brownell	Convertible-ST	E	31'	32	1897	260 converted to double end control 1918
264-273	St. Louis Car	Convertible-ST	F	31'	32	1899	St. Louis Car Co. order #27
274-288	St. Louis Car	Convertible-ST	G	31'	32	1900	St. Louis Car Co. order #117
289-298	St. Louis Car	Closed-ST	H	31'	32	1902	St. Louis Car Co. order #303
299-308	St. Louis Car	Closed-ST	I	31'	32	1903	St. Louis Car Co. order #389A
309-318	St. Louis Car	Closed-ST	J	31'	32	1906	St. Louis Car Co. order #659
319	?	Closed-ST	K	?	?	?	Purchased from Cincinnati Traction Co. 1911 and rebuilt by SC&C shops. Double end control.
"Kentucky"	Brownell/SC&C	Parlor-ST		30'6"	18	1911	Rebuilt into parlor car by SC&C shops from SC&C 64
320-334	Cincinnati Car	Closed-ST	L	31'	32	1911	Cincinnati Car Co. order #1325
100-119	St. Louis Car	Closed-ST	M	31'	32	1912	St. Louis Car Co. order #929
120-139	Cincinnati Car	Closed-ST	N	31'	32	1914	Cincinnati Car Co. order #1760
500-524	Cincinnati Car	Closed-DT	O	45'	52	1917	Cincinnati Car Co. order #2175. Modified by the Cincinnati Street Ry. shops in 1936-37 for one-man operation. Seating capacity increased to 55 and length to 46'10".

(2) Self-Propelled Non-Revenue Equipment (As of August 1935)

Fleet Nos.	Builder	Model	Length	Built	Date Conv. by SC&C Shops	Rebuilt from:
1-4	Stephenson	Sweepers-ST	26'	1890-91	1895-1897	SC&C ?,?,?,?
"No. 1"	Laclede	Tool Car-ST	26'	1892	1911	SC&C ?
"No. 2"	Laclede	Tool Car-ST	26'	1892	1911	SC&C ?
5-6	Brill	Sweepers-ST	28'	1916		Purchased New
7	Laclede	Sand Car-ST	30'	1892	1921	SC&C 50
8	Brownell	Sand Car-ST	30'6"	1893	1921	SC&C 68
9	St. Louis	Line Car-ST	31'	1899	1933	CN&C 272
29	Stephenson	Salt Car-ST	26'	1891	1914	SC&C 29
30	Stephenson	Salt Car-ST	26'	1891	1914	SC&C 30
45	Laclede	Snow Plow-ST	30'	1892	1918	SC&C 45
52	Brownell	Welding Car-ST	30'6"	1893	1927	CN&C 52
65	Brownell	Work Car-ST	30'6"	1893	1912	SC&C 65
69	Brownell	Snow Plow-ST	30'6"	1893	1918	SC&C 69
"Testing Car"	Stephenson	Bond Test Car-ST	30'	1891	1904	SC&C 3
240	Brownell	Hose Bridge Car-ST	31'	1895	1927	CN&C 240
263	Brownell	Work Car-ST	31'	1897	1933	CN&C 263
(1)	?	Sprinkler Car-ST	?	?	?	SC&C ?

(Non-Self Propelled)

67	Brownell	Instruction Car-ST	30'	1893	1913	SC&C 67
(1)	?	Portable Sub-station-DT	30'	?	?	?
(2)	Stephenson	Dump Cars-ST	26'	1890-91	1911	SC&C ?,?
(1)	?	Concrete Mixer-ST	?	?	1913	SC&C ?
(1)	?	Trailer Flat-ST	?	?	1911	SC&C ?

Streetcar Trucks and Motors (as of August 1935)

	TRUCKS	MOTORS
220-253 (34 cars)	(23 cars) Peckham #7-B	(28 cars) - Westinghouse #3 (2 at 25 h.p. each)
	(11 cars) Brill #21E	(6 cars) - Westinghouse #49 (2 at 35 h.p. each)
254-298 (45 cars)	Peckham - #7-B	Westinghouse #49 (2 at 35 h.p. each)
299-308 (10 cars)	Peckham - #7-D	Westinghouse #49 (2 at 35 h.p. each)
309-318, 320-334 (25 cars)	Brill - #21E	Westinghouse #49 (2 at 35 h.p. each)
100-103,105-139 (39 cars)	Brill - #21E	Westinghouse #49 (2 at 35 h.p. each)
500-524 (25 cars)	Cincinnati Arch Bar (two per car)	Westinghouse #506 (4 at 25 h.p. each)

Appendix G

Buses Of The Dixie Traction Co. 1922-1955
(Wholly Owned Subsidiary Of CN&C After 1940)

(1) Gasoline and Diesel Powered Transit Buses

Fleet Nos.	Builder	Model	Serial Nos.	Seats	Built	Year Acq. (If used)	Remarks
101-103	Mack	AB	57785,57789,57884	?	1922		
104-106	Mack	AB	?	?	1925		
107	Studebaker	?	?	15	1927		Fremont body
108-110	Studebaker	76	3250502,3250919,3251064	25	1928		FitzJohn bodies
111-112	Studebaker	99	3251493,3251723	25	1929		FitzJohn bodies
113-114	Studebaker	111	3251889,3251888	25	1929		FitzJohn bodies
115	Studebaker	111	3252205	25	1930		FitzJohn body
116	Studebaker	111	3252162	25	1931		FitzJohn body
117	Studebaker	111	3252222	25	1932		FitzJohn body
118-121	Studebaker	111	?	25	?	(1933)	Southeastern Greyhound
122	Studebaker	111	?	25	?	(1935)	Southeastern Greyhound
123-127	Mack	6-CW-3S	1191-1195	25	1936		
128-130	Mack	6-CW-3S	1826-1828	25	1937		
131-135	Mack	LC-3G	1001-1005	31	1940		
101	World	DA-60	?	21	?	(1940)	Cold Spring Bus Co.
102	White	702	?	25	1935	(1940)	Cold Spring Bus Co.
103	White	706	?	23	1936	(1940)	Cold Spring Bus Co.
104	Yellow	733	?	21	1938	(1940)	Cold Spring Bus Co.
105	Yellow	1204	?	24	1938	(1940)	Alexandria Bus Co.
136-138	Mack	LC-3G	1269-1271	31	1941		
150-152	Mack	LD-3G	1271-1273	35	1942		
106-107	Mack	6-CQ-3S	1195-1196	31	1936	(1941)	CN&C 61-62
90-91	International		?	22	1936	(1942)	CN&C 74-75
108-109	Mack	6-CQ-3S	1198-1199	31	1936	(1942)	CN&C 64-65
110-111	Mack	6-CQ-3S	1728-1729	31	1939	(1945-46)	CN&C 66-67
170-176	Twin	38-S	102-108	36	1946		
153-156	Mack	LD-3G	1183-1186	35	1942	(1947)	CN&C 374-377
190-196	GM	TDH-4008	1644-1650	39	1948		
157-161	Mack	LD-3G	1179-1182, 1187	35	1942	(1950)	CN&C 370-373, 378
177	Twin	38-S	?	36	1948	(1950)	Demo?
212-215	GM	TD-4007	195-198	39	1945	(1952)	CN&C 212-215
162-164	Mack	CM-3G	1151-1153	39	1940	(1953)	CN&C 400-402
165-167	Mack	CM-3G	1156, 1159, 1161	39	1940	(1954)	CN&C 405, 408, 410
501-508	GM	TDH-5105	596-603	51	1954		Delivered in CN&C paint scheme

(2) "Airporter" Service Buses

Fleet Nos.	Builder	Model	Serial Nos.	Seats	Built
41-42	Flxible	21B1	8264-8265	21	1948
43-44	Flxible	21C1	8275-8276	21	1948
45	Flxible	21C1	8988	21	1949
46	Flxible	21C1	8996	21	1950
47	Flxible	182B1	30060	24	1950
48-49	Flxible	182B1	30208, 30308	24	1951
50-52	Flxible	182F1	30453, 30455,30456	24	1952
53	Flxible	182B1	30672	24	1953
54-55	Flxible	182B1	30720-30721	24	1954
56-57	Flxible	218F1	30823-30824	29	1954

Certainly among the most interesting cars in the CN&C roster (opposite page) were the double-truckers. In the snap at **left** we see car 507 on the Ft. Mitchell line in front of the Green Line (and allied Union Light, Heat and Power Co.) headquarters in June of 1932. The motorman is leaning out the front window to throw a switch, using his iron. Note the smokestack on the car that vented a coke-fueled heater installed to supply warm forced-air for the passengers. The car has not yet been converted to one-man operation, and passenger entry is through the double folding doors on the rear platform.
James Gibson.

Appendix H

Buses Of The Green Line: 1936-1972
(Cincinnati, Newport & Covington Railway Co. 1936-1955)
(Cincinnati, Newport & Covington Transportation Co. 1956-1972)

(1) Gasoline and Diesel Powered Transit Buses

Fleet No.	Builder	Model	Serial Nos.	Seats	Built	Year Acq. If Used	Remarks
11-14	Yellow	Z-AZ-290	110059-110062	25	1928	(1936)	Cincinnati Street Railway 221-224
51-55	Mack	6-CW-3S	1210-1214	25	1936		
61-65	Mack	6-CQ-3S	1195-1199	31	1936		
60	Mack	6-CT-3S	1151	35	1936	(1937)	Demo
10	Yellow	Z-AZ-290	?	25	?	(1937)	Citizens-Merchant Bus Line
15-17	Intl.	?	?	22	1935	(1937)	Peoples Central Transit Lines; Beck bodies
18-19	Intl.	?	?	22	?	(1937)	Citizens-Merchant Bus Line; Union City bodies
20-22	Mack	AB	?	22	?	(1937)	Kentucky Motor Coach
23	Mack	AB	?	24	1929	(1937)	Ludlow Transit; Buick engine 1939
24	Mack	AB	?	22	1926	(1937)	Ludlow Transit; Buick engine 1939
25-26	Mack	AB	?	24	1929	(1937)	Ludlow Transit
27-29	Mack	AB	591628,591643,591666	24	1925	(1937)	Ross Motor Coach
30-32	Intl.	?	?	22	1935	(1937)	Citizens-Merchants Bus Lines; Superior bodies
33	Ford	?	?	20	?	(1937)	Ludlow Transit; Beck body
34	Ford	?	?	22	?	(1937)	Ludlow Transit; Hackney body
35	Ford	?	?	20	?	(1937)	Ludlow Transit; Union City body
36	Ford	?	?	25	?	(1937)	Ludlow Transit
37-38	Intl.	?	?	27	?	(1937)	Peoples Central Transit Lines
39-40	Intl.	?	?	29	1936	(1937)	Peoples Central Transit Lines; Beck bodies
41-42	Mack	BK	?	29	?	(1937)	Kentucky Motor Coach
43	Mack	AB	591688	29	1926	(1937)	Ross Motor Coach; BC Engine 1937
44-47	Mack	BC	?	29	?	(1937)	Ross Motor Coach
48-49	Twin	[40]	?, 544	33	1929	(1937)	Ross Motor Coach
70	Ford	70	?	25	1937		Ordered by Ludlow Transit
50	Mack	6-CY-3S	1006	25	1938	(1938)	Demo
66-67	Mack	6-CQ-3S	1728-1729	31	1939		
71-72	Dodge	JE	?	22	1929	(1940)	Black Diamond Stages; Superior bodies
73	White	805M	?	22	1936	(1940)	Black Diamond Stages
74-75	Intl.	?	?	22	1936	(1940)	Black Diamond Stages
76-77	Mack	AB	?	29	1930	(1940)	Black Diamond Stages; CU engines
78	Mack	AB	591677	29	1926	(1940)	Black Diamond Stages
350-354	ACF	36-S	194-198	35	1940		
399	Mack	CO-3G	1002	35	1939	(1940)	Demo
301-307	Mack	LC-3G	1006-1010,1016,1017	31	1940		
400-411	Mack	CM-3G	1151-1162	39	1940		
360-364	Mack	LD-3G	1046-1050	35	1941		
412-413	Mack	CM-3G	1846-1847	39	1941		
56-58	Mack	6-CW-3S	1191, 1193, 1196	25	1936	(1941)	Dixie Traction Co. 123, 125, 128 - Leased from Dixie Traction 11/39 - 4/41
370-378	Mack	LD-3G	1179-1187	35	1942		
414-423	Mack	CM-3G	2150-2159	39	1942		
430-437	Mack	C-41-G	1333-1340	41	1946		
330-340	Brill	C-36	1178-1188	36	1947		
380-386	Twin	38-S	223-229	36	1947		
440-459	Mack	C-41-GT	2483-2502	39	1947		GM 6-71 diesels (1955-57)
480-483	Twin	41-S	1198B-1201B	39	1948		
201-211	GM	TDH-3612	560-570	35	1950		
251-253	GM	TDH-4509	1337-1339	39	1951	(1951)	Twin Cities Motor Coach Co. (Benton Harbor, Mich.) 300D-302D
212-215	GM	TD-4007	195-198	39	1945	(1951)	Waterloo, Cedar Falls & Northern Railroad Co. 64-67
261-272	GM	TDH-4509	2300-2311	39	1952		
273-276	GM	TDH-4512	404-407	39	1954		
501-508	GM	TDH-5105	596-603	51	1954	(1955)	Dixie Traction Co. 501-508
150-152	Mack	LD-3G	1271-1273	35	1942	(1955)	Dixie Traction Co. 150-152
153-161	Mack	LD-3G	1179-1187	35	1942	(1955)	Dixie Traction Co. 153-161, nee CN&C 370-378
162-164	Mack	CM-3G	1151-1153	39	1940	(1955)	Dixie Traction Co. 162-164, nee CN&C 400-402
165-167	Mack	CM-3G	1156,1159, 1161	39	1940	(1955)	Dixie Traction Co. 165-167, nee CN&C 405, 408, 410
170-176	Twin	38-S	102-108	37	1946	(1955)	Dixie Traction Co. 170-176
177	Twin	38-S	?	36	1948	(1955)	Dixie Traction Co. 177

Fleet No.	Builder	Model	Serial Nos.	Seats	Built	Year Acq. If Used	Remarks
190-196	GM	TDH-4008	1644-1650	39	1948	(1955)	Dixie Traction Co. 190-196
212-215	GM	TD-4007	195-198	39	1945	(1955)	Dixie Traction 212-215, nee CN&C 212-215
438	Mack	C-41-GT	2600	39	1947	(1955)	Monmouth Street Merchants, GM 6-71 diesel (1959)
277-283	GM	TDH-4512	2633-2639	39	1958		
460-479, 484-487	Twin	41-S	?	39	1947	(1959-60)	Niagara Frontier Transit System
551-557	GM	TDH-5301	1247-1253	51	1960		
701-705	GM	TDH-4517	581-585	45	1960		
706-710	GM	TDH-4517	640-644	45	1960	(1961)	Harrisburg Railways Co. 501-505
284-288	GM	TDH-4512	130, 128, 131,129,132	45	1953	(1961)	Harrisburg Railways Co. 1253, 1251, 1254, 1252, 1255
434-437, 439	Mack	C-41-GT	2538-2542?	41	1948	(1963)	GM 6-71 diesels (1958); Akron Transportation Co. 263-267?
470-474, 476, 478-479	Twin	41-S	23-26, 17, 19,21-22	39	1946	(1964)	Southern Coach Lines 410-413, 404, 406, 408, 409
475, 477	Twin	41-S	43, 46	39	1947	(1964)	Southern Coach Lines 414, 417
289-295	GM	TDH-4512	222-228	45	1953	(1964)	Virginia Transit 922-928
552	GM	TDH-5301	1532	53	1960	(1964)	TriBoro Coach Corp. 772
296-299	GM	TDH-4512	1698, 1694,1692,1697	45	1956	(1965)	Youngstown Transit Co. 105,101, 99, 104
476, 478, 479	Twin	41-S	44, 49, 47	39	1947	(1965)	Southern Coach Lines 415, 420, 418
300-304	GM	TDH-4512	148-152	45	1953	(1966)	C&CDT 515-519
305-309	GM	TDH-4512	190, 192, 193,196,199	45	1953	(1966)	Columbus Transit Co. 361, 363, 364, 367, 370
215-218	GM	TDH-3714	394, 396-398	36	1954	(1967)	Nashville Transit Co. 311,313-315
558-564	GM	TDH-5303	6034-6040	51	1967		AC
310-315	GM	TDH-4512	008, 014, 015,021-023	45	1953	(1968)	San Diego Transit Corp. 862, 868, 869, 875-877
316-318	GM	TDH-4512	1381-1383	45	1956	(1968)	Metropolitan Tulsa Transit Authy. 657-659
319	GM	TDH-4512	2268	45	1957	(1968)	Metropolitan Tulsa Transit Authy. 783
320-322	GM	TDH-4512	1315, 1316,1321	45	1956	(1969)	Cleveland Transit System 303,304, 309

(2) Trolley-Coaches

Fleet No.	Builder	Model	Serial Nos.	Seats	Built	Year Acq. If Used	Remarks
600-620	Brill	T-40		40	1937		GE 125 h.p. motor, Order No. 23516
630-639	Mack	CR-3S	1224-1233	40	1939		GE 140 h.p. motor
651-655	Marmon	TC-44	15022-15026	44	1951		GE 140 h.p. motor
661-666	Brill	TC-46	026-031	44	1952		GE 140 h.p. motor

(3) "Airporter" Service Coaches

Fleet No.	Builder	Model	Serial Nos.	Seats	Built	Year Acq. If Used	Remarks
46	Flxible	21C1	8996	21	1950	(1955)	Dixie Traction Co. 46
47	Flxible	182B1	30060	24	1950	(1955)	Dixie Traction Co. 47
48-49	Flxible	182B1	30208, 30308	24	1951	(1955)	Dixie Traction Co. 48-49
50-52	Flxible	182F1	30453, 30455,30456	24	1952	(1955)	Dixie Traction Co. 50-52
53	Flxible	182B1	30672	24	1953	(1955)	Dixie Traction Co. 53
54-55	Flxible	182B1	30720-30721	24	1954	(1955)	Dixie Traction Co. 54-55
56-57	Flxible	218F1	30823-30824	29	1954	(1955)	Dixie Traction Co. 56-57
58	Flxible	218F1	30845	29	1955		
59-60	Flxible	218F1	30879-30880	29	1956		
61-62	Flxible	218GM1	31002-31003	29	1958		
63-66	GM	PD-4104	3869-3870, 4316-4317	41	1959		Delivered as CN&C 91-94
67-68	GM	PD-4104	4910-4911	41	1960		
69-70	GM	PD-4106	492-493	38	1961		
69	GM	PD-4104	4213	41	1959	(1963)	Delaware Bus Co. 3741; nee Harrisburg 4113
101-102	GM	PD-4107	098, 099	38	1966		Delivered as CN&C 71, 72
103-104	GM	PD-4107	100,101	38	1966	(1966)	Atwood's Transport Lines 103-104
106	GM	PD-4107	103	38	1966	(1969)	Atwood's Transport Lines 106
107-108	GM	PD-4107	299-300	38	1966	(1969)	Delaware Bus Co. 107-108
109-110	GM	PD-4107	295-296	38	1966	(1969)	Penn Stages 109-110
111	GM	PD-4107	297	38	1966	(1969)	Keystone Charter Service 111

Appendix I

Buses Of The Transit Authority of Northern Kentucky (TANK) 1972-2000

Fleet No.	Builder	Model	Serial Nos.	Seats	Built	Year Acq. If Used	Remarks
201, 203, 209	GM	TDH-3612	560, 562, 568	35	1950	(1972)	CN&C 201, 203, 209
215, 218	GM	TDH-3714	394, 398	36	1954	(1972)	CN&C 215, 218
262-265, 268, 270, 271	GM	TDH-4509	2301-2304, 2307, 2309-2310	39	1952	(1972)	CN&C 262-265,268,270,271
285, 286, 288-313, 315-320, 322	GM	TDH-4512	(See Appx. H)	45	1953-1956	(1972)	CN&C 285, 286,288-313,315-320,322
558-564	GM	TDH-5303	6034-6040	51	1967	(1972)	CN&C 558-564
701-703, 705-710	GM	TDH-4517	581-583, 585, 640-644	45	1960	(1972)	CN&C 701-703,705-710
800-819	GM	TDH-5105	(See Note)	51	1956-1957	(1972-73)	Kansas City Area Transit Authority
1902-1975	AMG	10235-8	000001-000074 (in reverse)	41	1975		
101-104	HWP	TC-25	25881-25884	25	1975		
1976-1985	GM (Canada)	TDH-5307A	B3500578-587	49	1981		
1986-1995	Gillig	3596TB6V92	D1080454-463	39	1983		
949-973	Gillig	3596TB6V92	J1082262-286	38	1988		
974-975	Gillig	3596TB6V92T	J1082419-420	38	1988		
936-940	Gillig	3596TB6V92TA	M1084305-309	37	1991		
941-942	Gillig	3596TB6V92TA	N1084310-311	37	1992		
943-948	Gillig	3596TB6V92TA	N1084321-326	37	1992		
1996-2005	Flxible	40102-6T	ND103817-826	44	1992		
1916-1935	Flxible	35096-6T	ND103794-813	37	1992		
1913-1915	Flxible	35096-6T	PD104486-488	37	1993		
2006-2015	Gillig	M11T40102	S1085881-890	44	1995		
1907-1912	Gillig	M11T3596	S1085891-896	38	1995		
1901	AMG	10235-8	000045	41	1975	(1995)	Rebuilt from 1930
2016-2025	Gillig	C21B102N4	V1089011-020	40	1998		
301-312	Orion	02.501	P6005737-748	22	1993	(1998)	Central Fla. RTA 101-112
313-318	Orion	02.501	W6006076-081	22	1998		
2101-2112	Gillig	G18D102N4	Y1071064-075	40	2000		Low-Floor
2113-2127	Gillig	G18D102N4	Y1071365-379	40	2000		Low-Floor

Note regarding units 800-819

TANK No.	Builders No.	Date Built	KCATA No.	TANK No.	Builders No.	Date Built	KCATA No.	TANK No.	Builders No.	Date Built	KCATA No.
800	2579	1957	200	809	2573	1957	194	818 *	2193	1956	212
801 *	2198	1956	217	810 *	2244	1956	263	819 *	2188	1956	207
802 *	2196	1956	215	811 *	2251	1956	270				
803 *	2558	1957	179	812 *	2223	1956	242				
804	2201	1956	220	813 *	2243	1956	262				
805	2554	1957	175	814	2191	1956	210				
806	2230	1956	249	815	2561	1957	182				
807	2545	1957	166	816	2218	1956	237				
808	2578	1957	199	817 *	2195	1956	214				

* Leased to Southwest Ohio Regional Transit Authority (operating as Queen City Metro) from January to June, 1977.

The arrival in 1975 of the 74 AM General buses allowed the disposal of the entire remaining Green Line fleet, save for the 7 air-conditioned GM TDH-5303s built in 1967. This image shows No. 563; it and its sisters were operated by TANK until 1981. Incidentally, these were the only ex-Green Line buses to receive the TANK "rainbow" paint scheme. *Tom McNamara.*

OPPOSITE

A history of the Green Line in a nutshell thanks to a selection of vintage letterheads ending with one from TANK.

THE SOUTH COVINGTON & CINCINNATI
STREET RAILWAY COMPANY
INCORPORATED
COVINGTON, KENTUCKY

LAGOON AMUSEMENT COMPANY
INCORPORATED

MEMBER
NATIONAL AMUSEMENT PARK
ASSOCIATION
NEW YORK OFFICE
933 & 934 KNICKERBOCKER THEATRE BLDG.

========= LESSEE OF =========
BEAUTIFUL LAGOON

Telephone, S. 900 and 1330.

Ludlow, Ky., opposite Cincinnati, O.,

THE UNION LIGHT, HEAT & POWER CO.
INCORPORATED

JAMES C. ERNST.
PRESIDENT
ALBERT SILVA.
SECY. & TREASURER

COVINGTON, KY.

THE CINCINNATI, NEWPORT & COVINGTON RAILWAY CO.
INCORPORATED

COVINGTON, KENTUCKY

THE DIXIE TRACTION CO.
INCORPORATED

ELSMERE, KENTUCKY

THE CINCINNATI, NEWPORT & COVINGTON RAILWAY COMPANY
INCORPORATED

AMERICAN TRANSPORTATION ENTERPRISES, INC.

14 EAST 75th STREET ● NEW YORK 21

THE CINCINNATI, NEWPORT & COVINGTON TRANSPORTATION COMPANY

ELEVENTH AND LOWELL STREETS
NEWPORT, KENTUCKY

HEmlock 1-7000

TANK
TRANSIT AUTHORITY OF NORTHERN KENTUCKY

Appendix J

Bibliography

I. Books

Blakley, Stephens L. (ed.) *The Cincinnati, Newport and Covington Railway Company of Ky.: Organization, Franchises, Ordinances, Contracts [and] Agreements.* Cincinnati: Johnson and Hardin, 1929.

Dawson, Albert F. *Columbia System: A History.* New York: I. J. Little and Co., 1938.

Hopkins, C. M. *City Atlas of Covington*, Philadelphia: F. Borquin's Press, 1877.

Kulp, Randolph L. *History of Lehigh Valley Transit Company.* Allentown: Lehigh Valley Chapter N.R.H.S., 1966.

Reis, Jim *Pieces of the Past.* Covington: Kentucky Post, 1988.

Wagner, Richard and Wright, Roy, with McNamara, Thomas *Cincinnati Streetcars.* Cincinnati: Wagner Co., (published in 10 sections) 1968-1997.

II. Newspapers and Periodicals

Various issues from:
  Cincinnati Enquirer, 1867-2000.
  Cincinnati Times-Star, 1890-1958.
  Kentucky Post, 1892-2000.
  Kentucky State Journal, 1879-1889.
  Newport Local, 1877-1879.
  Street Railway Journal, 1889-1907.
  Street Railway Review, 1891-1896.

III. Company Documents

Cincinnati, Newport and Covington Railway Co. (and predecessor companies). Affidavit of William Purser detailing construction of streetcar tracks in Northern Kentucky between 1867 and 1892, sworn to March, 1916.

_____ Analysis of Plant and Equipment Account - From Inception to December 31, 1931.

_____ Compilation of Ordinances and Resolutions, 1930 to 1954.

_____ Dixie Traction Co. Corporate Minutes, 1940 to 1955 (two volumes).

_____ Depreciation Schedule, Dec. 31, 1959.

_____ Employees' Manual, Feb. 4, 1932.

_____ Evaluation report prepared by MacConnel and Co., Jan. 1, 1952.

_____ Equipment Registers, April, 1965, 1968, 1970, Sept. 1, 1972.

_____ *Hail Columbia* (company newsletter) monthly 1920-1929.

_____ Letter of C. Pebworth to P. G. Vondersmith re: Early horsecar routes and operating practices, Jan. 27, 1932.

_____ Letter of Charles W. Reynolds M. D. to P. G. Vondersmith re: Covington locations of car houses and stables, April 2, 1946.

_____ Letter of David L. Ringo to Marc Haas re: Conversion of trolley-coach routes to motor coach routes, June 22, 1957.

_____ Operator Instruction Manual on Issuance of Transfers, circa 1950.

_____ Operator and Public Timetables, various years 1939-1971.

_____ Proposal by C. S. Warner and Co. to Purchase CN&C and Dixie Traction, Jan. 13, 1941.

_____ Report by Marc Haas on the CN&C, Aug. 12, 1945.

_____ Record book re: Acquisition, repair, modification and disposal of transit cars and buses, 1892-1950.

_____ Record book re: Engineering drawings of all CN&C trackage, 1920-1929.

_____ Record book re: Engineering drawings of Kenton Co. CN&C trackage, 1931-1936.

_____ Record book re: Engineering drawings of projects concerning the Dixie Terminal and the Newport and Covington car barns, 1933-1937.

_____ Record book re: Floods of 1933, 1937, 1940 and 1944.

_____ *The O-K News* (company newsletter to employees) (weekly 1930-1944).

_____ *The GreenLiner* (company newsletter) (bi-monthly 1946-1959).

Transit Authority of Northern Kentucky. Equipment Lists, July, 1996 and November, 1998.

_____ Operator and Public Timetables, 1973-2000.

_____ Pullout assignments, Aug. 19, 1996.

IV. Legal Cases and Documents

Bellevue v. CN&C, 284 Ky 764 (1941).

CN&C v. Brumleve, 302 Ky 477 (1946).

Covington et al. v. CN&C Ry. Co., 71 F.2nd 117 (6th Cir. 1934); (also transcripts and exhibits).

Devou v. Cinti., Cov. and Erlanger, 162 F. 633 (6th Cir.), *cert. denied* 212 U. S. 577 (1908); (also transcript, briefs of all parties and exhibits).

Red Star Trans Co. v. Red Dot Coach Lines, 295 S. W. 419 (1927).

South Cov. and Cinti. St. Ry. v. Covington, 235 U. S. 537 (1915).

South Cov. and Cinti. St. Ry. v. Kentucky, 252 U. S. 408 (1918); (also original trial transcript and exhibits).

South Cov. and Cinti. St. Ry. v. Newport, 259 U. S. 97 (1922).

South Cov. and Cinti. St. Ry., No. 3073 (E.D. Ky. 1920)); (also all briefs and exhibits).

V. Regulatory Cases and Documents

A. Interstate Commerce Commission Published Reports.

In Re: Allen & Co. - CN&C - LVT, 57 M.C.C. 41 (1950).
In Re: ATE - Delaware Bus Co., 80 M.C.C. 18 (1959).
In Re: Cold Spring Bus Co., 4 M.C.C. 141 (1938).
In Re: Control Black Diamond, 15 M.C.C. 644 (1939).
In Re: Dixie Traction Applications, 2 M.C.C. 455 (1937).
In Re: Ex-Parte No. MC-8, 4 M.C.C. 539 (1938).
In Re: CN&C Railway Co., 25 M.C.C. 213 (1940).
In Re: Purchase of Dixie Tr. Co., 35 M.C.C. (1940)
In Re: Control - Allen & Co., 39 M. C.C. 699 (1944).

B. Other Interstate Commerce Commission Documents

MC-503 Dixie Traction, 1940-1955 (sub. 1 to sub. 5)
MC-50909 CN&C, 1938-1972 (sub. 1 to sub. 19).

C. Miscellaneous Regulatory Agency Documents

City of Cincinnati - order of the Dept. of Public Utilities, May 15, 1936.
Kentucky Public Utilities Comm. - Appendix to rate case filed by CN&C Ry. Co., July, 1929.

VI. Miscellaneous Sources

A Report to the City of Cincinnati, Ross W. Harris, C. E., Aug. 31, 1912.
Census Bureau data for 1860 and every 10 years thereafter.
Deeds, Mortgages and Subdivision plats (Campbell Co. and Kenton Co. Recorder's Offices).
Letter of John R. Blakely, Esq., detailing both his experiences as counsel for Green Line and as a young passenger on the streetcars, received November, 1989.
Letter of John Hoschek concerning Green Line operations, received March, 1990.
Letters of David L. Ringo (10), detailing his recollections of Green Line System affairs and analysis of various documents, received October, 1987 to January, 1997.
Letters of Albert C. Meier (7), detailing acquisition and disposal of motor coaches by American Transportation Enterprises, received August, 1990, to October, 1994.
Letters of James K. Gibson (4), detailing CN&C operations during the 1930-1945 period, received June, 1992, to January, 1997.
Sanborn Fire Insurance Maps, 1895, 1910, 1930 (and updates to 1950).
St. Louis Car Co.: PCC blueprint for Cincinnati St. Ry., December 2, 1939.
St. Louis Car Co.: Specifications for Cincinnati St. Ry. trolley-coaches, Janury 1946.
Transportation Study: Covington, Ky., Northern Kentucky Area Planning Commission, December, 1966.
"Where the Cars Run" (author and publisher unknown - cover and first page missing), circa 1905.
Williams City Directories for Northern Kentucky, 1884 to 1920.

Future Author Gets Door-to-Door Service

Here is a photograph we simply couldn't leave out. To augment the CN&C bus fleet in 1947 seven Twin Coach model 38-S units (380-386) were acquired. Brand-new Green Line 381 has been exhibited in Dayton earlier in the day and now driver Jake Cook draws up to 319 W. 11th St. in Newport. In a moment future co-author Terry W. Lehmann will emerge and board the bus for a short trip to the Newport garage. *Motor Bus Society.*

Appendix K

These tracings of the elevation and floor plan of Cincinnati, Newport & Covington single-truck car on this page and a 500-series car on page 237 were made in 1947. The scale is not given. Each plan has a list of dimensions. After 1937, the CN&C basically operated only these two types of cars. Although there were several subclasses of single-truckers, the drawing below appears to be a generic composite.
Both: George Krambles Collection.

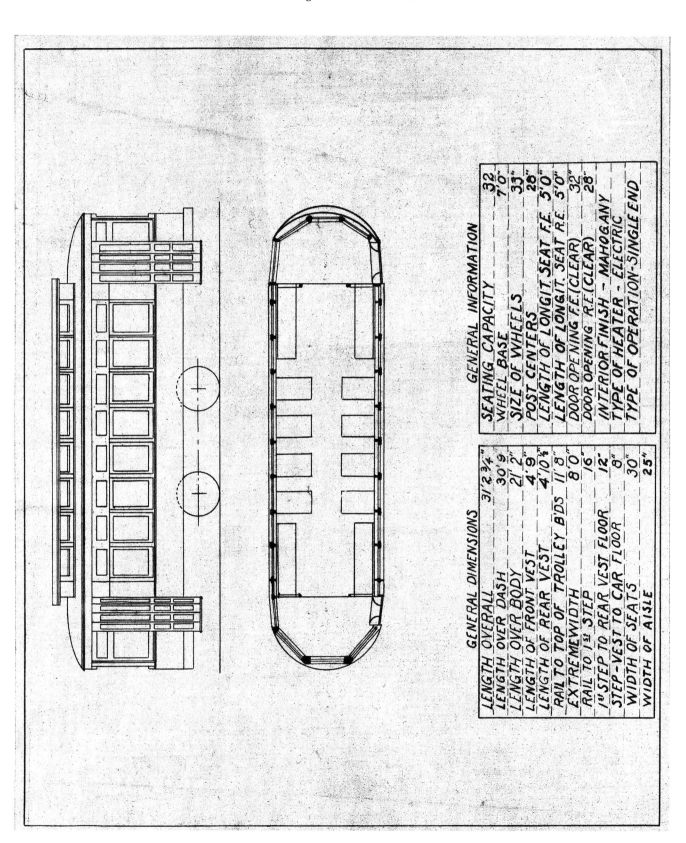

GENERAL INFORMATION	
SEATING CAPACITY	32
WHEEL BASE	7'0"
SIZE OF WHEELS	33"
POST CENTERS	28"
LENGTH OF LONGIT SEAT F.E.	5'0"
LENGTH OF LONGIT. SEAT R.E.	5'0"
DOOR OPENING F.E. (CLEAR)	32"
DOOR OPENING R.E. (CLEAR)	28"
INTERIOR FINISH – MAHOGANY	
TYPE OF HEATER – ELECTRIC	
TYPE OF OPERATION-SINGLE END	

GENERAL DIMENSIONS	
LENGTH OVERALL	31'2¾"
LENGTH OVER DASH	30'9"
LENGTH OVER BODY	21'2"
LENGTH OF FRONT VEST	4'9"
LENGTH OF REAR VEST	4'10½"
RAIL TO TOP OF TROLLEY BDS	11'8"
EXTREME WIDTH	8'0"
RAIL TO 1ST STEP	16"
1ST STEP TO REAR VEST FLOOR	12"
STEP-VEST TO CAR FLOOR	8"
WIDTH OF SEATS	30"
WIDTH OF AISLE	25"

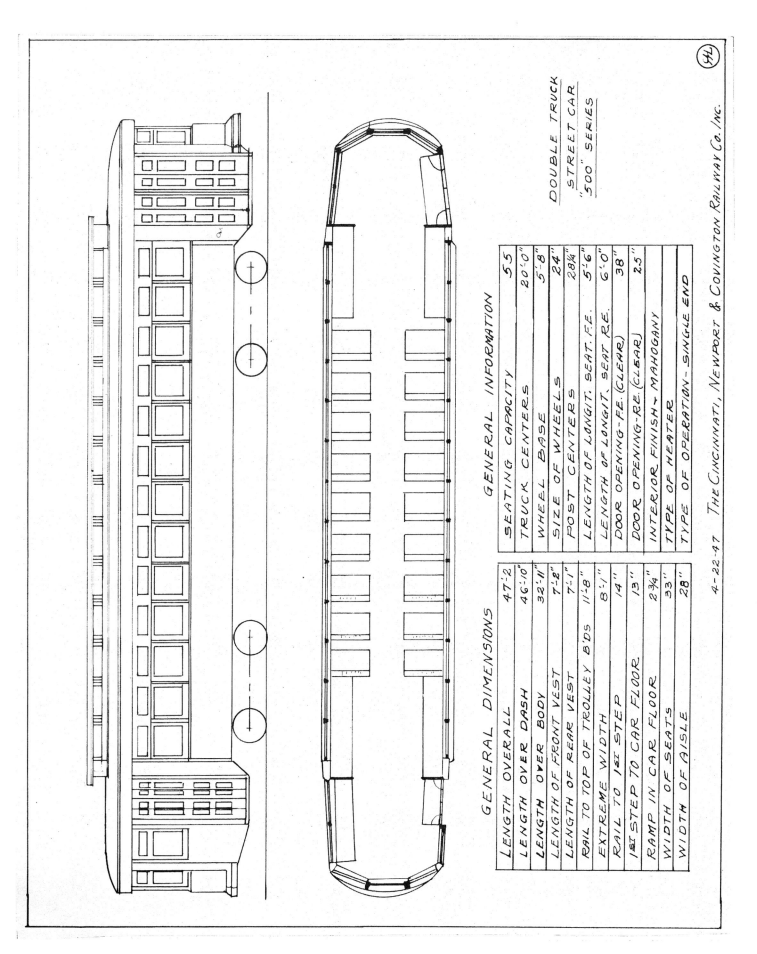

GENERAL INFORMATION

SEATING CAPACITY	55
TRUCK CENTERS	20'-0"
WHEEL BASE	5'-8"
SIZE OF WHEELS	24"
POST CENTERS	28¼"
LENGTH OF LONGIT. SEAT. F.E.	5'-6"
LENGTH OF LONGIT. SEAT. R.E.	6'-0"
DOOR OPENING-F.E. (CLEAR)	38"
DOOR OPENING-R.E.(CLEAR)	2.5
INTERIOR FINISH→MAHOGANY	
TYPE OF HEATER	
TYPE OF OPERATION-SINGLE END	

GENERAL DIMENSIONS

LENGTH OVERALL	47'-2"
LENGTH OVER DASH	46'-0"
LENGTH OVER BODY	32'-11"
LENGTH OF FRONT VEST	7'-2"
LENGTH OF REAR VEST	7'-1"
RAIL TO TOP OF TROLLEY B'DS	11'-8"
EXTREME WIDTH	8'-1"
RAIL TO 1ST STEP	14"
1ST STEP TO CAR FLOOR	13"
RAMP IN CAR FLOOR	2¾"
WIDTH OF SEATS	33"
WIDTH OF AISLE	28"

DOUBLE TRUCK
STREET CAR
"500" SERIES

4-22-47   THE CINCINNATI, NEWPORT & COVINGTON RAILWAY CO. INC.

Index

TO TEXT AND MAPS

High-Tech for its Day: the Nachod Signal

A bit of street railway technology is demonstrated in the picture at **right.** A 500-series car heading for Ft. Mitchell is leaving single track on Montague St. in Covington to enter Park Hills on the CN&C's private right-of-way. At this point double track begins. The Nachod block signal, which protects the blind single track on Montague, can be seen on the pole at the top left of the photo. The Nachod signal was widely used in the industry; this one has red and green aspects. *Earl Clark Collection.*

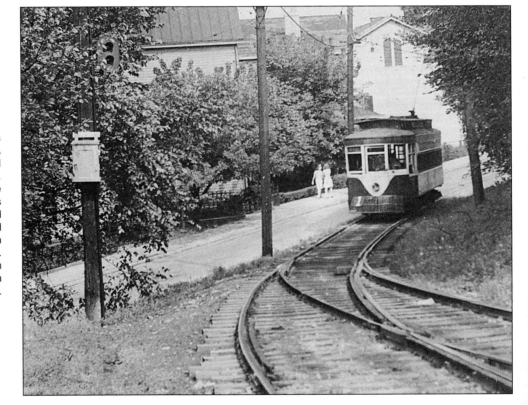